The Gospel Challenge

30 Years of Practical Application
of
the Christian Social Teaching
in the Nigerian Context

Adonis & Abbey Publishers Ltd and Skylark Publications (Ghana)

24 Old Queen Street,
London SW1H 9HP
United Kingdom
Website: http://www.adonis-abbey.com
E-mail Address: editor@adonis-abbey.com

Website: http://www.adonis-abbey.com
E-mail Address: editor@adonis-abbey.com

Nigeria:
Suites C4 – C6 J-Plus Plaza
Asokoro, Abuja, Nigeria
Tel: +234 (0) 7058078841/08052035034

Copyright 2022 © **George Ehusani**

British Library Cataloguing-in-Publication Data
A catalogue record for this book is available from the British Library

ISBN: 978-1-913976-13-2

The moral right of the author has been asserted

All rights reserved. No part of this book may be reproduced, stored in a retrieval system or transmitted at any time or by any means without the prior permission of the publisher

The Gospel Challenge

30 Years of Practical Application of the Christian Social Teaching in the Nigerian Context

George Ehusani

Foreword by Matthew Hassan Kukah

Table of Content

Acknowledgment...ix
Foreword...x
Fundamental Principles of Christian Social Teachings...............xv
Introduction..xii

Chapter One
Let Your Light Shine 21

Chapter Two
Moment of Truth..25

Chapter Three
WANTED: A New Generation of Nigerians...................29

Chapter Four
NIGERIA: The Wage of Sin is Death..............................33

Chapter Five
Light Your Own Candle..37

Chapter Six
Exploiting the Nigerian Malady 41

Chapter Seven
The Shock of the Moment...43

Chapter Eight
June 12 Election Annulment: Matters Arising................45

Chapter Nine
The Inviolability of Truth..47

Chapter Ten
Saving Our Educational System.....................................51

Chapter Eleven
When Will Abacha Go?..57

Chapter Twelve
Nigeria Shall Rise Again...61

Chapter Thirteen
Youth and the Future of Our Nation................................65

Chapter Fourteen
Nigeria: Salvaging the Future...71

Chapter Fifteen
Authentic Religion Saves a Nation 77

Chapter Sixteen
Nigeria: Investing in the Future......................................85

Chapter Seventeen
We Need Dreamers..91
Chapter Eighteen
A Reflection on Godly Leadership...................................95
Chapter Nineteen
In Search of Moral Sanity in Ebiraland...........................101
Chapter Twenty
Towards A More Peaceful Society..................................107
Chapter Twent- One
The Triumph of Mediocrity..113
Chapter Twenty-Two
That Tomorrow May Not Be Lost...................................119
Chapter Twenty-Three
A Nation on Trial...127
Chapter Twenty-Four
The Challenge of the Pope's Visit...................................129
Chapter Twenty-Five
Royalty and the Crisis of Relevance................................133
Chapter Twenty-Six
The Place of the Handicapped in the New Nigeria..........137
Chapter Twenty-Seven
The Role of Religion in the Evolution of a Just Democratic Society...143
Chapter Twenty-Eight
Sanitising Our Security Agencies 155
Chapter Twent-Nine
Alleviating the Plight of Widows in Nigeria....................159
Chapter Thirty
Responding to the Challenge of University Cults............163
Chapter Thirty-One
Between Reconciliation and Disintegration....................173
Chapter Thirty-Two
Jubilee, Forgiveness and National Reconciliation...........177
Chapter Thirty-Three
The Social Challenges of Jubilee 2000............................181
Chapter Thirty-Four
Moral Imperative of National Rejuvenation....................185

Chapter Thirty-Five
Nigerians: Stop the Madness!...187
Chapter Thirty-Six
Catholic Lawyers and National Re-Awakening...............191

Chapter Thirty-Seven
Building Peace through Justice, Love and Forgiveness..................197
Chapter Thirty-Eight
John Paul II: Hope in a Dying World..209
Chapter Thirty-Nine
Politics and the Manipulation of Religion in Nigeria 219
Chapter Forty
Mother Teresa: A Challenge for Nigerians..................................223
Chapter Forty-One
Social Instability and the Quest for Peace in Nigeria...................227
Chapter Forty-Two
Death Penalty and the Imperatives of Change 235
Chapter Forty-Three
Inter-Religious Dialogue in Nigeria: Present Challenges and Future Prospects...241
Chapter Forty-Four
Religious Organisations and the Challenge of Fighting Corruption.....249
Chapter Forty-Five
Nigeria and the Leadership Challenge..259
Chapter Forty-Six
Christmas and My Prophetic Imagination..................................265
Chapter Forty-Seven
The Good Shepherd and the Nigerian Situation..........................269
Chapter Forty-Eight
Dress Codes and Social Dislocation in Nigeria............................273
Chapter Forty-Nine
Religion and National Integration: Past Experiences, Present Realities and Future Prospects...283
Chapter Fifty
Need to Re-invent the Nigerian Police..289
Chapter Fifty - One
Lent: A Time for Repentance...293
Chapter Fifty - Two
It's Another Good Friday..295
Chapter Fifty-Three
The Challenge of Easter...297

Chapter Fifty-Four
The Mass Media and Social Responsibility: the Case of Religious and Cultural Symbols 301
Chapter Fifty-Five

The Nigerian Political Elite: A Plea for Compassion......................307
Chapter Fifty-Six
Towards the Globalisation of Human Solidarity: The Challenge
of Social Responsibility..311
Chapter Fifty-Seven
Christian Development Professionals as Champions of 'Transcendent
Humanism'..321
Chapter Fifty-Eight
Education for National Development: The Challenge before
Christians and Christian Bodies..335
Chapter Fifty-Nine
The Challenge of Electoral Reform in Nigeria.............................341
Chapter Sixty
LET THE SEED GROW: The Challenge of Mentoring
the Future Generation in Purposeful Existence........................347
Chapter Sixty-One
Citizenship Rights and the Imperative of Constitutional Reform 355
Chapter Sixty-Two
Sacrificing for Others: Way to Lasting Happiness.......................361
Chapter Sixty-Three
Meeting the Challenge of Environmental Justice........................367
Chapter Sixty-Four
The Christian Elite and the Challenge of Saving Nigeria.................375
Chapter Sixty-Five
Moral and Ethical Formation of Christians in Nigeria....................381
Chapter Sixty-Six
Easter and the Challenge of National Security 387
Chapter Sixty-Seven
Ethical and Moral Imperative of Credible Elections.......................391
Chapter Sixty-Eight
Nigeria at 54: Renewing Our Hopes..399
Chapter Sixty-Nine
The Role of Law in the Promotion of Justice and National
Development..401
Chapter Seventy
John the Baptist and Authentic Religion in Nigeria........................409
Chapter Seventy-One
The Common Good and Leadership Formation in Africa...............421
Chapter Seventy-Two
The National Question and Nigeria's Stability..................................433

Chapter Seventy-Three
The Critical Role of Faith Communities in the Task of Building
a Nation of Freedom, Security and Peace..................................445
Chapter Seventy-Four
The Nigerian Christian and the Imperative of Judicial Activism
for National Transformation...453
Chapter Seventy-Five
Beyond Ballots and Numbers: The Imperative of Credible
Elections...461
Chapter Seventy-Six
Finding Happiness and Salvation Through Work.........................469
Chapter Seventy-Seven
Information as Public Good and Press Freedom.........................475
Chapter Seventy-Eight
Strategic Communication in Governance and Security: The Role
of Traditional and Religious Institutions..................................485
Index..491

Acknowledgement

The process of putting together in book form this collection of articles, essays and public lectures, under the title, *THE GOSPEL CHALLENGE: 30 Years of Practical Application of Christian Social Teaching in the Nigerian Context* has been a rather difficult one, involving the very painstaking work of sorting through hundreds of my writings, covering a period of thirty years (from 1991 to 2021). The process was rendered more difficult because the papers were not originally filed away in any specific order or classified under any particular headings or themes. Therefore, the task of sorting through the tons of papers, and identifying which ones could be identified as part of the "practical application of the Christian social teaching in the Nigerian context," was an enormous one.

It is therefore with immense gratitude that I acknowledge the very painstaking groundwork done on the raw articles and papers by Rex Emma Odoemenam over a period of nearly two years. Next is the very rigorous task of organising and re-organising the originally selected papers by my good friend Dr. Anthony Okeregbe of the University of Lagos.

As the manuscript began to assume some discernible shape, I must acknowledge the diligent editorial work carried out on it by my brother, Fr. Richard Ehusani, and the intense proof-reading work executed by the indomitable Editor-in-Chief of Lux Terra Publications, Mr. Greg Aiyemo. I must also express my gratitude to Mike Egbe for typesetting the book, and to Prof. Jideofor Adibe of Adonis & Abbey Publishers, who organised the professional indexing of the book.

I want to thank my life-time friends and close collaborators in the practical application of Christian Social Teaching in the Nigerian context, Bishop Matthew Hassan Kukah and Msgr. Prof. Francis Obiora Ike, for taking time out of their very tight schedules to write the Foreword and the Introduction to this publication. I thank them both, not only for their contributions to this book, but even more for their life-long friendship and support.

Above all, to the One in Whom, according to St. Paul, "we live and move and have our being," to our Almighty God who has revealed himself definitively in Christ Jesus, and whose civilisation of love is expressed in the many elements of the Christian Social Teaching; to Him be honour and glory for ever and ever. Amen.

--Rev. Fr. George Ehusani

Foreword

Fr George Omaku Ehusani has earned brownie points for himself as a rigorous scholar, theologian and, to use the most abused word, an activist. Using street jargon, it is easy to call him an activist in cassock. To be sure, when these labels are bandied around, they are an evocation of sentiments of perception, how people see, analyse or interpret what we do or say. Unlike yours sincerely, Fr. George has focused on the critical Scriptural exegesis, challenging the foundations of our Christian conviction and calling largely to the Christian community to live up to its faith. Consequently, he has not stirred many hornets' nest enough to be subjected to public crucifixion as this writer. But, no matter.

Today, as a result of years of intense reflections on Christian life and witness, Fr. Ehusani has consistently been driven by a deep, passionate, intestinal sense of revulsion against the social and moral order in Nigeria. He speaks from the pit of his stomach with a pungent clarity that is at best, a call to a verdict for the reader. His sermons and speeches shatter the walls of ambiguity and suggest very clearly that the Christian today cannot equivocate over decisions of moral choice and conduct. It is, as in Joshua's admonition, to: *Choose today whom you will serve…Put aside the gods that your fathers served* (Joshua 24: 14).

Choosing whom to serve is part of the essence of our faith as Christians. The God we worship is a jealous God (Exodus 34: 14). In his letter to the Churches, the writer of the book of Revelation had some harsh words for the churches but the message to the Church in Ephesus is spectacular because it draws a line. Punishment is coming because you are neither hot nor cold and the result is that you will be spit out (Rev. 3: 16). Therefore, the greatest threat to Christianity is those who simply speak with their mouths and reject commitment to the words and commandments of God.

For the Christian, the narrative of Moses to the people of Israel drips with what today the world will call prophesy. Ours has become a world of fortune seekers and fortune-tellers, a world of opportunists, chancers, and guesswork, as our people struggle for power. A **"Betnaija"** culture has elevated what they call prophesy to a new level. Therefore, we are constantly staking our fortunes on who might be able to arm-twist God to secure what we want for us. In the book of Deuteronomy, Moses warned the people of Israel about what would happen as opportunities for wealth and power open up in the course of their occupation of the promised land. He said: *When you have all you want to eat and have built good* *houses to live in and when your cattle and sheep, your silver and gold and all other possessions have increased, make sure that you do not forget the Lord your God who rescued you from Egypt where you were slaves* (Deuteronomy 8: 12-14). Fr Ehusani has constantly attacked the carefree lifestyle of the rich and powerful whose questionable sources of wealth have continuously widened the scope of poverty and squalor.

Over the years, Fr. Ehusani has been trenchant in his criticism of the state and religion. He has denounced the oppressive structure of the state and charged it with inefficiency and corruption. In all, his arguments are based on the fact that genuine and committed Christian believers have left the doors open to scoundrels and charlatans to take over the management of our resources. He has denounced a Church that has chosen to sit on the fence and outsourced its prophetic voice or urgency to rudderless pastors or "men of God" who hawk the rotten fruits of material prosperity as the essence of God's love or his answer to prayers. He has drawn his preachings extensively from both Scripture and the teachings of the Catholic Church and used them as a mirror to challenge a decayed state to look at itself.

The Catholic Church has had a long history. Due to its longevity, its exposure, and its experience in wrestling with temporal power, the Church had suffered a lot of physical injuries and scarifications. However, with time, the Church learnt its lessons regarding the many consequences of embracing temporal power, especially on the purity of the faith. In the romance between Caesar and God, something had to give. Drawing from its extensive experience, the Catholic Church would painstakingly weave together a beautiful tapestry, a corpus of teachings on how best to create a world that fits into the image of God the Creator. These teachings have challenged the Church itself, and they have wrestled with and exposed the structural and institutional weaknesses of the state, laying a pathway for the achievement of what it has come to refer to as the **common good**. The Church teaches that if the state is to be legitimate, the pursuit of the common good must be at the heart of governance.

Bringing together his writings over the years, Fr Ehusani offers his readers and the wider society, a sumptuous intellectual feast. The Catholic Church in Africa has done a lot of talking over the years. Loosely, the Statements or Communiques of the Bishops and other Church leaders, are often referred to as *speaking truth to power*. However, over the years, it would seem tempting to say that the cutting edge of the power of the prophets has proved ineffective in dethroning the empire of evil. The essence of the state is as the founding fathers of the United States said in their 1776 Declaration of Independence: *We hold these truths to be self-evident that all men are created equal, that they are endowed by their Creator with certain unalienable rights, that among these are Life, Liberty and the pursuit of happiness.*

It is now time for the Catholic Church to step up and perhaps soil its hands directly or indirectly in shaping the political options for our country and continent. We have often mistaken participation in politics as a dirty game that only the fraudulent can undertake. But, time has run out and it must be clear to us that this neutral option is the most dangerous position to take. It is now time for us to step up and provide alternative routes for Catholics to lead the way in the formation of a good society in Nigeria. The Laity must be re-energised to move from being bystanders to participants. The Leadership of the Church must participate by offering moral clarity and directions.

We have done a lot of talking. Now, an action plan is a necessary option. The prophets of old did no less. God said to Ezekiel, *dig through the wall* (Ez. 8:7), God told him; *Take the scroll and eat* (Ez. 3:1). He was further told: *You will be tied with ropes, and you will not be able to go out in public* (Ez. 3: 25). *Zechariah was told he would be dumb for doubting the promise of the birth of John the Baptist* (Lk. 1: 20).

Our Justice, Development and Peace Commission must do more than just be spectators to processes such as Election monitoring. Election monitoring is not a goal. Happily, Fr. Ehusani's book is very timely because, thanks to a robust collaboration between the Kukah Centre and the Catholic Theological Association, the draft proposal of a Vade Mecum of the Social Teachings of the Church is now available in simple language for all Catholics. The CBCN reviewed and approved the document for public use in 2019. One of the greatest developments, thanks to the enthusiasm of Archbishop Matthew Man'so Ndagoso, Chairman of Church and Society for the CBCN, is that the Catholic University, Veritas, has now introduced a course of study on the Church's social teachings.

No doubt, Fr. Ehusani's book will add to the much-needed material for a wide spectrum of Christians who will be exposed to this much hidden treasure. We are hopeful that in a few years, the Social Teachings of the Church, more than the Manifestos of the Political parties, will constitute the bedrock and part of the syllabi of political education in Nigeria.

We owe Fr. Ehusani a debt of gratitude for a work that should become a reference point to all those who wish to understand the mind of the Church in the formation of a good society. This is a valuable text for not only clerical and lay leaders of the Church, but for all Christians and indeed all Nigerians.

+Most Rev. Matthew Hassan Kukah
Catholic Bishop of Sokoto, Nigeria

Fundamental Principles of Christian Social Teachings

1. Human Dignity and Inviolability
2. Human Solidarity
3. Participation of all in the Affairs of Society
4. Priority of the Common Good Over Individual or Group Good
5. Preferential Option for the Poor
6. Sanctity and Integrity of the Family
7. Stewardship of the Natural Environment
8. Subsidiarity

Introduction

One of the most enigmatic and charismatic personalities of our contemporary Catholicism in the later part of the 20th and currently in our 21st century in the Nigerian society, and one whose leading voice, intellectual sharpness, educational involvement, pastoral impact and ethically exemplary influence continue to adorn the modelling of youth and the consciences of many people within the African continent, especially Nigerian Christians and the socio-political elite in general is Father George Ehusani. Ordained priest in 1981, George has made the Social Teaching of the Church and its ethical compass the anchor for his academic, social, cultural, and pastoral life and activities.

The book in your hands of over four hundred pages, containing written reflections, articles, points of view, well arranged in seventy-five reflections spanning a period of thirty years from 1991 till 2021. These articles are now compiled and put into one volume as legacy for posterity to cherish, read and learn from as a good guide for ethical living and teaching.

In a letter from the author dated 10th October 2021 and inviting my humble self to write the introduction to this book, he mentioned the judgment of history as one of the compelling reasons why he wants a documentation of these thoughts and reflections with the following words:

> As Nigeria's corporate existence and our mutual co-existence in peace remain in contention; as democracy remains on trial; and as issues of social injustice, executive lawlessness and impunity, citizenship and "indigenship," and lately as ethnic and religious discrimination, resulting in renewed agitation for self-determination persist; I have become convinced that the social commentaries that some of us have made over the years need to be documented or put on record. Someday, students of social history, social psychology and political economy may be interested in tracing the trajectory of our unfortunate political history, and what role if any, people like you and I played in the unfolding of events. Perhaps it will be a useful accompaniment to the compendium of the social teachings of the Church for the teaching or propagation of the social imperatives of the Gospel of Christ - in the Nigerian context. My request is that you do a quick glance through and write an introduction for the work.

I have accepted the honour to write this introduction for someone whose thoughts and area of specialisation resonate with mine. We are dear to each other and are colleagues that have been sharing and working together since four decades, and knowing fully well the African thought which is found also in other ancient cultures as a proverbial guide, namely:

> If you plan for one year plant rice. If you plan for ten years plant trees. If you plan for One hundred years build houses. If you plan for one thousand years write books. And if you plan for eternal life, practice love.

This adage resounds also in the words of Pilate who as Judge ordered the crucifixion of Jesus Christ on Golgotha when he said to the sponsors of the judicial killing: "What I have written, I have written". In other words, *"Vox auditaperit, littera scripta manet"* meaning "The spoken word disappears, but the written word remains". You have in your hands the written words of a much sought-after public speaker, teacher, pastor and writer. The work bears the title: *"The Gospel Challenge: 30 Years of Practical Application of the Christian Social Teaching in the Nigerian context"*.The Reverend Father Dr George Ehusani celebrates his fortieth anniversary as a servant of God, a dedicated priest of the Catholic Church and a preacher of the Good News with the gift of this Book to humanity.

The contents are expressed as invitation to each person and every reader to let our light shine in the world around us through better behaviour. There is a situation globally of enveloping darkness upon humanity that has caused so much pain, violence, unnecessary deaths, travails, and burdens, especially on the poor and the most vulnerable. This unacceptable situation continues globally and in various sectors of the human enterprise and is often caused by wickedness or the choice of evil over the good. If each person, particularly Christians allowed the light in them to shine as the Master Jesus Christ invited and challenged all to be and to do (in Matthew 5:14 to 16), we would have a better world.

I have taken enough time to read through every line and paragraph of the entire work. The topics span around concerns for the Future, the Youth, Peace and Justice, Prophetic witnessing, Religion and Society, Reconciliation and the Challenge of an Authentic National Renewal in Nigeria. Other topics focus on the need for Mutual Respect and Interreligious Dialogue, Leadership and Education, Human Rights and Dignity, the Rule of Law, the Preservation of our Ecological Environment, Press Freedom, and Lessons from Love which makes eternity and all things possible. These discussions demonstrate that many of our common problems are solvable because they are man- and woman-made.

The submission is that "Living faith" leads directly to "Loving Action" for the transformation of the world. Such a world view is to be found in the great wisdom embedded in our Christian Social Teaching, a great source of light and faith, capable of changing the evil intentions and actions of humankind through the light of the gospel preached by the Lord Jesus Christ. Under this light, the human person's dignity and fundamental rights are recognised and respected; society has order; justice, peace and love are not illusions or mere pep talk; freedom and responsibility are seen as complementary sides of one coin; and life has meaning and purpose. We cannot easily convince others or lead them rightly if we do not know the way. We cannot find the way if we have no faith. We cannot easily work for the unity of all if we are arrogantly and selfishly preoccupied with our private interests and affiliations and intolerant of other groups. The call is for us to open up, to learn, to live, and to love.

What we need is the faith, the will, and the courage to carry out such necessary actions that serve the common good. The leadership and the elite are central to these discussions because they bear particular responsibility to lead by example.

Therefore, the author has specifically beamed the concentration of his many speeches and reflections on the responsibility of the Christian in a world of global change. Pope John XXIII in his famous Encyclical Letter *"Mater et Magistra"* had stressed this fact in the following words:

> It is not enough to formulate a Social Doctrine. It must be translated into reality. And this is particularly the Church's Social Teaching, the light of which is truth, justice its objective, and love its driving force.

The premise is simple and logical: If we have faith, then we must be concerned for justice. Once justice is secured, we have laid the necessary foundation for the effective expression of Christian love.

Without falling into the temptation of repeating in this introduction, the erudite writings contained in the following pages of the authors work, mention must be made of the foundational ethical teaching of Christian Social Principles. These teachings and principles emphasise acknowledgment and respect for every Human Life and the Dignity of the Person. All other Human Rights are derived from this first principle. Specifically, the inalienable rights of all persons and their equality before the law as willed by their creator is a cardinal teaching of Christian Social Thought. The right to a Free and well-informed Conscience, including the Freedom of Religion and its exercise, the Practice of Subsidiarity which allows competencies at each lower level function, and Solidarity which calls for support where the lower levels cannot help each other, etc., remain strong teachings that have helped many civilised societies reach to the heights.

Furthermore, Christian Social Teaching calls for a Fundamental Option for the Poor, the Priority of the Common Good over personal and group interest, Stewardship as a manner of caring for creation and all resources in creation, and the Right of Participation by everybody, irrespective of gender and class in the ordering of society in the light of natural law. Such (natural) law is inspired by the Creator and known to all through sound reason and common sense. Christian Social Principles allow space for all to work and have a dignified existence without oppression, and adequate security is offered under governance structures that encourage the use of the talents and capabilities of all to promote the Justice that is essential for lasting Peace.

Reading the several pages of this book, one is fascinated by the involvements of the author who has turned every available opportunity offered to him by any audience to contribute his wealth of experience and knowledge to build up the thinking and models of action for his listeners. It is not easy to write and painstakingly express thoughts in such logical and clear manner which distinguishes this work as a book of inspiration.

I have read other works of the author such as *A Prophetic Church*. I have also read his doctoral thesis of the 1980's, submitted to Howard University in the United States of America, which already then called for inculturation of the Christian message into local contexts of our various cultures so that Christ and context are one, and people are not alienated by their faith.

It is clear to me that the challenges confronting humanity today are a compelling call for leadership to transform the many crises of our day into opportunities. As a member of the World Academy of Sciences, promoting Leadership in Thought that leads to Action, I have had several encounters with colleagues and our *Cadmus Journal* (Volume IV) issued in June 2020, containing ideas that resonate with what Father George Ehusani has been working to achieve through his Lux Terra Leadership Foundation. This book is one of such initiatives. I will now quote the following from the Journal:

We all need local and global leadership with a transboundary vision: leadership that can sense the rising social energies and seize the occasion to convert these energies into effective transformative social power; leadership to forge alliances across borders, disciplines and other types of walls; leadership which can learn from the past and creatively apply its poignant lessons to unlock the future; leadership with the individuality and courage to spearhead a global social human-centred movement; leadership to seize this unique planetary moment to unleash the planetary momentum to create the future NOW.

The Gospel Challenge:30 Years of Practical Application of the Christian Social Teaching in the Nigerian Context is a call to such Leadership which essence is to offer an ethical guide and compass for a people in need and in quest. Pessimism is not an answer to the current problems facing us in our country Nigeria. Hope is the adequate response, and this hope is founded on solid grounds. It is the hope of the *"Adumbratio"*, the pre-shadow of the already begun, but not yet fulfilled understanding of the *kerygma* of the Gospel. Our journey of life is made easier and more meaningful with a living faith and some loving action that flows from such faith. It is with great delight that I recommend this book very highly to all people of Good Will.

Msgr. Francis Ike Obiora
Professor of Social Ethics and Director, Globethics.net
Geneva, Switzerland

CHAPTER ONE

Let Your Light Shine
(Written on November 17, 1991)

In the Gospel of St. John (8:12) Jesus told his disciples "I am the light of the world, anyone who follows me will not be walking in darkness but will have the light of life." Jesus also told his disciples that: "You are the salt of the earth. But if salt loses its taste, what can make it salty again? It is good for nothing and can only be thrown out to be trampled under people's feet. You are the light of the world. A city built on a hill-top cannot be hidden. No one lights a lamp to put under a tub; they put it on the lamp stand where it shines for everyone in the house. In the same way your light must shine in people's sight, so that, seeing your good works, they may give the praise to your father in heaven" (Matthew 5:13-16).

Now how are we expected to shine this light? It is by a life of faith, trust, hope, fortitude, and perseverance, even at times of great tribulation. It is by living a life of love and justice, and by taking seriously the message of Jesus in Matthew 25:31-46: that is, caring for the poor, the hungry, the weak, the orphan, the despised, the stranger, and the victims of all sorts of injustice. Our light must shine through the pursuit of human rights, the defence of human dignity and the promotion of freedom and abundant life for all in our society. The Christian is called upon to be a sign of contradiction in a world of darkness and sin. For a corrupt, violent, materialistic, hedonistic, and consumeristic society, the Christian is called upon to shine out the light of holiness, love, purity of heart, mercy, kindness, and peacefulness. This is the way to be the salt of the earth and the light of the world.

The circumstances of today's Nigeria challenge those of us who constitute the Christian elite to act as the conscience of the nation. The Nigerian Christian elite must assume their responsibility as salt of the earth and light of the world. The Christian elite must be forthright and consistent in denouncing individual evil and evil structures in our society. The Christian elite must cry out loud enough for the leadership of Nigeria to be compelled to do something about our primitive penal system, our inhuman prison conditions, and our treatment of ex-convicts. The Christian elite must stand alongside the oppressed, the impoverished, the marginalized, those denied their just rights and those discriminated against.

The Christian elite is called upon to champion the cause of the handicapped and the homeless and the destitute. We are called upon to defend the right of poor workers to just wage, to health insurance, and to adequate retirement benefits. We are called upon to be in the forefront of the struggle to rid Nigeria of military dictatorship and the structural injustices that have constituted a superstructure of violence over our motherland.

The Christian elite must always resist the temptation to apathy and despondency. We must always rise and be counted on the side of reason, truth and justice, for we are the salt of the earth and the light of the world. The Christian elite must be patriotic but fearless Christians who will demonstrate to the men and women of this land that a true patriot is one who cares deeply about the happiness and well-being of his country and all its people; not one who sings the praises of the leaders. We must demonstrate love for our country not by sycophancy, not by paid solidarity visits, but by demanding the highest standards from our leaders and by accepting nothing but the best for and from our people. We must be ready to stand up and be counted on the side of truth, even as falsehood reigns in the land.

Many Nigerians want to live in a land where there is justice, democracy, good governance, and prosperity, but they are not prepared to make the necessary sacrifices. Many Nigerians want peace to reign in this land, but they are unwilling to pay the high price which the pursuit of peace demands. The cost of peace is a lifestyle of sacrifice. Peace does not come on a platter of gold, but through a crown of thorns. The peacemaker must be ready to pay the costly price of atonement for the multiple violence that currently make peace impossible in our land. Being salt in a corrupt society and being light in a world of darkness is no easy task. The cost of maintaining truth in a world of falsehood is quite high. Yet the true disciple of Christ cannot run away from this sacrifice.

True, many Nigerian Christians have paid only lip service to the social imperative of the Gospel of Jesus Christ. We have often lived like hypocrites, preferring to have our little pleasures and comforts, rather than rocking the boat and getting hurt. We have often avoided as much as possible any occasion of confrontation with the status quo, even when we can see clearly that the status quo is made up of unjust and evil structures. To that extent we have betrayed our Christian prophetic calling. We have often forgotten the beatitude, "Blessed are those who are persecuted for righteousness' sake, for theirs is the kingdom of heaven" (Matthew 5:10).

Jesus Christ had warned all disciples of truth that, "You will be delivered up even by parents and brothers and kinsmen and friends, and some of you they will put to death; you will be hated by all for my name's sake. But not a hair of your head will perish. By your endurance you will gain your lives" (Luke 21:12-19).

The Christians of Nigeria have for too long been complacent, conformist, apathetic and despondent. They have been too weak to stand up and be counted on the side of truth. But today we are being challenged to abandon the posture of complacency. The embarrassing socio-political realities of our day are a constant reminder that if we do not stand up for something we shall fall for anything. Many Nigerians, including many highly placed Christians have fallen by the wayside. They have fallen for power, they have fallen for pleasure, they have fallen for money. Greed for money and lust for power have robbed many of our brothers and sisters of their Christian consciences. That is why they offer themselves as instruments in the hands of known oppressors of God's children. That is why they do not hesitate to be in solidarity with deceitful leaders. That is why they applaud fraudsters and sing the praises of dictators.

The resurrection of Christ should however always be a reminder to Christians that truth has overcome falsehood, and that though liars may prosper in an evil age, the reign of falsehood is short-lived. Christians must be convinced that evil doers shall share the fate of Satan, the patron of evil, that liars shall perish with the devil the father of lies. It is the prerogative of Christians to study the phenomenon of fraud and falsehood in our socio-political and economic set-up, to identify the lie wherever it rears its head, to warn society of its devastating potential, and to champion the cause of combating and dislodging the structures of falsehood.

The Nigerian Christian elite have a responsibility to shape the direction of their society. We cannot be passive onlookers in the unfolding of events in our country. We must keep up the light even amid the storm. We must keep the dream of justice alive for as long as the darkness lasts. We must continue to hunger for righteousness even as we are daily confronted with endemic corruption and chronic oppression. We must dissociate ourselves from the prevalent structures in our country that are structures of violence and death. We must not only denounce all authority structures that oppress, intimidate, alienate, and impoverish people, but also, we must make a definite commitment to the evolution of alternative social, economic, and political structures that will make for justice, good governance, peace, and prosperity.

Those of us who genuinely seek peace for our country must be ready to pay the price for peace, which sometimes may include martyrdom. We must reject the culture of indiscipline, crass materialism, conspicuous consumption, greed, selfishness, economic exploitation, social discrimination, arbitrary rule, false propaganda, capital punishment, etc., which today make peace impossible. We must take up the challenge of conceiving, promoting, and enthroning alternative socio-economic and political structures which will make for peace, with all the resources at our disposal. We must be ready to commit our resources to programmes and projects aimed at educating and empowering the poor, freeing those unjustly held captive, pulling down walls of hatred and building bridges across the rivers of ethnic, religious, and social hostilities.

Finally, we recognise along with the Psalmist that unless the Lord builds the house, the labourer labours in vain, and unless the Lord watches over the city, the sentries watch in vain (Psalm 127:1). And indeed, Jesus told his disciples in John 15:5 that "cut off from me you can do nothing." We believe that the Lord who enabled his disciples to bear fearless witness to His name, will grant committed Nigerian Christians the abiding presence and power of the Spirit which they need to be authentic witnesses for truth and justice in this country. Even as we struggle through the present darkness, may those committed to His name find His light and His peace. Amen.

CHAPTER TWO

Moment of Truth
(Written on May 24, 1992)

In the weeks following Easter, Nigeria was clearly in a state of emergency, whether the authorities accept this fact or not. Beginning in Lagos, and spreading like wildfire through Benin to Kaduna and Zaria, there occurred what looked like the people's revolution that did not quite succeed, or was it just gathering momentum? Workers went on strike, students staged demonstrations, street people went on the rampage, tribesmen declared war, and blood-thirsty religious fanatics had a field day. The complacency of government in the face of the death-dealing economic hardship brought about by the deregulation of the Naira, and further exacerbated by the unprecedented nationwide fuel shortage, sent the hungry and angry mobs unto the streets in several cities. They had had enough, and they were poised to kill, to maim, and to destroy.

As the embittered students, the aggrieved workers, the hopeless applicants, and the murderous fanatics could not get at the authorities, they made for public structures, company buildings, government vehicles, petrol stations and tankers, and alas, the precious blood of their fellow sufferers. In Kaduna State, the crisis assumed the dimension of a full-scale war, as the long-standing ethno-political and religious tension between the natives of Zangon-Kataf and the Hausa and Fulani settlers blew up, and spread to Zaria and Kaduna, where recent history repeated itself, as Churches, shops, and private homes were burnt, and hundreds of human beings lay dead. And the dust has not quite settled.

The truth of the moment is that the government has not only lost credibility, but has lost control. The primary reason why governments exist is to ensure the safety and well-being of the citizens. If in any political entity this safety and well-being cannot be ensured, then the government of such a political entity exists only in name. It appears to us that just as the authorities of Nigeria have lost control of the economy, so have they lost their grip on the polity. What we are witnessing in present-day Nigeria, as the events of the last few weeks typify, is anomy, or is it anarchy? The truth of the moment is that those at the helm of affairs are only serving their own selfish interests, and not the interests of the people.

With the institutionalisation of corruption and the widespread abuse of the people, through the trading of lies, open robbery and victimisation, the authorities seem to have planted seeds of violence that have matured and are now bearing fruits in the form of reckless murder and arson. Propaganda as a machinery to keep the people docile under these structures of violence, has failed, as the ugly events of the last few weeks are able to show. The truth of the moment is that, while some of the people can be deceived some of the time, all the people cannot be deceived all the time. The poor of Nigeria are beginning to take to the streets as their counterparts did only a few years ago in Eastern Europe. Like their comrades in misery who, in different parts of the world at different times, have braved it through a procession of tanks and artillery, Nigerians are beginning to react to the structures of violence that have suppressed them for so long. And they are doing it fearlessly, for the truth of the moment is that, when life is worthless, fear is banished.

Much of the reaction of the aggrieved poor in the last few weeks, however, is senseless and misguided. What is the sense in the hungry and angry Nigerians pouncing on their fellow sufferers and killing or maiming them? Why will they burn down public buildings and vehicles, procured with the resources of their motherland? What is the rationale behind the burning of churches? Is the Christian God to whom these buildings are dedicated suspected of being a secret accomplice in the destitution of the people? Or is it that the oppressors have succeeded in turning people against themselves, while they continue business as usual? But if this trend continues, no one is going to be spared. The impending doom is in the form of collective decay. Is there no one then to halt the process of decomposition of the Nigerian society? Is there no balm in Gilead, at least to sooth the multiple wounds, if the cancer cannot be entirely removed?

Faced with the threat of decay, we are reminded that Christians are the salt of the earth, whose role is precisely to fight against decay, by resisting the agents of decomposition. And in today's Nigeria, the agents of decomposition are greed, avarice, selfishness, slothfulness, thoughtlessness, as well as religious and ethnic bigotry, which is increasingly narrowing itself down to senseless clannishness. Yes, these are the agents of decomposition, now rife in the sick organism called Nigeria, which must be destroyed if the country is to survive as an entity.

They are lethal viruses against which a war must be fought and won if Nigeria is to live again.

Christians as the light of the world must never adjust to a life of darkness. As darkness engulfs the society, we call on Christians to rise and shine in fidelity to their name and calling, and live above greed, avarice, and selfishness. We call on Christians to reject the indignity of political, ethnic or religious bigotry. We call on Christians to reject violence as a way of life, and to demonstrate to the confused world that the way of justice and love is the way of peace. It is, above all, the responsibility of Christians to witness to government and the powerful people of the land, that unjust policies will destroy not only the weak, but also the powerful policy maker, that unfair distribution of resources will destroy not only the poor victim, but also the rich perpetrator, and that those who engineer the destruction of others' lives and property will, before long, become victims of the same machinery of destruction. Under these circumstances of present-day Nigeria, Christians must be men and women of thought and imagination, for where there is no vision, the people do perish!

CHAPTER THREE

WANTED: A New Generation of Nigerians
(Written on June 20, 1992)

In the wake of the recent riots across the country, by which many Nigerians registered their protest against the injustice of the prevalent economic structures, and after the crisis of Zangon-Kataf, that quickly spread through the whole of Kaduna State, leaving thousands of people dead, and millions of naira worth of property destroyed, and as tension still mounts in the Northern part of Nigeria, there is a general feeling of insecurity, accompanied by widespread discouragement and disillusionment about the trend of events in the society, and particularly the blatant hypocrisy of the Nigerian leadership. Even among pious believers, there is frustration that arises from the apparent failure of Christian groups and individuals to make any serious impact on the morale of the citizens.

It is becoming clear to many of us that the present adult population of Nigeria is chronically and perhaps terminally ill. It is as if all known treatments have been attempted and they seem to have been to no avail. Shehu Shagari's Ethical Revolution failed, because in the context of that corrupt regime, no idea could be as devoid of meaning. Muhammed Buhari's War Against Indiscipline failed, because it became more of an instrument of repression than of discipline. And Ibrahim Babangida's MAMSER is presently hanging in the balance because nothing could be more hypocritical than the noise they make, amid official corruption, abuse of human rights, and the systematic destitution of the peasantry.

Furthermore, many Nigerians have become apprehensive about change in regime, even as the country prepares for a return to democracy. Past records and present political developments indicate that it would be naïve to continue to think that a change in government would amount to an improvement in the living conditions of the peasant population. What has become true, sadly enough, is that a change of baton catapults a new set of scavengers into positions of power, from where, like the pigs of the Animal Farm fable, they feed on the carcasses of their erstwhile fellow sufferers. It is unfortunate but true, that what Ayi Kwesi Armah said of Ghana in the 1960s is applicable to the present-day Nigeria: that "The Beautiful Ones Are Not Yet Born."

The failure of parents and leaders to inspire the young people in right living has given birth to a brood of deviants, who now constitute a nuisance in our homes, our schools, our offices, and on our streets. The irrational pursuit of material goods, the enthronement of money as king in many hearts and homes, coupled with the gratification of the flesh through illicit and scandalous sexual unions, have robbed many parents, teachers and leaders, of the moral authority that should accompany their position in society. They have largely lost their rightful place as moulders of conscience. Many parents, teachers, and leaders have become objects of ridicule, rather than points of light for the young ones. The violence that rages on in the society, has made life very unsafe, even in remote villages. Many young people are discouraged and have lost hope. Others have lost the sense of meaning and direction. And still others protest the evil of society and the hypocrisy of the leaders, by resorting to hard drugs and getting involved in all sorts of pervert and anti-social behaviour. The whole system is collapsing.

Yet, we are where we are today largely because we have lost our traditional sense of God and of the sacred. We are in this mess because just as we have lost the sense of God, we have also lost the sense of the value of the human person. If armed robbery has become so rampant, if political thuggery has become the order of the day, and if bribery and corruption in public office are part of business as usual, the reason is that money and pleasure have become our god, and foolishness has ascended the throne, while reason is on recess. Yes, the multiple ailments of the Nigerian organism are symptoms of widespread godlessness, a situation which cannot sustain for too long before a total collapse occurs.

We call for a new generation of God-fearing Nigerians to arise from the debris of the multitude that are a lost generation, as far as justice, discipline, integrity, and peaceful co-existence are concerned. We call for a new generation of Nigerian Christians out of the millions that fill our churches every Sunday, but whose lives do not distinguish them as the light and the salt amid a dark and decaying society. We challenge the thoughtful few, the remnant of the Lord, to take the bull by the horn, and pilot this country along the path of sanity and probity. As the country prepares for the various elections in the Federal Legislature and Executive, we challenge aspiring leaders to abandon clannishness and selfishness in favour of true patriotism and public accountability, and to give God his rightful place in public and private life. We call on the emerging generation of Nigerians to appreciate the wisdom of Proverbs 1:7 that "The fear of the Lord is the beginning of wisdom," and of

Matthew 16:26 which asks: "What does it profit a man if he gains the whole world but loses his soul?"

There is a saying that each time a new child is born to us, it is evidence that God has not yet despaired of the world. The same could be said of each sunrise. Our God is a patient and long-suffering God. His anger lasts for a moment, but his mercy for all eternity. Shall we allow the beautiful ones to be born in us, or do we still prefer to join the bandwagon in a life of bribery and corruption, of clannishness and selfishness, of blind pleasure and crass materialism, and of ethnic bigotry and political violence? Shall we allow the sun of righteousness to rise in us, or shall we rather perish in the darkness of a long night? I believe that Christians have no choice in these matters if they are to remain true to their calling. The new generation must turn their backs on the prevalent life of darkness and foolishness. They must be men and women of reason and imagination. They must hold the torch, or at least the light, for where there is no vision, the people do perish!

CHAPTER FOUR

NIGERIA: The Wage of Sin is Death
(Written on July 10, 1992)

St. Paul says that the wage of sin is death. The Nigerian civil service is now harvesting the wage of sin, the reward for corruption and indiscipline, as Mike Wallace, the *C.B.S.* presenter recently demonstrated to the entire world in a *60 Minutes'* show of shame. It is incredible but true, that with cash in hand a foreigner could enter Nigeria without travelling documents, and if he wants, he could obtain a Nigerian passport. With enough cash, a traveler could import just anything into Nigeria, including hard drugs, guns, and grenades. And he would be sure to pass through all the security checks. Yes, with money in hand, a foreign national visiting Nigeria for the first time could obtain a birth certificate showing that he was born in Nigeria. He could obtain a citizenship certificate testifying that he hails from the remotest district in Nigeria!

True, the punishment for sin is death. For the cumulative effect of large-scale corruption on the part of our Immigration Officials, Customs Officers, Police Officers, and other agents of the law, is the social decay projected to the entire world on the *C.B.S.* programme. The rest of the sane world was shocked and bewildered when they watched on screen the abnormal level of corruption in Nigeria. They must be asking whether all Nigerians are crazy. The civilized world must be asking whether there are no good people left in the land. The Christian world must be asking whether only pagans live in the land. They must be asking whether there are no prophets, no visionaries, and seers in the land. Yet after the show of shame at which ours was proclaimed "the most corrupt nation on earth," Nigerians have continued business as usual. There is yet no sign of repentance, there is no sign of regret. And so, death continues to reign in the land.

Indeed, the harvest of sin is death. For today there is death on our highways in the hands of reckless drivers who have no regard for highway codes. There is death in the hands of trigger-happy policemen who lack the proper morale, training, and technical equipment to man roadblocks. There is death on our highways at the hands of vengeful youths otherwise known as armed robbers. There is death on our township roads at the hands of vindictive youths otherwise known as "area boys." There is death in our institutions of learning at the hands of mischievous youths who have become dare-devil secret cultists. There is death in our hospitals at the hands of careless and reckless practitioners who have no regard for the ethics of their profession. It is all part of the culture of death, the harvest of sin.

Alas, the reward of sin is death. For all over the land there is the foul smell of decay. Human life in Nigeria is cheap, very cheap, and easily expendable. With the slightest provocation, an irate mob has often burnt fellow citizens to death with tires, petrol, or acid, with no recourse to any law. Such dead bodies sometime are left to decompose on our roads, with no individual, group, or agency taking responsibility for their removal. The remains are often run over by motor vehicles until they become indistinguishable from the tar. Passers-by would put up with the stench rather than make a move to take the shame away. Now and again, we hear of babies being abandoned by young mothers who reject motherhood. It is all part of the culture of death, the reward of sin.

Oh yes, the wage of sin is death, for Nigerians heard of the three-and-a-half-year-old child in Ibadan, Bosede, who had a six-inch nail driven through her skull and was left in the bush on New Year's Eve. Many people expressed outrage. They called it a sinister act, a most callous act. "The perpetrators must be brought to book." "The police must track down the scoundrels." But after a few weeks, the noise about Bosede has died down. And now it is business as usual. Not long ago we heard of the beheading of a man in Kano, for an alleged desecration of the Quran. The angry killers paraded the head round the city. Noise about this incident has also died down. And now it is business as usual. These things happen every day. Only a few are picked up by the press. The truth is that Nigeria has become a very violent country. Nigerians are sick in the mind. The Nigerian dog has tasted blood and has gone berserk. Nigerians are adjusting fast to the culture of violence. They are fast losing their traditional reverence for life and are now eating each other's flesh raw. That is all part of the culture of death, the wage of sin.

No doubt, the harvest of sin is death, for our streets are lined up with children, beautiful children and even toddlers who, ever before they know what life is, must put up with the indignity of begging for a living. Nigerians are witnesses to the pitiable sight of fine children, whose daily preoccupation is to scavenge through one refuse dump after the other in search of rotten fruits, sour food, and used clothes. Nigerians are putting up with the ugly sight of young boys and girls dangerously running after moving vehicles, to sell some miserable wares. That is all part of the culture of death, the harvest of sin.

For sure, the payment of sin is death, for while the poor are under the constant threat of death by starvation, the rich themselves are often subjected to deadly harassment by angry youths who have nothing to lose. The rich and powerful Nigerians are experiencing death in numerous other ways. Thus, no one is spared. The rich and the poor alike, oppressors as well as the oppressed, must face up to the dire consequences of sin. We've got to drink from our own wells or otherwise swim in our own mess. That is the oracle of God for an unrepentant generation.

Alas, the wage of sin is death. And the fulfillment of this oracle is manifested in the disorder that is apparent everywhere, for as the political climate is polluted by primitive feudalism, military dictatorship, lust for money, and greed for power, so is the economy destroyed by the sheer lawlessness and thoughtlessness of the Nigerian opportunist, who loots all available resources of the land to emerge a multi-millionaire overnight, while the multitude starve to death. Our autochthonous conquerors may be celebrating their loot in palatial mansions and state-of-the-art gadgets, but God's oracle concerning the wage of sin is quietly but surely being fulfilled in our land. Those fraudsters who in the face of a national tragedy are feasting sumptuously, and are shamelessly parading the spoils of corruption, may be under the illusion that cheating pays. But they are mistaken. Those who are having the best of times during this period of agony and desperation in our land, may be under the illusion that true life can be lived amidst a culture of sin. But they are mistaken, for there is no rest for the wicked. Instead, the reward of sin is death.

Indeed, the reward of sin is death. The Nigerian leadership shall yet answer for their flirtation with death in the form of corruption, fraud, deceit, and mischief. Our political elite shall yet pay for their romance with death by way of ideological prodigality, greed for money, lust for power, large-scale mismanagement, and blatant wastage. Our economic elite shall get the appropriate reward for their entanglement with death in the form of massive fraud, exploitation, and economic sabotage. Our military elite shall reap the harvest of their courtship with death in the form of oppression, intimidation, social abuse and widespread violation of human rights and dignity. Our military dictators have enthroned violence in the land, in as much as they have attempted to rule by the force of the gun, instead of the people's consent. Military dictatorship is by its very nature primary violence. It is structural violence. It generates and nurtures an environment of tension, fear, anxiety, oppression, aggression, and intimidation.

There can be no peace in the land if we continue to live under the dictatorship of the gun, for the old adage remains true that he who lives by the sword perishes by the sword. Yes, the harvest of dictatorship is the reign of a culture of death, in which armed robbery, street violence, violent demonstrations, jungle justice, arson, murder, abortion, suicide, child abuse, drug abuse, and rape, are an everyday occurrence. Those who have been wooing the angel of death by a lifestyle of corruption, oppression, and injustice, shall pay for their prodigality, for as you lay your bed, so do you lie on it. The Fathers of the Second Vatican Council assert that all acts of indignity against human life and against the human person debase the perpetrators more than the victims. The oracle of God remains true, I say, that the harvest of sin is death.

The Nigerian problem appears at first sight to be complex and multifaceted. Perhaps a closer look will reveal that it is not that complex. The solution can be quite simple too. Enormous human and material resources have been expended on all sorts of experimentation and adventure in political engineering and economic reconstruction. But they have led us nowhere. Perhaps the simple solution to our problem is a return to the basics. Our political, economic, and social structures, in as much as they are based on foundations of falsehood, selfishness and injustice, can only lead to death. A return to the basics shall entail repentance from falsehood, selfishness and injustice, and conversion to truth, love, and justice.

As a corporate entity, we are moving along the path of destruction, and if we do not change our course, we are bound to end up where we are headed. The moment has come for us Nigerians to look critically at our past and honestly acknowledge the immense damage wrought by our individual and communal sins. We must have a rethink. We must make a change of course. However difficult the turnaround may be, we must act now, while the sun still shines over our heads. It does not matter how challenging the call may be. We must make the move while the leaves are still green. Christians call this rethink *repentance*. We call this change of course *conversion*. What Nigerian Christians must do now is to take the lead in this penitential revolution. All baptised people in this country must champion this penitential revolution, for where there is no vision, the people do perish!

CHAPTER FIVE

Light Your Own Candle
(Written on July 30, 1992)

Today's Nigerians are a grumbling lot. Practically everyone is complaining about everything and everyone else, but hardly anyone is doing something concrete towards changing anything. Everyone seems to recognise that things are not the way they should be. We all seem to know that the evils that plague our society are, among others, selfishness, greed, avarice, and religious and ethnic bigotry. Our leaders are largely self-seeking, whether they rule by the gun, or they claim the mandate of the electorate. By means of a combination of propaganda and brutal force, the people are brought to submission. Then, a culture of violence is nurtured. Everybody complains, but, with time, more and more people dip their hands in the blood. And they are no longer innocent.

Our health institutions are themselves in a state of infirmity. Precious human lives are wasted, not only due to the lack of basic equipment and services in our public hospitals and clinics, but also due to the lack of commitment among health workers. Everybody complains, but soon, more and more people dip their hands in the blood. And they are no longer innocent. Our public utilities are largely in a state of disuse. The people suffocate in their own stench, for, though they know what could be done, no one would lift a finger. Our educational institutions suffer multiple debilities, including the menace of secret cults, drug abuse, examination malpractice, sexual harassment, and what could be described as a loss of vision in the ivory tower. We all know this, and we have all turned professional critics, but who will bell the cat?

Nigerians often complain as if the country is not a sovereign nation. They complain about the situation as if their rulers were vassal kings or hirelings who have little concern for the welfare of the indigenous population. Yet, Nigeria is no longer a colony of any nation. The Nigerian government is run by sons and daughters of the soil. Our depressed economy is managed by our brothers and sisters, our sick institutions are manned by our kith and kin. So, whom are we complaining about? The better to light a candle than to curse the darkness. Too many Christians sit by, as it were, helplessly, and watch the Nigerian organism degenerate under the combined forces of its multiple maladies. And it is a sad legacy that most of those who are loudest critics today soon turn out to be among the greatest culprits. The Nigerian university students of today, and the so-called new breed politicians, will soon turn out to be corrupt government officials, negligent professionals, irresponsible parents, and reckless rulers.

We challenge Nigerian Christians to stop complaining and begin to do something positive, both individually and collectively, towards salvaging the nation. Nigerian Christians must start somewhere, no matter how humble, for charity begins at home. Nigerian Christians have to take the bull by the horn, in accordance to their divine mission as the salt of the earth and the light of the world. Christians are not helpless before the forces of destruction in Nigeria. With the spiritual and moral resources available to us in Jesus Christ, we can fight back the collective decay that presently threatens the Nigerian nation, and champion the cause of justice and fair play in the country, beginning from our homes, our schools, our churches, unto our villages, our towns, and the nation at large.

We cannot all be presidents, governors, or legislators, but, rather than sit idly and complain endlessly about the deplorable state of our country, we should get into action in whatever way is open to us and ignite our Christian candles to fight the darkness of the country, whether as responsible parents or respectful children, devoted teachers or diligent students, God-fearing doctors or dedicated nurses, dutiful administrators or faithful labourers. Indeed, if every Christian teacher were highly dedicated, if every Christian doctor were really God-fearing... then Nigeria would not be the sick organism that it is today. Yes, if every Nigerian Christian lit just one little candle, what a bright country this would be!

There is an urgent need for Christians who are apostles of Truth to minister the truth that sets people free to Nigerians who today are in the captivity of greed and selfishness. There is a crying need for Christians who are apostles of Peace to minister the message of peace to Nigerians who today are in the bondage of a culture of violence. There is a desperate need for Christians who are apostles of Life to minister the message of life to Nigerians who today are wasting away their lives under a covenant of death. These apostles must rise from among the present generation of Nigerians Christians, and shine, for, where there is no vision, the people do perish!

CHAPTER SIX

Exploiting the Nigerian Malady
(Written on September 1, 1993)

The chronicle of callous intrigues, and mind-boggling subterfuge is unending. True, the Nigerian politician has a strange complex. Practically every one of them believes that he is the best. If he does not win an election, then that election must have been rigged, and so it must be canceled. If he cannot become president, then no civilian should; he would rather subscribe to military dictatorship. Babangida and his Machiavellian junta knew this very well. They exploited this psycho-political malady to prolong their stay in power, forming political associations and proscribing them, scheduling elections and canceling them, banning politicians and unbanning them, all at their whims and caprices.

At the close of the June 12 presidential elections, participants from the two official parties, and observers from within and outside the country testified that this was one of the most free and fair elections ever conducted in Nigeria; one in which ethnic and religious sentiments were for the first time apparently played down. Nigerians were congratulating themselves for after all they were able to conduct elections without the bitterness and violence that characterized previous attempts. But suddenly on June 23, Babangida nullified the elections in the most uncivilized manner, in total disregard for the will of 14 million voters. And rather than be outraged by this assault on their people's dream for freedom, and with unified force kick the devil out of office, they began to sing discordant tunes. Rather than face the generals and with one voice say "Enough is Enough," and "No More Dictatorship," sections of the political class, especially of the losing party began to sing the Babangida refrain, calling for another round of elections, and soliciting their people's support for an interim government, and finally asking the dictator to stay on for yet another term!

Since the onset of this multiple injustice Nigeria has not known peace, true to the proverbial saying that a nation without integrity can have no peace, or "when the wicked rule, the people groan." Even the delicate peace we used to enjoy has given way to an abiding state of tension and anxiety. The mass movement of Nigerians to their places of origin and the near paralyses of the entire social and economic structure smacks of anarchy or chaos, all because of the assault on democracy in which our politicians are active collaborators. This is the shame of Nigerian politics.

To us the most embarrassing dimension of this whole shameful drama is that there are Christians among the political elite. Nigerian Christians in politics are either active participants in the criminal conspiracy to despoil this nation, or they act as passive and as it were helpless on-lookers as the forces of darkness manipulate the poor of Nigeria like pawns on a chessboard. Either posture is inadmissible, for an account will be required of their stewardship.

A great challenge now lies ahead for Christians interested in partisan politics: they must act as sentries, prophetic voices, and visionaries in the blind alley of Nigerian politics. They must take very seriously the words of Jesus Christ in Matthew 5: 13 and14, "You are the salt of the earth...You are the light of the world," or be considered irrelevant in the scheme of God.

I join my voice to that of the Bishops' Conference of Nigeria and other well-meaning Nigerian groups and individuals, to call for serious prayers for a nation adrift in a sea of confusion, for unless the Lord builds the house, the labourers labour in vain (Psalm 127:1-2). I challenge Christian politicians to take the bull by the horn and address the truth of our corporate existence. We have lived a lie for too long. Our hope is that the moment of truth has finally come. We trust that the Lord is with us, and that he is in control. We trust that he will raise up for this country, God-fearing men and women to lead in the way of a politics of righteousness in place of what is today only a legacy of shame, for where there is no vision, the people perish!

CHAPTER SEVEN

The Shock of the Moment
(Written on September 5, 1993)

The political class has shocked right-thinking Nigerians to the bone. The sharp twists and turns, the devilish maneuvers and deadly intrigues that characterized Nigerian politics in the last few months portray the Nigerian political class at best as a set of unprincipled and irresponsible leaders, and at worst as a gang of greedy opportunists, reckless plunderers, and mindless looters. They have shown that they are manipulators who will use and abuse poor Nigerians repeatedly, exploiting the ignorance of the majority of the people, and cashing in on the existing ethnic and religious polarities when it pays them to.

After eight years of Machiavellian dictatorship, fraudulent governance, and murderous misrule, during which time the people of this country suffered all sorts of indignities, what General Babangida and his military cabal needed was to be disgraced out of office, but once again the political elite has shocked the rest of us with a display of political immaturity to an unprecedented degree.

True, greedy people always work against themselves, and at the end they lose both ways. Our politicians were in such a hurry to share the booty that they failed to finish prosecuting the war against the military. At the end of the day what left the rest of us speechless was that a good number of the politicians queued up at the dictator's door in groups, asking him to stay on to head the interim government in order to finish the good work he began. And to add insult to injury, they did not go as individuals, no, they presumed to go in their official capacities as representatives of Nigerian voters, as the voice of the voiceless grassroots poor!

It is said that politics is not about permanent friends or enemies, but about permanent interests. In trying to apply this principle to the Nigerian situation we are at a loss as to defining a more overriding principle or permanent interest in contemporary Nigerian politics than money. What has come to be known as "settlement" is nothing but bribery, large scale bribery. It is the looting of the national treasury for use in buying heads and minds and consciences and hearts. It is the use of the God-given resources of our land to further enslave a people who have already been stretched to breaking point under the draconian decrees, organized inflation, and official thuggery of the Babangida administration. "Settlement" has made sycophants, bootlickers, praise singers, and vile propagandists out of our politicians. But "settlement" is betrayal of public trust, and much more. "Settlement" is an act of thievery.

For all those involved in this "settlement", it is a conspiracy to steal not only the people's goods, but more seriously a conspiracy of the powerful to steal away the right of the poor to decent living, and peaceful existence. "Settlement" is a damnable sin in view of its terrible consequences on the agonizing poor of Nigeria. The sequence of political events since the cancellation of the June 12 presidential election, culminating in the swearing in of an interim government that is more or else a stooge or surrogate of the established dictator, convinces us that the politicians have indeed sold the country out to military plunderers, or at least that they are active collaborators in the grand conspiracy to rob the generality of Nigerians of freedom and well-being.

CHAPTER EIGHT

June 12 Election Annulment: Matters Arising
(Written on September 23, 1993)

After eight years of fraudulent governance, during which he presided over the devastation of a once vibrant economy and polity, General Babangida finally surrendered to internal protests and external pressures, and on August 25, 1993, bowed out of the presidential villa. But instead of respecting the will of the people as expressed at the presidential election of June 12, 1993, the dictator left as untidily as he came in. He instituted what to many observers is a surrogate contraption tagged "interim government" headed by Chief Ernest Shonekan, the same person who led the inconsequential "Transitional Council" for eight months. The interim government which is supposed to lead Nigeria out of the ongoing political quagmire has as many as six members of the defunct Babangida administration, including the Information Secretary, Uche Chukwumerije whose pro-Babangida propaganda was seen by many as capable of inciting citizens to war.

The hand-picked government also has on it General Babangida's Justice Secretary who churned out for suffering Nigerians the most repressive of military decrees. But the interim government, which has a seven-month tenure that expires on March 31, 1994, is faced with a herculean task making itself accepted by Nigerians and recognized by foreign governments and agencies. While many Nigerians celebrate the termination of the eight long tortuous years of dictatorship, they are nevertheless not satisfied with the interim arrangement which for them is a smokescreen or a charade. Many see it as another assault on democracy. Some individuals and organizations within and outside Nigeria have expressed the opinion that what Nigerians want now is a complete change, but that with the interim arrangement, nothing has really changed. They therefore call for an immediate termination of the tenure of the Shonekan-led government.

The Commonwealth Secretary-General, Chief Emeka Anyaoku reacted to the new arrangement by saying that the installation of an interim government "does not shed any more light on the in-comprehensible political developments in Nigeria beginning with the annulment of the democratic election held there on June 12, 1993." He asked the Interim

Government to "consider the full implications of permanently setting aside the June 12 presidential election that was nationally and internationally acclaimed to be free and fair." Virtually all the Human Rights organizations in the Country have denounced the installation of an interim government, calling on Nigerians to continue their civil disobedience, and make the country ungovernable until justice is restored, and the June 12th election is affirmed.

Dr. Beko Ransome Kuti, leader of the human rights organisation, Campaign for Democracy, just released from detention (along with Gani Fawehinmi, and Femi Falana) has warned foreign governments and agencies not to recognize the Interim National Government, for as he says, "It is an extension of military rule." Segun Jegede, the national administrative secretary of the Committee for the Defense of Human Rights, in a press release described the arrangement as "fundamentally defective and a misnomer as it lacks the people's mandate."

Meanwhile, the international community is reacting to the new development in Nigeria with caution. No definite pronouncements have so far been made by any foreign government in favour of the interim national government. Meanwhile the tension in the country has not subsided. Only few of those who moved their families and property to their villages of origin for fear of the outbreak of war have returned to base. The indications are that with so many cracks and bumps and holes in the interim arrangement, true peace is not yet in sight.

CHAPTER NINE

The Inviolability of Truth
(Written on September 24, 1993)

Nigerians are now daily agonizing under the enormous burden of the superstructure of lies deliberately put in place to suppress the truth of their communal existence. The nullification of the June 12th election, the vicious propaganda and the campaign of calumny against individuals and sections of the polity, and the subsequent imposition of an Interim National Government, are the latest additions to this burdensome structure of lies. The untidily constituted Interim National Government itself is a smokescreen designed to suppress the full expression of the truth of democracy in this land, but the charade has not quite succeeded. Instead, tension has continued to mount in the country. And realizing that they are enthroned on a pile of explosives, the members of the Interim National Government have resorted to begging for acceptance. They have spent the last one month traversing the land and using the remnant of our traditional feudal institutions, professional sycophants, and other prostitutes of power. They are begging us to forget the truth and settle for a lie. But just as the ING and its cronies are pleading passionately for recognition, so are the defenders of truth and protectors of freedom campaigning relentlessly for a return to the June 12th election.

The ongoing drama of shame in Nigeria is an expression of the resilience of truth. Truth is inviolable. Yes, immortal truth is indomitable. As often as it is crucified, so often shall it rise again. Persecutors of truth always end up being confounded and humiliated by the obstinacy of truth. Truth is a child of freedom, and it remains free despite all pretensions to cage or imprison it. Truth is inflammable, it is highly combustible. Those who attempt to seal up or suppress truth often discover in truth a potent explosive, which is less dangerous when exposed and contended with, than when sealed up or set aside. Like truth, the truth-bearer is a child of freedom too and shall always remain free despite the efforts of the enemies of truth to use all the available instruments of coercion to imprison, proscribe or silence him. As long as he remains on the side of truth, he shall remain free. The ongoing attempt in Nigeria to suppress truth and discredit, malign, and when possible, silence the bearers of truth will surely have a boomerang effect: Truth shall bounce back with a vengeance.

Many leaders, elders, and politicians in this country are habitual violators of truth. They have repeatedly sought to sacrifice truth on the altar of greed and lust for power. They have regularly attempted to mortgage truth for a life of debauchery. They have repeatedly attempted a definition of truth along the parameters of political expediency and economic gain. Now and again, our leaders have painted for the people the picture of a state of affairs which is antithetical to the reality on the ground. They have told us that black is white when we can see clearly that only the contrary is true. They have told us that what we have in Nigeria is one nation and one destiny, when our chequered political history shows that the contrary is true. But the violation of truth carries with it unwholesome consequences not only for the victims but also for the perpetrators. We are told to settle for a lie in order to avoid the outbreak of violence. But falsehood is itself primary violence, and when that falsehood is built into the political, social and economic structure of society, an explosion of violence soon occurs, as is cleverly demonstrated in the Biblical epic of the Tower of Babel (Genesis 11:1-9). To build a nation on a foundation of lies is to sow in the emerging nation the seed of its own destruction.

These days the agonizing masses of Nigeria, who are suffering the multiple violence of starvation, fear, and anxiety, compounded with the vexatious fuel shortage, are being told that the Interim National Government is meant to preserve the peace and unity of the country. They are told that those calling for justice by way of a return to the June 12th election, are dissidents, fomenters of trouble, unpatriotic elements, and enemies of peace. But what manner of peace are we seeking for Nigeria? Is it the false peace that comes via the suppression of the people's will or the fragile peace that thrives amidst the silencing of legitimate democratic aspirations? What manner of unity do we want for our country? Is it the false unity that comes via the intimidation of minority groups and opinions, or the fragile unity that thrives amidst primitive ethnicism, senseless statism and irrational religious bigotry?

We know that lasting peace can only be built on truth and justice. In fact, true peace, the state of affairs pictured in Isaiah 11:1-9, and the type of peace that the Lord Jesus declares in Luke 4:18 and John 14:27, is the fruit of justice. Lasting peace in any society is the reward for a consistent life of truth and justice. True peace is achieved by a people who know and live by the fact that righteousness exalts a nation, and that greed and avarice destroy a people. Democracy in its true expression is the mutual acknowledgement of certain fundamental truths, including the truth of the dignity, equality and freedom of all in a society. In Nigeria, democracy will only germinate and thrive upon the mutual recognition and acceptance of the truth that all the inhabitants of the geographical entity we call Nigeria must enjoy equal dignity and opportunities; that all who qualify to be called Nigerians by birth or naturalization must enjoy equal protection of the law, irrespective of ethnic origin, religious affiliation, or political preference.

Jesus Christ identified Himself as the Truth and the Life (John 14:6); to accept Him is to know the truth that sets one free (John 8:32). He came into the world to bear witness to the truth, and only those on the side of truth really hear His voice (John 18:37). Christians are by their very calling champions and prime defenders of truth. No one therefore qualifies to bear the name "Christian" if he does not defend the truth at all times - in season and out of season, welcome or unwelcome. No one should presume to be in the sheepfold of Christ if he compromises truth in fear or for selfish gain. No one who settles for a lie is worthy of Christ.

As the pressure mounts daily, and more and more people settle with the idea of an Interim National Government, Christians who under pressure compromise the truth should know that they not only shirk their responsibility to be salt for the earth and light for the world, but also by the very act of compromising truth, they pitch their tent against truth. Such persons are offenders and violators of truth. Those who are promoting the idea that under the present circumstances, "in order to avoid chaos and anarchy," we should accept one more structure of lies, are under the peculiar delusion that the flower of peace can emerge from the debris of lies, injustice, corruption and manipulation. But this is only a delusion. The authorities may succeed for a while in silencing truth. They may win over all the royal fathers, elder statesmen, and the so-called honourable and eminent personalities and groups, but the indomitable truth shall resurrect and bounce back, but this time with a vengeance. As we write, the country remains on the edge of a precipice. To escape the vengeful judgement of crucified truth, Nigerian Christians must stand up and be counted on the side of truth, for where there is no vision, the people perish!

CHAPTER TEN

Saving Our Educational System

An Address Delivered at the Public Presentation of the book:
Education In Kogi State by Dr. A.A. Olagboye, in Lokoja,
On Thursday, October 7, 1993.

I congratulate Dr. Amos Olagboye for his commitment to education in Kogi State, which has led him to put together this fine book on Education in Kogi State. I commend his research efforts in tracing the development and maintenance of the various administrative and management structures for education on the State level, from the old Kabba Province of Northern Nigeria, through the creation of Kwara State in 1967 and subsequently Benue State in 1976, to the creation of Kogi State in 1991, with the consequent re-union of parts of the old Kwara-Benue factors and structures. Ladies and gentlemen, you will agree with me that at these critical times in our country, when "survival" seems to be all that matters, anyone who commits his time and scarce resources to such an unprofitable venture as the writing of a book, at a time when education has lost almost all its glory, deserves our unreserved commendation and encouragement. It is my hope that the efforts of Dr. Olagboye will inspire other eminent academics and educationists in Kogi State whose talents are currently being buried in the sand, to put some of their thoughts together for posterity. In the civilized world, books are indispensable. They are the principal source of acquiring and imparting knowledge in the Arts and Sciences. The acute shortage of books and other reading materials in our schools and colleges, and the gradual disappearance of a reading culture in the wider society, spells doom for the future of scholarship in Nigeria.

Too many things have happened within the last fifteen years to the structure, the management, the administration, the supervision, and the financing of State schools and colleges, culminating in a serious dislocation of our educational system, whose symptoms are the much-decried fall in academic standards, widespread indiscipline, examination malpractice, frequent riots and violent demonstrations. Perhaps an even greater dislocation has occurred in the psyche of the contemporary Nigerian teacher, whose morale is now judged to be at its lowest in the history of education in Nigeria. The senseless politicization of education at the Federal, State, and Local Government levels, the gross neglect of education in the allocation of funds by successive governments, and the shabby treatment of teachers of all cadres, have combined to rob education and the teaching profession of their traditional pride, dignity, and honour. It is as if a tragic war is being deliberately waged against the destiny of the people through the destruction of education, the very organ in which resides the hope of tomorrow.

The quality of life and work in our public schools and colleges has become a thing of shame and a source of embarrassment to many of us who have an idea of what educational institutions should look like. I consider myself fortunate for going through secondary school at the time I did. The economy of the country was buoyant, and education was considered a viable venture worth investing upon. Though there has always been corruption in this country, but by the time I went through primary and secondary schools, corruption in public life, and especially that aspect of corruption which involves the appropriation of public funds for private use had not assumed the crisis dimension of today. By then government schools were fairly well funded.

Today, almost all State and Local Government-run schools and colleges are in a deplorable state. Most of the physical structures are in a state of total neglect and disrepair. The schools lack basic textbooks, laboratory equipment and other tools for imparting knowledge. At a time when developments in educational technology have made computers, video recorders and projectors necessary tools for adequate instruction in schools, our public schools often lack such elementary tools as the chalk or duster. Some schools are unable to procure their class registers and record of work books several weeks into the term, while others often have to write their terminal or sessional examinations on the chalkboard, as there are no funds for the required stationery.

The library shelves are virtually empty. Staff quarters, in schools where they used to exist, have now been abandoned by the staff to annual bush fires as the authorities have left them un-maintained and uncared-for for ages. Very few schools have staff buses, and even fewer staff members have vehicles, to the effect that many often need to trek for several kilometers to school on empty stomachs. Arriving in school tired and haggard, they are often unable to perform. I salute all those currently serving as teachers in State-owned schools, for their resilience in the face of discouraging and demoralizing circumstances. In almost all State-owned schools, the teachers are faced with the onerous task of molding bricks without straws. If some of the erstwhile colonial administrators or missionaries who founded some of these schools should visit any of them today, they would weep at the devastation we have unleashed upon the projects of their pride.

Imagine what has become of the once imperial Provincial Secondary School Okene, now Abdul Azeez Atta Memorial College. Think of what has become of the once prestigious Women Teachers' College Kabba, now Kabba Teachers' College. See what has become of the once elegant Crowder Memorial College. Ladies and gentlemen, we have so destroyed the school system and the teaching profession, that the remnant of Nigerian teachers is now made up largely of a bunch of disgruntled, disillusioned, frustrated, and depressed professionals. Lacking in motivation or encouragement, their output in terms of teaching, research, and publication, is understandably low.

The cumulative result of all this is not only that we are producing graduates of secondary schools, polytechnics, and universities, who cannot compete on equal terms with their counterparts trained elsewhere, but more painfully, that education is gradually losing its pride of place in the Nigerian society, and that the teaching profession has lost much of its status of honour and has rather become a despised and derided profession. Outside the schools, there is hardly any reading culture. At ten or twelve Naira and at twenty or thirty naira respectively, local Newspapers and Magazines are beyond the reach of the average Nigerian, and such international Magazines as *Time* or *Newsweek* can no longer be found, even on university library shelves.

The project of education is supposed to be the promise of the future in any society, yet comparatively speaking, teachers are the least remunerated workers in the Nigerian economy. It is unusual today for a young graduate to wish to make a career out of teaching. Many pick up the chalk as a last resort, when all efforts to secure other employments fail, and they remain in teaching only for as long as they are unable to find better jobs. Practically every other job is better than teaching in today's Nigeria: A PhD holder in History or Mathematics will rather queue up for a job with the Customs Department, than take his chair at the University or College of Education. Also, a PhD holder in Economics will prefer the job of a counter cashier in a Commercial Bank, rather than become a university teacher. True, what the headmaster of a primary school with thirty years cognate experience takes home at the end of the month, is often not as much as the total remuneration of a newly employed messenger in an Oil

Company. And with the Structural Adjustment Programme, the teacher's monthly salary is hardly enough for a week.

Teachers often cannot measure up with their colleagues in the civil service of the same state, as they are often denied the regular promotions that are their due. (I am aware of several graduate teachers who have remained on the same salary grade level for nine or ten years!). The result is that the Nigerian teacher has become notorious for poverty, and this erstwhile noble career now attracts only drop-outs, failures, and unlucky people. This situation cries out for immediate rectification, for when the institutions set up for the pursuit of knowledge are despised and the instruments that transmit this knowledge from one generation to the other are in disrepute, the future is in jeopardy. If the current trend in educational degeneration is allowed to continue, the impending doom shall be in the form of collective decay. No one shall be spared; not even the children of the rich who are sent overseas or who attend Capital Schools, Command Secondary Schools, or Federal Government Colleges.

But is there no balm in Gilead? Is there no one to halt this process of decomposition in the Nigerian society? If what is happening to education today is a deliberate attempt by the powers that be to destroy the machinery of education so that they may constitute an uninformed and therefore submissive citizenry, then they have got more than they bargained for: in the process of destroying education, a culture of violence is set in train, and an angry mob is being made of the young population. The failure of government and the leaders of society to inspire the young people in the pursuit of higher values, has left us with a brood of deviants, addicts, and outlaws, who now constitute a nuisance in our homes, schools, and offices. An unprecedented wave of violence now rages through the land and threatens the very foundation of our society. Life is becoming very unsafe even in remote villages. Many young people see the mess their leaders have made of the society, and they are discouraged. Others have totally lost the sense of meaning and direction. And still others protest against the evil of the society and the hypocrisy of their leaders by resorting to hard drugs and enlisting in secret cults that unleash indiscriminate violence on society. The whole system appears to be collapsing, yet our leaders seem completely oblivious of the fact.

We must say that the crisis in the Nigerian educational set-up is an index of the country's socio-political equilibrium. Yes, the rupture in our institutions of learning is a measure of the communal health of this country. Indeed, the rapid deterioration of our public schools is an indictment on all Nigerians, and particularly on our leaders for their carelessness, their thoughtlessness, their recklessness, and their outright prodigality with the project of education in this country. Nigeria does not lack the human and material resources necessary to redeem our educational enterprise. Nigeria does not lack the technical know-how to turn things around for the better. Nigeria has the means to establish and run schools that are schools, not breeding grounds for thieves, thugs, and touts. What Nigeria lacks is the political will to make things happen. We must summon this will and act now, if we are not to kill tomorrow before today's sun sets.

I seize the opportunity of the presentation today of Dr. Olagboye's book: *Education in Kogi State*, to call for an urgent re-orientation of the Nigerian citizenry on the place of education in the collective destiny of a people. We call for de-politicization in the establishment and administration of schools, and in the hiring and firing of teachers. We call for a re-prioritization in the allocation and management of our human and material resources, thus giving education the pride of place it deserves. And finally, we call for a re-formulation of our educational goals, principles, and policies, with the aim of demolishing sterile and superfluous structures, of decentralizing the management set-up, and of reducing to the barest minimum the usual bureaucracies of government as far as education is concerned.

CHAPTER ELEVEN

When Will Abacha Go?
(Written on February 28, 1994)

The traditional role of the military is to defend the state against external aggression and internal subversion. In the enlightened societies of the modern world, the army performs this task at the orders of, and in strict obedience to an elected government. The soldiers, armed with guns that are purchased with the resources of the nation, are trained to shoot the enemy at wartime, and in peacetime to oil their machinery and stay on guard, or perform such constructive tasks as may be assigned to them by the civil authority. The military has no business whatsoever in politics. Military intervention therefore under whatever guise is a stumbling block on a nation's way to economic development, social progress, and political maturity. Military governments are, to say the least, a derogation from the democratic development of any country.

The twenty-three years in which Nigeria has been subjected to different shades of military dictatorship are years eaten by the locust. Those twenty-three years are years during which the Nigerian soul has been obfuscated, the Nigerian people emasculated, and the Nigerian landscape devastated. As a nation we have made no gains whatsoever from the flirtation of the military with the unfamiliar terrain of political governance. Instead, what we have is a near total destruction of the Nigerian psyche, a reckless despoliation of our human and natural resources, and the consequent diminishment of our national potential.

Late last year, the Chief of Army Staff, Major General Chris Ali delivered an address to Nigerian soldiers in which he congratulated the army for its commitment to "democratic ideals," and applauded its role in maintaining unity, stability, and peace in Nigeria. Speaking at the end of 1993, the year in which the military presided over the enactment of a national disgrace, and the same year in which unarmed civilians dared artillery guns and tanks, and kicked the accomplished military despot out of power, General Chris Ali was deluded into asserting that the army enjoys the support and concern of Nigerians. Only recently the Abacha regime marked its first 100 days in office. And as has become customary in these fraudulent days, sponsored editorial comments and news analyses especially from government-owned media houses applauded the regime and congratulated the key actors for delivering Nigeria from the dark days of 1993, into the new dawn of peace and progress. There can be no greater insult to the sensitivities of Nigerian citizens!

The sycophants, bootlickers and praise singers presume that we all have short memories. But they are mistaken. Many of us still remember that it is the military, especially under Ibrahim Babangida which has so masterfully divided the constituent segments of Nigeria against themselves while trying to hold on to power at all costs. We still remember that it is the military which set the entire country on fire by purportedly annulling a free and fair presidential election. If the ship of the Nigerian state is today on the edge of the precipice, many of us still remember that it is the military which brought us thus far. Yes, many of us remain convinced that the werewolves of institutionalised corruption, economic plunder and political ruination were conceived, gestated, and delivered in Nigeria under the large eyes of the military dictators. For any military cabal therefore to parade themselves as messiahs in Nigeria soon after the shame of 1993, is not only ironical but insulting.

General Sanni Abacha might well be sincere in his messianic mission to turn Nigeria around and see us through the transition from the darkness of near disintegration to the new dawn of peace and prosperity, but we have reason to remain sceptical. As a key player in all the regimes preceding his own, including the illegal Interim National Government, the new occupant at Aso Villa will have a hard time convincing principled Nigerians that he has any more credentials to rule than the instruments of coercion presently at his disposal. As one who worked hand-in-hand, step-by-step, and neck-to-neck with General Babangida to run a government that plundered this country to shreds, the new Strongman shall be continually haunted by the ghost of yesterday's pillage. As an intrinsic part of the intricate plot to perpetuate the military in power, which in 1993 was violently resisted by those on whom sovereignty really resides, the new dictator shall be hard-pressed convincing doubting Nigerians that he is a worthy midwife of the desired democracy. And as an eminent player, faithful supporter, and prime beneficiary of the regime of corruption and destruction that Ibrahim Babangida presided over for eight years, General Sani Abacha shall find it difficult to prosecute any war against corruption and indiscipline. The reason is that Nigerians know only too well that the leopard does not change its spots so easily. They know very well too that he who comes to equity must come with clean hands.

Indications from the first 100 days of the Abacha regime do not encourage even the most generous of Nigerians to entrust their destiny and the destiny of their fatherland into the hands of war tacticians. The shady agenda of the regime, the silence over the length of its tenue, the refusal to probe the last military regime, the awkward circumstances surrounding the promulgation of the first ten decrees released by the administration, and the undemocratic manner by which it appears to be going about the proposed Constitutional Conference, are some of the handwritings on the wall.

True, Nigerians have seen enough mercenaries that come in the name of messiahs. Nigerians have had enough of military tacticians who parade themselves as a political think tank. Nigerians will do well without another set of wolves in sheep's clothing. It is time to tell the truth as it is, namely, that a military-organised form of democracy is no democracy. Do we need to waste another eight years to be convinced of this fact? No, we need to be rescued, or rather to rescue ourselves from the vicious circle of false and endless transitions. For too long we have been rotating on the same axis, running in circles, and moving nowhere.

What we need today is a Sovereign National Conference, at which forum the various ethnic republics, political interest groups and religious bodies in the geographical space we call Nigeria, would decide if they want to travel in the same ship of state, and on what terms. But the proposed Constitutional Conference as conceived and teleguided by Abacha's team, may, like similar ventures in the past, prove to be much ado about nothing. It may turn out to be an unnecessary diversion. As money-seeking and power-hungry Nigerians scuttle for positions in the proposed Conference Hall, the military is bidding its time, and few people are asking the very vital question: "When will Abacha go?" Yet no real progress is possible until the military is out of the stage.

We call on Nigerian Christians to pray fervently against the perpetuation of dictatorship in this land. As Easter approaches and Christians look forward to the victory that lies beyond Calvary, we urge Nigerian Christians to keep the dream alive. Our salvation is not in any gun-toting cabal, no matter their pretentions to benevolence. Our salvation is in Christ the Truth, by whose truth alone we shall be free. As lies are daily traded across the land, Nigerian Christians must stand up and be counted on the side of truth, for where there is no vision, the people do perish!

CHAPTER TWELVE

Nigeria Shall Rise Again
(Written on June 30, 1994)

These are trying times for Nigerians. We have remained at the edge of a precipice for quite a while. As a social entity we have been teetering on the brink of collapse for over one year. Yet the storm is not over. Rather than subsiding, it appears to be gathering more strength. The ship of state, battered by multiple assaults, is being dragged along rather recklessly by men in obvious alliance with the angel of death.

Countless Nigerians have lost their lives amid the storm. Some have died of hunger and starvation. Some were murdered in cold blood by armed robbers and hired assassins. Some were victims of the anarchists holding the reins of power, or the thugs in uniform. A few Nigerians have escaped. Others are struggling to escape. They are seeking asylum in some foreign lands – whichever country is generous enough to accept them despite the stigma they carry as a crooked, fraudulent, drug-pushing and troublesome people. The rest of the people, starved not only of food and drink, but also of truth and freedom, are daily derided and harassed by those who rule with the gun.

Many of the surviving Nigerians have unfortunately lost their hope, and they are giving in, individually and collectively to a death wish. They resolve to "sidon look" or succumb to the social pathology of corrupt enrichment, sycophancy, and drug-pushing. We are indeed living through trying times. That is why many are subjecting themselves to the proverbial death wish. Many have accepted the chronic aberration of military dictatorship as a tolerable "child of circumstance." They know that democracy cannot be erected, nor can it thrive upon deceit, disinformation, manipulation, coercion, and subterfuge. But they close their eyes to the illegality of yet another teleguided Constitutional Conference.

Corruption has become for many the way to survive in Nigeria. They seem to have resolved that the clean way to do business and the honest way to run the civil service will not work in Nigeria. Nigerians are getting used to crisis situations. They queue up for days in petrol stations and are no longer complaining. Rather, they rejoice and thank their stars when they get a litre of gasoline for ten naira. Even when the rate of inflation for consumer goods has reached an all-time high, Nigerians anticipate that prices will rise even higher, so they hoard the goods. As the peasant poor starve to death, many clever Nigerians are becoming millionaires overnight. They fail to see the contradictions inherent in their apparent success. What should be seen as a state of emergency is fast becoming the Nigerian way of life.

And the young people? They are on the one hand frightened and confused, and on the other hand angry and vengeful. They see the situation as a hopeless one, and with what energy remaining in them, they are visiting violence on the callous adult society that has stolen away their national pride. They are visiting their anger on the adult society that has denied them their right to adequate nourishment, good education, functional health care and social services. And so, they turn our universities to theatres of war, and our social gatherings to arenas of violent encounter. From what they see of the adult society, they often do not believe that there is any reward for hard work, nor punishment for criminals. So, they cheat at examinations and forge certificates, passports, and visas.

The current situation challenges the very will to live of even the most resolute Nigerian. Yet there are those, albeit very few, who reject the death wish, and instead prefer to dream about national pride, to dream about economic well-being for all, and to dream about democracy and the rule of law. There are still a few Nigerians who hunger and thirst after truth and justice, and they are persistently agonising over the disorder of the day. Yes, there are a few people among us who know that government by coercion violates the fundamental freedom bestowed by God on individual persons and human communities, and so they are ready to continue the struggle.

As Abacha and his criminal gang roll out the tanks and brandish the guns against unarmed protesters, this category of Nigerians recall that the principle of "might is right" is only applicable in the jungle. Their hearts bleed as they see their fatherland taking on the character of a jungle, where lawlessness is the norm. This category of people have been harassed and lampooned by the violent usurpers of power. They are called enemies of peace and anarchists who should be tried for treason.

We are indeed living through trying times. But we rejoice that all is not lost. We rejoice that God has left among us a remnant few. God has left among us some men and women of vision, whose martyrdom today constitutes the seed of a better tomorrow. These men and women are a beacon of light amid the darkness, constantly reminding us that what we have today is not a social order, but a pack of cards destined to crumble. The presence of these remnant few from east to west and from north to south, is the hope of survival that this nation has.

The adult generation in Nigeria may be a lost generation, judging by the level of greed, corruption, social injustice, and lawlessness among our leaders. In all of history, greed, corruption, and injustice engender social decay, for they are a cancer that eventually eats up its host. Nigeria will not be an exception to this historical process. We cannot run away from the impending judgement. In fact, the visitation of justice is no more an article of faith, but a reality that has already set in for Nigeria. So, the pack of cards erected on Aso Rock or those erected on Victoria Island Extension, will surely crumble. Yet our hope is that out of the rubble, a new nation shall emerge. Our hope is that out of the debris of the lost generation, a new Nigerian nation shall be born; one that will have justice and truth as its foundation; a nation that will have a place for sages and visionaries, and for true nationalists and patriots; a nation that will provide for the poor, the weak and the meek. Our hope is that soon, very soon, this nation so richly endowed by God, but now so terribly desecrated by treacherous stewards and battered by callous usurpers of power, will rise again on the path of peace and progress.

We need a revolution of hope in Nigeria, for the cost of widespread apathy, disillusionment, and despair, is too great to be imagined. We need a revolution of hope, radical enough to take us through the shame of the moment. We need to bestow on our young people who today are wasting at home or languishing in exile, the sense of a homeland. We cannot all run away from Nigeria, so we need a powerful orientation on the culture of life to surmount the prevailing culture of death. Christians must be in the forefront of this revolution of hope, for we are indeed a people of hope. We believe in a God of miracles, who can put back flesh on dry bones. We believe in Jesus Christ who raised Lazarus from the dead even after four days in the tomb. Nigerian Christians must therefore champion this revolution, for where there is no vision, the people do perish!

CHAPTER THIRTEEN

Youth and the Future of Our Nation
(A talk delivered at the speech and prize-giving ceremony of Community Secondary School, Magongo, Kogi State, on July 13, 1994).

I have said much and written a lot about the youth and the Nigerian nation, yet this time it was not easy, deciding what to say to this audience about the youth and the future of Nigeria. I must confess that with recent happenings in the country, I am no longer sure what to think, much less what to say about our country at a gathering like this. I believe that thinking Nigerians have been so shocked, mesmerized and flabbergasted by the turn of events in Nigeria that they have now gone underground.

Ladies and gentlemen, the issue of our youth as builders of the nation or leaders of tomorrow cannot be adequately addressed unless we make an honest assessment of where we are and what has led us thus far. For without a keen sense of history, the nation has no future. I am a Christian, so faith in the resurrection is central to my life and perception. That is to say that no matter how bad things are today, there is nevertheless the hope of redemption, of resuscitation and of rejuvenation. As a Christian I believe that even from the wreckage or rubble of our devastated land, a new great nation can emerge, by the power of God who creates and re-creates. I believe that from the broken bricks that are today littered around the landscape, a new united country can emerge, by the power of God who puts back flesh on dry bones. And I believe that from the battered bodies that parade the land today, a new peaceful nation can emerge, by the power of God who makes all things new.

Yet this kind of rejuvenation only comes about with atonement. Redemption comes only after a sincere acknowledgement of sin, followed by a true repentance. Thus, the much hoped-for rejuvenation of the Nigerian nation will not come about until Nigerians, and especially the Nigerian leadership acknowledge the sins that have robbed them of greatness and identify the demons that have led them along the path of economic depression, political anarchy, and social disintegration. My own reflection is that the Nigerian elite has shown itself to be a set of unprincipled leaders, greedy opportunists, reckless plunderers, and mindless looters. In my judgement, most of those who have paraded themselves as our leaders, whether they be military dictators or civilian politicians, are largely manipulators who use and abuse poor Nigerians repeatedly, exploiting the ignorance of the majority of the people, and cashing in on the existing ethnic and religious polarities when it pays them to do so.

Before we talk of how the youth can build tomorrow, we need to know that the collective suffering and pain which we experience in Nigeria today is not God's will for us, but the onset of the process of retribution. The degeneration of the Nigerian economy and the disintegration of the Nigerian polity which we witness today is not the design of God, but the inevitability of nemesis catching up with the offender. For God has provided this land with enormous resources. We are so richly endowed that we could indeed have become the giant of Africa. But today we are paying dearly for our undisciplined and unprincipled lives. As a people, we are today atoning for our collective greed, our criminal avarice, and our blind consumerism. Yes, we are paying today for our collective profligacy.

When we see thousands of people dying at home or in the hospitals because they cannot afford to eat good food or buy drugs to cure minor infections, we need not ask our stars for the reason. When we see thousands of our people suffering depression, becoming lunatics, and roaming about the streets, we do not need a seer to tell us why. When we see our young people becoming beastly in hate, ruthless in violence, and reckless in consumption, we do not need to ask too many questions. We are in this mess today because we have plundered the inheritance of our fatherland and squandered the resources of our motherland, and we have engaged in a life of debauchery and prodigality. Like the prodigal son in the parable of Jesus, we have left our palace of pride to dwell in the pit of shame. We have thrown decency and integrity to the dogs and flushed justice and truth into the septic tank. We have violated love and trampled on the poor and the weak. We have enthroned bribery and corruption in our public life, and with reckless abandon, we have perpetuated that act of thievery now known as "settlement." We have neglected our educational institutions and made our teachers objects of ridicule in the eyes of society.

Our schools and colleges in turn have lost the sacred character of formation centres, and have rather become breeding grounds for thieves, touts, secret cultists, gangsters, rapists and prostitutes. We hear these days of school children beating up their teachers, sacking their principals, and burning up their libraries. Examination malpractice in some of our schools has now assumed the frightening dimension whereby teachers and principals organise cheating at external examinations, and parents annually contribute money to "settle" supervisors and invigilators. As our leaders and parents have become more enterprising in greed and political mischief, and as they fail to inspire the young people in the pursuit of higher values, we have lost control of our young generation.

Many of our young graduates from secondary schools, universities, and polytechnics, are deviants, addicts, and outlaws, who now constitute a nuisance in our homes, our schools, and our offices. With juvenile bravado many of these young people are constantly visiting their vengeance on an adult society that has failed to give them a sense of direction. So, they cheat and steal, they rob and rape, and they kill and maim. Many of these terrible crimes are committed with such mastery that they could win a place in the Guinness Book of Records or be considered good enough for replication by the James Bond team at Hollywood.

The time has come for a rethink. Our problems are not from God. Neither are they caused by some mysterious hand from outer space. No, our problems are man-made. Our misery has been brought upon us by our kith and kin. We are dying slowly at the hands of our own brothers and sisters, who have been blinded by greed for power and lust for money. Yes, the fault is not in our stars, but in ourselves.

In the mid-1960s Hubert Ogunde, the guru of Nigerian theatre, saw the trouble in the west and the lasting consequences of the devilish maneuvers and intrigues in the political set-up, and called on his people to think (*"Yoruba Ronu"*). The situation in today's Nigeria is a lot worse than it was with the west in the mid-1960s. The situation is nothing short of an emergency. We seem to have lost a generation already - the generation of our successive leaders who brought us to this point. Since they have never publicly repented of their sins against this nation, but instead have continued the plunder, there does not seem to be any hope for them.

But another generation is on the verge of being destroyed. This time it is the generation of the young people whose teeth are on edge because their fathers have eaten sour grapes. We are about to lose millions of young people. They are full of energy and endowed with numerous talents, but they lack the necessary pride in their fatherland. They are devoid of any sense of direction. They have not been adequately taught, nor have they seen practical examples of justice, truth, love, compassion, patriotism, and altruism, sufficient to motivate them. What is more, our young people are beginning to lose hope. And this is the greatest danger. It is the absence of hope amid hardship that has led many of our young unemployed people into the now widespread township thuggery, armed robbery, drug peddling and drug addiction.

My dear principal, staff, and invited guests, there is work to be done by all of us who belong to the adult society in Nigeria, if we are not to kill tomorrow before today's sun sets. We must own up before our young people that we have betrayed our fatherland and failed to lay the foundation for a prosperous future. We are guilty to the extent that we have contributed in some way to the mess of the moment by our corrupt and selfish lifestyle. As parents, teachers, and elders, we have often failed to inspire our young people to live lives of integrity. As leaders we have often failed to be a beacon of light. Instead, we have often been a source of scandal for our own children and the children of our country.

The time has come for a rethink. For us believers, the situation may be bad enough but not hopeless. Redemption is possible. Yes, we can experience a rejuvenation, if today we begin to retrace our steps, and get back to the basics. From the rubble of our shattered fatherland, a rich, powerful, peaceful, and united country can emerge, if we identify and get rid of the demons that have bewitched this land since independence. The ongoing constitutional conference may not succeed in doing this because it is plagued by greed, manipulation, deceit, mischief, and subterfuge - the same evil forces that have brought us to our knees.

Those who seek to bestow hope on the rising generation must be committed to a life of truth, justice, and integrity. Parents must be ready to make sacrifices for the sake of their children. Teachers must recognize that they teach more by their lives than their lessons. We talk too much about love and compassion. What young people need however is to know that love and compassion are possible at home, between their fathers and mothers, and between their elder brothers and sisters. Their young minds are confused when they notice an abiding hatred among some of the elders in society. We talk too much about truth, honesty, and fairness. What young people need instead is to see this truth, honesty, and fairness at work in the civil service, in the award and execution of contracts, in the process of governance and in the examination hall.

Young people are constantly let down and disappointed when their leaders are fraudulent or when they see teachers assisting unscrupulous students to cheat at examinations. They are shocked when they discover that their governors, local government chairmen, parents, or teachers are liars. Then they wonder whether a life of truth is possible in this world. Their trust is violated when they themselves or their peers are sexually exploited, harassed, or abused by leaders, elders, or teachers. When they see the hypocrisy of the adult society, they convince themselves that there is no truth or justice in the world. They make up their minds that there is no such thing as love and compassion. They then conclude that the world is one big jungle, largely inspired by the principle of mutual exploitation and governed by the law of the survival of the fittest and the triumph of the villain. Ladies and gentlemen, there is work for the adult society to do if we must bestow hope on our young people.

I want to end this reflection by challenging our young people gathered here, especially the graduating class, not to join the bandwagon in a life of greed and graft. I want to challenge our young people here and everywhere to reject the foolish pattern of life which has led Nigeria to the mess of the moment, and instead to seek after higher values that will guarantee peace and prosperity. I challenge you students to start now cultivating the virtues of sacrificial love, truth, justice, discipline, and patriotism. I challenge you to shun materialism, for it blinds people and enslaves them. I challenge you all to seek wisdom, knowledge, understanding, and the fear of the Lord.

It is becoming fashionable for young people to reject God who is the source of their being, their peace, and their fulfillment. But that is part of the madness of the day. I challenge you to take your spiritual and moral development seriously, and to appreciate the words of our Lord that "man does not live by bread alone," and "what does it profit a man if he gains the whole world but loses his soul?" I believe that if you cultivate these virtues, and shape your lives along this way, then tomorrow will not be lost. I believe that if today you choose the culture of life in place of the prevailing culture of death, then you shall have a bright future ahead of you.

I believe that with God on our side, we shall one day sing our National Anthem with a sense of respect for our past heroes, a sense of pride in our fatherland, and a sense of belonging to a nation bound in freedom, peace and unity. God bless you all.

CHAPTER FOURTEEN

Nigeria: Salvaging the Future
(Written on August 5, 1994)

Today's children they say, are the leaders of tomorrow. Young people in any society, are an embodiment of tomorrow's promise. Just as morning shows the day, the seed of peace and prosperity, or on the other hand the germ of discord and misery, is already sown in the youth of today. This is why so much premium is placed on children and the youth in all sane societies. Human beings generally find a great measure of fulfillment in the assurance that they are leaving behind them a veritable legacy by way of a disciplined, principled, knowledgeable, united, progressive and peace-loving progeny. On the other hand, they experience a deep sense of frustration and disillusionment when they see that their offspring are criminals, drug addicts, thugs and touts.

If in any society, parents, teachers and leaders, do not invest enough spiritual, moral and material resources on the training of their youth, that society shall have much to regret. Young people are often a mirror of the adult society to such an extent that the success of a generation of human beings can be measured by the quality of life to be found among its youth. In Nigeria however, the young people have been utterly scandalized by the corrupt and selfish lifestyle of the adult generation. Over the years, the Nigerian elite has shown itself to be in large measure a set of unprincipled leaders, greedy opportunists, reckless plunderers and mindless looters. Our experience is that most of those who have paraded themselves as our leaders, whether they be military dictators or civilian politicians, are largely manipulators who use and abuse poor Nigerians over and over again, exploiting the ignorance of the vast majority of the people, and cashing in on the existing ethnic and religious polarities when it pays them to do so. The children and young people have seen all this, and they have taken scandal.

On their part, the young people are becoming beastly in hate, ruthless in violence, and reckless in consumption. Our educational institutions which we have neglected for so long are losing their sacred character as formation centres. They are becoming breeding grounds for thieves, thugs, touts, secret cultists, gangsters, rapists and prostitutes. As our leaders and parents have become more enterprising in greed and political mischief, and as they fail to inspire the young people in the pursuit of higher values, we have lost control of the young generation. Many of those who today graduate from secondary schools, universities and polytechnics, are deviants, addicts, and outlaws. They now constitute a nuisance in our homes, on our streets, and in our offices. With juvenile bravado, many of the young people are constantly visiting vengeance on an adult society that has failed to give them a sense of direction. So, they cheat and steal, they rob and rape, they kill and maim. And they carry out these acts with such mastery and sophistication that could put the Italian Mafia to shame.

The embarrassing truth is that the collective psyche of our young people has been so seriously wounded, and their delicate conscience so brutally battered by the crimes of their leaders and elders, that we now stand the chance of losing tomorrow altogether. Yet we should continue to hope, even against hope. Though the dark tunnel is a long one, and there does not seem to be any sign of light, yet we should continue to believe that there is the possibility of redemption, of resuscitation and of rejuvenation for Nigeria. As men and women of faith we should believe that even from the wreckage or rubble of our devastated land, a new great nation can emerge. We should believe that from the broken bricks that are today littered around the national landscape, a new united country can emerge. Yes, there is reason to believe that from the battered bodies that parade the land today, a just, peaceful and prosperous nation can emerge.

However, in Christian theology, this kind of rejuvenation only comes about with atonement. Redemption comes only after a sincere acknowledgement of sin, followed by a true repentance. Thus, the much hoped-for rejuvenation of the Nigerian nation will not come about until Nigerians, and especially the Nigerian leadership acknowledge the sins that have robbed them of greatness. The redemption of the Nigerian nation shall remain an empty dream unless the demons that have led us along the dark alley of economic depression, political anarchy and social disintegration, are identified and cast out.

Therefore, as we reflect on the place of the Nigerian youth today, and the quality of life and leadership we expect from them in the future, we must put into proper focus not only the socio-political events of the recent past, but also the moral climate and the values or vices that we have pursued in the past. Indeed, no society can make progress or find peace unless it possesses a keen sense of history. No society can forge ahead on the path of greatness unless it acknowledges its past mistakes, repents of its sins, and makes a definite commitment to such values as will guarantee peace and prosperity. We in Nigerian are in urgent need of an examination of our individual and collective conscience, if we are to have any future.

We must acknowledge that the collective suffering and pain we experience today is not God's will for us, but rather the onset of the process of retribution. The degeneration of the Nigerian economy, the disintegration of the Nigerian polity, and the disorientation of the Nigerian youth which we witness today, is not the design of God but the inevitability of nemesis catching up with the offender. For God has provided this land with enormous resources, both human and material. We are so richly endowed that we could indeed have become the giant of Africa. But today we are paying dearly for our unprincipled and undisciplined lives. As a people, we are today atoning for our collective greed, avarice and crimes against the poor. We are paying today for our collective profligacy.

We are in this mess today because we have plundered the inheritance of our fatherland and squandered the resources of our motherland. We have engaged in a life of debauchery and prodigality. And like the prodigal son in the story of Jesus, we have left our palace of pride to dwell in the pit of shame. We have violated love and trampled on the poor and the weak. We have enthroned bribery and corruption in our public life, and with reckless abandon, we have perpetuated that act of thievery called "settlement." Thus, the time has come for a rethink. Our problems are not from God. Neither are they caused by some mysterious hand from outer space. No, our problems are man-made. Our misery has been brought upon us by our kith and kin. We are dying slowly at the hands of our own brothers and sisters, who have been blinded by greed for power and lust for money. Yes, the fault is not in our stars, but in ourselves. The time has come for a rethink. The day has indeed dawned when Nigerians as a people must make a collective examination of conscience, as the first step in the journey towards redemption.

The situation in today's Nigeria is a lot worse than it was with the west in the mid-'60s. The situation is nothing short of an emergency. We seem to have lost a generation already - the generation of our successive leaders who brought us to the present state of political anarchy and economic doom. Since the leaders have never publicly repented of their sins against this nation, but instead have continued the plunder, there does not seem to be any hope for them. We should be glad to be rid of that generation of deceit and mischief who stole food off the plate of their own children. But alas, another generation is on the verge of being destroyed. This time it is the generation of the young people whose teeth are on edge because their fathers have eaten sour grapes. We are about to lose millions of young people. They are full of energy and endowed with numerous talents, but they lack the necessary pride in their fatherland. They are devoid of any sense of direction. They have not been adequately taught, nor have they seen practical examples of justice, truth, love, compassion, patriotism and altruism, sufficient enough to motivate them. What is more, our young people are beginning to lose hope. And this is the greatest danger. It is the absence of hope in the midst of hardship that has led many of our young unemployed people into the now widespread township thuggery, armed robbery, drug peddling and drug addiction.

There is work to be done by all of us who belong to the adult society in Nigeria, if we are not to kill tomorrow before today's sun sets. We must own up before our young people that we have betrayed our fatherland and failed to lay the foundation for a prosperous future. We are guilty to the extent that we have contributed in some way to the mess of the moment by our corrupt and selfish lifestyle. As parents, teachers and elders, we have often failed to inspire our young people to live a life of righteousness. As leaders we have often failed to be a beacon of light. Instead, we have often been a source of scandal for our own children and the children of our country.

The time has come for a rethink. Terrible as the situation may be, it is nevertheless not hopeless. Redemption is possible. We can experience a rejuvenation, if today we begin to retrace our steps, and get back to the basics. From the rubble of our shattered fatherland, a rich, powerful, peaceful and united country can emerge, if we identify and get rid of the demons that have bewitched this land since independence. The ongoing constitutional conference may not succeed in doing this because it is itself plagued by greed, manipulation, deceit, mischief and subterfuge - the same evil hands that have brought us to our knees. Those who seek to bestow hope on the rising generation must be committed to a life of truth, justice, and righteousness. Parents should be ready to make sacrifices for the sake of their children. Teachers must recognize that they teach more by their lives than their lessons.

We talk too much about love and compassion. What young people need however is to know that love and compassion is possible at home, between their fathers and mothers, and between their elder brothers and sisters. Their young minds are confused when they notice an abiding hatred among some of the elders in society. We talk too much about truth, honesty and fairness. What young people need instead is to see this truth, honesty and fairness at work in the civil service, in the award and execution of contracts, in the process of governance and in the examination hall. They are constantly let down and disappointed when their leaders are fraudulent or when they see teachers assisting unscrupulous students to cheat at examinations. They are shocked when they discover that their governors, parents or teachers are liars. Then they wonder whether a life of truth is possible in this world. Their trust is violated when they themselves or their peers are sexually exploited, harassed or abused by leaders, elders or teachers.

When they see the hypocrisy of the adult society, they convince themselves that there is no truth or justice in the world. They make up their minds that there is no such thing as love and compassion. They conclude that the world is one big jungle, largely inspired by the principle of mutual exploitation and often governed by the law of the survival of the fittest and the triumph of the villain. There is work for the adult society to do if we must bestow hope on our young people.

To salvage the future, the young people themselves have some work to do. Young Nigerians must be careful not to join the bandwagon in a life of greed and graft. They must reject the foolish pattern of life which has led us to the mess of the moment, and instead seek after higher values that will guarantee peace and prosperity. Young Nigerians must start now cultivating the virtues of sacrificial love, truth, justice, discipline and patriotism. They must shun materialism, for it blinds people and enslaves them. They must seek wisdom, knowledge, understanding, and the fear of God.

It is becoming fashionable for young people to reject God who is the source of their being, their peace, and their fulfillment. But that is part of the madness of the day. In order to salvage the future, young people must take their spiritual and moral development seriously, and appreciate the words of Jesus Christ that "man does not live by bread alone," and "what does it profit a man if he gains the whole world but loses his soul?" If our young people cultivate these virtues, and shape their lives along this way, then tomorrow will not be lost. If today our young people choose the culture of life in place of the prevailing culture of death, then they shall have a bright future ahead of them. Yes, if our young people embrace the culture of life and truth, they shall one day sing their National Anthem with a sense of respect for their heroes past, a sense of pride in their fatherland, and a sense of belonging to a nation bound in freedom, peace and unity.

CHAPTER FIFTEEN

Authentic Religion Saves a Nation
Presented at the Annual Conference of the Catholic Laity Council of Nigeria (Kaduna Province) in Idah, Kogi State, on August 20, 1994

The Visitation of Decay

IN his letter to the Romans, St. Paul declares that "the anger of God is being revealed from heaven against all the impiety and depravity of men who keep truth imprisoned in their wickedness." Though they know God, he observes, they have refused to honour him. Instead, they have made nonsense of logic, and their minds are darkened. For that reason, he says, "God has abandoned them... God has left them to their irrational ideas and to their monstrous behaviour. So they are steeped in all sorts of depravity, rottenness, greed and malice, and addicted to envy, murder wrangling, treachery and spite. They are libelers, slanderers, enemies of God, rude, arrogant and boastful, enterprising in sin, rebellious to parents, without brains, honour, love or pity." He says that the verdict of God against the individuals or generations that are so enterprising in sin is very clear: "...they deserve to die" (Romans 1:18-32. See also Romans 6:23 "the wages of sin is death").

Nigeria is passing through the worst of times. All over the land, and in every sphere and dimension of our national life, there are ominous signs of the visitation of decay. From north to south and from east to west, we are affronted with the odious stench of the seamless rot in the land. From politics to economy and from education to health care, we are witnessing what appears to be a grand conspiracy of the combined forces of decomposition and degeneration against the nation. The grim reality now taking shape in the Nigerian landscape is the tragic loss of our collective soul. If Nigeria had only lost control of its economy, there could be hope that someday economic sanity will be restored. If it were only our educational enterprise that is bankrupt, we could nurture the hope that someday wise counsel will prevail. And if all we suffered were political doctoring by fakes and quacks, we can hope that with time, true philosopher-kings shall emerge to take control of the reins of power. But when a nation loses its soul to debauchery, that nation experiences decay that is often irreversible.

Amidst the prevailing socio-political and economic crises, Nigerians seem to be losing their humanity. They are losing their humanity because their leaders and elders are trading the characteristically human sense of justice, of compassion, of remorse, and of neighbourliness, for greed, hatred and subterfuge. Having mixed up the concepts of right and wrong, foul and fair, truth and falsehood, honour and shame, Nigeria as a corporate entity now teeters on the brink of decay. It is a nation simply gone mad. All values have been upturned. According to the law of nature, light chases out darkness. But what do we find in skewed Nigeria? Here the absurd is the rule, and only the silly and the crazy, the crook and the thief, the brigand and the hooligan seem to be "getting on" and finding their way to the top. In this skewed society, the true patriot is condemned to discomfiture, while the betrayer of trust, the slave of perfidy, and the architect of injustice occupies the citadel of power. These constitute themselves into parasites - worms, rats and locusts - that devastate the national organism.

The impression given today is that our nation has been conquered by greed, selfishness and corruption. We have a parade of bandits in the corridors of power, and to be acknowledged in Nigeria, one has to be on the highest rungs of the brigade of bandits. Yes, our power structures are dominated by a group of opportunistic and myopic maniacs whose motto is "politics without morality." They are the morally bankrupt and depraved functionaries who cannot distinguish between personal interests and the national good. And operating from what appears to be an absolute lack of principles, they have ended up making a virtue out of banditry and villainy. They not only loot the resources of the land, but they also arrogate to themselves the prerogative of deciding for the rest of the society what is good and what is evil, what is true and what is false, what is fair and what is foul. This is the game of deceit that the power brokers in Nigeria have called governance for nearly one decade. But the lie will not last. Operating our entire social system on a structure of lies carries with it unwholesome consequences not only for the victims but also for the perpetrators.

The Wages of Sin is Death

When falsehood is built into the political, social and economic structure of society, an explosion of violence soon occurs in such a manner that no one will be spared. This idea is cleverly demonstrated in the Biblical epic of the Tower of Babel (Genesis 11:1-9). Truth, on the other hand, is resilient. Truth is irrepressible. If assaulted, truth bounces back with a vengeance.

And that is exactly what is happening today. To build a nation on a foundation of lies is to sow in the emerging nation the seed of its own destruction. What we have experienced since June 1993 is nothing short of the visitation of nemesis on a nation that has imprisoned truth and violated justice. Nigeria has thrived on falsehood for too long. Now it is caught up in its own web of deceit. Nigerians have thrived on corruption for too long. Now they are swimming in their own mess. The Nigerian leadership has all along fed fat on the crisis. Now it is constipated by myriad crises.

Yes, indeed, the wages of sin is death. As a corporate entity, Nigeria seems to be undergoing the process of death and decay in payment for the multiple assaults on all the principles and virtues that make for peace. Many delude themselves that there is a government in Nigeria that is keeping the peace. But that is far from the truth. The truth of the day is that there is no one in charge. Considering the amount of violence on the ground, the collapse of the economy and the educational system, the ever-increasing number of endless strikes in the most essential sectors of the economy, and the consequent loss of security everywhere, we must admit that what we have today is nothing short of anarchy. True, the "giant of Africa" is dying. But what hope of resurrection is there for our country? What hope of re-creation is there for the devastated landscape? What hope of redemption is there for the battered socio-economic structures? How can Nigeria be saved?

Righteousness Exalts a Nation

The theme of this conference, "Authentic Religion Saves a Nation" is, for me, a call for an honest assessment of the quality of Christian discipleship and witnessing within the Nigerian polity. It is also a call for a renewed commitment on the part of all men and women that profess the Christian religion, especially among the Catholic laity to be the salt of the earth and the light of the world (Mt.5:13-14), in fidelity to their true vocation in the world. The theme of this conference confronts Nigerian men and women, and particularly Christians, with the Biblical wisdom that righteousness exalts a nation, but that sin destroys a people. Prophet Jeremiah warns that there will neither be peace nor security for a nation that has lost integrity (Jer.6:1-15), while Isaiah says that the wicked person will not enjoy peace (Is.48:22). The prophets saw the rise and fall of ancient Israel as closely related to her fidelity or infidelity to the covenant of love and justice which Yahweh established with her.

Also, studies have shown that about 26 civilisations have risen and collapsed in the course of human history. Most of these civilisations did not collapse due to external attacks or invasion. Their destruction was due to what St. Augustine calls "the want of order in the soul." They were destroyed by internal decay, whose worms are violence, hatred, oppression, avarice, greed and promiscuity. Our Judeo-Christian faith teaches us that fidelity to God's covenant of love and justice results in abundant blessings of peace, security and prosperity, whereas a lifestyle of violence comes with a curse (Mt.6:33; Dt.29:8-28). For Moses, being faithful to the covenant of Yahweh means life and prosperity, whereas the violation of the covenant by way of a sinful lifestyle means death and destruction.

Nigeria shall not be saved until Nigerians individually and collectively repent of the atrocities they have committed against their neighbours and against a just and loving God. The dynamics of salvation and peace involve a rejection of the logic of the prince of this world - the logic of inordinate pride, pleasure and power. The dynamics of peace involve a creative revulsion against the values of an acquisitive, oppressive, and militarised society. Peace will not just occur in Nigeria. The prevailing order is an order built on long-standing injustice. Until this order is demolished or reversed, peace will not come. Our socio-economic structures are largely structures of violence, which by their very nature are bound to beget further violence if they are not urgently replaced. The continuous attempt to suppress the collective will of a people, through a multiplicity of draconian decrees, through the callous detention of opinion leaders and the closure of media houses shall not bring peace.

Nigeria shall not be saved unless the leadership repents of its greed for money and power. Nigeria shall not know peace until Nigerians repent of the falsehood that has characterised the art of governance in this land, for a nation without integrity neither deserves nor shall it ever find peace. God does not save a people without their cooperation. So peace will not just occur in Nigeria. It will not come without some striving on the part of those who seek it. Jesus Christ has shown us that peace does not come on a platter of gold but instead through a crown of thorns. The peacemaker must be ready to pay the costly price of atonement for the multiple violence that has brought us to the mess of the moment.

A Time for Stocktaking

True, the near absence of any impact of a Christian conscience in the political culture of Nigeria continues to be our greatest source of frustration, embarrassment and scandal. Christians claim 45 per cent of the population of Nigeria, and there are many Christians among the corrupt politicians and military dictators that have brought upon the poor of Nigeria the agony and misery of today. The ongoing drama of shame in Nigeria is perhaps the first serious test of the impact of the over one hundred years of Christian evangelisation in Nigeria. What has become of the Christian moral education which many of those who have served as public officers received? What does the average Christian or Catholic lay person who is a public officer make of the moral and spiritual lessons that are regularly taught in the Sunday liturgy?

Has the Christian message of peace through justice really failed to save the Nigerian soul, or has it been ignored by the Nigerian elite? Why is it that the life of many Nigerians remains untouched by the social principles of Jesus Christ, in spite of the fact that millions of people go to church and celebrate the word and the sacraments? Why is it that in our society, in spite of the ideals of the gospel, the affluent and the poverty-stricken, the oppressor and the oppressed, the unjust judge and the helpless widow, the fraudulent businessman and the exploited consumer, the greedy politician and the innocent victim of greed, the ethnic bigot and the victim of ethnicism, do sit down together in church or partake in the same Eucharist, without their relative positions being seriously challenged by the gospel?

The time has come for an honest assessment of the part Christians have played in the entire game of mischief and deceit and thievery and roguery, which we have called politics in the last 34 years. We must admit that Christian politicians have either been active participants in the criminal conspiracy to despoil this nation, or they have acted as passive onlookers as the forces of darkness manipulate the poor of Nigeria like pawns on a chessboard, thereby shirking their responsibility of being light and leaven for society. Either posture is inadmissible, for an account will be required of their stewardship.

A Call to Radical Discipleship

Dear brethren, I want to use this forum of the lay leadership of the Catholic Church of Northern Nigeria to remind all Nigerian Christians that they shall have questions to answer on what role they played in the Nigerian drama of death. Christian leaders have perhaps been too diplomatic in their public statements against the injustices of the day. But this is not a time for niceties. We have nearly reached rock bottom, and so the time has come for us to call a spade a spade rather than calling it an agricultural implement. True, the time has come in Nigeria for Christian leaders to name the demon in order to free the demoniac. The nation has had enough of self-proclaimed messiahs who turn out to be looters, opportunists, and architects of discord. The nation is in dire need of the prophets of peace. We are at a critical point in history. We are at the edge of a precipice. Yet Nigeria can be saved if Christians wake up to their calling and are ready to pay the price for radical discipleship of Jesus Christ in a society dominated by forces of darkness. Nigeria can be saved if Christians, true to their Christian calling, refuse to adjust to injustice or to compromise truth. Nigeria can be saved if Christians take up their prophetic role and act as sentries and "watchmen" for their generation.

Christians should never adopt a passive approach or take a defeatist posture before the forces of darkness that unleash multiple plagues on the society. We have been empowered by Jesus Christ, who has commissioned us to go and teach the whole world the truth (Mt. 28:19-20). We possess the authority to cast out demons and trample upon snakes and scorpions (Mk.16:17-18). The Lord has promised to send Christians power from on high, to abide with us forever. He has promised that we shall do what the world considers impossible if we abide in Him. Besides, he says nothing shall ever harm us, especially when we are actively and faithfully engaged in dislodging darkness and spreading the light (Lk.10:19).

It is the special prerogative of Christians to study the phenomenon of falsehood and fraud in our socio-political and economic setup, to identify the lie whenever and wherever it rears its head, to warn society of its devastating potential, and to champion the cause of combating it. Christians cannot succumb to the feeling that truth does not pay. We must not fall for the illusion that truth has vanished. Rather, we must reproach, deplore, and denounce falsehood. We must be ready to put our life on the line for the sake of the truth. Individual Christians and such Christian Organisations as the Catholic Bishops Conference of Nigeria, the Nigerian Clergy Association, the Laity Council, the Catholic Men Organisation (CMO), Catholic Women Organisation (CWO), the Knights, the Catholic Youth Organisation of Nigeria (CYON), and yes, the Nigerian Federation of Catholic Students (NFCS), must be ready to "stick their necks out" in defence of truth. The truth must be taught and preached, no matter how bitter it may be; that political deceit, even when adorned in gold, is sin; that dishonesty in business, even when justified by the laws of economics is sin; and that civic lying, even when it is the order of the day, is sin.

Nigerian Christians must start from somewhere, no matter how humble, for charity begins at home. We must take the bull by the horn, in accordance with our divine mission, as salt of the earth and light of the world. Christians must re-assert their authority to teach the world the way of life and the way of peace. We are not helpless before the forces of destruction in Nigeria. With the spiritual resources at our disposal in Christ Jesus, we can fight back the collective decay that consistently threatens the Nigerian nation. Beginning from our homes, our schools, our villages, and then onto our towns, our states and the nation at large, we must champion the cause of justice and fair play.

We cannot sit idly and complain endlessly about the deplorable state of affairs in our country. We must get into action in whatever way is open to us and ignite our Christian candle to fight back the forces of darkness and decay, whether as responsible parents or respectful children, devoted teachers or diligent students, God-fearing doctors or dedicated nurses, dutiful administrators or faithful labourers. If a sufficient number of Christians lit their candles in this way, then we can be sure that dying Nigeria shall rise again to greatness by the power of God who raised Jesus Christ from the dead. As Christians, we believe that even from the wreckage or rubble of our devastated land, a new united nation can emerge by the power of God who creates and re-creates. We believe that from the broken bricks and battered bodies that are today littered around the national landscape, a just, peaceful and prosperous nation can emerge by the power of God, who makes all things new. This will come about if a sufficient number of Nigerian Christians today answer the call to radical discipleship of Christ.

Only an authentic discipleship of Jesus Christ, the Prince of Peace, will guarantee peace for Nigeria. Christians must present the true Jesus to the men and women of this country. This is the only solution to the multiple problems that today plague our nation. No one lights a lamp and puts it under a bed. Christians must therefore rise and shine out the light of Christ in this dungeon of economic prodigality, political bigotry and military banditry. Yes, we must act quickly at this time to be counted on the side of truth, justice and sanity.

CHAPTER SIXTEEN

Nigeria: Investing in the Future
(Written on February 6, 1995)

I have said much and written a lot about the place of our youth in nation-building, yet these days I find it difficult to know what to think when it comes to the issue of our youth as leaders of tomorrow. I believe that thinking Nigerians have been so shocked, mesmerized and flabbergasted by the turn of events in Nigeria that many have simply gone underground. True, thinking Nigerians seem to have been beaten hands down by the sharp twists and turns, the devilish maneuvers and deadly intrigues and the monumental greed that have characterized Nigerian politics and economy in the last few years.

The issue of our youth as leaders of tomorrow cannot be adequately addressed unless we make an honest assessment of where we are and what has led us thus far. For without a keen sense of history, our nation has no future. As a Christian, faith in the resurrection is central to my life and perception. That is to say that no matter how bad things may be today, there is nevertheless the hope of redemption, of resuscitation and of rejuvenation. As a Christian I believe that even from the wreckage or rubble of our devastated land, a new great nation can emerge, by the power of God who creates and re-creates. I believe that from the broken bricks that are today littered around the landscape, a new united country can emerge, by the power of God who puts back flesh on dry bones. And I believe that from the battered bodies that parade the land today, a new peaceful nation can emerge, by the power of God who makes all things new.

Yet this kind of rejuvenation only comes about with atonement. Redemption comes only after a sincere acknowledgement of sin, followed by a true repentance. Thus the much hoped-for rejuvenation of the Nigerian nation will not come about until Nigerians, and especially the Nigerian leadership acknowledge the sins that have robbed us of greatness, and identify the demons that have led us along the path of economic depression, political banditry and social disintegration. My own reflection is that the Nigerian elite have shown themselves to be a set of unprincipled leaders, greedy opportunists, reckless plunderers and mindless looters. In my judgment, many of those who have paraded themselves as our leaders, whether they be military dictators or civilian politicians, are largely manipulators who use and abuse poor Nigerians over and over again, exploiting the ignorance of the vast majority of the people, and cashing in on the existing ethnic and religious polarities when it pays them to do so.

We must appreciate the fact that the collective suffering and pain which we experience in Nigeria today is not God's will for us, but the onset of the process of retribution. The embarrassingly poor quality of governance, the near collapse of the economy and the widespread insecurity of lives and property which we witness today are not the design of God, but the inevitability of nemesis catching up with the offender. For God has provided this land with enormous resources. We are so richly endowed that we could indeed have become the giant of Africa. But today we are paying dearly for our undisciplined and unprincipled lives. As a people, we are today atoning for our collective greed, avarice and profligacy.

When we see thousands of people dying at home or in the hospitals because they cannot afford to eat good food or buy drugs to cure minor infections, we need not ask our stars for the reason. When we see thousands of our people suffering depression, becoming lunatics, and roaming about the streets, we do not need a seer to tell us why. When we see our young people becoming ruthless in crime and reckless in violence, we do not need to ask too many questions. We are in this mess today because we the political and economic elite of this country have plundered the inheritance of our fatherland, and squandered the resources of our motherland. We the elite have engaged in a life of debauchery and prodigality. Like the prodigal son in the parable of Jesus, we have often left our palace of pride to dwell in the pit of shame. We have often thrown decency and integrity to the dogs and flushed justice and truth into the septic tank. We have often violated love and trampled on the poor and the weak. We have often enthroned bribery and corruption in our public life, and with reckless abandon, we have perpetuated that act of thievery called "settlement." In the process we have often neglected our educational institutions, and made our teachers objects of ridicule in the eyes of society.

Our public schools and colleges in turn have lost the sacred character of formation centres, and have rather become breeding grounds for thieves, thugs, touts, secret cultists, gangsters, rapists and prostitutes. We hear these days of school children beating up their teachers, sacking their principals, and burning up their libraries. Examination malpractice in some of our schools has now assumed the frightening dimension whereby teachers and principals organise cheating at external examinations, and parents annually contribute money to "settle" supervisors and invigilators. As our leaders and parents have become more enterprising in greed and political mischief, and as they fail to inspire the young people in the pursuit of higher values, we have lost control of our young generation.

Many of our young graduates from secondary schools, universities and polytechnics, are deviants, addicts, and outlaws, who now constitute a nuisance in our homes and our offices, and a terror on our streets and highways. With juvenile bravado many of these young people are constantly visiting their vengeance on an adult society that has failed to give them a sense of direction. So they cheat and steal, they rob and rape, and they kill and maim. Many of these terrible crimes are committed with such mastery that they could win a place in the Guinness Book of Records, or be considered good enough for replication by the James Bond cast at Hollywood.

The time has come for a rethink. Our problems are not from God. Neither are they caused by some mysterious hand from outer space. No, our problems are man-made. Our misery has been brought upon us by our kith and kin. We are dying slowly at the hands of our own brothers and sisters, who have been blinded by greed for power and lust for money. Yes, the fault is not in our stars, but in ourselves. In the mid-'60s Hubert Ogunde, the guru of Nigerian theatre, saw the trouble in the west and the lasting consequences of the devilish maneuvers and intrigues in the political set-up, and called on his people to think (*"Yoruba Ronu"*). The situation in today's Nigeria is a lot worse than it was with the west in the mid-'60s. The situation is nothing short of an emergency. We seem to have lost a generation already - the generation of our successive leaders who brought us to this point. Since they have never publicly repented of their sins against this nation, but instead have continued the plunder, there does not seem to be any hope for them.

But another generation is on the verge of being destroyed. This time it is the generation of the young people whose teeth are on edge because their fathers have eaten sour grapes. We are about to lose millions of young people. They are full of energy and endowed with numerous talents, but they lack the necessary pride in their fatherland. They are devoid of any sense of direction. They have not been adequately taught, nor have they seen practical examples of justice, truth, love, compassion, patriotism and altruism, sufficient enough to motivate them. What is more, many of our young people are beginning to lose hope. And this is the greatest danger. It is the absence of hope in the midst of hardship that perhaps has led many of our young unemployed and unemployable people into the now lucrative business of kidnapping, political thuggery, armed robbery, drug peddling and drug addiction.

There is work to be done by all of us who belong to the adult society in Nigeria, if we are not to kill tomorrow before today's sun sets. We must own up before our young people that we have betrayed our fatherland and failed to lay the foundation for a prosperous future. We are guilty to the extent that we have contributed in some way to the mess of the moment by our corrupt and selfish lifestyle. As parents, teachers and elders, we have often failed to inspire our young people in the righteousness which exalts a nation. As leaders we have often failed to be a beacon of light. Instead we have often been a source of scandal for our own children and the children of our country.

The time has come for a rethink. For us believers, the situation may be bad enough but not hopeless. Redemption is possible. Yes, we can experience a rebirth, if today we begin to retrace our steps, and get back to the basics. From the rubble of our shattered fatherland, a rich, powerful, peaceful and united country can emerge, if we identify and get rid of the demons that have bewitched this land since independence. The ongoing electoral reform and constitutional amendments may not succeed in doing this as long as the environment remains overburdened by monumental greed, manipulation, deceit, mischief and subterfuge - the same evil hands that have brought us to our knees.

Those who seek to bestow hope on the rising generation must be committed to a life of truth, justice, and righteousness. Parents must be ready to make sacrifices for the sake of their children. Teachers must recognize that they teach more by their lives than by their lessons. We talk too much about love and compassion. What young people need however is to know that love and compassion is possible at home, between their fathers and mothers, and between their elder brothers and sisters. Their young minds are confused when they notice an abiding hatred among some of the elders in society. We talk too much about truth, honesty and fairness. What young people need instead is to see this truth, honesty and fairness at work in the civil service, in the award and execution of contracts, in the process of governance and in the examination hall.

Young people are constantly let down and disappointed when their leaders are fraudulent or when they see teachers assisting unscrupulous students to cheat at examinations. They are shocked when they discover that their governors, their parents, their priests or their teachers are liars. Then they wonder whether a life of truth is possible in this world. Their trust is violated when they themselves or their peers are sexually exploited, harassed or abused by leaders, elders or teachers. When they see the hypocrisy of the adult society, they convince themselves that there is no truth or justice in the world. They make up their minds that there is no such thing as love and compassion. They conclude that the world is one big jungle, largely inspired by the principle of mutual exploitation and often governed by the law of the survival of the fittest and the triumph of the villain. Ladies and gentlemen, there is work for the adult society to do if we must bestow hope on our young people.

I want to end this reflection by challenging all young people, especially Christian youths, to prepare themselves for a life of meaning and purpose, and to let the conduct of their lives bear fruits towards a wholesome society. The scandalous conduct of the adult society – the lost generation – notwithstanding, young people must strive to imbibe the following lessons: that It Pays to Work Hard; that Honesty is the Best Policy; that Discipline is the Cornerstone of a Successful Life; that There is Dignity in Labour; that Contentment is the Secret of Happiness; that Violence Begets Violence; that Without Justice There Can Be No Peace; that Cleanliness is Next to Godliness; that Where There is No Vision the People Perish; and that Greed, Tribalism and Religious Intolerance Do Destroy a People. Yes, if we are to have a wholesome future, our young people must imbibe the humanistic and Christian virtues of Love, Mercy, Compassion, Humility, Chastity, Frugality, Prudence, Courage, Dignity and Self Confidence.

I challenge the upcoming generation – our young people, to lead a purpose-driven life, and pursue meaning over and above wealth, power and pleasure. To this end I propose the following pledge to be constantly said by all our youths who want a better future for themselves and their country:

1. I will keep my heart pure and my conscience free
2. I will fill my life with love; I will make no room for hate, resentment and bitterness
3. I will always think of others before myself
4. I will be optimistic and hopeful; I will spread sunshine around
5. I will be contented with who I am & what I have, even as I aim at excellence
6. I will do what I love doing and love what I do
7. I will spend my life working to improve the world around me
8. I will live simply so that others may simply live
9. I will be thankful for even the smallest favour received

I challenge all Nigerian young people not to join the bandwagon in a life of greed and graft; rather to reject the foolish pattern of life which has led Nigeria to the mess of the moment; and to seek after higher values that will guarantee peace and prosperity. I challenge Nigerian youths to shun materialism, for it blinds people and enslaves them, and instead to start now cultivating the virtues of sacrificial love, truth, justice, discipline and patriotism. Yes, if we are not to lose tomorrow before today's sun sets, I challenge everyone to seek wisdom, knowledge, understanding, and the fear of the Lord.

It is unfortunately becoming fashionable for young people to reject God who is the source of their being, their peace, and their fulfillment. But that is part of the madness of the day. I urge our youths to take their spiritual and moral development seriously, and to appreciate the words of our Lord that "man does not live by bread alone," and "what does it profit a man if he gains the whole world but loses his soul?" True, if today our youths choose the culture of life in place of the prevailing culture of death, they shall have a bright future ahead of them. If they allow these positive sentiments to germinate and take root in them, then as a people, with God on our side, we shall one day sing our National Anthem with a sense of respect for our heroes past, a sense of pride in our fatherland, and a sense of belonging to a nation bound in freedom, peace and unity.

CHAPTER SEVENTEEN

We Need Dreamers
(Written on July 6, 1995)

Dreamers are a vital force in society. They are the visionaries of their time. When all others are blind, dreamers are the ones granted to see the handwriting on the wall, to interpret the signs of the times, and to see the light beyond the tunnel. Equipped as they are with superior perception, dreamers analyze the situation on the ground in the light of the common good and of the true goal of the human person and the society. Dreamers possess the vision of life as it ought to be, and with this vision they give the much needed hope to a suffering people.

Dreamers often proclaim the inevitability of nemesis. They constantly warn the men and women of society of the impending doom if they do not change their course. They are also constantly pointing to the direction where society is supposed to be heading. Dreamers refuse to be defiled by the corruption of the moment or be engulfed by the darkness of the surrounding environment. As prophets they are endowed with rare courage not only to denounce evil in general, but also to name the specific human agents of evil in society. They remind society that peace is the fruit of justice, and warn evil doers of the inevitability of nemesis. Dreamers give reason to hope. They assure "the remnant" who hunger and thirst for righteousness, that all is not lost.

In an environment such as ours, there is very little room for the dreamer. In a land of greed and graft, of lies and subterfuge, there is hardly any place for the dreamer. In a country where lawlessness is the norm and corruption has acquired the status of a virtue, the dreamer is something of an eccentric. Amidst a harvest of debauchery, and widespread apathy and despondency, the dreamer is an object of scorn. And in a generation that is almost fully surrendered to the mundane, where progress is defined only along the parameters of the moment, the dreamer is considered a nonentity.

Yet the dreamer is essential for the very survival of human society. Humanity owes its continued existence to generations of dreamers who lamented over the triumph of conquerors and agonized over the humiliation of the vanquished. The human species would have been wiped off the face of the earth, but for the dreamers who constantly gazed beyond to seek the stars, as their fellow wayfarers submerged themselves in the fleeting pleasures of the day. Biblical literature gives the examples of Noah, Joseph, John the Baptist and Jesus Christ. And down through the centuries, there have been dreamers who tread the path of these pioneers.

Humanity has never understood its dreamers, for they always dreamt dreams that were "unrealistic" for their contemporaries. Their dreams of love and brotherhood, and of justice and peace, when not aborted, were often stillborn. Yet many have continued to conceive dreams, and it is their dreams that have held us together to this day.

One such dreamer was Dr. Martin Luther King Jr., the African American Civil Rights leader and Nobel Prize winner. The greatest legacy of Dr. King is perhaps the famous speech delivered at the Lincoln Memorial, Washington D.C., on August 26, 1963, titled: "I have a dream." He says in part: "I say to you today even though we face the difficulties of today and tomorrow, I still have a dream...I have a dream that one day this nation will rise up and live out the true meaning of its creed...I have a dream that one day every valley shall be exalted and every hill and mountain shall be made low. The rough places will be made straight...we will be able to hew out of the mountain of despair a stone of hope...we shall be able to transform the jangling discords of our nation into a beautiful symphony of brotherhood...we will be able to work together, to pray together, to struggle together...to stand up for freedom together, knowing that we will be free one day."

Martin Luther King was not deluded. His dream might have sounded unrealistic at the time, but it was not an empty dream. It was a dream based on faith. Martin Luther King's dream was based on a strong faith in the fundamental equality of all men and women before God. His dream was based on faith in the fact that the just shall overcome someday. It was based on the belief that all appearances to the contrary notwithstanding, light conquers darkness, and truth overcomes falsehood.

The recent history of our country effectively demonstrates how the lack of knowledge can destroy a people. As a people, Nigerians are groaning under the weight of collective myopia. There is an acute shortage of vision, intellectual rigour and critical thinking even in academic circles. What appears to be in place is the cult of mediocrity, whereby professors of political science for whom democracy is an article of faith, legal luminaries who hold the title of "Senior Advocate of Nigeria," and who have sworn to defend the rule of law, and highly respected religious prelates, who are expected to hold truth as sacred, now bow before ruthless feudal lords and callous military despots. Many of those whom Nigerians look up to for a sense of direction, have become sycophants, praise singers and propagandists for the oppressors of the Nigerian people. Their action is a serious betrayal of their education and the mission they owe to succeeding generations of Nigerians.

In the face of this national embarrassment, Nigeria is in dire need of dreamers, seers and visionaries, who will liberate our people from bondage, and open the way for justice, peace, and abundant life. Our people have never in history witnessed this degree of impoverishment, oppression, enslavement and betrayal. That is why we need citizens endowed with the wisdom of the sage, equipped with the vision of the prophet, and propelled by the passion of the true nationalist, to make a powerful intervention now on behalf of the distressed people of our land. We need patriotic but fearless Nigerians who will demonstrate to the men and women of this land that (in the words of Chinua Achebe in *The Trouble With Nigeria*) "a true patriot is one who cares deeply about the happiness and well-being of his country and all its people; not one who says he loves his country... A true patriot will always demand the highest standards of his country and accept nothing but the best for and from his people. He will be outspoken in condemnation of their shortcomings without giving way to superiority, despair or cynicism."

Our land has not been altogether bereft of dreamers. Like other nations, Nigeria has been blessed with a few. But their dreams have often been broken by multiple distractions. The faint voices of Nigerian dreamers have had to contend with the vicious demons of oppression and military dictatorship. Through the course of the years, Nigerian dreamers have been presented with too many challenges. Right now, the challenges are such that their very capacity to dream dreams has been stretched to near-breaking point by incessant harassment and detention. Yet the country must learn to tolerate the dreamer and his dreams, if we are not to be totally consumed by the plague of collective myopia.

CHAPTER EIGHTEEN

A Reflection on Godly Leadership
(Written on the Feast of Christ the King, November 26, 1995)

We celebrate today the feast of Jesus Christ the Universal King. We declare to the world today that the one who stood condemned before Pilate, the one who suffered the greatest humiliation of death on the cross of Calvary, the one who at the last supper gave up his body as food and his blood as drink; that it is the same one who was raised from the dead and given a name that is higher than every other name, with sovereignty and power and glory (Philippians 2:6-11). Jesus' own authority is the one acquired through sacrificial love, his power is one acquired through humility and obedience. It is by virtue of his absolute love for human beings that Jesus exercises absolute authority over them. Earthly authorities like Herod and Pilate may destroy his flesh, but he cannot be vanquished. Jesus' kingship is of a different kind. His glory is beyond the reach of earthly trials and failures. His divine kingship may not save him from physical pain and death, but he is nevertheless victorious. It is through the suffering of pain and physical death out of love for humanity that he has triumphed. Jesus presents for us a radically different and perhaps contradictory model of leadership than we are today familiar with in the world, and particularly in our country Nigeria, plagued as it is by brutal dictators, callous scavengers, and merciless looters.

Jesus is the leader who is meek and humble of heart, whose yoke is easy, and whose burden is light (Mt.11:29-30). Jesus is the leader who takes pity on his suffering people, a leader whose compassion for the poor, weak and the distressed moved him to perform miracles for healing and for feeding the people (Mk.1:40-45; 6:30-44). Jesus is the king whose leadership means service. He did not come to be served, but to serve. He told his disciples that among the pagans the rulers lord it over them, and their great men make their authority felt. He warned that this should not happen among them. Instead, he said:

anyone who wants to be great among you must be your servant, and anyone who wants to be first among you must be your slave, just as the Son of Man came not to be served but to serve and to give his life as a ransom for many (Mt20:24-27).

Christ's model of leadership is one of compassion and solidarity with the poor, not one that alienates and further impoverishes the poor. Christ's kingship is one that frees the oppressed, it is not one that oppresses, intimidates and terrorizes the weak and the lowly. Christ's model of leadership is one that is assumed through suffering, not one that is usurped through the naked display of power. The throne of Christ is not erected with the crushed bones of the poor. His throne is rather the wooden cross of Calvary. The palace of Christ is not built up with the broken bodies of the lowly. His palace is rather built with his own body, broken for the salvation of his people. The palace of Christ is painted not with the blood of the poor, but with his own blood, the blood which he offered in sacrifice for the salvation of mankind. Yes, Christ is the leader, the king, whose body was broken, and whose blood was shed for the salvation of his people (Matthew 26:26-28; Mark 14:22-24; Luke 22:19-20).

The kingship of Christ is one of purposeful leadership, a leadership with vision, with the fear of the Lord, and with commitment to the well-being of the people. Our celebration today challenges the current Nigerian situation of oppression, social injustice and the widespread abuse of human rights. The kingship of Christ challenges the apathy and acquiescence of Christians in the face of social manipulation, political deceit and false propaganda in the leadership of this country. The kingship of Christ poses a great challenge for a society where leaders have often appropriated the resources of the land for selfish use, while the multitude of the people languish in misery. The kingship of Christ calls to question the posture of intimidation, harassment and coercion towards opposition voices which we witness in this country.

Christians cannot afford to be passive onlooker in the unfolding of events in their country. They cannot afford to bury their talents in the sand, for on the last day they shall be called upon to give an account of their stewardship. By divine mandate, Christians are to teach the world the way of life and truth (Matthew 28:20). By God's imperative, Christians are the salt of the earth and the light of the world (Matthew 5:13-14). Christians have an immense responsibility in the project of transforming their country from a less human to a more human society. They must employ every peaceful means available to change the course of events in their country.

Chapter Eighteen | George Ehusani

They must do everything possible under God's inspiration to influence the pattern of leadership of their society. They must not only pray for God's kingdom to come, but also work hard towards its emergence.

As we celebrate the feast of Christ the King, and reflect on Christ's model of leadership, this is a most opportune time to look critically at the quality of leadership in our society and denounce all authority structures that oppress, intimidate, alienate and impoverish the people of God in our society. This is a time for Christians to propose alternative structures of leadership for our society. Nigerian Christians form a sizeable proportion of the population of this country. The socio-political and economic direction of their country should be of utmost concern to them. This is the time for the Christian elite in Nigeria to commit their God-given resources into setting up structures that would challenge in every peaceful manner dictatorship, arbitrary rule, mismanagement, corruption and fraud in our country.

This is the time for the Christian elite in Nigeria to commit their resources into programmes and projects aimed at the promotion of human dignity and the respect for human rights. The time has come for our Christian elite to stand up and be counted on the side of the poor, the oppressed and the downtrodden. As we hear in today's Gospel, the Lord identifies Himself intimately with the hungry, the thirsty, the naked, the homeless, the sick, and the prisoner. These are the least of His brethren, and what we do to them we do to Jesus. Our admission into heaven where Jesus reigns supreme shall be determined to a large extent by how we treat the poor, lowly and voiceless people in our midst. Our practice of charity and our passion for justice shall be the yardstick for judgement on the last day.

Under the circumstances of mass destitution, ignorance and disease in our country, the Christian elite cannot pretend to be helpless. The Christian elite cannot afford to be an idle onlooker under our present circumstances. Yes, the time has come for the Christian elite who is endowed with intelligence and some material resources to establish programmes and projects aimed at educating and empowering the poor, freeing those held captive, and denouncing the unjust structures of leadership at all levels. This is the best way to celebrate the feast of Christ the King.

The very tendency to over-indulge in food, in drink, in the pursuit of pleasure, and in the accumulation of material wealth, is often a defence mechanism, an attempt to camouflage the void within. The inordinate ambition for power, the desire to dominate and control others is often a way of concealing the fear, insecurity, and emptiness inside. For example, following the revelations of the large-scale looting of the national treasury by the late General Sani Abacha and his comrades in crime, Nigerians are today able to see that for five years they had an insane man as head of state. Sixty-four billion naira is said to have already been recovered from his family. Did he intend to buy up the Nigerian nation or the entire West African Sub-Region? What could have been the true state of mind of Abacha before his death? Indeed, many wise men and women today acknowledge that the satisfaction of the profound hunger in the human heart will not come about through the acquisition of more and more money, power, and technical gadgets. Nor will it occur through the plastic wings of aberrant sex or the stupefaction of drugs.

In my solitude, I took a closer look at the Nigerian society and its problems, and I saw that we are truly suffocating under the enormous weight of the seven deadly social sins identified by Mahatma Gandhi as: Politics without principles; wealth without work; commerce without morality; pleasure without conscience; education without character; science without humanity; and worship without sacrifice. I reasoned that the only way forward is the way of repentance and conversion. No amount of rhetoric will change our situation if the demons of hatred, greed and ethnic bigotry are not exorcised.

Apparently overcome by mental exhaustion or fatigue, many Nigerians are too weak to keep their dreams, too hungry to hold on to their principles, and too blind to see beyond the madness of the moment. So, they adjust their lives to the prevalent injustice, they join the bandwagon that make falsehood a way of life, they lend their voices to the chorus of confusion, they contribute their talents towards oiling the machinery of misinformation, they enlist in the ever-increasing army of sycophants and bootlickers, they embrace the culture of death and subscribe to all forms of violence, both conventional and novel. The result of all this on the national landscape is the glorification of mediocrity, the institutionalisation of corruption, the banishment of truth, honesty, fairness and hard work, and the progressive degeneration or decay of the moral fibre of society.

As a people, we seem to have abandoned the pursuit of excellence in politics, education, economics, health care, and social infrastructure, and settled for expediency, mediocrity and charlatanism. As a nation, we appear to have made up our mind that the price to be paid for honesty, fidelity, truth and justice in governance and social contracts is too high. So, we settle for the short cut and the quick fix, and we resort to mutual betrayal, calumniation, opportunism and manipulation. We seem to think that high standards of democracy and social accountability are unattainable in our land, so we settle for what we call "home-grown" democracy that is actually a gunpoint democracy, by which a hundred million people are hoodwinked and bamboozled into a transition to democracy programme that is anything but democratic.

For example, faced with the challenge of the criminal neglect of certain minority areas in the distribution of resources, as a result of which there is an incessant craving for the creation of more states and local government areas, Nigerians lacked the political will to address the problem of inequitable distribution of resources and uneven development of the various segments of the nation. Instead, we chose to create more and more states, and make every village and hamlet a local government area, notwithstanding the fact that most of these entities are not viable. At the end of the day, the statutory allocation from the federation account to these states and local government areas can barely take care of the cost of running the emerging bureaucracies, with little or nothing left for the physical development of the areas and the improvement of the quality of life of the people.

Nigerians saw this after the creation of states exercise in 1976. We saw it again in 1988. And again in 1991. Yet we continue to think that even at a time of great economic distress, the solution to the problem of uneven development and inequitable distribution of resources is the creation of more states and local government areas. We have indeed settled for the quick fix - a momentary opiate to keep the people quiet, if only for today! Of course, the beneficiaries of the new states and local government areas are killing themselves with joy over the new dispensation, and organising countless solidarity visits to the great benefactor, though the celebrations may soon give way to mass retrenchment, forced relocation, and other attendant sorrows. This display of collective myopia and minimalism is part of the symptoms of the chronic pathology that exists on the level of our communal psyche.

CHAPTER NINETEEN

In Search of Moral Sanity in Ebiraland
(Paper delivered on February 17, 1996)

Let me begin by congratulating the Ebira Muslim Association of Nigeria (EMAN) for the efforts put into organising this one-day National Seminar on the theme: "The Search for Moral Sanity in Ebiraland," as part of the programmes to mark the end of this year's Ramadan season and the celebration of *Eid al-Fitr*. I am highly gratified to know that many men and women of Ebiraland, of both Islamic and Christian affiliations are not only expressing serious concern about the present degenerate moral climate of our motherland, but also engaging in serious reflection, study and dialogue towards finding lasting solutions to our critical social problems. I am even more gratified to realise that many of those engaged in this endeavour are not the usual politicians who may only wish to use such media to score political points for themselves, but young people, who are genuinely seeking a wholesome, veritable and peaceful future for their homeland. I thank the members of this Association for giving me an opportunity to share a few thoughts with you on these issues of social dislocation in our land. By inviting me to partake in this discussion, the organisers have demonstrated clearly that the crisis before us is a serious one, one which calls for the positive input of every enlightened son or daughter of Ebiraland, whether Christian or Muslim or even Traditional Religionist. May Allah, Most Beneficent and Merciful, grant success to your sincere efforts. May He grant you the grace of filial cooperation with other concerned citizens, towards the much-desired moral regeneration and social transformation in Ebiraland.

A critical reflection on the sociological developments in Ebiraland within the last sixteen or seventeen years shows that somewhere along the way we have lost our social cohesion. A serious dislocation seems to have occurred in the life of Ebira people who used to be known nationwide as a hard-working, kind-hearted, hospitable, and peace-loving group of people. Within the last sixteen or seventeen years, there seems to have occurred an acute disruption of the organic unity of Ebiraland. Our image as a people is so severely dented today that many men and women of this land are suffering a crisis of identity. Ebira people today clearly lack the sense of a common purpose. In all these years, our young people have suffered criminal neglect. Many of them have been allowed to grow up as thugs and touts, hoodlums and bandits. The mere sight of a crowd of Ebira youths now frightens a lot of people, especially visitors in our land, because it is believed the young people could break lose anytime and become violent.

The adult elite have been tragically overwhelmed by moral bankruptcy, social ineptitude, and political fragmentation. They have often engaged in a politics of bitterness, to the extent that the young people could hardly find sufficient motivation from their socio-political conduct. Many of those who belong to the elite class among our people have failed Ebiraland woefully in as much as they have not assumed their social responsibilities towards the future generation of Ebira people. And so today our young people have not been adequately prepared to face the challenges of the modern competitive society where only hard work and optimum productivity can win one a place. Our young people are simply groping in the darkness, and becoming increasingly hateful, resentful, angry and depressed. The cumulative effect of all this is the high rate of violent crimes which we witness every day in our land, and more painfully the brutal assaults and barbaric acts that are now associated with the traditional festivals of *Echanne* and *Ekuechi*.

This is rather unfortunate for a land that is so abundantly blessed by the Creator with immense human and natural resources. It is sad to note that a land which only twenty-five years ago held so much promise of greatness should today be in this mess. With the siting of the nation's first major Iron Ore and Steel Companies in Ajaokuta and Itape twenty-five years ago, Ebira people had the singular opportunity of establishing their weighty presence in the Nigerian social, political and economic landscape. We were offered the chance to make a major contribution in terms of natural resource and manpower to the industrial development of Nigeria. But we have lost this chance to the dirty politicking and the rancorous infighting that have surrounded the appointment and tenure of nearly all the Ebira people who have held important positions in the two companies since their inception. After twenty-five years, Ajaokuta has not much to show for all the billions of dollars expended on the project. Ebiraland has little to show after all these years, except of course the increase in crime and social insecurity. Yet with nearly two million people, Ebira people constitute a formidable ethnic group in the country. They rank among the first nine most populous language groups in this country, so they should ordinarily be among the movers and shakers of Nigeria. But our lack of social cohesion and unity of purpose has robbed us of our greatness.

Part of the social dislocation in Ebiraland can be traced to the loss of a moral fibre in the society. A land without integrity can neither have peace nor progress. We seem to have lost sight of the spiritual and moral principles and values that held our ancestors together for so long; those principles and values that gave them so much power and confidence that they were never conquered in history. We have lost our sense of respect for life, human life, which our ancestors saw as the centrepiece of God's creation. We have ignored the philosophical import of such names as "*Ozovehe*", "*Ozavize*", "*Ozohu*" and "*Oziohu*", "*Ozavisa*" and "*Ozavinoyi*" – all of which point to the immense dignity of the human person. We have ignored the eternal message in such wise sayings of our ancestors as: "*Aa kuozanyariozi, oza o ma kuozanyariekehi*" and "*Oza o ma siozamoenyi re*," a proverb which teaches that no amount of money could be compared to one single human being. We have sacrificed our traditional valuation of life on the altar of mammon and exchanged wholesome family life for material gain. The thirst for power, greed for money and lust for pleasure have taken away from the Ebira people the love of family, the joy of community and the sense of solidarity for which they were so well known in ages past.

My dear friends, the root of our problem is excessive materialism, and the pursuit of power and pleasure at all costs. Ebira politicians have largely practised a "do-or-die" kind of politics in the last two republics. Our politics has been characterised by such bitter rivalry and hatred that it is impossible to have peace and moral sanity in the land after all the mess, unless we repent of our sins, ask for God's forgiveness, make restitution where necessary, and learn a new politics of mutual respect and tolerance for opposing views and divergent opinions. We must note too that the social dislocation in Ebiraland has also been exacerbated by the tension that seems to exist between certain sections of the Islamic community and adherents of the traditional religion who engage in ancestor veneration in the form of afternoon or night masquerading. Ebiraland has not been spared of the credal bigotry and religious fanaticism that has so seriously threatened the peace in many parts of this country. But for the restoration of sanity in Ebiraland, credal bigotry and religious fanaticism must be halted.

Humanity has gone beyond the age of violent crusades and jihads. In medieval Europe, all who belonged to the Empire had to adopt the religion of the king. There was no freedom of conscience. The conscience of the king was synonymous to the conscience of the nation. There was a time when Christians fought religious wars and when they carried out crusades as an act of devotion to God. Today Christians think differently. There was a time too when Muslims fought religious wars and carried out jihads in God's name. Today the majority of Muslims think differently. Islam, they say is submission to Allah. The word "Islam" comes from the same root as the Hebrew Shalom, Salaam or Salem, meaning "peace." No sane person can engage in reckless killing of fellow human beings who are created in the image and likeness of God and still claim that he is serving the God of peace. Modern society recognises that all human beings, including those whom we may refer to as "infidels" have a right to life. All human beings enjoy freedom of conscience. All human beings enjoy freedom of religion. These rights are inviolable. Each human being is a subject of these rights by virtue of his or her humanity. They are recognised as God-given rights, and even atheists who do not believe in God still enjoy these rights.

More and more human beings are becoming conscious of these rights each day, and so whenever the rights are denied anyone anywhere, tension erupts, and society loses peace. If moral sanity is to be restored in Ebiraland, those who have engaged in religious bigotry and fanaticism, whether Christian or Muslim, must be stopped henceforth. Such people are the greatest enemies of our land. They have brought nothing but tears to our people. They must not be allowed to continue their campaign of hatred. They must be made to realise that the world is now at the threshold of the twenty-first century, and Ebira people cannot be left behind. They must be educated that in the civilised world, evangelisation and proselytisation for Christians or Muslims is done by persuasion and not by the force of arms. Violence must always be condemned. Violence has never brought any good to humanity anywhere. Rather violence begets further violence, and society degenerates in the vicious circle of violence.

For peace and sanity to reign in our land, leaders of the various religions must open up the channels for dialogue. Serious dialogue must be encouraged among the leaders of the various Christian groups, among the various sects within Islam, and between Christians and Muslims. Dialogue must also be initiated between Christians and traditional religionists, and between Muslims and traditional religionists, especially the patrons, caretakers, custodians and organisers of the Echanne and Ekuechi festivals. It must be recognised that those who have not accepted Islam or Christianity have a right to worship God or venerate their ancestors in the way they think best, as long as they do not thereby violate the rights of others in society. When such an understanding exists among the various segments of society, peace will not be far away.

The lack of love in the family and in the community is a major source of our social dislocation. It is the absence of love that is the cause of so much tension in our land. The absence of love and the reality of hatred and wickedness is responsible for so much suffering in our society. The absence of genuine love between husband and wife has led to widespread divorce and broken marriages in Ebiraland. A number of Ebira men marry too many wives to the extent that many children grow up lacking not only food and clothing but also sufficient parental love, care and affection. Modern psychologists are agreed that a child that grows under such an environment will have all sorts of complexes. If a child grows with hostility they say, he will learn to be aggressive. Many of our children today are growing amidst a very hostile parental environment. Many are growing up under circumstances of near destitution. We know that reasonability is an attribute of wholesome humanity. When people are living under sub-human conditions, they cannot be expected to behave reasonably.

Our society is becoming insensitive to the suffering of poor relations, especially the widows, the orphans, the sick, the handicapped and the disabled. A lot of our youth are living in deplorable conditions at home or in school. Many of them are entirely abandoned to the streets, so they adopt a crisis morality and an emergency ethic. Our streets are now full of mentally handicapped people whom we have neglected to care for. Many people are dying everyday of poverty, whereas there are some among us who have so much money that they engage in conspicuous consumption, while others engage in useless celebrations. The Koran says "Have you thought of him that denies the Last Judgement? It is he who turns away the orphan and does not urge others to feed the poor... Woe to those who pray but are heedless in their prayer, who make a show of piety and give no alms to the destitute" (Q. 107:1; 107:7).

So, what can we do to halt the decay? Let me use this forum to plead with wealthy sons and daughters of Ebiraland to invest their resources on the children of today who are the leaders of tomorrow, by giving scholarships, and equipping our primary and secondary schools with books and equipment. They can also help our young people by investing in wholesome recreational facilities in our towns and villages. When young people have no opportunity for healthy recreation, they often engage in crime. I plead with wealthy Ebira sons and daughters to invest their money in projects that will provide employment opportunities for our energetic men and women and promote the people's empowerment. I plead with the generality of Ebira men and women to be more responsible to their families and to their children. I plead with the men especially not to marry more wives than they are able to cater for. I wonder how anyone can really cater for more than one wife. I call upon the young people in Ebiraland not to follow the example of the elders who are living scandalous lives, elders whose long years in the world have been our years eaten by the locust. I call upon the young people to look instead at the few among the Ebira elite that continue to make us proud and follow their example.

Finally, I call upon all Ebira people to return to the true worship of God, for the fear of the Lord is the beginning of wisdom. "Unless the Lord builds a house the labourers labour in vain. And unless the Lord watches over a city the sentries watch in vain." May Allah the Compassionate, Beneficent and Merciful God bless you all.

CHAPTER TWENTY

Towards A More Peaceful Society
(Written on October 21, 1996)

Peace is a dynamic process. It does not just happen. Peace is the fruit of justice. Peace does not occur irrespective of the moral disposition of the individuals in society. It is predicated on a prior commitment on the part of human agents to truth and justice. Those who work against peace never find peace. Peace is the treasure found only by seekers of peace. It is the graceful harvest of those who work tirelessly for peace. Peace is found only by makers of peace. Peace is never brought about by the hangman's noose or the executioner's sword. Peace does not result from military conquest or from a successful coup d'etat, for as it is said, all who take the sword will perish by the sword. Peace cannot be decreed by sword-brandishing bandits or gun-toting dictators, for the prophet says that there is no peace for the wicked, and that a nation without integrity cannot know peace. True peace is to be distinguished from the "pax Romana" of medieval Europe. It is different from the balance of terror that was called nuclear deterrence in 20th century Europe. And peace is not the silence of the graveyard that we witness in the present Nigerian dispensation.

There is no true peace where a multitude of people are subdued by military or political might. There is only a superficial peace where the security of a people rests on oppression and injustice. The peace that is based on fear is the peace of the graveyard. Where millions of people are starving to death in a land so richly endowed as ours, peace is only a dream. Where millions of people are plagued by the diseases of malnutrition just as others are engaged in conspicuous consumption, peace is a mirage. Wherever human life is fractured by hunger, disease, oppression, intimidation and coercion, peace is broken. Yes, peace, like freedom, is indivisible. We either all have it, or no one has it. Peace cannot be privatized. It either goes round or no one has it. Human life has a powerful corporate dimension. Our life has a strong imperative for corporate responsibility. There is no room for pockets of peace in a land that is so broken and so distressed.

Though peace appears to be an urgent concern to every Nigerian, few among us are ready to pay the price for the peace that lasts. While many pay lip service to the concept of peace, they pursue war rather than peace. Though many pray for peace, they are unwilling to abandon the selfish, greedy, and manipulative lifestyles that lead to violence and war. Their violent lifestyles, their corrupt social habits, their unjust economic choices and their oppressive political decisions, are often in pursuance of death and doom rather than peace and prosperity. Peace will be long in coming if Nigerians continue to abuse, oppress and manipulate each other. Peace will not come until Nigerians are ready to pay the price for peace, which includes the pursuit of justice, equity and fairness. Peace will not just occur. It demands repentance on the part of individuals and social groups for the atrocities they have committed against their neighbours, especially the poor, the weak and the lowly. The dynamics of peace involve a creative revulsion against the values of an acquisitive, aggressive and militarized society. The dynamics of peace involve a reappraisal of the values and principles that sustain our individual lives and determine our communal existence.

The present political order in our country is an order built on long-standing injustice. Unless this order is reversed, peace shall not come home. Our socio-economic structures are largely structures of violence, which by their very nature, are bound to beget further violence, if they are not urgently replaced. The suppression of the collective will of the people through a multiplicity of draconian decrees and ouster clauses, and the concentration of executive, legislative and judicial powers in one man, do not make for peace. The coercion and intimidation of the people, and the perpetration of acts that amount to state terrorism, will not attract peace. What is more, the institutionalization of corruption, the trading of lies in official circles, and the open encouragement of political sycophancy, which together make today's Nigeria a nation without integrity, shall not bring peace home.

Peace shall be long in coming, unless the leadership of Nigeria repents of its lust for power, and its greed for money. Peace shall delay in coming unless our leaders repent of the falsehood and fraudulence that now constitute the character of Nigerian governance. Peace shall continue to elude us, until the citizens banish sycophancy and courageously embrace truth, that truth which sometimes must confront the status quo. Yes, peace is not without a price. It will not come without some striving on the part of those who seek it. Peace is costly. The cost of peace is a lifestyle of struggle and of sacrifice. The cost of peace is the unrelenting pursuit of the principles of justice that make way for peace. Peace does not come in a platter of gold, but through a crown of thorns. Under the present circumstances in our country, peace will not come if we continue business as usual, for as it is said, "unless a people change their course, they are bound to end up where they are headed."

Nigerian peace seekers must stop paying lip-service to the search for peace. Nigerian peace seekers must themselves operate from a thoroughly disarmed heart, and be ready to pay the price of atonement for the multiple violence, including the primary violence of oppressive structures that currently crush the people and make peace impossible in our land. They must be prepared to suffer martyrdom, which is the lot of peace seekers of all times. That is to say they must be ready to follow the example of Jesus of Nazareth, Mahatma Gandhi of India, Martin Luther King Jr. of America, Steve Biko of South Africa and Oscar Romero of Argentina. Those who sincerely seek peace must reject the prevalent culture of violence and death, which include crass materialism, conspicuous consumption, greed, selfishness, economic exploitation, social discrimination, arbitrary rule, false propaganda and capital punishment.

Nigerian peace seekers must dissociate themselves from the prevalent structures that are structures of violence and death. They must not only denounce all authority structures that oppress, intimidate, alienate and impoverish people, but also they must make a definite commitment to the evolution of alternative social, economic and political structures that will make for peace. They must take up the challenge of conceiving, promoting and enthroning these alternative structures with all the resources at their disposal. They must use all the peaceful means available to build a peaceful nation. Nigerian peace seekers must be ready to commit their resources into programmes and projects aimed at educating and empowering the poor, freeing those unjustly held captive, pulling down walls of hatred and building bridges across the poisoned rivers of ethnic, religious and social hostilities. This is the way to promote a just, humane and peaceful Nigeria. For indeed, peace is not only a desirable condition but also an enormous task. It is not only a goal but also a serious striving. Peace is not only a fact but also a dynamic process.

Today, more and more Nigerians are calling for fasting and prayer in order that our country may find peace. Churches are organising prayer vigils, individuals and organisations are staging regional or national prayer sessions. Even governments are said to be hiring pastors, imams and "dibias" to organise prayers for Nigeria, since only God can save Nigeria. It is a good thing that at times of crisis such as this, Nigerians know that they should turn to God, for as the Psalmist says, "unless the Lord builds the house, they labour in vain who build; and unless the Lord watches over a city, the sentries watch in vain." Jesus Christ, who Himself is the Prince of Peace, taught his disciples that with God "all things are possible," and so he challenged them to turn to God the Father through Him in prayer when they are in great need.

In spite of our belief in the efficacy of prayer and in the truth that only God can save our land, we remain highly suspicious of the ongoing clarion call for prayer in Nigeria. We suspect that some of our countrymen and women are manipulating the logic of "only God can save Nigeria," to a ridiculous extent that is tantamount to magic. They are using the logic of "only God can save Nigeria" to promote a feeling of utter helplessness in the face of an otherwise contrived evil, and justify the now widespread disposition of indifference, inertia, inaction and apathy in the people of Nigeria. Once again, religion is being utilised to keep the people quiet while sustaining the status quo of injustice, oppression, human degradation and abuse. This is the type of religion that was identified as the opium of the people, one that lends itself to manipulation by oppressive forces in society to sustain the structures of injustice.

It is true that only God can save Nigeria. Yet God will not save Nigeria without Nigerians! God does not impose himself on anyone. The Christian God that we worship does not save human beings against their will. Persons who are beneficiaries of His salvific acts are never treated as helpless objects. They are always seen as participating agents in the process of their own salvation. God indeed does not save anyone without his or her cooperation. In the same way He will not save Nigeria without Nigerians. Those who are calling on Christians to pray for God to save Nigeria must recognise that within the context of a society that stinks with sin, Christian prayer is only efficacious when it is preceded by true repentance and conversion. Nigerians must recognise that at the root of our nation's multiple ailments is sin, individual as well as social sin. This sin manifests itself by way of primordial greed and avarice, exaggerated selfishness and crass individualism, ethnic bigotry and religious intolerance.

God will not save Nigeria if Nigerians continue business as usual; if they continue to cover one lie with another, and erect one unjust structure upon another. God will not save Nigeria if Nigerians individually and collectively do not adjust their corrupt, greedy and avaricious lifestyle. God will not save Nigeria if Nigerians as individuals and as corporate entities do not make the necessary change of behaviour and attitude that will make for peace and prosperity. God will not save Nigeria if the structures of injustice that are at the root of our multiple crises remain in place. Yes, God will not save Nigeria until Nigerians repent of their individual and social sins, and acquire the spiritual vision and the moral virtues, the socio-economic values, and the political attitudes and disposition that are the foundation of peace.

A genuine call for prayer is not an invitation to indolence and apathy. Rather it is a call to action by way of repentance and conversion which are always a painful experience. It is a call to action by way of the mutual forgiveness of past hurts. Those who are calling for prayer must be ready to face squarely the truth of our national existence, and where necessary summon the moral courage and political will to redress the long-standing injustices that have bred so much resentment in the land. Since the God we serve is the God of truth, prayer to Him is most efficacious when truth ascends the throne in the lives of the supplicants. Those calling for prayer must be committed to truth. They must not only live the truth, but courageously proclaim the truth in season and out of season. In this way our prayers shall be efficacious, and God will indeed save our land, for in Second Chronicles the Lord promised that "if the people who bear my name humble themselves, pray and seek my presence and turn from their wicked ways, I myself will hear from heaven and forgive their sins and restore their land." I believe that only God can save Nigeria, but not without some striving on the part of Nigerians. God has in fact already offered His recipe for salvation. What we need today from Nigerians are gestures of acceptation. May we be ready to make the necessary sacrifices that will constitute the much-needed gestures of acceptation of God's salvation.

CHAPTER TWENT- ONE

The Triumph of Mediocrity
(Written on January 23, 1997)

The times are hard for the generality of our countrymen and women. But for thinking Nigerians, they are turbulent times. It is simply incredible what our saints and scholars, and seers and dreamers are going through during these times when the champions of virtue and the crusaders of justice seem to have been gagged, harassed and coerced into submission or forced to beat a retreat. Mere survival has become an uphill task for dogged champions of the principles of civility. We have indeed been through many lean years, and they have taken their toll even on the saints and scholars of our land. How does the crusader thrive in an environment of rampant sycophancy and idolatry? How does the idealist bloom in a society of charlatans, minimalists, and champions of mediocrity? What place has the man or woman of principles in a land of duplicity, where compromise is king? What chances of survival have saints and scholars at a time when corruption is clothed in purple and adorned with gold? How does the dreamer dream his or her dreams in the midst of a generation that is plagued by collective amnesia and corporate myopia?

The distress of the moment perhaps has done greater damage to the Nigerian psyche than many realise. One can readily see the economic, political and social dimensions of our nation's distress, but the negative transformation of the Nigerian psyche in the last few years has been subliminal and silent, but nevertheless progressive and phenomenal. The unwholesome psyche manifests itself in the widespread apathy, helplessness, and hopelessness which we witness today. Apparently overcome by mental exhaustion or fatigue, many Nigerians are too weak to keep their dreams, too hungry to hold on to their principles, and too blind to see beyond the madness of the moment. So, they adjust their lives to the prevalent injustice, they join the bandwagon that make falsehood a way of life, they lend their voices to the chorus of confusion, they contribute their talents towards oiling the machinery of misinformation, they enlist in the ever-increasing army of sycophants and bootlickers, they embrace the culture of death and subscribe to all forms of violence, both conventional and novel. The result of all this on the national landscape is the glorification of mediocrity, the institutionalisation of corruption, the banishment of truth, honesty, fairness and hard work, and the progressive degeneration or decay of the moral fibre of society.

As a people we seem to have abandoned the pursuit of excellence in politics, education, economics, health care, and social infrastructure, and settled for expediency, mediocrity and charlatanism. As a nation we appear to have made up our mind that the price to be paid for honesty, fidelity, truth and justice in governance and social contracts is too high. So, we settle for the short cut and the quick fix, and we resort to mutual betrayal, calumniation, opportunism and manipulation. We seem to think that high standards of democracy and social accountability are unattainable in our land, so we settle for what we call "home-grown" democracy that is actually a gunpoint democracy, by which a hundred million people are hoodwinked and bamboozled into a transition to democracy programme that is anything but democratic.

For example, faced with the challenge of the criminal neglect of certain minority areas in the distribution of resources, as a result of which there is an incessant craving for the creation of more states and local government areas, Nigerians lacked the political will to address the problem of inequitable distribution of resources and uneven development of the various segments of the nation. Instead, we chose to create more and more states, and make every village and hamlet a local government area, notwithstanding the fact that most of these entities are not viable. At the end of the day, the statutory allocation from the federation account to these states and local government areas can barely take care of the cost of running the emerging bureaucracies, with little or nothing left for the physical development of the areas and the improvement of the quality of life of the people.

Nigerians saw this after the creation of states exercise in 1976. We saw it again in 1988. And again in 1991. Yet we continue to think that even at a time of great economic distress, the solution to the problem of uneven development and inequitable distribution of resources is the creation of more states and local government areas. We have indeed settled for the quick fix - a momentary opiate to keep the people quiet, if only for today! Of course, the beneficiaries of the new states and local government areas are killing themselves with joy over the new dispensation, and organising countless solidarity visits to the great benefactor, though the celebrations may soon give way to mass retrenchment, forced relocation, and other attendant sorrows. This display of collective myopia and minimalism is part of the symptoms of the chronic pathology that exists on the level of our communal psyche.

Another example of the triumph of mediocrity in our land is the trash that "30 million viewers nationwide" often receive via the N.T.A. In an ideal situation, where there is regard for excellence, and where public-owned agencies and parastatals are accountable to the people, this medium is supposed to be not only educative, informative and entertaining, but also objective and sensitive to the various socio-political currents of the land. But before our very eyes the N.T.A. has often been used in a most blatant manner as the propaganda machine of the ruling class, and Nigerians who are ever ready to adjust to irregular situations, and to settle for less, have accepted the situation as normal, since they say, "He who pays the piper dictates the tune." But this mode of operation is far from being normal, for it violates certain fundamental principles of journalism, and disregards prudence, decency and civility.

On many occasions, the nine o'clock network news is like a drilling session for the 30 million viewers in the art of propaganda absorption. After taking in the N.T.A. dose on such occasions, I often wonder whether to laugh or to cry. Gazing at the tube and trying to make meaning out of the vanity on display, I often remain for a long time in a state of perplexity. In my amazement I have often cried out: "What am I hearing?" "What am I seeing on screen?" "Are other Nigerians hearing this?" "Are they seeing it?" "Do they believe what they are hearing?" "Does the Newscaster herself believe what she is reading?" Indeed, my moral sensibilities have been terribly insulted for the umpteenth time by the N.T.A. My passion for truth and objectivity has often been severely affronted by this medium. My commitment to peace and non-violence has often been seriously violated through this medium.

My sense of decency and civility is slighted for example when N.T.A. aids and abets the ever nauseating "rent-a-crowd" syndrome and helps to elevate sycophancy to a ridiculous extent that is tantamount to idolatry. Not long ago the medium featured a crowd of placard carrying demonstrators in Oshogbo, the Osun State capital, and highlighted a particular placard which read, "No Abacha, No Nigeria." I was frightened. I was thrown off-balance that evening and I cried, for that image immediately reminded me of King Louis XIV the celebrated monarch who came to a point where he declared that "I am the state." Also, my passion for truth and objectivity was affronted for example when on January 6, 1997, the N.T.A. carried the story of the seizure of a truck of arms and ammunition that was coming into the country through the border with Benin Republic. The story which was relayed with an official commentary was not attributed to anyone. A few days later, a Beninois Minister denied that any such incident involving the border with Benin happened. When journalists approached the minister of information for comment, he sent them away with the excuse that the story did not originate from him. Since then, those arms and ammunition have been paraded daily before Nigerians as part of the activities of dissidents and traitors, aimed at destabilising the country. Yet no one has fully established the veracity of the story, and N.T.A. has made no effort to demonstrate the objectivity of its report. This is journalism at its lowest level, and yet the citizens who own the medium cannot complain.

Since Nigerians seem to have abandoned the pursuit of excellence, lost sight of the ideal, and settled for expediency and mediocrity, they have begun to accept as normal, outrageous violations of human dignity and rights. For example, besides extorting money at gunpoint from innocent citizens, it is now commonplace for the numerous security agents along our highways and within our cities to point fully-loaded guns menacingly at every oncoming vehicle, as if all Nigerians were hardened criminals to be hunted and hounded down. The havoc caused by armed robbers and other criminals in our society today is no excuse for all of us to be treated so shabbily. And except in war ravaged Rwanda, Burundi and Liberia, there is hardly any place we know in the modern (civilized) society where such practice is condoned. Yet Nigerians who are ever ready to settle for less than the ideal, have adjusted themselves to this indignity and primitivity.

Nigerians are putting up everyday with sub-standard services and shabby treatment from NITEL, from NEPA, from the Water Corporation, and other public agencies and parastatals, and are not complaining. In the Lagos area for example, officials of NITEL would toss the telephone line of a subscriber before he or she ever gets the bill for the month. In many parts of the city, the subscriber never ever receives the bill in his house. It is after the disconnection that the subscriber has to go and look for his or her bill, settle the bill in a bank, and go to NITEL to present evidence of payment and reconcile the account. Only after this will the line be re-activated. But this process can take a full week, during which the person's business is grounded. The following month he or she would be required to go through the same ritual. Even if a subscriber has one million naira credit in his or her account with NITEL, he or she often has to go through this ritual every month. This is how far we have degenerated. For many Nigerians, it appears that the worst is not bad enough, as we seem ever ready to adjust to the rot.

As I brood and ruminate over the decay in the land, the reality of our collective amnesia and myopia and the triumph of mediocrity and minimalism, I keep wondering about the level of my sanity. If Nigerians carry on business as usual and they are thriving under circumstances that I consider inhuman, indecent, undignified and uncivilized, then perhaps I am an odd person. What is happening to my motherland? What is happening to me? Are all these abnormalities part of a prolonged nightmare on my part? Am I existing all these years in a land of dreams? What is the state of my mental health? Do I need to be examined by a psychiatrist? Perhaps I need some expert assistance in the dynamics of adjustment to injustice. Perhaps I need to be schooled in the dynamics of duplicity and compromise. Perhaps I need to take lessons in the dynamics of settlement and realism. Perhaps someday I shall be able to live comfortably, eat well, and laugh in the midst of these abnormalities. But when that day comes, and when the internal transformation takes place, shall I still answer my name? Shall I still be the same person? Ah, my story must sound lunatic. Yet how sane is life in Nigeria? When the entire society seems lunatic, whence lies madness?

CHAPTER TWENTY-TWO

That Tomorrow May Not Be Lost
(Written on September 30, 1997)

We celebrate this week thirty-seven years of our liberation from colonial rule, and our independence as a nation. Under normal circumstances this week is supposed to be a week of rejoicing, a week of national celebration. Under normal circumstances, our land is supposed to be agog this week with festive parades, fireworks, parties, picnics and sundry activities. But as has become the norm in the last ten or so years, we are going to have very little of celebration. Our circumstances are far from normal. Instead of festivities, what we have is widespread anxiety, fear, uncertainty and a sprinkling of anti-climactic hope. Looking at the past thirty-seven years, Nigerians are filled with regret and nostalgia about broken promises, dashed hopes and shallow dreams of a land of peace and prosperity. For many, the story of Nigeria is that of a paradise lost.

Many Nigerians are overwhelmed with a sense of betrayal and frustration as they mark this independence anniversary, for at the threshold of the twenty-first century, while the rest of the world is competing in digital technology and flying high at jet speed in business and economics, our own country is crawling behind, weighed down by ethnic bigotry, endemic corruption, and political subterfuge. At the threshold of the twenty-first century, while many countries have reached a very high level in the provision of quality education and social infrastructure for their citizens, the Nigerian educational system has virtually collapsed due to criminal neglect of infrastructures and senseless disregard for intellectualism. At the threshold of the twenty-first century, while the rest of the world is making spectacular advances in the appreciation and application of democratic principles, and in the recognition and respect for the rights and dignity of every human person, Nigeria still groans under the awesome burden of military dictatorship with the attendant violation of fundamental human rights and the extreme militarisation of society. We mark the thirty-seven years of our independence with the fear of being sidetracked or left on the margins of the twenty-first century human civilization.

October 1st, 1997 therefore, is to be for many thinking Nigerians, a day for sober reflections on why our thirty seven years of independence have been a dismal failure, how we ended up in this mess, where we went wrong, where we must go from here, or how we must work towards a more wholesome future?

Our independence anniversary is nevertheless still an occasion for thanksgiving. We thank God that we are alive to bemoan our plight. We thank God that we are not yet dead, or rather that we have not yet been killed. We owe our continued existence to God's mercy and compassion. We believe that it is by virtue of his mysterious love that we have been spared the trauma of another civil war, and the sordid experience of the sister countries of Somalia, Bosnia, Burundi, Rwanda, Liberia and Sierra-Leone. We have enough reason to thank God. Though we may be psychologically deflated and morally demented, we thank God that we are still alive. Though we may be politically humiliated and economically impoverished, we thank God that we are still alive. Though may be brought low in the sight of the world, we thank God that we are still alive. Though we may be lacking pride in ourselves and in our country, and living daily with a sense of shame, we thank God that we are still alive. Though we may be locked up in the pit of decay where we are devoid of clear vision, we thank God that we are still alive, for life after all is better than death, and when there is life, there is hope. Since we are alive, we continue to nurture the dream and keep up the hope that the eclipse of reason over our land shall someday give way and wisdom shall reign.

The embarrassing truth we must acknowledge today is that many of those who constitute the Nigerian elite have over the last thirty-seven years been largely blind guides, unprincipled leaders and greedy opportunists. Many of our successive leaders have turned out to be reckless plunderers and mindless looters. True, our experience of leadership in this country, whether at the hands of military dictators or civilian politicians is one of large-scale deceit, manipulation and exploitation. Poor Nigerians have been used and abused many times over. Our leaders have often exploited the poverty and ignorance of the vast majority of Nigerians and cashed in on the existing ethnic and religious polarities when it paid them to do so.

We must acknowledge the fact that the collective suffering and pain which we experience in Nigeria today is not God's will for us, but rather the onset of the process of retribution. The depression in the Nigerian economy and the distress in the Nigerian polity which we witness today is not the design of God, but perhaps the inevitability of nemesis catching up with the offender. For the Creator has provided this land with enormous resources. We are so richly endowed by God that we could indeed have become the giant of Africa. But today we seem to be paying dearly for our undisciplined and unprincipled lives. As a people, it is as if we are now atoning for our collective greed and avarice.

When we see thousands of people dying at home or in the hospitals because they cannot afford to eat good food or buy drugs to cure minor infections, we need not ask our stars for the reason. When we see thousands of our people suffering depression, becoming destitute, and roaming about the streets, we do not need a seer to tell us why. When we see our young people becoming beastly in hate, ruthless in violence, and reckless in destruction, we do not need to ask too many questions. We are in this mess today because we have plundered the inheritance of our motherland and squandered the resources of our fatherland.

Nigerians have engaged in a life of debauchery. Like the prodigal son in the parable of Jesus, we have left our palace of pride to dwell in the pit of shame. We have often thrown decency and integrity to the dogs and flushed justice and truth into the septic tank. We have often violated love and trampled on the poor and the weak. We have enthroned bribery and corruption in our public life, and with reckless abandon, we have perpetrated that art of thievery called "settlement." We have neglected our educational institutions and made our teachers an object of ridicule in the eyes of society.

Our schools and colleges in turn have lost their sacred character as formation centres, and have rather become breeding grounds for thieves, thugs, touts, secret cultists, gangsters, rapists and prostitutes. We hear these days of school children beating up their teachers, sacking their principals, and burning up their libraries. Examination malpractice in some of our schools has now assumed the frightening dimension whereby teachers and principals organize cheating at external examinations, and parents annually contribute money to "settle" supervisors and invigilators.

As we the leaders and parents have become more enterprising in greed and political mischief, and as we fail to inspire the young people in the pursuit of higher values, we have lost control of the younger generation. Many of our graduates from secondary schools, universities and polytechnics, are social deviants, drug addicts, and secret cultists, who now constitute a nuisance in our homes, our schools and our offices. With juvenile bravado many of these young people are constantly visiting their vengeance on an adult society that has failed to give them a sense of direction. So they cheat and steal, they rob and rape, and they kill and maim. And they commit these crimes with the sophistication of the Italian mafia. The truth is that the collective psyche of our young people has been so seriously wounded, and their delicate conscience so brutally battered by the crimes of the adult society, that we now stand the chance of losing tomorrow altogether.

We are about to lose millions of our young people whose teeth are on edge because their fathers have eaten sour grapes. We are about to lose millions of young people who are constipated because their mothers have eaten the forbidden fruit. Our young people are full of energy and endowed with numerous talents, but they lack the necessary pride in their fatherland. Our youths are resourceful and ingenious, but they are devoid of any sense of direction. Our children have not been adequately taught, nor have they seen practical examples of justice, truth, love, compassion, patriotism and altruism, enough to motivate them. What is more, our young people are beginning to lose hope. And this is the greatest danger. It is the absence of hope in the midst of hardship that has led many of our young unemployed people into the now widespread township thuggery, armed robbery, drug peddling and drug addiction.

The progressive degeneration of our national landscape in the last thirty seven years has some important lessons for all men and women of reason, namely, that greed is a cancer that eats its own host to death; that lies, corruption, and political subterfuge have never, and will never nurture a people; that thievery, robbery and roguery, by whatever name else it is called, when it becomes king in a land, that land rots; that when hooliganism and banditry get into high places, the superstructure soon comes crashing down; and that where lawlessness becomes the norm, and illegality becomes the rule, the people soon perish.

There is work to be done by all of us who belong to the adult society in Nigeria, if we are not to kill tomorrow before today's sun sets. We must own up before our young people that we have betrayed our fatherland and failed to lay the necessary foundation for a prosperous future. We must own up to the fact that we have often stolen food off the hands of our children. Each one of us is guilty to the extent that we have contributed in some way to the mess of the moment by our corrupt and selfish lifestyle. As parents, teachers, preachers and elders, we have often failed to inspire our young people to live a life of righteousness. As leaders and elders we have often failed to be a beacon of light. Instead, we have often been a source of scandal for our own children and the children of our country.

The time has come for repentance. For us who are believers in God, the situation may be bad enough but not hopeless. We should believe that redemption is possible for our land by the power of God who creates and recreates. We can experience a rejuvenation, if today we begin to retrace our steps, and get back to the basics. We should believe that from the rubble of our shattered motherland, a rich, powerful, peaceful and united country can emerge, by the power of God who puts back flesh on dry bones. This will happen if we identify and get rid of the demons that have bewitched this land since independence.

Our endless transition programmes to democracy often fail in as much as they are plagued by greed, manipulation, deceit, mischief and subterfuge. The redemption of the Nigerian nation shall remain a mirage, an empty dream, unless the demons that have led us along the dark alleys of economic depression, political anarchy and social disintegration are identified and cast out. As we reflect on the way towards a more wholesome future, we must put into proper focus not only the socio-political events of the recent past, but also the moral climate and the values or vices that we have pursued in the past.

In the past we have seen too many leaders and elders that are habitual violators of truth. Leaders and elders in this country have over and over again sacrificed truth on the altar of greed and lust for power. However, those who seek to bestow hope on the coming generation must recommit themselves to a life of truth, justice, and righteousness. Parents must be ready to make sacrifices for the sake of their children. Teachers must recognize that they teach more by their lives than by their lessons. The world has too many teachers and preachers. What the world needs today are living witnesses to love, compassion, truth and justice.

We talk too much about truth, honesty and fairness. What young people need instead is to see this truth, honesty and fairness at work in the civil service, in the award and execution of contracts, in the process of governance and in the examination hall. They are constantly let down and disappointed when their leaders are fraudulent or when they see teachers assisting unscrupulous students to cheat at examinations. They are shocked when they discover that their governors, ministers, parents or teachers are liars. Then they wonder whether a life of truth is possible in this world. Their trust is violated when they themselves or their peers are sexually exploited, harassed or abused by leaders, elders or teachers.

When our young people see the hypocrisy of the adult society, they convince themselves that there is no truth or justice in the world. They make up their minds that there is no such thing as love and compassion. They conclude that the world is one big jungle, largely inspired by the principle of mutual exploitation and often governed by the law of the survival of the fittest and the triumph of the villain. Ah, there is work for the adult society to do if we must bestow hope on our young people.

Lasting peace in any society is the reward for a consistent life of truth and justice. True peace is achieved by a people who know and live by the fact that righteousness exalts a nation, and that greed and avarice destroy a people. Democracy in its highest expression is the mutual acknowledgement of certain fundamental truths, including the truth of the dignity, equality and freedom of all in a society. In Nigeria, democracy will only germinate and thrive upon the mutual recognition and acceptance of the truth that all the inhabitants of the geographical expression we call Nigeria must enjoy equal dignity and opportunities. For democracy to thrive in our land, all who qualify to be called Nigerians by birth or naturalization must enjoy equal protection of the law, irrespective of ethnic origin, religious affiliation, or political preference.

For a peaceful and prosperous future, thinking Nigerian have work to do. Those endowed with vision in Nigerian must resist the temptation to apathy and despondency. We must rise up and be counted on the side of reason, truth and justice. We must refrain from joining the bandwagon in a life of greed and graft. We must reject the foolish pattern of life which has led our nation to the mess of the moment. Instead, we must seek after higher values that will guarantee peace and prosperity. We must start now cultivating the virtues of sacrificial love, truth, justice, discipline and patriotism which alone can bring peace and prosperity. If today we cultivate these virtues, then we would have laid the foundation for a more wholesome future for our country.

The upcoming generation, the youths themselves, must shun materialism, for it blinds people and enslaves them. Instead of seeking escape in the plastic wings of sexual pleasure and hard drugs, and the illusory power of secret cults and satanic confraternities, our young people must seek the fear of the Lord, which is the beginning of wisdom. If today our young people allow their lives to be shaped along the way of these higher values, then tomorrow will not be lost. If today our young people choose the culture of life in place of the prevailing culture of crime, violence and death, then they shall have a bright future ahead of them. Yes, if our young people embrace the culture of life and truth, they shall one day sing the National Anthem with a sense of respect for our heroes past, a sense of pride in our fatherland, and a sense of belonging to a nation bound in freedom, peace and unity.

We all have work to do, and we must begin from somewhere. It is not enough to identify the problems, for most Nigerians already know what the problems are. We must do something about the problems. We cannot sit idly by and complain endlessly of the deplorable state of affairs. It is better to light a candle than to curse the darkness. Thinking Nigerians, both young and old must all be committed to the all-important task of national rejuvenation. We must light the candle of hope in our homes, in our offices, and in our schools. We must do this by struggling to lead a life of truth, justice, honesty and discipline. We must embrace a new a new ethic of life, and pursue it relentlessly, for indeed "where there is no vision, the people perish."

CHAPTER TWENTY-THREE

A Nation on Trial
(Written on January 22, 1998)

The news of a coup d'etat, planned, aborted, executed, failed, or foiled is not new to Nigerians. We have had a haversack full of them in our four decades of national independence. What is new in our multiple coup legacy is the hi-tech coup monitoring and the selective video entertainment that has characterised the latest episode. However, with yet another coup scare what Nigerians must do is to rise beyond the hysteria generated by official propaganda and take a pensive moment to ponder the root causes of the various destabilizing events in the land, including coup d'etat and election annulment. Nigerians must engage in sober reflection on questions fundamental to the country's political unity, social harmony and economic progress.

Nigerians must ask searching questions why after 12 unbroken nightmarish years of transition we remain in an economic and political wilderness. Nigerians must ask why it must take so long to reach the promised land. If it takes all night to rehearse our play of national unity, then when shall we enact the drama? Nigerians must examine critically the underlying issues that excite widespread resentment, open and hidden angers, mutual distrust and widening divides. Nigerians must seek to know why so much remains unsettled in our body politic to warrant the degree of distress, disaffection and dissatisfaction in evident in the land.

The alleged coup plot presents an occasion for serious stocktaking, for if in fact at this stage in what has been highly touted as our final transition, military personnel of the calibre of the accused are linked to a plot to topple the applecart they helped to set up and oil, an administration in which they were known to be active participants, a government whose decisions, popular or unpopular, appeared to Nigerians to have received their full backing, if in spite of all these a violent change of government was yet in the offing, then the damning revelation means that there remain fundamental structural defects in Nigeria's nation state. It means that there remain elements of inherent instability even among the leadership. It means that Nigerians remain bound on a jerry-built national merry-go-round. It means that Nigeria is in a greater mess than many imagine.

Is this the will of God, or are we being driven into perdition by a band of demoniacs? Is it God that is directing the Nigerian roller-coaster or are we by our evil machinations - our greed, our treachery, our intrigues, our prejudices, and escapism bent on riding to self-destruction? Is it providence that is steering the Nigerian ship of state or are we by our collective amnesia, our corporate myopia and mutual delusion, set on a blind course and headed for a national shipwreck?

With the latest report of coup-plotting and the subsequent video show, details of which are said to be despicable, it is the Nigerian nation that is really on trial, for beyond the hysteria attending the official propaganda at this time, is the very serious question of what hope there is for the realisation of a free civil political future for the country. Why is our claim to national unity still so illusory? Why has Nigeria remained a broken dream and an empty promise? Why is Nigeria all motion and no movement? Who will guarantee that there will be no more coups and coup trials? Who will lead Nigeria towards the promised land of peace and prosperity?

CHAPTER TWENTY-FOUR

The Challenge of the Pope's Visit
(Written on August 20, 1998)

The visit of Pope John Paul II to Nigeria this week promises to be a remarkable event, one that will draw worldwide attention as his trips always do. Nigerians remember vividly the energy and charismatic effusion among the crowds with which a much younger and more ebullient pontiff covered a busy itinerary countrywide in 1982. In this second visit to Nigeria, the Pope's main pastoral assignment, the beatification of Father Cyprian Michael Iwene Tansi will hold centre stage, but it cannot be divorced from the social and political environment in which it is happening.

As the Chief Shepherd of the world's flock of 900 million Catholics, the Pope personifies the Good News and the salvific message of Christ in our human experience. In championing Christ's mission of total liberation of humankind, the Pope confronts the elements that impact humanity on the spiritual and material levels. And when he speaks, the world sits up and listens. Pope John Paul II could be said to have provoked the demise of Communism in his homeland Poland and effectively catalysed the same event all over former Communist Europe.

His recent visit to Cuba has been no less dramatic. It has already inspired very significant changes in that country's political and religious landscape. For the first time in decades, Fidel Castro's government declared a national holiday at Christmas and re-opened air traffic between Cuba and the United States. Christians flocked back to churches in a season of relaxed worship. On the social front, the Pope's visit paved the way for the re-union of Cuban families long separated by the clampdown of the totalitarian regime of Fidel Castro. As many as 300 political detainees have been released. There are now indications that the United States may soon review its trade embargo on Cuba, a case that the Pope constantly referred to during his visit as unethical.

The Pope's travelling anywhere has always been a memorable event for the world, and particularly for his hosts. But beyond the euphoria over the Pope's visit within and outside the Catholic Church, we need to examine Nigeria's preparedness for the reception of the pontiff. What is the prevailing social, political and economic environment, and what are its implications for the visit? While we spruce up our streets and alleys of material dirt - the heaps of garbage that are veritable landmarks in our towns and cities, how do we clean up the labyrinths of immorality and debauchery that criss-cross our national life? While we stretch our hands to greet the Pope and open our doors to make him welcome, how do we open our hearts to embrace our fellow Nigerians kept at bay by our ethnic, political and social divides? While we prepare the guns to salute the Holy Father, how do we silence the cannons of dissent and conscientious objection rumbling in the background, signifying the disquiet in the land? While we sing or chant the national anthem, mouthing the ideals, principles and values of believers in God, how do we match these attributes with appropriate actions to present a country worthy of the Pope's commendation?

The pastoral nature of the visit notwithstanding, we Nigerians should be concerned about the impression we are making on the pontiff and what parting gift the Nigerian society will want him to cherish as he leaves our shores, perhaps for the last time. True, Nigerians should be concerned about the extent to which we have improved our social rating in the eyes of the Pope and other observers since 1982 as a God-believing and God-fearing nation.

The Pope is an agent of peace and reconciliation, but can we camouflage our prevailing peace of the graveyard or negate the dialogue of the deaf that characterise our pretention to stability? The Pope is a promoter of human dignity and civil rights, but can we justify our incarceration of dissenters and the flight from state terrorism into self-exile of prominent citizens? The Pope is a defender of the poor and oppressed, but can we claim improvement in the fortunes of the masses in recent memory? The Pope is a crusader for good governance, but can we claim the same under three military juntas since his last visit to a civilian-run Nigeria in 1982? The Pope is a supporter of democratic values, but can we explain away the near fascist dispensation we have today and the attendant repression of opposition?

What impression do we then expect to make in our convoluted national environment on such a colossal world leader who commands a great following everywhere and always casts his vote on the side of the poor and under-privileged? To what can we ascribe with any iota of conviction the outrageous disparity between the rich and the poor, the 'haves' and the 'have-nots' of this country? We can, with pride, point to our abundant blessings in natural and human resources, yet how do we explain that only a tiny minority have access to the good life while the rest of the people languish in so much squalor and distress?

While the Pope may view with sympathy and compassion, a similar situation of deprivation in a run-down decrepit banana republic, a country like Nigeria cannot easily be forgiven for harbouring and cultivating a ballooning population driven to the fringe of starvation and misery while at the same time scandalously promoting a class of privileged and favoured citizens faltering on the economic spoils of the land. How do we as a nation face the challenge of the Pope's visit? How do we acknowledge its indictment of the social and political structures presently foisted on the land?

Given the Pope's known disposition on socio-political and economic situations worldwide, his visit affords us a chance for critical self-examination. More than any other, Pope John Paul II has produced numerous encyclicals dealing with the social issues of justice, violence, war, peace, ethnicity, family, poverty, gender, culture, ecology, labour and capital, and their impact on the spiritual life of peoples around the world. His contributions in these areas, and particularly his consistent defence of human rights and the inviolability of human dignity, have for long earned him international acclaim.

Indeed respect for the pontiff as a champion of the poor nations and peoples of the world cuts across colour, race, state, religion and cultural boundaries. Pope John Paul II stands out as a stout defender of a new kind of Christian humanism that embraces all of God's human creation. John Paul II cannot be identified with a religion that is the "opium of the people." Instead, this Pope is a man who preaches with passion Christ's message of release for captives. When, if not on this auspicious visit, can we demonstrate solidarity with him by the release of our own kith and kin who we have put behind bars?

This Pope asked that his potential executioner Ali Agca be shown mercy as Christ Jesus on the cross asked God's forgiveness for his crucifiers. When, if not in contemplating his Christian humanism, can we accord him on this visit a stately honour by a declaration of general amnesty for all the perceived enemies of the state who are wasting away in our detention cells? The Pope nurtures a unique sentiment with regard to the oppressed and the marginalised. When, if not now, can we welcome him with a cheering pronouncement on human rights? The white stripe of our national flag denotes peace. When, if not on this Pope's visit, can we adorn our country with the flag of peace and genuinely proffer the olive branch to our perceived detractors in the international community?

The Pope's pastoral assignment on this upcoming visit presages the global identification and recognition of the Nigerian nation with saintliness. The beatification of Father Tansi as a prelude to his canonisation represents for Nigeria a positive dimension to the Nigerian character, which has suffered severe damage worldwide from the anti-social propensities of the country's nefarious elements. In contrast, Father Tansi through a life of piety, prayer and spiritual fidelity lived within and outside the shores of this country, has done great honour to Nigeria's image and in death has proved a worthy and saintly ambassador because his great spirit which is being honoured by the Pope's visit rose from the Nigerian soil.

As the Pope comes, therefore, we are challenged to do an examination of conscience and to undergo a deep spiritual cleansing to exorcise the numerous demons bedevilling our society. We can resolve to make truth our guiding article of faith so that those held under the yoke of falsehood may be unchained. We can resolve to make justice our weapon for social equity so that those touched by justice will find succour and remain in gracious appreciation. We can resolve to make freedom of thought, of expression, of association, and of lawful assembly our national credo so that no citizen will suffer the pangs of exclusion and alienation. We can resolve to have a change of heart, to cultivate the spirit of love, forgiveness and mercy towards all, so that Christ's peace and the civilisation of love which the Pope preaches may flourish in our land. Only in this way shall we be giving the acclaimed agent of peace and reconciliation a befitting welcome to our land.

CHAPTER TWENTY-FIVE

Royalty and the Crisis of Relevance
(Written on October 15, 1998)

The institution of Traditional Rulers in Nigeria - of Emirs, Obas, Obis, Ezes, and other categories of chiefs, used to be seen and treated as a sacred institution. Traditional rulers appeared to many as representing all that was good, honourable and memorable about our culture and tradition, including, truth, discipline, courage, industry, probity, sacrifice and responsibility. Though the history of our country reveals that various traditional rulers from north to south and from east to west, aided and abetted the notorious trans-continental slave trade and the infamous colonial system that robbed the land of enormous human and material resources, and dealt incalculable damage to the psyche of the surviving generations, many still looked upon the institution with a sense of awe and reverence. Since most of the rulers were also chief priests of the traditional religions, who regularly offered sacrifices on behalf of their people, they often benefited from the reverence and awe due to the gods.

As legitimate representatives of their people, traditional rulers were adept at gauging the feelings of those in their domain, and in situations of conflict the positions they took were hardly controversial. Giving allowance for few exceptions here and there, they were generally not known to betray their people for selfish monetary gains. They owned large farms and livestock that were tended by those over whom they were chiefs. In other words, their material well-being and that of their large families were generally guaranteed by their "subjects," such that they did not need to play the sycophant in order to make a living. They were not greedy mercenaries. They largely operated from a truly nationalistic or patriotic disposition. Some of them were reputed to have such courage, fortitude, and sense of sacrifice that they actually died or lost members of their immediate families in the cause of pursuing the interest of those in their domain.

The above image of the traditional institution was before the neutralizing force of military dictatorship that in the last thirty years has overwhelmed and decimated practically every institution and authority structure in the country. The above image of traditional rulers was before the coming of the Petro-Naira whose corrupting potential has been the prime instrument of the total subjugation of the Nigerian polity. The above image of our kings and chiefs was before the conquerors acquired the right and prerogative to hire and fire Sultans and Emirs, to install and dethrone Obis and Ezes, and to promote and demote Obas and Bales.

When those who seized the keys of the national treasury by force of arms decided to grade the traditional rulers, fix fabulous salaries, build palaces, and dole out cars and miscellaneous allowances for them, the chiefs were immediately faced with a crisis of allegiance, since as they say, he who pays the piper dictates the tune. What we witness today among many traditional rulers is the dramatic orchestration of this crisis of allegiance that is soon to transform into an acute crisis of relevance.

Recent activities and pronouncements of individual chiefs and Councils of Traditional Rulers from various parts of Nigeria on such controversial issues as the alleged self-succession bid of the present leadership of the country, and the alleged coup plot of December 21, 1998, begs the question whether traditional rulers now speak on any platform representative of the people. Some of them present the image of government employees or civil servants who must defend the status quo at all costs, and who could be summoned at very short notice to the state capital or to the federal capital for briefing or de-briefing by whoever happens to be in power, no matter the moral credibility of the individual or the legitimacy of the regime. On their own, some of these rulers routinely engage in making solidarity statements and visits where they mortgage their people's political expectations.

What is becoming clear to thinking Nigerians is that many traditional rulers now seem to sway wherever the wind of fortune blows. Lacking a clearly defined ideological thrust, and settled with all manner of inducements, some of them carry sycophancy to a ridiculous extent that is tantamount to idolatry. They feel obliged to defend an unwholesome status quo, to lobby one regime after another, and to offer themselves and their exalted positions as rallying points for government support, in exchange for reward and rehabilitation. Thus, they unwittingly play into the hands of the ruling force which now regards the traditional institution as the second estate of the realm.

But the danger in their unabashed sycophantic expressions is that they undercut the people's collective will, they perpetrate the cruel dispensation of tyranny that has caused so much distress in the land, they sow the seeds of insecurity and instability, and they cultivate the virus of disintegration. Indeed, the conduct of many royal fathers in the last few years is something of an embarrassment for many in their immediate constituencies who hold royalty in high regard. The reaction of the public to the rather unguarded statements of some of these rulers in the last few weeks is very instructive. From Lagos to Enugu, and from Calabar to Kaduna, many Nigerians have expressed shock and outrage at the all too patronizing posture and the unguarded statements of some of these rulers. In the evolving tragedy of greed and avarice, deceit and mischief, betrayal and treachery, manipulation and subterfuge, the combination of which we call Nigerian politics, many traditional rulers, along with some religious prelates and some of those called leaders of thought in our country, seem to betray such gullibility and naivety that they have been too easily conscripted as pallbearers in the triumph of mediocrity that defines the present-day Nigerian governance.

In the past our feudal societies engaged in tribal warfare and skirmishes under a largely illiterate band of traditional rulers who luxuriated in the deference and awe of an equally illiterate, ignorant and superstitious population. Now the field is crowded by a growing crop of Nigerian elite, including military retirees with newly acquired titles. One would have thought that the injection of the elite would enhance dignity, prestige and honour for the traditional institution and a new destiny for the common folk. Instead, what we have seems to be the enthronement of greed and avarice; what we see appears to be the perpetration of treachery in high places; what we witness is more like the elevation of sycophancy into a royal art. A whole new sordid dimension is emerging in the extended feudal system. Abetting this culture of servitude are people with severely short attention span who stoically accept any insulating position and ignore the distress of the neighbour.

True, from recent developments nationwide, one begins to wonder if these leaders have not transformed themselves into mercenaries with questionable constituencies and ideological leanings. Beyond influence peddling and the execution of sundry survival strategies, what positive impact have these rulers in the complex politics of our nation? In the changing dynamics of modern political systems, can we carve out a role in our nation's body politic for such traditional institutions? In other words, within the context of the modern democratic society which has developed a heightened sense of popular participation in the running of public affairs, what place really has the feudal structure we refer to as traditional rulers?

Ours is a generation that jealously guards what has come to be known as the Fundamental Human Rights of all persons, which include the right of individuals to equal hearing, the right to equal representation, the right to equal treatment, the right to conscientious objection, and the right to dissent. In the midst of such an enlightened society, has the traditional institution of Emirs, Obas, Obis, Ezes, and other categories of chiefs in our day become an anachronism? True, the entire institution of Royal Fathers and the context in which the people do set about preserving it, demand periodic appraisal, otherwise those regarded as custodians of culture and tradition will systematically bastardize what should be a sacred responsibility. Perhaps what we have today camouflaging as royal sycophancy in our nation's body politic is a crisis of relevance that must be courageously addressed.

CHAPTER TWENTY-SIX

The Place of the Handicapped in the New Nigeria
(Written on December 14, 1998)

Since our independence from colonial rule in 1960, and in spite of the enormous human and material resources with which our country has been endowed by the Almighty Father, we can say without any fear of contradiction that no government has succeeded in articulating, let alone implementing any radical programme that is capable of transforming the plight of the disabled and handicapped people of our society. Instead, with the passage of time, the plight of these least of brethren in our society has increasingly worsened, to such an extent that today a large proportion of them are condemned to the indignity of a beggarly existence. Pushed out of their homes by the reality of economic depression and social neglect, most of our disabled clan now constitute themselves into the army of beggars that have taken over our highways and motor parks.

The tendency to disregard the travails of the handicapped in society is a worldwide phenomenon. Too often people are inclined to sidestep disturbing sights and occurrences by whatever way caused. Ensconced in the comforts of our situations and environment the natural inclination is for us to wish away anything we consider unsightly, anything that confronts our social comfort, anything that rocks our emotional balance. And "anything" here often includes members of the society who suffer from various forms of disabilities, physical, mental or generational. But whatever the nature of such disabilities, and by whatever means they are induced or incurred - whether by natural causes or self-inflicted, many societies are today overrun by the sheer numbers of people whose lives have become degraded from one form of disability or the other.

All through the course of history, disabled or handicapped persons have been the object of one form of indignity or the other, ironically at the hands of the more endowed members of the human society whose responsibility it should be to defend and uplift the less able. The handicapped have suffered perhaps more than any other category of persons the social consequences of a humanity that has often rejected the dynamics of Christian compassion and violated the golden rule. The handicapped have suffered immensely at the hands of a society that discountenances the logic of the civilization of love by which human progress, advancement or development is measured by how well the society takes care of its most vulnerable members - the orphan and the widow, the physically and mentally handicapped, the sick and the aged, indeed how the society threats those of its members who are not useful or productive in the narrowest sense.

Even from biblical accounts we learn of the social stigma associated with physical deformity and such diseases as leprosy. In many parts of the world the handicapped have continued to suffer the indignities of isolation and ostracism. Yet all through the ages, the handicapped, battling physical disabilities and social stigma, have recorded remarkable achievements to confound the world. Like breaking through the sound barrier, the handicapped have sometimes excelled beyond the capacity of normal human endeavour. From the polio victim who became United States president to the blind music maestro whose compositions and piano renditions shall ever remain classics, and from the armless artist who paints award-winning pictures with the brush stuck to his or her mouth or toes, to the paraplegic athlete who achieves incredible feats in sports, the handicapped have continued to struggle for relevance and for a place in the sun.

A society that looks after its own develops social structures to support the handicapped. The ordered society creates the enabling environment that encourages the handicapped to maximize their residual endowments to the best advantage for living wholesome and meaningful lives. But how do we cope with the disabled of our society Nigeria? How many of our leaders, military or civilian have made any serious attempts to envision and articulate a formidable advancement programme for the disabled? How ready are the various organs in society to assist public spirited persons and organisations that attempt to set up projects and programmes for the disabled? From our observation, depending on the degree of incapacitation, the handicapped in Nigeria are treated often as social irritants, sometimes as objects of humiliation and scorn and at other times they are conveniently ignored or abandoned.

We do not need to look into established institutions to locate our country's handicapped persons. Those institutions are few and far between and quite a number are best discounted. Our handicapped are to be found on our streets, in towns and villages, in our homes and in self-organised beggar colonies under urban bridges and motor parks. Those suffering from various levels of mental disorders often constitute a dangerous nuisance let loose by an indifferent and uncaring society. The physically handicapped, bereft of any rehabilitation, are left to loiter, hobble and grope as they ply the begging trade, sometimes perilously in the thick of traffic. The weak and elderly on their part, often lacking family support are driven by hunger, neglect and want to join the homeless and helpless in the streets or are left to die silently.

Yet all human beings, the handicapped inclusive, are created in God's image and likeness. They are an important part of God's creation and therefore they have an inalienable right to life and a right to dignified existence. Among factors distinguishing us from the lower order of creation are our endowment with good reasoning and judgement, our capacity to make an act of will to love (even when the object of love is not always attractive), and our ability to harness our human emotions for good initiative. A society with any claim to being civilized must accord a basic recognition to the primary needs of every one of its members. But have we in this country shown any commitment to the social advancement of our people? Those who have unilaterally appropriated leadership have had neither the time nor the disposition for the social necessity to upgrade the lives of the people, let alone care for the handicapped. We have seen to what degree they have succeeded in their single-track mind-set in destroying the moral and material fabric of the country. Most affected by their mindless enterprise are the people on the fringe of society, including the physically and mentally handicapped, the sick, the aged, and the poor.

We are at the threshold of a new socio-political dispensation after a long and painful military interregnum. One of the major platforms for political reformation is the urgent and ardent need for national reconciliation - a tacit acknowledgement of the traumatic consequences of unguided military adventurism in Nigeria's politics and leadership. Also, a guiding light for social change is the degree of articulation of development programmes of aspiring political parties. Meanwhile our politicians are preoccupied with jockeying and jostling for positions and offices, making little or no concrete statements of socio-political and economic intent. We have recently concluded the local government elections and put in motion the machinery for other elections on the state and federal levels, with hardly any discernible programmes of socio-economic change articulated by any of the political parties vying for the people's votes. Nigerians do not seem to be bothered at all that we are once again engaged in politics without principles which Mahatma Gandhi identified as one of the seven deadly social sins. Such politics which amounts to a social engineering without any ideological framework will take us nowhere, and at the end of the exercise it may be all motion but no movement.

True, any serious political campaign must go beyond the frontiers of personality cult to include the articulation of projects and programmes aimed at the betterment of those that for too long have been left at the margins of the Nigerian society. Genuine political organisations must include in their programmes for the masses the prosecution of measures specifically designed for the enduring benefit of the handicapped, for a society without a serious programme for the handicapped where social security is guaranteed cannot be a fully reconciled society. It is not enough to construct lofty edifices as a showcase for national development. It is indeed a falsity and an aberration to project a nation awash in conspicuous consumption in the midst of abject poverty and deprivation. A truly reconciled society must therefore incorporate its lowliest members.

In the emerging democratic society, the handicapped themselves must be assisted by all men and women of goodwill so that they can be principal agents of their own development. The handicapped, to whatever degree they are capable, must be made to appreciate their inalienable rights, including their right to elect leaders of their own choice to rule them. Secondly, the handicapped must recognise the power of their votes. They and their benefactors and sympathizers nationwide must insist that before any politician benefits from their votes, such a politician should demonstrate beforehand their vision of a better social environment for the handicapped, and what programmes and projects for capacity development they plan for those who are disabled in our society.

To ameliorate conditions for the handicapped, Nigerian leaders must assume the moral responsibility for adequate planning, prosecution and monitoring of long-term relief and social security. Too often in Nigeria, programmes are designed ostensibly only for propaganda effect and as channels for graft and corruption. Is this not why for example food meant for prisoners allegedly end up in markets and in pantries outside the prisons? Ill-managed and un-sustained, fancy programmes end up fading into antiquity. At the rural level, which is the point of first contact with victims of abject poverty, ignorance and disease, rural dwellers fulfil their role to some degree by keeping and caring for their handicapped within the limitations of their poverty. Government must recognise this responsibility and reach out to them to augment their effort. In the cities and urban centres where distress for the handicapped is perhaps more evident and more acute, individuals and organisations are inspired from time to time to undertake aid and rehabilitation initiatives in support of the handicapped. These vacuum-filling efforts are crucial and particularly important as government hardly ever devotes adequate attention and resources to the voiceless in society. These noble private initiatives must be recognised and encouraged through active and sustained government assistance and coordination of programmes.

Government at various levels must embrace the care of the handicapped as a cardinal responsibility for social development. A world leader has posited that how a nation treats its prisoners shows how it treats its citizens at large. The disabled in a sense are prisoners of their handicaps. How we treat our disabled therefore is a reflection of the degree of spirituality, humanity and civilization of our nation.

CHAPTER TWENTY-SEVEN

The Role of Religion in the Evolution of a Just Democratic Society
(Written on March 7, 1999)

Introduction

The place of religion in the conduct of the State has become a matter of public discourse in Nigeria in recent times, especially towards the end of the draconian regime of the late General Sani Abacha. There are those who were irked by the public posture of some religious personages, especially those who came out openly to denounce what they perceived as unjust policies on the part of the state machinery, or the foul conduct and lack of vision of the political class. We remember the protracted "KUKAH DEBATE" in *The Guardian On Sunday* that spanned between February and May, 1996. And following the publication of my book, A Prophetic Church, that same year, a number of critical articles appeared in various papers on the so-called Liberation Theology. Some of them sought to present the Latin American initiative as a veiled form of atheistic communism that preaches class struggle and promotes violent revolution. The writers therefore felt obliged to warn innocent but ill-informed Nigerian believers to beware of religious leaders who pose as social crusaders.

Along with other religious leaders who are also social crusaders, we have often been accused of dabbling into politics which is supposed to be a secular domain that should not be mixed with religion. These critics often advise religious leaders to stick to the pulpit and to concentrate on prayer, their true vocation, and leave politics to the politicians. The critics sometimes remind the preachers that Jesus Christ said one should give to Caesar what is Caesar's and to God what is God's. On Sunday September 28, 1997, Colonel Peter Ogar, then Military Administrator of Kwara State, reacted rather strangely against the alleged involvement of clerics in politics. After a communique of the Catholic Bishops' Conference of Nigeria was read, in which they opposed the bid for General Abacha's self-succession as president, the Administrator was alleged to have taken over the pulpit and lambasted the Bishops for misinterpreting the Bible and for abandoning their role of worship and prayer to be involved in dissident politics.

Of Caesar and God

The logic of giving to Caesar what is Caesar's and to God what is God's which Jesus Christ enunciated in the gospel of Matthew (Mt.22:15-22) has been given a variety of interpretations all through the history of Christendom. The discourse on the payment of taxes to Caesar and the celebrated response of Jesus Christ in the Gospel of Matthew is certainly one of the most controversial texts of the New Testament. It has served as a veritable justification on the one hand for those who wish to engage in spiritual and ideological syncretism, and on the other hand by those who perceive human existence in terms of two separate and unrelated compartments - the spiritual and the material, the sacred and the secular, the religious and the political, the Church and the State. One interpretation of this text has been identified as *the altar and the throne theology,* which is the extreme separation of religion and politics to the ridiculous extent whereby religious leaders are not supposed to have any say whatsoever on how civil society is run.

This kind of thinking reached its peak during the Nazi period in Germany when religion was kept so completely out of politics and politics was so devoid of religion and morality that an evil genius (or do we say a devil incarnate) such as Adolf Hitler, could rule a so-called Christian Germany, pontificating over the Jewish holocaust and supervising the Auschwitz torture chambers that remain the greatest shame of modern humanity. True, in the history of humanity, politics and religion have often been uncomfortable bed-fellows. They do not always make a good mix, yet they must both exist, and one must exert its influence on or impact the other in some way. The issue is not about forgetting one or ignoring the other. It is not about one overthrowing or subduing the other. It is about putting first things first and allowing other things to follow. It is about serving the Supreme God and at the same time giving due regard to the exigencies of human existence, with particular reference to the authority structures of society, and how the common good is promoted.

It is true that Caesar has a limited sphere of authority. Caesar has some control on human beings and human society. Yet the limited control which Caesar exercises over human beings, he exercises on behalf of God to whom Caesar is ultimately accountable, since according to the Judeo-Christian and also the Islamic tradition, God is the only true ruler of his people. Caesar's authority is as it were a delegated authority that is valid only if its exercise is subject to, and in accordance with the will of the one who delegates the authority. Caesar, that is the State and its authority structure, must maintain law and order and promote the security and welfare of the citizens. To the extent that Caesar pursues this agenda truthfully, judiciously and responsibly, the citizens owe Caesar obedience and respect in return. Since just and God-fearing rulers share in the authority of the Supreme God, they deserve the obedience of citizens.

A real problem however arises in the case of unjust rulers, oppressors, tyrants, dictators and impostors when there is often an obvious clash of interest between Caesar and God. Here we are faced with a troublesome dilemma, for this kind of rulers do not share legitimately in the authority of God whom Christians know as the Good Shepherd. This kind of rulers are simply usurpers of the place of God and of the people's sovereignty. They are the ones referred to by Jesus as thieves, rogues and brigands. The majority of Christians and Muslims believe that where there is a clash of interest between Caesar and God, they must choose to obey God rather than men!

When in the New Testament of the Christian Bible St. Paul says that all authority comes from God, it is not to be understood as a blanket approval of, and sheepish submission to all forms of rulership in the human society. The authority that comes from God and is exercised in the name of God is not to be understood to include genocidal dictatorship, murderous tyranny and repressive militarism, the type the world has witnessed in Adolf Hitler's Germany, in Apartheid South Africa, in Idi Amin's Uganda, in Kamuzu Banda's Malawi, in Ferdinand Marcos' Philippines, in Pinochet's Chile, in Fara Aideed's Somalia, in Sese-Sekou's Zaire, and in Sani Abacha's Nigeria. In the unfortunate circumstances such as the above listed, Caesar did not accept his limitations. He did not take what belongs to him alone. He took everything. In such circumstances Caesar usurped God's place and arrogated to himself the power of life and death, of hunger and satisfaction, of freedom and imprisonment, of prosperity and doom and of war and peace. The resulting holocaust, genocide, starvation, impoverishment and massive degradation of human life and destruction of the environment in these places, are not an act of God, but that of some evil genius. The authority they exercised is not that of God, but that of the devil who in the words of Christ "only comes to steal, to cheat and to destroy." Yes, the authority that abuses, manipulates, degrades and destroys the people is not from God, for God (as we Christians know him), is the true Shepherd who lays down his life for His sheep.

The religious person who lives in a land where such rulers exist who have overstepped their bounds and taken the place of God is really faced with a tricky dilemma. The religious leader in such circumstances is compelled to reflect upon and provide suitable answers to the same questions that the followers of Jesus Christ asked him about paying taxes to an oppressive occupation force symbolised by Caesar. When faced with this dilemma, it is often difficult to define what exactly belongs to Caesar, for as the Psalmist says "the Lord's is the earth and the fullness thereof." We are obliged to render to Caesar only the things that are Caesar's, not the things that are God's. The power of life and death for example belongs to the Supreme God, not to Caesar, and so when a human authority ascribes such power to itself, it may be pointed out that such a human authority is overstepping its legitimate bounds.

Shall the messengers of God sit and fold their arms when they see Caesar usurping God's sovereignty and appropriating the things that belong to God, or shall they just pray? What about prophetic denunciation, the type for which John the Baptist was beheaded? Reacting to the abuses of the leaders of Israel in his day the prophet Ezekiel warned that the curse of Yahweh is upon the shepherds who instead of feeding the sheep under their charge, feed fat on the sheep, and treat them harshly and cruelly. True, God's authority comes with a corresponding responsibility. God's authority comes with a divine imperative, the imperative of service and not lordship over the people.

When responding to the tricky question of whether or not to pay taxes to an oppressive political structure such as the Roman occupation force in the Israel of his day, Jesus told his adversaries to render unto Caesar what is Caesar's and to God what is God's. It is to be noted that Jesus himself did not carry on him the coin which has Caesar's image on it. For him, anyone who is willing to carry around the coin which has Caesar's effigy or image on it should be willing to give back to Caesar what truly belongs to Caesar. Yet he challenged his adversaries and his disciples with a more fundamental obligation - they were obliged to recognise God as the Supreme Sovereign and render Him his due.

Rendering to God his due has many implications that go beyond praying in Church and Mosque, and offering sacrifices to Him. Giving God his due is more than just paying one's tithe. If (as we Christians believe), every human being has been created in the image and likeness of God, and if everyone is a child of God, dear to His heart, then giving God his due implies also respecting the image of God in the neighbour. Since our faith tells us that God has identified himself closely with the poor, the hungry, the thirsty, the naked, the stranger, the prisoner, the sick (see Mt.25:31-46), giving God his due implies that we recognise the dignity of even the least of our neighbours in our society and treat them with utmost respect. Therefore to treat the neighbour unjustly or cruelly, to oppress or marginalise the neighbour, to abuse or dehumanise the neighbour, to cheat or manipulate the neighbour, and to kill or maim the neighbour will be to deny God His due, a serious offence that carries with it unwholesome consequences for the culprit. The offence of denying God his due is particularly grave when committed by those in authority, since by such conduct they challenge the very sovereignty of God.

Our country has seen too many people who profess the Christian or Islamic religion, but whose conducts in political and economic affairs are often clearly at variance with the moral principles of the religion they profess. Ours is a country with the sad history of a corrupt and irresponsible leadership, yet a large percentage of our successive leaders have been religious people. What it means is that they have often given more to Caesar than he legitimately deserves. Religious people in positions of authority in this country have often been too greedy to fight for the poor, too timid to stand up for truth and justice and too cowardly or faint-hearted to deny Caesar his unjust claims and render to God the things that truly belong to God. Yes, religious people and their leaders in this country have often been too apathetic to speak out for the poor, too complacent to champion the cause of the oppressed, and too frightened to risk comfort in the defence of truth and justice.

The Nigerian Predicament

The dialectics of rendering to Caesar what is Caesar's and to God what is God's has been perhaps the main predicament of the Nigerian political, social and economic life in the last few years. True, the problematic of giving to Caesar what is Caesar's and to God what is God's is a major part of the exigencies of our troubled motherland. The erection and maintenance of structures of violence and of unredressed injustices; the violation of truth and the manipulation of the population; the widespread denial of the inalienable rights of free human beings created in the image and likeness of God; the appropriation by a greedy few of the abundant resources bestowed by God on our land and the consequent progressive impoverishment of the multitude of Nigerian people who are dear to God's heart -- all this and others together constitute a reckless, reprehensible and damnable usurpation by Caesar of God's sovereign position.

No society which nurtures these evils can prosper. The empire which neglects the spiritual, moral and religious dimension of human existence is surely on its way to ruin. The empire which gives everything to Caesar and neglects to pay God his due is digging its own grave. The fate that has befallen atheistic communism in our own century is a case in point. The Communists thought that they could build an utopia in this world, all on their own, without reference to God and with no recognition for the place of religion in wholesome human existence. But they were deluded. St. Augustine of Hippo had said that the greatest threat to human fulfilment and societal prosperity is the want of order in the soul. We also learn that human history has recorded the rise and fall of about twenty six or so civilizations. Their successive collapse was not due to external attack, but internal decay.

It is this and similar thoughts that were put together by Mahatma Gandhi, the legendary Indian nationalist and philosopher in what he identified as THE SEVEN DEADLY SOCIAL SINS: politics without principle; wealth without work; commerce without morality; pleasure without conscience; education without character; science without humanity; and worship without sacrifice. At a Workshop in 1996 on Justice and Peace in Africa held in Harare, Robert Mugabe the Zimbabwean President, asserted that without the moral vision such as the one provided by religion, governments will often fail to achieve their social targets. He noted that "governments have a great potential for mischief, abuses and excesses, unless they are guided by basic beliefs resting on deep morality." This is how to render to Caesar what is Caesar's and to God what is God's.

Christians and Muslims in Nigeria who fill our churches on Sunday and our mosques on Friday must surely have big problems convincing themselves that they are doing well as religious people while we live in a society and practice our religion in an environment that is plagued by poverty, disease, widespread abuse of human rights, structural injustice, dictatorship, large-scale corruption, unemployment, ignorance, occultism, violent crime and capital punishment. As religious people we are confronted with a socio-cultural context that is not only distressed but even traumatized. We can no longer pretend that all is well. We have a responsibility in transforming the country from a less human to a more human society. Since we are adherents of the God who is Creator of all and light over all, we can bring into the social realm of our country the light of love, truth, justice mutual forgiveness and human solidarity.

Our God, a God of well-being and liberation

The Old Testament reveals that the God of Abraham, Isaac and Jacob, develops an intimate relationship with his people, and takes a caring interest in the day to day life of his people here on earth. For a pilgrim people, He is a pilgrim God, who travels with them and shows them the way. He establishes a covenant with Abraham in which he promises prosperity to him and his descendants. He commits himself to be a friend of those who treat Abraham well, and a foe of those who curse Him:

> Now the Lord said to Abraham, "Go from your country and your kindred and your father's house to the land that I will show you. And I will make you a great nation, and I will bless and make your name great, so that you will be a blessing. I will bless those who bless you, and curse him that curses you; and by you all the families of the earth shall bless themselves" (Genesis 1:1-3).

The God of Moses, Joshua and the Judges is for us Christians not an abstract, impersonal entity. He is a compassionate God who hears the cry of his oppressed people and is moved to action to free His people from oppression, and to give them back their dignity. He says to Moses:

> I have seen the affliction of my people in Egypt and have heard their cry of complaint against their slave drivers, so I know well what they are suffering. Therefore I have come down to rescue them from the hands of the Egyptians....Indeed the cry of the Israelites has reached me, and I have truly noted that the Egyptians are oppressing them. Come now! I will send you to Pharaoh to lead my people, the Israelites, out of Egypt (Exodus 3:7-10; See also Exodus 2:23-24; Judges 3:9-10; and Judges 3:15).

As stubborn Pharaoh would not let the suffering people go, Yahweh intervened with a powerful hand. He brought them out after inflicting a number of plagues on the Egyptians, and made them cross the red sea on dry ground, while their enemies who gave them chase perished in the sea (Exodus 8,9,10,12; Exodus 14:26-31). In their long road to freedom, Yahweh accompanied the people in the form of a pillar of cloud by day, and a pillar of fire by night. When in hunger and thirst they cried to him in the desert, Yahweh intervened by providing manna and quail, and water from the rock of Massah and Meribah (Exodus 16,17).

The God of Samuel, David and Solomon, lives as king among his people, showing them the way. He is the conscience of the nation, who defends the weak and lowly against the excesses of the rich and powerful. A good example of this is the story of David's sin against Uriah, the assignment of prophet Nathan, the repentance of David, and the death of the child born to David on account of the sin (2 Samuel 11&12). The God of Elijah, Isaiah and Amos, is the God of holiness and justice. He is the defender of the poor and the weak, and the protector of the widow and the orphan. Through the prophets, he exposes the injustice in the political and economic structures of the society, and denounces the hypocrisy of the religious leaders who not only fail in their duty as shepherds, but are also often a tool in the hands of the kings for the maintenance of unjust structures (See the story of Naboth's vineyard in I Kings 21). The God of the prophets is a God who provides food for the poor widow of Zeraphtah, and who removes the shame of leprosy from Naaman the Syrian Army Commander (I Kings 17, 2 Kings 5).

The God of the Virgin Mary, of John the Baptist and of Simon Peter, is one who in Jesus Christ takes flesh and lives among his people.

> In the eyes of the Virgin Mary,
> He has shown strength with his arm, He has scattered the proud in the imagination of their hearts, He has put down the mighty from their thrones, and exalted the lowly; He has filled the hungry with good things, and sent the rich empty away... (Luke 1:51-55).
>
> In John the Baptist the Lord confronts the powerful but corrupt Herod who unjustly takes his brother Philip's wife. He confronts the soldiers, the tax collectors, and religious bigots who cheat, defraud and intimidate the people (See Matthew 3).
>
> In Jesus Christ, God comes:
> ...to preach the good news to the poor
> ...to proclaim release to captives
> and recovery of sight to the blind
> to set at liberty those who are oppressed,
> to proclaim the acceptable year of the Lord (Luke 4:18).
>
> In Jesus Christ, God comes that his people might have life, and have it to the full (John 10:10). For the sick he brings comfort by performing miracles of healing; for the possessed or demonized he brings freedom by performing exorcism; for the hungry he brings satisfaction by

multiplying loaves and fish; and for the oppressed and marginalized in society he brings relief by challenging the power structures that perpetuate the injustices against them. He does not rationalize their material or physical condition, nor does he encourage blind resignation to their suffering. He does not abandon them to their plight, nor does he simply prepare them for heaven. Rather, in each case, he does something concrete to alleviate the pain of those who suffer, while promising full and definitive victory in the Kingdom of God. He gives the poor, oppressed and marginalized people of today reason to hope, when he tells them:

Blessed are you that hunger now for you shall be satisfied.
Blessed are you that weep now, for you shall laugh....
But woe to you that are rich, for you have received your consolation.
Woe to you that are full now, for you shall hunger.
Woe to you that laugh now, for you shall mourn and weep... (Luke 6:20-26).

In Jesus Christ, God demonstrates a special love for, and affinity with the poor, the lowly, the stranger, and the sick. He goes as far as to say that our admission into the Kingdom of God depends on how we treat these classes of people, for what we do to them, we do to him (Matthew 25:31-45). This is the foundation for what we in the Catholic Church understand as Jesus' preferential option for the poor. Jesus opted for the least of the brethren, because they are easily the most vulnerable in society. They are always the greater victims of oppression, abuse and injustices of all sorts. In the New Testament of the Christian Bible, St. James teaches that the practice of religion which is not accompanied by a commitment towards a more wholesome humanity is "worthless." He says that "pure, unspoiled religion in the eyes of God our Father is this: coming to the help of the orphans and widows in their hardships (Jas.1:27).

Time for Action

Under the prevalent circumstances in Nigeria, the men and women of religion are called upon to show utmost concern for the poor, the hungry, the weak, the orphan, the despised, the stranger, and the victims of all sorts of injustice. The religious person must demonstrate his or her belief in the God of mercy and compassion through the pursuit of human rights, the defence of human dignity and the promotion of freedom and abundant life for all in our society. The religious person must be a sign of contradiction in a world of darkness and sin. For a corrupt, violent, materialistic, hedonistic and consumeristic society, the religious person is called upon to shine out the light of holiness, love, purity of heart, mercy, kindness and peacefulness. This is the way to make religion relevant in the contemporary society.

The circumstances of today's Nigeria challenge religious people to do much more than they have done in the past if they are truly to be the conscience of the nation. We must be forthright and consistent in denouncing individual evil and evil structures in our society. We must cry out loud enough for successive rulers of this country to be compelled to do something about our primitive penal system, our inhuman prison conditions, and our treatment of ex-convicts. Religious people must stand alongside the oppressed, the impoverished, the marginalized, those denied their just rights and those discriminated against. Religious people are called upon today to champion the cause of the handicapped and the homeless and the destitute. We are called upon to defend the right of poor workers to just wage, to health insurance, and to adequate retirement benefits. We are called upon to be in the forefront of the struggle to rid Nigeria of rogue leadership and the structural injustices that have constituted a superstructure of violence over our motherland.

Religious people in this country must be both patriotic and fearless. We must be ready to demonstrate to our countrymen and women that a true patriot is one who cares deeply about the happiness and well-being of his or her country and all its people; not one who sings the praises of the leaders. We must be ready to demonstrate love for our country not by sycophancy, not by paid solidarity visits, but by demanding the highest standards from those who want to rule us and by accepting nothing but the best for and from our people. We must be ready to stand up and be counted on the side of truth, even in the midst of falsehood.

Many Nigerians want to live in a land where there is justice, democracy, good governance and prosperity, but they are not prepared to make the necessary sacrifices. Many Nigerians want peace to reign in this land, but they are unwilling to pay the high price which the pursuit of peace demands. The cost of peace is a lifestyle of sacrifice. Peace does not come on a platter of gold, but often through a crown of thorns. The peacemaker must be ready to pay the costly price of atonement for the multiple violence that currently make peace impossible in our land. Being a sign of contradiction in a corrupt world, and being light in a world of darkness is no easy task. The cost of maintaining truth in a world of falsehood is quite high. Yet the truly religious person cannot run away from this sacrifice, for as Christians and Muslims know, sacrifice is part of the very essence of religion.

The price which those of us who genuinely seek peace for our country must be ready to pay includes a rejection of the culture of indiscipline, crass materialism, conspicuous consumption, greed, corruption, selfishness, economic exploitation, social discrimination and arbitrary rule, which before now have made peace impossible in our land. With the aid of experts from various fields of human endeavour, religious leaders must take up the challenge of conceiving, promoting and enthroning alternative socio-economic and political structures which will make for justice, reconciliation, good governance, peace and prosperity. We must be ready to pursue this commitment with all the resources at our disposal. Christian and Muslim individuals and groups must be ready to commit their resources to programmes and projects aimed at educating and empowering the poor, pulling down the walls of hatred in our land and building bridges across the rivers of ethnic, religious and social hostilities.

The exploiters, manipulators and oppressors of the Nigerian people have often capitalised on the existing ethnic polarities. They have often cashed in on the age-old ethnic sentiments and clannish antipathies when it pays them to do so. And at times of great distress, rather than address critically and objectively their condition of economic deprivation and social degradation, poor Nigerian victims often recourse to religious fanaticism, primitive clannishness and ethnic hatred. We see such misplaced aggression in such far flung ethnic clashes as between Fulani herdsmen and Hausa farmers, between the Ife and the Modakeke, between the Ijaw and the Itsekiri, between the Bassa and the Ebira-Toto, and between the Tiv and the Jukun.

Faced with the enormous challenges of building a new Nigeria, religious people must begin to work together and cooperate in projects that are aimed at liberating the human person, the whole person - mind and spirit, body and soul; the whole person, with his or her daily concerns and aspirations, and his or her dreams and ultimate fulfilment. The time is ripe for Christians and Muslims to design joint projects that are geared towards redeeming our devastated environment. Yes, as men and women of vision, we must do something to defend the defenceless in our society, including the unborn children, orphans, widows, the aged, handicapped people, the sick, prisoners, strangers and refugees.

Our sense of solidarity as people who worship the God of Abraham, should spur us on to do something about the economic structures of our country which leave the majority of people permanently on the margins of society. We must work together in collaboration with the sundry human rights organisations and NGOs that now exist in Nigeria towards evolving a democratic culture for our country. Religious leaders have a very significant role to play in the task of laying down the structures and statutes that would protect the dignity and rights of the citizens of our country against the excesses of those in power. We must find ways of educating our adherents that sovereignty belongs to the people, not to the person in power; that leadership is for service, not for domination and exploitation. We need to set up structures that will support human rights advocacy, protection and promotion. As the Catholic Bishops said at the end of their last plenary meeting whose theme was "Corruption in Nigeria: its implications for nation-building," religious organisations should see it as their principal role to inculcate in their members the fear of God and the values of truth, honesty, hard work, accountability and concern for the common good.

This is not the time for religious fanaticism, creedal parochialism or sectarian bigotry. Instead the exigencies of the times demand that we be engaged in constant dialogue as we work towards the emergence of a more just, equitable and humane society, for no individual or group can on their own achieve the much desired peace for our land. It is a project in which everyone must be involved, and so the greater dialogue, collaboration, cooperation and solidarity we can achieve, the easier the task of building a just, democratic society, for as they say, united we stand, but divided we fall.

CHAPTER TWENTY-EIGHT

Sanitising Our Security Agencies
(Written on October 15, 1999)

In recent times the various security agencies in Nigeria and the manner of their operation have come under the searchlight of the critical segment of the Nigerian polity. The attention of Nigerians has also been drawn to the deplorable condition of the nation's prisons and detention centres, with many concerned individuals and agencies calling for a complete overhaul of our penal and prison systems, which today are a structure of violence and a legacy of shame. In 1996 a Newspaper report alleged that an average of 10 inmates died every week at the *Kirikiri* medium security prison alone. They died by instalment through malnutrition, starvation, disease and physical torture at the hands of security agents in the process of obtaining confessional statements.

Very recently President Obasanjo granted amnesty to hundreds of long-term detainees - those awaiting trial on account of minor crimes for over two years. This is a step in the right direction, but it only scratches the surface of the problem, because the overwhelming majority of long-term detainees in our nation's prisons fall into categories that are not covered by the amnesty. So they are bound to remain in prison custody under the most deplorable conditions. Nigeria has indeed been operating a security system that is, to say the least, brutal. Whether they are officers and men of the regular Nigerian Police Force, the Mobile Police, the State Security Service, members of the armed forces, or the numerous Task Forces that now exist, they all operate like an occupation force that is designed to beat the local people into submission.

The ad-hoc task forces that sprang up in many states during the last military dispensation are government-sponsored terrorist squads that were designed to constitute a balance of terror in the wake of the rising crime rate in many urban centres. Coming out with such code names as Operation Crush, Operation Wedge, Operation Flush and Operation Sweep, these killer squads were often mandated to shoot suspects at sight. And they often did their job with utmost recklessness, killing and maiming helpless Nigerians in a manner that violated all norms of civility and humanity. Like trained bullies, they drove around with a loaded gun in one hand and a horsewhip in the other, destroying wares, tearing human flesh, breaking human bones, and framing up outrageous charges against some innocent citizens. We would never know the number of innocent Nigerians who were sent to their early graves as a result of the activities of these state-sponsored bandits.

In accordance with international juridical standards, suspects are presumed innocent until proven guilty of an offence in a court of law. Those to be arrested, interrogated or detained therefore are supposed to be treated with utmost respect until they are convicted of a crime through the due process of law. But the Nigerian security agencies operate like an aberrant order, intimidating, coercing and brutalising Nigerian citizens in total disregard of all constitutional provisions regarding the limits of their powers or the rights of citizens. There has not been any marked difference in operational style between the Colonial Police Force that was put together for the sole purpose of subjugating the Nigerian people or coercing them into submission, and the post-Independence Nigeria Police. Perhaps no conscious efforts have been made since independence to transform the Nigeria Police into a civil agency that is aimed at maintaining order and protecting lives and property. Thus, for the slightest misdemeanour they often deal with "bloody civilians" in the bloodiest manner. At Police Stations, at public functions, and at regular checkpoints or emergency roadblocks, they harass, extort, brutalise and torture innocent Nigerians mercilessly.

The Nigeria Police officer is far from being "your friend." One only needs to see the Mobile Squad or the Anti-Riot Police at work, to recognise that they are not trained to keep law and order, but rather (as they have come to be known among Nigerians) to "kill and go." The whole operational style of the security agencies is often belligerent, aggressive and vindictive. Before them the life of the Nigerian suspect is cheap and easily expendable. They have often deployed tanks and armoured carriers, and used live bullets to suppress students' demonstrations and disperse mass rallies. No wonder the young segment of our society has come to see the police as their foremost enemy. Security agents who accompany top government officials in escort vehicles, and those of them who accompany cash-carrying bullion vans, are often armed with guns, clubs and horsewhips, with which they whip and bash fellow citizens out of the road. The recklessness with which they drive their siren-blaring vehicles, and the brute force and bravado with which they send other road users off the highway whenever they are passing, constitute nothing but a reign of terror. Recently an NTA report showed a line of vehicles battered by men of the Rapid Response Squad while the law-abiding owners or drivers were trapped in a typical Lagos traffic jam. It was presumed that the squad was on its way to quell the ethnic riots in Ajegunle. But in the process they brought blood and tears to many innocent road users. This type of scenario is very common in our country.

It is true that violent crime has increased in Nigeria, but there are numerous international conventions regarding the fundamental human rights of suspects, who must be presumed innocent until they are proven guilty through the due process of law. So which law permits the Nigeria Police to parade mere suspects before TV cameras everyday? Which law permits the police, the vigilante groups or the public to kill criminal suspects and set those alleged to be armed robbers on fire? Which law permits the police or the prison authorities to keep an armed robbery suspect in detention without trial for four or five years? Which law permits the officers and men of the regular Police Force who mount road blocks to harass or brutalise motorists over vehicle particulars? Which law permits a military officer, a government official or a cash-carrying bank chief to force other road users off the public highway with sirens, guns and horsewhips? Our nation's constitution provides for the equality of all citizens under the law. Even in the process of fighting crime, there are international conventions regarding the rights of suspects and the rights of convicted persons. Persons convicted of violent crimes nevertheless have certain elementary rights that are inviolable. There are international conventions on the treatment of prisoners of war, including provisions that forbid the application of torture in an attempt to obtain information. Nigeria, along with other segments of the civilised world, is a signatory to most of these international conventions.

As we transit towards genuine democracy, this is the time to reflect upon and take urgent action towards the modernisation of the Nigerian security and penal systems, since we cannot lay claim to democracy if the fundamental human rights of everyone, including criminal suspects, are not respected. The time has come for us to go beyond mere rhetoric, and do something urgently about the much talked about re-orientation of the nation's armed forces, to make them subservient to the constitution and accountable to the people. The time has come for us to put the mechanism in place for the civilianisation of the security agencies, particularly the Nigeria Police Force, and the de-militarisation of the Nigerian psyche.

CHAPTER TWENT-NINE

Alleviating the Plight of Widows in Nigeria
(A paper presented at the Widows Safety Nest workshop in Lagos, October 24, 1999)

Our widows are often classed among the poorest of the poor because we live under a patriarchal and patrilineal social system with structures that tend towards being inherently evil, unjust and inequitable, to the extent that they support the domination, degradation, subjugation and dehumanization of society's weaker members. In our country as in many parts of the world women have no tangible rights of their own, particularly when they become widows due to no fault of theirs. Whatever peripheral rights they assume are bestowed by virtue of their attachment or relationship to their husbands and/or their children. Whatever residual privileges the woman enjoys are given because of the labour she provides in many forms. The sources of economic security, remain in the hands of the man because he virtually controls all the means of production. The woman's labour may be utilized but that hardly ever bestows on her any share in the ownership of the means of production or the wealth they generate.

When therefore the husband is lost, the widow loses her place in society. She falls several rungs in the ladder of the community and becomes an unwilling candidate for marginalization and destitution. The most precarious situation is that of the childless widow - often accused of killing the husband, of being a witch, or of being a greedy usurper eyeing the family wealth. In such circumstances she often gets thrown out of the matrimonial home and loses the security of the extended family, often after being subjected to traumatizing physical and mental torture. She then becomes an emotional, economic and social wreck.

In the typical traditional African setting there are still no juridical structures that ensure next-of-kin status for the widow, there are no reassuring means of inheritance for her and there is no painless process to bequeath property to her. That is to say traditionally, our society does not yet recognise the wife as a normal, natural extension of the husband, showing in effect that the wife is more of a property than a partner of the husband. In a fundamental way, marrying therefore equates to acquiring additional property - one reason perhaps why polygamy remains attractive as a measure of clout in the society.

Our society has come a long way with modernization and the campaign on women liberation, but we have a lot more ground to cover when it comes to breaking our entrenched attitudes and orientations with regard to widowhood. Properties are still recorded in the name of husbands, and of the sons, and sometime of the brothers, but hardly of the wives. Traditionally the woman is married not by the man alone, but by the larger family. There are many things good in this concept when we consider the unity, communal love, sharing in joy and pain and in material things it evokes. Yet a lot of times this concept of marriage is heavily abused, especially when the husband dies. The extended family structure is supposed to be a safety nest for the wife but because of outrageous customs which linger due to greed, lust and hunger, because of lack of education and lack of status on the part of the women, the custom involving widowhood rights remains a burden for the bereaved woman who is often heavily traumatized by the agonizing rituals she is put through upon losing the husband. These may include:

- oath swearing over the corpse of the husband
- drinking the bath water of the corpse
- imposed confinement, sometimes lasting for months
- not bathing for a specified period
- wailing rites
- trial in the court of the dead
- dressing in black and leaving the hair unkempt.

Those suspected or accused of witchcraft are 'tortured' severally as above, while normal widows come under less severe sanctions.

The bottom line to all these practices is the lack of acknowledgement of equal dignity of man and woman. In our march towards spiritual liberation and structural emancipation, it is imperative that we begin to systematically dismantle the superstructures of traditional imprisonment for our creator did not mean that we remain chained to ungodly practices. We must therefore start to change our concept of womanhood and recognise the equal dignity God has given all human beings. We must begin to destroy the abiding myth of female inferiority and the evil of male chauvinism. We must begin to promote the notion of complementarity in the talents and geniuses of the male and female species; to recognise that God has given to each gender certain unique traits and talents, not to be subservient but to be complementary to one another. We must begin to respect and defend the equal dignity and value of men and women, while conceding the distinctions in physical, reproductive, social, and economic functionalities and roles.

We must begin to accord equal educational opportunities to all children, male or female, as the lack or shortfall of education for women tends to unfairly enhance the position of men over women. We must begin to create equal job opportunities to accommodate the unique skills of the genders and pay equal wages for equal work. We must open up equal opportunities for promotion to ensure that women are no longer the subject of frustration and victimization. We must begin to showcase those business and other organisations under female management to demonstrate the latent abilities of women in management. We must begin to encourage capable women to consider careers in politics, so that they can aspire to policy-making positions where they can directly effect the desired change. All this will enhance the bargaining power of women and place them at par with the men.

Presently, women's liberation groups are often un-coordinated and need to go beyond the level of sloganeering and elite posturing to the level of concrete women's rights advocacy work. We need a paradigm shift, not just in advocacy but in practical action on the ground. To this end there is a real need to domesticate all international conventions on women's rights. There is a need for advocacy groups to take on women's social, political and economic rights which together touch on the dignity of womanhood. There is the urgent need for advocacy groups to take on specific aspects of women's issues and thus give them the grounding they deserve. Some of these issues will include child labour, child marriage and widowhood practice. There is also the need to push for constitutional recognition of women as the equal of men. This means quantifying and placing monetary values on household chores performed by the wife - in other words ascribing a family wage to the wife's special responsibilities of child bearing and child raising and other functions that would otherwise attract a wage for a housekeeper. This would be a form of insurance in widowhood.

There is the need for a retirement benefit for older women as people who have contributed in various unquantifiable ways to the development, sustenance and maintenance of society throughout their productive years. Advocacy groups need also to look into divers ways of encouraging economic security for women, the need to discourage girls marrying too young (with the attendant serious consequences) and the need to discourage marriages between couples with sub-normal age disparities. There is also the need to advocate a widespread practice of writing wills which will invariably protect women from total disinheritance.

The input from government and its agencies will include establishing poverty alleviation programmes; guaranteeing social security for widows; ensuring constitutional provisions for concessionary public housing for widows. Nigeria has the resources and the managerial skills for establishing and sustaining a comprehensive social welfare structure for the poorest of the poor, including our widows who undergo tormenting emotional and economic stress in widowhood. What has always been lacking is the political will to do what is good and just.

The Christian community can be actively involved in setting up counselling units for groups and individuals; organising support groups for widows; providing temporary and long-term shelters for displaced widows and children; sponsoring widows' children, initiating poverty alleviation programmes; intensifying gospel preaching on equity, love and justice, and regularly presenting God as the friend of the poor, the father of orphans and the defender of widows. Jesus indeed has made it clear that what you do to the least of his brethren, you do unto him (Mt.25:31-46).

The Christian Bible presents God as the friend of the poor, the father of the orphan and the defender of the widow (see Psalm 68:5-6; Psalm 146:9; Baruch 6:37). In Exodus 22:22-24, the Lord said "You must not molest the stranger or oppress him, for you lived as strangers in the land of Egypt. You must not be harsh with the widow, or with the orphan; if you are harsh with them, they will surely cry out to me, and be sure I shall hear their cry; my anger will flare and I shall kill you with the sword, your own wives will be widows, your own children orphans." Members of the above listed classes of people are acutely vulnerable in different ways but we want to turn our attention to widows who belong to the poorest of the poor. It is therefore particularly obligatory that we who believe in God and recognise Him as father of all, must show a high level of commitment to the plight of widows in our society.

CHAPTER THIRTY

Responding to the Challenge of University Cults
(Presented at a Public Forum organised by the University of Lagos, November 3, 1999)

We are recording each day in Nigeria a number of casualties of the soaring violence, including acid attack, armed robbery, hired assassination, cult violence in our tertiary institutions, and ethnic violence that now threatens the very foundation of our nation state. After seven students were murdered in cold blood at the Obafemi Awolowo University, in July this year, Nigerians who seemed to have suddenly woken up from their long stupor were shocked and outraged and with a united voice called for an end to violent cultism in our institutions of higher learning. Some people prescribed the death penalty for convicted cultists. Others were advocating a "shoot at sight" policy as a way of combating violent cultism on our campuses. Since then university authorities have been up and doing, beefing up internal security, organising mass rallies, workshops, religious services and enlightenment campaigns to highlight the evil of secret cults. Many Vice Chancellors announced an instant dismissal sanction for anyone caught in the act, and called upon repentant cultists to make a public renunciation of their membership. Most of the universities have recorded appreciable success if media reports of public confessions and renunciations by former cult members are anything to go by.

Yet Nigerians did not just wake up one morning to discover that their otherwise peaceful educational institutions have been overtaken by bloodthirsty bandits. No. The handwriting has been on the wall for a long while. Though today we shout and curse and swear at the dangerous turn of events in our educational institutions and the danger it portends for the future, the multitude of our countrymen and women can however not absolve themselves of responsibility for the cult violence in our universities and for the banditry that has taken over most of our towns and villages. Many of us actually have our hands painted red with blood. We have for a long while been wooing the angel of death by the way we manipulate and abuse the structures of power, the way we violate and jettison the rule of law, and the way we organise our society around the pursuit of wealth and pleasure. We seem to have elevated material wealth to the status of a deity and sacrificed all spiritual, human and social values on the altar of this deity. Now we are face-to-face with the realities of the Hobbesian state, where life is nasty, brutish and short. It is the expression of this national malaise among the restive youth population which is concentrated in our tertiary institutions that has come to be known as student cultism.

In this modest contribution, I wish to reflect on the phenomenon of violent cults in our tertiary institutions within the context of our degenerate social system, our collapsed state machinery and our national death wish. Violent cults blossomed within the ambience of the prevailing culture of death in the wider Nigerian society, manifested in political thuggery, harassment, detention and even elimination of perceived enemies of government, widespread armed robbery, hired assassination, ritual killings, bomb explosion, police brutality and extra-judicial killings by security agencies and sometimes by an angry mob. The Nigerian state had in the recent past become a monumental fraud as a result of a prolonged military adventurism that was an exercise in roguery, banditry and debauchery. Over the years, Nigerians lost faith in governance and in the rule of law. They were only hounded and banded together by the state instruments of coercion which had been domesticated by one maximum ruler. Nigeria was indeed a jungle ruled by bandits who only recognised the law of the survival of the fittest.

Individuals and groups took care of their own security by hiring police escorts, constituting vigilante groups or even forming private armies which operated largely outside the law. To combat the growing crime in our cities, state governments constituted terrorist squads that were worse than the notorious "kill and go" arm of the police force. These killer squads adopted such code names as "Operation Sweep," "Operation Crush," Operation Wedge," and "Operation Flush." They were often mandated to shoot suspects at sight, and they did their job with utmost recklessness. We would never know the number of innocent Nigerians who were sent to their early graves as a result of the activities of these state-sponsored bandits.

While today we are experiencing some calm and quiet in the tertiary institutions, the youths of the Niger Delta are at war with the Federal Government, with the Oil Companies and with one another, killing, abducting, maiming, raping and harassing innocent people. From Bori to Eleme and from Bomadi to Warri, the impression is that no one is in control. Instead, what we are confronted with is total lawlessness or anarchy. In Lagos too the youth wing of the Oodua Peoples Congress has been credited with several killings at various locations in the city, including the latest mayhem at Ajegunle in which they were pitched with the Ilaje and Ijaw youths. We are all familiar with the violent exploits of the "Area Boys" who command the streets of our major cities, harassing, extorting and terrorizing members of the public. Thus it appears that through all the years of debauchery, an incalculable damage has been done to the psyche of the Nigerian youth. They no longer seem to be able to distinguish between good and bad, between virtue and vice, and between right and wrong. They seem to have lost faith in the adult society, in the leadership and even in their parents and teachers.

How indeed could the young people have learnt the lesson on the sanctity of life when daily they heard of adults and children being kidnapped, killed and dismembered for ritual purposes by members of the adult society? How could they have come to appreciate the truth of the inviolability of life when daily they were confronted with the reality of human corpses that are left to decompose and decapitate on our streets, while thousands of people pass by and only block their noses against the stench? How could our young people have accepted that violence is evil when everyday they watched the rich and powerful crush the poor and lowly with all the instruments of violence at their disposal, and when such criminals were treated as successful members of society? How could they have accepted the truth of human transcendence when they heard that government agents were sometimes involved in the sordid conspiracy that we call ritual murder?

How can you demonstrate to our young people that human life is not cheap, expendable and disposable when (without any functional film censorship) even the youngest and the most vulnerable among them are exposed to the most outrageous celebration of violence on TV and home videos? How can they accept the rule of law and respect the rights and freedoms of their neighbours, when everyday they watch innocent people humiliated, tortured and eliminated, while the culprits who are often well connected, go scot-free? How can our young people be made to value human life and respect the rights and dignity of persons when their leaders and elders have demonstrated to them that wealth and power are the ultimate values, when these leaders and elders would stop at nothing in the pursuit of these values, when they would blackmail, kidnap, torture or even eliminate anyone who may be in their way to the acquisition of maximum wealth and power. How can they accept that secret cults are bad when they observe that access to wealth and position is often guaranteed and safe passage through the corridors of power is often secured through one's enlistment in one of such adult cults as the Ogboni Confraternity?

How can you make the young people to sit down and concentrate on their studies when the leaders have messed up the educational set-up to such an extent that universities have been shut on more than one occasion for upward of six months, and there was no provision for any profitable engagement of their young minds during the period? Do we not say that the devil makes use of the idle mind? How can our students be eager to study, to pass their examinations and to graduate from the university, when there are no jobs awaiting them, when even for the mandatory Youth Service Scheme they sometimes have to bribe their way to be able to find placement, after having been deployed to places such as Lagos, Abuja, Port Harcourt and Warri? How can they value life amidst acrimonious poverty, when many young people are reduced to a state of destitution, when they are made to struggle with malnourishment, and when they have to study in an environment that is degenerate and decrepit, while they watch in amazement the conspicuous consumption of those who have stolen food off their hands?

True, we have not given our young people reason to live. So they easily fall into the hands of the angel of death. It has been observed that "when life is worthless, fear is banished." Young people are highly impressionable. They are easily scandalised They can easily be led astray. It is only by practical example from members of the adult society that they will learn that the fear of God is the beginning of wisdom; that human life is sacred, unique and inviolable; and that money, power and position are not the highest values for which other values may be so easily sacrificed.

The foregoing seeks to demonstrate that the Nigerian state particularly under both the evil genius and the expired maximum ruler was itself a monumental fraud and a violent cult. Under these two despots the Nigerian state was effectively privatised, and state power, state policy and state resources were totally domesticated by the one who held the country hostage. Thus, before his sudden expiration in June 1998, General Sani Abacha had constituted himself into such a vengeful demigod that only those who prostrated before his altar could live safely and prosper in the land. All others, especially the vocal opposition, were either hunted and hounded into detention, or they were blasted out of existence, or even ritually sacrificed so that the luciferan regime could last for ever. It did not matter if the victim was a renowned artist, a scientist of international repute or even a Nobel Laureate. If his head was required to keep the cult of the maximum ruler going, it was promptly delivered.

With the above scenario I wish to make the point that cult violence in our tertiary institutions was only an attempt by the youth population to replicate in their own immediate environment, the banditry that characterised Nigerian life and governance for so many years. The result of course is that our centres of learning and culture were transformed into a jungle whose only law is the survival of the fittest. And as we noted earlier, whereas the university variant of this national malaise is secret cultism, the malaise manifested itself in the form of big time thuggery and extortion at the hands of the "Area Boys" in our major cities, in the form of hijack, kidnap and vandalisation by the angry youths of the neglected Niger Delta region, and by way of ethnic cleansing at the hands of militant youths of the Oodua Peoples Congress in many parts of Lagos.

Thus I believe that the scourge of university cults cannot be studied, let alone dealt with in isolation from the wider socio-economic and political environment and the moral climate within which it thrived. Violent cultism arose in our universities and colleges within the general framework of a Nigerian state that was in many ways itself a monumental fraud as well as a violent cult. The ongoing anti-cult campaign around the universities which has attracted unprecedented media coverage and public interest is highly commendable. It is however my humble opinion that if the gains of the moment are to be consolidated for the long run, and if we are to make real progress beyond the show business of rallies and renunciation of cult membership before TV cameras, then the cult phenomenon in our tertiary institutions should be studied and tackled from a holistic or multi-dimensional perspective.

The liberation of our ivory tower from the stranglehold of violent cultists along with the redemption of the Nigerian nation shall truly begin when the demons that have led us along the dark alleys of economic depression, political anarchy and social disintegration are identified and cast out. As we reflect today on the way forward in our march towards a more wholesome future for our young people, we must put into proper focus not only the socio-political events spanning the thirty nine years of our independence, but also the moral climate and the values or vices that we have pursued in the past.

The embarrassing truth we must acknowledge is that many of those who constitute the Nigerian elite have over the years been largely blind guides, unprincipled leaders and greedy opportunists. Many of our successive leaders have turned out to be reckless plunderers and mindless looters. True, our experience of leadership in this country, whether at the hands of military dictators or civilian politicians, is one of large scale deceit, manipulation and exploitation. Poor Nigerians have been used and abused over and over again. Our leaders have often exploited the poverty and ignorance of the vast majority of Nigerians, and cashed in on the existing ethnic and religious polarities when it paid them to do so. We have neglected our educational institutions, and made our teachers objects of ridicule in the eyes of society. When therefore we see our young people becoming beastly in hate, ruthless in violence, and reckless in destruction, we do not need to ask too many questions.

Our schools and colleges have lost their sacred character as formation centres, and have rather become breeding grounds for thieves, thugs, touts, secret cultists, gangsters, rapists and prostitutes. We hear these days of school children beating up their teachers, sacking their principals, and burning up their libraries. Examination malpractice in some of our schools has now assumed the frightening dimension whereby teachers and principals organize cheating at external examinations, and parents annually contribute money to "settle" supervisors and invigilators.

As we the leaders and parents have become more enterprising in greed and political mischief, and as we fail to inspire the young people in the pursuit of higher values, we have lost control of the younger generation. Many of our graduates from secondary schools, universities and polytechnics, are social deviants, drug addicts, and secret cultists, who now constitute a nuisance in our homes, our schools and our offices. With juvenile bravado many of these young people are constantly visiting their vengeance on an adult society that has failed to give them a sense of purpose and a sense of direction. So they cheat and steal, they rob and rape, and they kill and maim. And they commit these crimes with the sophistication of the Italian mafia.

The truth is that the collective psyche of our young people has been so seriously wounded, and their delicate conscience so brutally battered by the crimes of the adult society, that we now stand the chance of losing tomorrow altogether. We are about to lose millions of our young people whose teeth are on edge because their fathers have eaten sour grapes. We are about to lose millions of young people who are constipated because their mothers have eaten the forbidden fruit. Our young people are beginning to lose hope. And this is the greatest danger. It is the absence of hope in the midst of hardship that has led many of our young unemployed and unemployable people into student cultism and the now widespread township thuggery, armed robbery, drug peddling and drug addiction.

There is work to be done by all of us who belong to the adult society in Nigeria, if we are not to kill tomorrow before today's sun sets. We must own up before our young people that we have betrayed our fatherland and failed to lay the necessary foundation for a prosperous future. We must own up to the fact that we have often stolen food off the hands of our children. Each one of us is guilty to the extent that we have contributed in some way to the mess of the moment by our corrupt and selfish lifestyle. As parents, teachers, preachers and elders, we have often failed to inspire our young people to live a life of righteousness. As leaders and elders we have often failed to be a beacon of light. Instead we have often been a source of scandal for our own children and the children of our country.

The time has come for repentance. For us who are believers in God, the situation may be bad enough but not hopeless. We should believe that redemption is possible for our land by the power of God who creates and recreates. We can experience a rejuvenation, if today we begin to retrace our steps, and get back to the basics. We should believe that from the rubble of our shattered motherland, a rich, powerful, peaceful and united country can emerge, by the power of God who puts back flesh on dry bones. This will happen if we identify and get rid of the demons that have bewitched this land since independence.

Those who seek to bestow hope on the coming generation must recommit themselves to a life of truth, justice, and righteousness. Parents must be ready to make sacrifices for the sake of their children. Teachers must recognize that they teach more by their lives than by their lessons. The world has too many teachers and preachers. What we lack are living witnesses to love, compassion, truth and justice. Young people need to see that truth, honesty and fairness are possible at work in the civil service, in the award and execution of contracts, in the process of governance and in the examination hall. Our youths are constantly let down and disappointed when their leaders are fraudulent or when they see teachers assisting unscrupulous students to cheat at examinations. They are shocked when they discover that their governors, ministers, parents or teachers are liars. Then they wonder whether a life of truth is possible in this world. Their trust is violated when they themselves or their peers are sexually exploited, harassed or abused by leaders, elders or teachers.

When these young people see the hypocrisy of the adult society, they convince themselves that there is no truth or justice in the world. They make up their minds that there is no such thing as love and compassion. They conclude that the world is one big jungle, largely inspired by the principle of mutual exploitation and governed by the law of the survival of the fittest and the triumph of the villain. Ah, there is work for the adult society to do if we must combat the angel of death and bestow hope on our young people.

I hereby call on all Nigerians to reject the foolish pattern of life which has led our nation to the mess of the moment. Instead we must seek after higher values that will guarantee wholesome living, peace and prosperity.

Chapter Thirty | George Ehusani

We must start now cultivating the virtues of sacrificial love, truth, justice, discipline and patriotism which alone can take us to the promised land. If today we cultivate these virtues, then we would have laid the foundation for a more wholesome future for our country.

I call on the upcoming generation, the youths themselves, to shun materialism, for it blinds people and enslaves them. Instead of seeking escape in the plastic wings of sexual pleasure and hard drugs, and the illusory power of secret cults and satanic confraternities, I call on the young people to seek the fear of the Lord, which is the beginning of wisdom. If today our young people allow their lives to be shaped along the way of these higher values, then tomorrow will not be lost. If they choose the culture of life in place of the prevailing culture of crime, violence and death, then they shall have a bright future ahead of them. Yes, if our young people embrace the culture of life and truth, they shall one day sing the National Anthem with a sense of respect for our heroes past, a sense of pride in our fatherland, and a sense of belonging to a nation bound in freedom, peace and unity.

Nigerians are good at identifying the problems. But we must do something about the solution. The time for action is now. We are not entirely helpless in the face of evil. We must begin from somewhere. As they say, it is better to light a candle rather than curse the darkness. Thinking Nigerians, both young and old must all be committed to the all-important task of national rejuvenation. We must light the candle of hope in our homes, in our offices, and in our schools. We must do this by struggling to lead a life of truth, justice, honesty and discipline. We must work hard towards sustaining a pro-life and pro-people culture in our national life. Our economic policies must be given a human face. We must all be ready to make the necessary sacrifices towards sustaining the sacred institution of marriage and family life, recognising that good and responsible parenting necessarily involves fidelity, mutual forgiveness and sacrificial love. We must work hard towards ameliorating societal and institutional poverty, and establish comprehensive welfare programmes for our teeming youth population.

Instead of engaging in prestige projects, we must set aside a sizable percentage of our national earnings for the education of our young people who constitute the nation's most valuable resource. We must begin to re-evaluate and re-conceive our educational curriculum, administration and management. We must fund our colleges and universities so adequately that they would provide the necessary infrastructures for wholesome learning and recreation. We must help the teachers to regain their lost glory, so that

they may command the respect of their students and the general public. We must sanitize the admission process into our universities. The realities of the day make it imperative that we establish counselling centres in all our schools for distressed students and lecturers. It has also become necessary that a programme of adoption of young students be introduced in our schools. Above all, we must embrace a new ethic of life, and pursue it relentlessly, for indeed "where there is no vision, the people do perish."
Let me end this reflection by proposing that Nigerian youths along with their teachers and parents should recite the following lines on daily basis, until all the manifestations of corruption and violence are wiped out of our land:

> I pledge my commitment to the emergence of a new Nigeria, recognising that greed and avarice are a cancer that eats its own host to death; that corruption ultimately kills not only the victims, but also the perpetrators; and that unless we change our course we are bound to end up where we are headed.

I pledge my commitment to the emergence of a new Nigeria, recognising that lies, manipulation, and political subterfuge have never, and will never nurture a people; that thievery, robbery and roguery, by whatever name else it is called, when it becomes king in a land, that land rots; and that when hooliganism and banditry get into high places, the superstructure soon comes crashing down.

I pledge my commitment to the emergence of a new Nigeria, recognising that where lawlessness becomes the norm, and illegality becomes the rule, the nation collapses; that righteousness exalts a nation, but that sin is a reproach to a people; and that where there is no vision the people soon perish.

Finally, I recognise with the Psalmist that unless the Lord builds a house, the labourers labour in vain, and unless the Lord watches over the city, the sentries keep watch in vain (Ps 127:). So help me God to use all the resources you have bestowed upon me to renounce the evils of the past, and to work towards a more wholesome and peaceful Nigeria.

CHAPTER THIRTY-ONE

Between Reconciliation and Disintegration
(Written on April 27, 2000)

At the end of May 2000, our fourth attempt at democratic governance shall be one year old. After years of military dictatorship, the worst form of which was manifested in the Abacha dispensation, Nigerians had hoped for a period of peaceful transition to a just, equitable, democratic, and prosperous society. We had hoped for a new Nigerian society where we shall once again have the opportunity to channel our enormous natural endowments to positive use for the advancement of our teeming population. We had hoped for a new Nigerian society where we can celebrate the richness of our diverse languages, cultures, and religions. We had hoped for a new Nigerian society where we can take our rightful place in the comity of nations.

It is with such hopes that we made May 29, 1999, a day of national celebration, with Abuja and every state and local government headquarters alive with festivities. Our new president, our governors and our local government chairmen took their oath of office, promising to serve the people with all honesty dedication and patriotism. One year has gone by and look at where we are. Rather than make progress towards the realisation of our dreams, see how far we have regressed. One year after the best of hopes were kindled in us, the Nigerian nation appears to be more fragmented than ever before, and as a people we seem to be more divided now than we ever were since our national independence.

The divisions and the resultant tensions are everyday played out on the streets, in marketplaces and in neighbourhoods, as Nigerians hound their fellow citizens to death and set their properties on fire at the slightest provocation. They are often reflected on the floor of the state and national assemblies, where the honourable men and women sometimes need the anti-riot police to keep the peace. They are implied in the frosty relationship between the executive and the legislature that is making the Nigerian brand of democracy look like an exercise in mutual acrimony. The multiple crises that have plagued post-military Nigeria, sufficiently demonstrate that we have been sitting on a pile of explosives that are now exploding in every direction, and there is no end to the crises.

We have been witnessing an orgy of violence: From the onslaughts of the angry Egbesu youths of the Niger Delta, to the atrocities of aggrieved OPC youths of the South-West, and from the senseless killings among the Ife and the Modakeke, to the crazy Sharia campaign in the North that has shaken the very foundation of the nation, it has been a season of blood and tears. Precious human lives have been destroyed in their thousands, and property worth hundreds of millions of naira have been set ablaze. We now have thousands of refugees and other displaced persons squatting in police and army barracks all over the place. As a result of these sad developments, investors have been scared away, and the economy remains comatose. With the circumstance of widespread violence and great insecurity in the land, potential investors seem to have decided to watch and see. Unemployment remains high and the mass of the people are plagued by acrimonious poverty, with the lot of many worsening by the day. Thus, one year after we said goodbye to military dictatorship, we are witnessing what appears to be another round of aborted dreams, broken promises, and dashed hopes.

The sad events of the last one year surely bring to the fore the imperative of genuine national reconciliation. Perhaps the people of Nigeria along with their leaders had underestimated the extent of the problems that had built up in the land over the years of debauchery, when social injustice, economic isolation and political banditry reigned, breeding widespread anger and resentment that were kept in check all the while only by military might. With sporadic skirmishes that erupt from North to South and from East to West, over unresolved ethnic, religious, political, and economic differences, Nigerians must now realise that there are lots of structural defects in the land that we must deal with courageously.

With so many un-addressed wounds and hurts over past injustices and inequities, our task of nation-building must begin with an elaborate programme of, and an honest commitment to national reconciliation, or else our new preoccupation with democratic governance will lack the much-needed foundation, and end once again in disaster. The conduct of many of these leaders in the last one year does not inspire sufficient confidence in the population on their ability to champion the much-needed reconciliation and national rebirth. For many it is business as usual, scheming for power and privilege, and sometimes manipulating the existing ethnic and religious divisions for their selfish gains. Yet these are unusual times for our country, times that call for immense sacrifices on the part of the leadership.

Elected representatives of the people who occupy both executive and legislative positions in the present political dispensation must consider themselves as part of a transitional government of national reconciliation. They must learn to feel the pulse of the nation, to hear the cry of the people, and to react with utmost sense of responsibility to the desires and aspirations of the constituent units of the country for a unity that is based on mutual understanding, and a peace that is built on justice. We can no longer run away from the idea of a national conference or whatever the experts call it. We surely need to have a forum at which we can attempt a re-negotiation of the conditions of our corporate existence as a nation. The marginalised majorities and the suppressed minorities of this country need to have a forum at which they can lay their cards open and discuss like civilised people issues relating to their self-determination.

Rather than resort to armed banditry which will do no one any good, the angry youths of the oil producing regions of the Niger Delta should be given the opportunity to come around the negotiating table along with their shopping list of demands, rather than transform their homeland into a war zone. The vengeful children of Oduduwa in the South-West should be encouraged to sheath their swords and come on board with their enlightened self-interest, instead of taking the law into their hands. The aggrieved Ndigbo zealots of the South-East should be given the chance to express their frustration with the rest of Nigeria in a legitimate manner and be helped to heal the wounds of the past, rather than be left to raise a new Biafran army to fight a second civil war that may be more brutal than the first. In the same way, the embittered champions of the Middle Belt agenda, along with the wounded Sharia Jihadists of the core North should be encouraged to come together with the rest of Nigeria for a true dialogue, in place of the multiple monologues that are now holding sway.

The challenge before the Nigerian leadership today is that of reconciliation or otherwise disintegration. The threat of disintegration in the land is real. There is sufficient anger in many individuals and groups over real or perceived injustices for which they seem ready to take up arms to tear the country to pieces. Our political elite must wake up to the fact that this time around it is not business as usual. They will be held responsible for whatever happens to Nigeria in the next few years. For God's sake, who has endowed this land with such enormous resources and opportunities which we have squandered for the umpteenth time, and for the sake of the one hundred and ten million people, the overwhelming majority of whom are poor, powerless, and helpless, our elected representatives must abandon their preoccupation with frivolities and take seriously the agenda for true national reconciliation.

Our honourable men and women in the executive and legislative arms of government must for once put selfishness and greed aside and work conscientiously towards the realisation of the Nigeria of our dream. Perhaps we have too many mercenaries parading as leaders. Such are the ones who make reconciliation impossible since they gain by the continued tension in the land. Such are the ones who fan the flame of ethnic and religious tension. Such are the one who would resist the idea of a national forum for reconciliation with all the resources at their disposal. The rest of Nigeria must become more discerning. We must constantly strive to identify genuine leaders and distinguish them from mercenaries who are out only to steal, to cheat and to destroy. Nigeria will only know peace and prosperity after we must have dealt with these mercenaries and put in place the proper structures that will make for justice, equity, mutual recognition, mutual respect, and ongoing dialogue. We must act now, or we shall soon answer the call to disintegration.

CHAPTER THIRTY-TWO

Jubilee, Forgiveness and National Reconciliation
(Written on May 15, 2000)

AT the end of May 2000, our fourth attempt at democratic governance shall be one year old. After years of military dictatorship, the worst form of which was manifested in the Abacha dispensation, Nigerians had hoped for a period of a peaceful transition to a just, equitable, democratic and prosperous society. We had hoped for a new Nigerian society where we shall once again have the opportunity to channel our enormous natural endowments to positive use for the advancement of our teeming population. We had hoped for a new Nigerian society where we can celebrate the richness of our diverse languages, cultures and religions. We had hoped for a new Nigerian society where we can take our rightful place in the comity of nations. However, one year has gone by after the best of hopes were kindled in us; rather than make progress towards the realisation of our dreams, the Nigerian nation appears to be more fragmented than ever before. As a people, we seem to be more divided now than ever, since our national independence.

The divisions and the resultant tensions are everyday played out on the streets, in market places and in neighbourhoods as Nigerians hound their fellow citizens to death and set their properties on fire at the slightest provocation. They are often reflected on the floor of the state and national assemblies, where the honourable men and women sometimes need the anti-riot police to keep the peace. They are implied in the frosty relationship between the executive and the legislature that is making the Nigerian brand of democracy look like an exercise in mutual acrimony. The multiple crises that have plagued post-military Nigeria, sufficiently demonstrate that we have been sitting on a pile of explosives that are now exploding in every direction, and there is no end to the crises.

We have been witnessing an orgy of violence: From the onslaughts of the angry Egbesu youths of the Niger-Delta, to the atrocities of aggrieved OPC youths of the South West, and from the senseless killings among the Ife and the Modakeke, to the crazy Sharia campaign in the North that has shaken the very foundation of the nation, it has been a season of blood and tears. Precious human lives have been destroyed in their thousands, and properties worth hundreds of millions of naira have been set ablaze. We now have thousands of refugees and other displaced persons squatting in police and army barracks all over the place. As a result of these sad developments, investors have been scared away, and the economy remains comatose. With the circumstance of widespread violence and great insecurity in the land, potential investors seem to have decided to watch and see. Unemployment remains high, and the mass of the people are plagued by acrimonious poverty, with the lot of many worsening by the day. Thus, one year after we said goodbye to military dictatorship, we are witnessing what appears to be another round of aborted dreams, broken promises and dashed hopes.

The sad events of the last one year surely bring to the fore the imperative of genuine national reconciliation. Perhaps the people of Nigeria, along with their leaders, had underestimated the extent of the problems that had built up in the land over the years of debauchery, when social injustice, economic isolation and political banditry reigned, breeding widespread anger and resentment that were kept in check all the while only by military might. With sporadic skirmishes that erupt from North to South and from East to West, over unresolved ethnic, religious, political and economic differences, Nigerians must now realise that there is a lot of structural defect in the land that we must deal with courageously.

Many in the Igbo nation are resentful of the rest of Nigeria for the injustices of the 1967 to 1970 civil war, the abandoned property imbroglio, and the post-war marginalisation of Igbo people in some vital segments of the national economy. Many in the Yoruba nation are angry with the rest of Nigeria for the injustices associated with the June 12 election annulment, and the alleged post-June 12 persecution and marginalisation of Yoruba people. The collocation of small ethnic nationalities, which we call the Middle-Belt, is today vexed by the alleged appendage status accorded them in the nation's constitution. Many of them allege that they have suffered numerous injustices for being falsely associated with the North, while they gained nothing from the Northern hold on political power. The citizens of the oil-producing Niger-Delta are poised for a showdown with the rest of Nigeria, and if recent clashes are anything to go by, their youths appear to be well equipped for war with the rest of Nigeria, because of the callous exploitation of their natural resources for decades, while they were abandoned in a state of destitution. Many among the Hausa and Fulani Muslims of the core North who desire to live under the supremacy of the Islamic Sharia are incensed the rest of Nigeria wants to jettison their religious freedom. Within each group, there is often bitterness over past hurts and wounds which have never been seriously addressed.

With so many unaddressed wounds and hurts over past injustices and inequities, our task of nation-building must begin with an elaborate programme and an honest commitment to national reconciliation, or else our new preoccupation with democratic governance will lack the much-needed foundation and end once again in disaster. The leadership of Nigeria must learn to feel the pulse of the nation, to hear the cry of the people, and to react with an utmost sense of responsibility to the desires and aspirations of the constituent units of the country for that kind of unity and peace that is based on mutual forgiveness for past hurts and wounds, and a mutual commitment to righting the wrongs of the past, and building our society on justice and fair-play.

Many concerned Nigerians have called for a National Conference to deal with the structural defects in our nation state. This may well be one way out of our protracted political crisis. However, Christians whom the Lord calls the light of the world have the imperative of forgiveness, the practice of which Pope John Paul II says is the only guarantee for lasting peace. He observed in the Encyclical *Dives in Misericordia* (published in 1980) that a world without forgiveness shall be a world of endless violence. It is with the Christian virtue of forgiveness that past wounds, bitterness and resentments could be adequately healed, and wholesome human relationships can once again begin afresh. As we celebrate the Jubilee Year, the Pope has given us an example by asking for pardon for the past hurts and wounds caused by people who acted on behalf of the Church. He also, on behalf of every Catholic, offered forgiveness for all the injustices the Catholic Church and its functionaries have suffered over the ages. He thus challenges everyone to do an examination of conscience, and to courageously address the hurts and wounds of the past; to offer forgiveness for these hurts and wounds, and to ask for forgiveness for those injustices which we ourselves have caused others.

Chapter Thirty-Two | George Ehusani

CHAPTER THIRTY-THREE

The Social Challenges of Jubilee 2000
(Written July 2, 2000)

On November 10, 1994, Pope John Paul II proclaimed the 2000th anniversary of this most blessed event of history, "an extraordinarily great jubilee," towards which elaborate preparations have been made within and outside the Church in the last six years. A most important document issued during the period of preparation is John Paul II's *"Tertio Millennio Adveniente,"* which spelt out the historical, theological, social and pastoral dimensions of the jubilee celebrations.

Following the biblical tradition from which the practise derives (see Leviticus 25: 1-23; Exodus 23:10-11; Deuteronomy 15:1-18; and Luke 4:18-19), the jubilee is a year-long holiday - a sabbath of sabbaths as it were. The jubilee year is a year of celebration, thanksgiving and praise. It is a period of rest, recuperation, rejuvenation and reconciliation for the human heart, for human relationships, for entire societies and for the natural environment. The jubilee year is meant to be a year when the land is allowed to lie fallow in every respect. It is a year when the people of God are engaged in some kind of retreat, to recollect themselves enough, so as to engage in a mission of repentance and reconciliation, offering and receiving forgiveness and proclaiming a general amnesty for offenders and transgressors.

The jubilee year is supposed to be a year when a moratorium is declared on all anger and vengeance, and when warring parties observe a ceasefire. During the jubilee year we are supposed to witness a cessation to oppression and exploitation, the proclamation of liberty to all bonded people, the cancellation of all bad debts, and the restoration of justice and the original balance in human affairs and in the natural environment.

The first Christian Jubilee was proclaimed by Pope Boniface VIII in the year 1300. Since then the universal Church has had about twenty-four other jubilee or holy years. Among the major features of these jubilee celebrations are the Opening of the Holy Door that represents

Christ the Way the Truth and the Life; Repentance for individual and social sins (or what Pope John Paul calls "the Purification of Memory;" Pilgrimages to Holy Places and Shrines; Indulgences; and a special Commemoration of and updating of the list of Martyrs whose blood constitutes the seed of the Church. This particular jubilee for the year

2000 has the special distinction of being highly universal, ecclesial, ecumenical, liturgical and sacramental.

The official opening of the Great Jubilee at the St. Peter's Basilica in Rome and in the various Cathedrals and Churches all over the world has been very well publicised. And beginning with the Jubilee of Children on January 2, 2000, various individual celebrations throughout the year shall highlight the major components of the Church, whose membership of the Body of Christ and whose assurance of salvation in Christ is the major reason for the jubilee celebration.

Dioceses, parishes and lay apostolate organisations within the Church have outlined various pastoral, liturgical and social programmes to mark the Jubilee. This is in order. We need to do even more to let the world know that we are celebrating a Jubilee on the occasion of the 2000th year of the birth of our Saviour Jesus Christ. We are called upon to use the occasion to glorify the God of eternity who intervened at a particular point in history by sending his Son into the world to bring about the salvation of humanity. It is an occasion to pray more fervently than ever before for the emergence of the Kingdom of God, the Kingdom which Christ preached, and towards which all Christian ministry is tended.

Yet beyond the liturgical and pastoral programmes already lined up by the various Churches for the year are the enormous social challenges of the jubilee celebration. If the jubilee is a time for forgiveness, healing, restoration and reconciliation, then what are the implications of all this for the socio-economic and political structures of our society and the existential fortunes of our people? What are the implications of these high points of the jubilee celebration for our individual and group relationships, and for our social habits and customs? What are the implications of the ideals of the jubilee tradition for the Nigerian society that is plagued by a scandalous disparity between the excessive affluence of a few and the acrimonious poverty of the multitude? How does the jubilee celebration challenge our circumstance of systemic corruption, widespread ethnic bigotry, religious intolerance and the resultant tension and strife in the land?

Looking at our circumstances in the world and in our country, we would say that the proclamation of Jubilee 2000 is most auspicious.

Believers in God who are nevertheless alienated from him due to sin need the forgiveness which the Lord generously offers during the jubilee year. African countries which are today groaning under the enormous weight of unpaid debts eagerly look forward to the cancellation of debts which is associated with jubilee celebrations. The men and women of the world who are torn apart by hatred, violence and strife need the reconciliation which is synonymous with the jubilee. The natural environment too, which is today seriously endangered as a result of irresponsible exploitation by human beings has been waiting for the restoration of creation which the jubilee is all about. The jubilee celebration should therefore offer all of us the providential opportunity to repent of the individual and communal sins of our society, and to make a new commitment to the individual virtues and social values that will make for peace, security and prosperity.

CHAPTER THIRTY-FOUR

Moral Imperative of National Rejuvenation
(Written on Oct. 1, 2000)

WE have come together today to reflect on the moral imperative of national rejuvenation. We speak of national rejuvenation or rebirth for our country because many of us believe that the Nigeria we have today is in large measure a failed state, its economy comatose, its polity fragmented, and its image severely damaged. Our forty-year sojourn as an independent nation has been a prolonged nightmare punctuated by a bitter civil war, and a succession of rogue leadership made up of military dictatorships and their civilian collaborators, featuring a culture of coups and counter-coups, the senseless shedding of blood and the sowing of bitterness and resentment in the land.

Since leadership in most of our nation's history has often been illegitimate, those at the helm of affairs have very often manipulated and orchestrated the existing ethnic and religious polarities and antipathies, causing tension and igniting violent skirmishes between the constituent groups who would otherwise have lived together in peace if we were blessed with a more visionary and less opportunistic leadership. The result of the long-standing discord sown in the land is that there is today a discernible absence of a sense of national cohesion, while at the same time ethnic cleavages across the land are waxing stronger by the day.

Part of the consequences of the failure of the Nigerian state is the emergence all over the place of ethnic militia and vigilante groups who have taken up the responsibility of the police and of the courts, arresting real or suspected criminals, judging them in jungle fashion and executing them in the most barbaric and dastardly manner imaginable. Even with the daily execution of scores of Nigerians in this most primitive manner, life and property remain very unsafe in our land. Indeed can we expect a better scenario in a land where poverty has assumed the moral equivalence of war? Can we expect to be more secure than we are today when close to 75 per cent of our able-bodied youth population are either unemployed or underemployed?

In spite of the enormous wealth bestowed on our land by way of natural and human resources, Nigeria is entering the 21st century as a beggarly nation, scored so low in modern development indices that it is described as the 13th poorest nation on earth, with no less than 75 per cent of its population living below the poverty line. Ironically Nigeria has some of the richest people in the world, with their foreign accounts swelling with stolen wealth. Thus we are classified by Transparency International as the most corrupt nation in the world.

At the end of the day, there is very little to be proud of in the political history, the economy and our social life in Nigeria as it is presently constituted. We need a new Nigeria which we can be proud of. We need a rejuvenated Nigeria, based on certain shared values, particularly moral values, without which we cannot move anywhere. If we are to arrive at the Promised Land, Nigerians and their leaders must come to recognise that greed and avarice are a cancer that eats its own host to death; that corruption ultimately kills not only the victims but also the perpetrators; and that unless we change our course, we are bound to end up where we are headed. To arrive at the destination of our dream, we Nigerians and our leaders must come to recognise that lies, manipulation, and political subterfuge have never, and will never nurture a people; that thievery, robbery and roguery, by whatever name else it is called, when it becomes king in a land, that land rots; and when hooliganism and banditry get into high places, the superstructure soon comes crashing down. To facilitate the emergence of a peaceful and prosperous nation, we must recognise that where lawlessness becomes the norm, and illegality the rule, the nation collapses; that righteousness exalts a nation, but that sin is a reproach to a people; and that where there is no vision, the people soon perish. When we as a people decide to wake up to these realities and live by these truths, our land, shall by the grace of the good Lord, experience rejuvenation, and the giant of Africa shall once again bounce back on its feet.

CHAPTER THIRTY-FIVE

Nigerians: Stop the Madness!
(Written on October 10, 2001)

Our country Nigeria has become a reservoir of violence and death. Peace as a national refrain is becoming a rare commodity, no matter how loudly we acclaim it. If anything, violence as a means of settling a variety of scores has become firmly entrenched, taking root like an incurable cancer that threatens to consume its host. From a distressed and traumatized national psyche, regimented under decades of military domination, what seems to have emerged is a convoluted sense of freedom under our strange version of democracy, that is interpreted by some as freedom in the extreme.

From North to South, and from East to West, our country is overrun by ethnic, religious and political conflicts that regularly explode in unrestrained violence, even as we are held under siege or enveloped in the dark aura or the brutality of armed robbery on the one hand, and the outrageous activities of sundry vigilante groups on the other. Think of the restiveness in the Niger Delta region that was once compounded by the state violence unleashed on Odi. The result of state intervention in that case was nothing short of genocide. Think of the Aguleri/Umuleri clashes in Anambra State, and the Ife/Modakeke crisis in Osun State in which hundreds of lives were lost and the towns were rendered desolate. We recall the O.P.C. crisis in some parts of the Southwest, especially Ajegunle and Ketu in Lagos, and the killings that occurred in Shagamu allegedly due to ethnic or religious sentiments. What about the never-ending ethnic feuds in Benue, Taraba, and Nasarawa States, which have not only devastated the areas concerned, but lately claimed the lives of some twenty Nigerian soldiers sent on peace mission.

For us the most troubling and frightening of this orgy of violence in Nigeria is the Sharia-induced slaughter of Christians and/or non-indigenes, the destruction of Churches, and the burning of shops and private homes in Kaduna, Bauchi, Plateau and Kano States, the recent occurrence in Kano being the most senseless, inexplicable, and outrageous of such attacks on Christians and non-indigenes and the disturbance of public peace. We seem to be riding a roller coaster of madness, violence, and death, and no one seems to be in control.

The Sharia crisis in many parts of the North have sometimes provoked reprisal killings in the South, generating a chain of events that are inimical to harmonious living in the country. People have been displaced, properties have been looted, businesses have been dislocated, and there is a general breakdown of trust and the rule of law, and the trading of fear and widespread insecurity. Indeed, the Sharia campaign triggered in Zamfara State has its special significance in raising the level of violence in Nigeria. The recent events in the land have created all manner of extremists, social deviants, ethnic militia, religious jihadists and crusaders, and societal malcontents, whose objectives are obscure, unlawful, and vicious, and who mete out violence on society in the most vicious and primitive manner. In such riotous environment, no investors in their right frame of mind would want to stake their resources in this country.

Among the remote and near causes of the topography of violence in Nigeria is the acrimonious poverty in the land, the visionless leadership that is ridden with kleptomania, the selfish motivations of the elite political class who often capitalize on the poverty and ignorance of the mass of the people, and exploit existing religious and ethnic sentiments for selfish ends. After long years of abuse, in which the population has shifted from one unrealized expectation to another, a restive population has been cultivated into an army of discontented elements, ready to be used to kill, to maim and to destroy. But while the nation burns and the people die in their thousands, our leaders at all levels have generally displayed a shocking degree of insensitivity.

Our leaders are busy amassing wealth and awarding national honours to themselves and their friends. They are busy bickering over political fortunes and investing in re-election to their high offices come the year 2003. They are busy travelling all over the world, claiming to be seeking investors, when all they needed to do was to ensure peace and security in Nigeria and investors will flood in. It is for us a sad commentary on the Nigerian style of leadership that when the Sharia riots of Kaduna broke out in February 2000, Governor Makarfi was out of the country. When in September this year the mayhem took place in Jos, Governor Dariye was out of the country. And as Kano was burning only two weeks ago, following the pro-Osama bin Laden demonstration of some Islamic fanatics, President Obasanjo took off for France.

What we have had is a classic display of the characteristics of a failed state, running on a cycle of violence where human life has lost all its value, and where government or leadership is, for all practical purposes, absent. We appear to be back to the jungle or to the Hobbesian state of nature where life is nasty, brutish and short. Is the security of lives and property not the first and most important duty of government? Our rulers must learn the art of true leadership. They must learn that they are not conquerors, but stewards and servants of the people. They must learn to be sensitive, responsive and accountable to those over whom they are placed as shepherds.

The irony of the Nigerian situation is that we claim to profess one form of religious belief or another. We claim piety and nearness to God, yet our actions underscore the gulf between believers and the primitive. For Christians the message is loud and clear. No one who claims any knowledge of God can justify the employment of violence as a weapon to settle scores. This message has been rung repeatedly by Pope John Paul II and by the Catholic Bishops of Nigeria. In a 1991 Encyclical Letter, John Paul II made a passionate plea against violence and war. He wrote: "Never again war! No, never again war, which destroys the lives of innocent people, teaches how to kill, throws into upheaval even the lives of those who do the killing and leaves behind a trail of resentment and hatred" (*Centesimus Annus*, 52).

In a statement issued after the February 2000 Sharia riots in Kaduna, the Bishops of Nigeria stated: "We condemn violence on whatever excuse, and from whatever direction. We condemn it above all when its perpetrators blasphemously and fraudulently claim religious justifications. Those who say they love God while hating their fellow human beings, even to the extent of killing them, are liars." And after the September 2001 Plenary Meeting of the Bishops, during which time the 9/11 Al-Qaeda attack on the World Trade Centre and Pentagon in the United States had just taken place, and the Jos killings were on, the bishops once again declared: "We totally condemn the use of violence in all its forms by adherents of every religious or ethnic group. For no destruction of human life can be justified in the name of religion. As an alternative to the use of violence as a means of settling issues in Nigeria and other parts of the world, we continue to propose dialogue, forgiveness and reconciliation."

I therefore call on all those who harbour violence as an offensive or defensive weapon to reflect on the sanctity and inviolability of human life. The road to anarchy and chaos is strewn with violence. We cannot ever make peace via the way of violence. Violence always begets violence. I call on Nigerians to stop the madness and abandon the culture of violence and death. I call on the Nigerian political and social elite to check ethnic bigotry, excessive sectionalism, and senseless parochialism. I call on religious leaders, especially of the Islamic fold to check the fanatics and extremists in their fold. I call on those who justify violence with religion whether they are Muslims or Christians, to stop the blasphemy, for anyone who kills in the name of God is giving religion a bad name. I call on the Press to report and comment on the various cases of violence with utmost care and prudence in such a way that one occurrence does not spark off another.

I call on the President of Nigeria, the Legislators, the Governors, and other political office holders to sit up and consider the project of national reconciliation of urgent priority. I call on all these leaders to stay at home, stay close to their constituencies, and become agents of the much-needed reconciliation in the land, rather than junketing round the world or running after the project of re-election in 2003, for if the present level of violence continues, there may even be no 2003 elections. After long years of military profligacy, social disintegration, and mass impoverishment, what Nigeria desires today are not mercenaries, contract chasers and feudal lords, but selfless leaders and shepherds who are ready to sacrifice not only their comforts, but, if necessary, their very lives in the pursuit of national reconciliation, social reintegration, and economic recovery.

Finally, our present leaders must note that they shall be held responsible in large measure for the death and destruction all over the land. If they do not put all their resources into arresting the present situation, and if we should descend further in anarchy and doom, posterity will judge them badly and consign them to the dustbin of history for squandering away a golden opportunity they had to rebuild Nigeria.

CHAPTER THIRTY-SIX

Catholic Lawyers and National Re-Awakening
(Paper presented to the first Convention of National Association of Catholic Lawyers, Lagos, February 16, 2002).

On behalf of the Catholic Bishops Conference of Nigeria, I congratulate you members of the National Association of Catholic Lawyers, for the hosting of your first full national convention, here in the Auditorium of Nigeria's premier Law School, where nearly all of you got your professional certification. I believe that for many of you it is a homecoming experience that is characterised by the joy of meeting old friends in an all too familiar territory.

For me the successful hosting today of a full national convention is the realisation of a longstanding dream. The inauguration of this Association on the national level took place on April 28 last year. Before this event I knew that a good number of well-known Nigerian lawyers were Catholics. I knew that Catholic lawyers formed a sizeable proportion of those who have been in the forefront in the struggle for democracy and good governance. I knew that groups of Catholic lawyers even existed in a few dioceses or states, some actively involved in the life of the church and society where they were. These individual Catholic lawyers and state or diocesan groups functioned with rather limited capacity to influence national policy or make any serious impact as Catholic lawyers on what direction the country takes in legal and constitutional matters, or in the struggle for a just, democratic society. This is due in large measure to the absence of a national platform or networking strategy, by which the immense potential for social change that such a strategic group of Christian professionals with shared values and a common moral vision has could be actuated.

At the inauguration of this Association in April last year, I remarked that one of the weaknesses of the Nigerian Church in the past is the poor recognition of expertise and the inadequate utilization of experts that abound in our Church. Part of the new thinking in the Catholic Bishops' Conference and the Secretariat, I said, is to bring on board the resources and expertise of individuals and groups among the faithful that will enhance the Church's mission of evangelisation and the spread of God's kingdom of justice, love and peace, in accordance with the spirit of the Second Vatican Council which defined the Church as "the people of God," of which lay persons involved in the social, economic and political affairs of life are an integral part.

Modern democratic governance is founded upon a popular constitution, and sustained by the rule of law. The Catholic Church recognises democracy as the best form of government available today, in as much as it acknowledges the equality of all men and women in society, and promotes the common good. Since 1891 when Pope Leo XIII issued the epoch-making encyclical on labour matters titled "Rerum Novarum," the teaching authority of the Catholic Church has taken enlightened stands on many issues that were previously thought to be purely social and political in nature. This is because it can be seen clearly today that socio-economic and political issues have moral implications that may not be ignored. Unfortunately these teachings are so little known by Christians, even among the most educated members of our Church. Yet they contain principles that are most relevant for the day-to-day conduct of their Christian life as Judges and Lawyers, as Doctors and Nurses, as Politicians and as Diplomats and as Entrepreneurs and working class people. The social teachings of the Church constitute the points of convergence between the fundamental planks of Christ's civilisation of love and the best tenets of democracy and the rule of law.

From 1891 when Pope Leo XIII issued the encyclical *Rerum Novarum*, to the present day when we have Pope John Paul II's *Evangelium Vitae*, the Magisterium has made pronouncements on a wide range of issues, including the Common Good and Human Solidarity, Violence and Nuclear War, the Sanctity of Life and the nature of Human Development, the Justice that makes for Peace, Fundamental Human Rights and Dignity, Freedom of Religion and Conscience, the Rights of the Child and the Family, nationalism, the right of minority cultures and communities, and the principle of subsidiarity, Imprisonment and Torture, Capital Punishment or the Death Penalty, socialism and capitalism, the right to work and just wages, workers' unionism and strikes, the arms race and international relations, etc.

A network of Catholic Lawyers as you are, shall be an immensely useful tool in the dissemination and promotion of the moral, spiritual and social values contained in the Social Teachings of the Church. Such a network of men and women of faith and vision on the national level, by virtue of your professional training as custodians of the rule of law and your religious commitment to the spread of God's kingdom of justice and peace, shall be in a position to engage the leadership and the citizens in the civilised dialogue that must replace the disparate voices and discordant tunes that today make governance such a nightmare and peaceful co-existence such a tall dream.

There are many issues today in our country calling for the attention of such a network of legal professionals with a common faith, morality and value system. We are challenged today by the problem of ethnicism and the lack of any discernible sense of national cohesion, due in large measure to a perceived absence of protective instruments in the constitution of the country for various ethnic and interest groups. We have the problem of the *Sharia* that has been proclaimed as state law in an otherwise secular country. We are challenged that the most fundamental rights of Nigerians, such as the right to basic education and elementary healthcare are not justiciable. We have the problem of resource control and the overbearing nature of the central authority, whereas ours was meant to be a federation whose constituent units are not meant to be just outposts of the central body. We have the problem of citizenship, whereby Nigerians born and raised in many parts of this country are not considered citizens of such places because their ancestors were born elsewhere. We remain challenged by the injustice of the forceful take-over of schools established by voluntary agencies, and today we are face-to-face with the threat of the legalisation of abortion, which the Church clearly acknowledges as murder. Finally, there is the perennial problem of corruption, the lack of transparency in governance, the problem of militarism and the prevalence of a command culture, even after we claim to have done away with military rule.

These and more are legal and constitutional issues that require to be dealt with decisively and objectively; and perhaps no one is better placed to address them than a national network of committed lawyers, who are driven by passion for the common good. I welcome you all to this inaugural convention and pray that this National Association of Catholic Lawyers may provide for each one of you another opportunity to utilise your God-given talents for the benefit of your country and in the light of your Christian faith.

The foregoing has been by way of introduction to the subject which I hope you will find time today to reflect upon, that is: the role of Catholic Lawyers in their individual and collective capacities in the project of national rejuvenation, a rejuvenation that must come first in the form of a national moral awakening, then will follow the task of building a modern civil society that is governed by laws and regulations, and not the whims and caprices of the one in power. It is only after Nigerians have experienced rebirth on these foundational levels that we can begin to speak of a new political culture that will bring about a just, democratic and peaceful society.

You will agree with me that in the beginning God endowed us with a land that is richly blessed. Materially Nigeria overflows with natural resources. The country harbours a large and active population that includes very talented people that can match their peers anywhere in the world. With such men and material, God placed Nigeria strategically in a position of regional and global prominence for her to wield great influence, a position designed by the creator to bring not just prosperity and well-being for the country's population but prestige and respect from a world that appreciates God's goodness. Thus, at independence in 1960, God set this country on the path of greatness. Yet in the four decades since then, Nigeria seems to have been so afflicted by the demonic forces spawning the moral, spiritual and material scourges of the day that today the land is in dire need of the services of the exorcist.

The multiple impact of the moral decay and the many levels of social, political and economic malfeasance in the land has generated the widespread disillusionment, devastation and desolation, such as is portrayed by the sight of Ikeja Cantonment and Oke Afa canal in Lagos after we exploded high calibre bombs on our own citizens on January 27, 2002, or the Idi-Araba environment in Lagos after the ethnic mayhem of February 2, 2002 that left nearly 200 people dead and millions of naira worth of property destroyed, or even the ultra-modern market in Jos that only a few days ago was reduced to ashes. We are today living through death, with corpses littering our highways and street corners, unattended. We are indeed living death as we vacillate between military dictatorship and political banditry, with mercenaries, scavengers and dogs of power ensuring that in either case they remain relevant. Yes indeed, we are living through death, as we are murdered, maimed, harassed and intimidated by armed robbers, and the security of many Nigerians is now in the hands of such groups of bandits as the Bakassi Boys in the East or the O.P.C. in the West, who have the mandate to arrest, interrogate, convict, execute and incinerate the bodies of those who fall into their hands.

The book of Proverbs says that where there is no vision, the people do perish. And to the Romans St. Paul says that the wages of sin is death. He warns the Galatians: "Don't delude yourselves into thinking that God can be cheated; where a man sows, there he reaps; if he sows in the field of self-indulgence, he will get a harvest of corruption out of it" (Galatians 6:7-8). Those who have been wooing the angel of death by a lifestyle of corruption, oppression and injustice, shall pay for their prodigality, for as you lay your bed, so do you lie on it. The Fathers of the Second Vatican Council assert that all acts of indignity against human life and against the human person debase the perpetrators even more than the victims. So, the oracle of God is true that the harvest of sin is death.

The Nigerian problem appears at first sight to be very complicated and multifaceted. Perhaps a closer look will reveal that it is not that complex. The solution can be quite simple too. Enormous human and material resources have been expended on all sorts of experimentation and adventure in political engineering and economic reconstruction. But they have led us nowhere. Perhaps the simple solution to our problem is a return to the basics. Our political, economic and social structures, in as much as they are based on foundations of falsehood, selfishness, greed and injustice, can only lead to death. A return to the basics shall entail repentance from falsehood, selfishness, greed and injustice, and conversion to truth, love and justice.

As a corporate entity, we have been functioning along the path of death and destruction, and if we do not change our course, we are bound to end up where we are headed. The moment has come for us Nigerians to look critically at our past and honestly acknowledge the immense damage wrought by our individual and communal sins. We must have a rethink. We must make a change of course. However difficult the turn-around may be, we must act now, while the sun still shines over our heads. However challenging the call may be, we must make the move while the leaves are still green. We must act fast before we lose another generation of young people. So many of them are today condemned to an existence devoid of hope and meaning.

As a people we need a national reawakening. As a country we need a national reorientation. As a political entity we need to embark on a reprioritization of our value system. As a corporate body we need a rebirth if we must survive the violence and trauma of the moment. Christians call this process repentance or conversion. What Nigerian Christians, and Christian professionals such as yourselves must do now is to take the lead in this penitential revolution, trusting God who is rich in mercy and compassion, and there is no better time than now, the season of Lent, to begin the cleansing process.

Learned Gentlemen, the recent history of our country sufficiently demonstrates how the lack of knowledge can destroy a people. There is an acute shortage of vision, intellectual rigour and critical thinking even in our academic circles. What appears to have been in place is the cult of mediocrity expressed most pathetically in what we call the politics of the belly that sustains sycophancy and political prostitution in our land. It is the cult of mediocrity that makes professors of political science for whom democracy is supposed to be an article of faith, and legal luminaries who hold the title of "Senior Advocate of Nigeria," and who have sworn to defend the rule of law, to bow before ruthless feudal lords and callous despots. Many of those whom Nigerians looked up to for a sense of direction became praise singers and pall-bearers for despots, and propagandists for the the oppressors of the Nigerian people. Their action is a serious betrayal of their education and the mission they owe to succeeding generations of Nigerian.

In the face of this national embarrassment, Nigeria needs learned men (and women) who will liberate our people from bondage and open the way for justice and peace. We need Christian lawyers, endowed with the wisdom of the sage, equipped with the courage of the prophet, and propelled by the passion of a true nationalist, to make a powerful intervention now on behalf of the distressed people of our land. We need patriotic but fearless Catholic lawyers who will demonstrate to the men and women of this land that (in the words of Chinua Achebe in *The Trouble with Nigeria*) "a true patriot is one who cares deeply about the happiness and well-being of his country and all its people; not one who says he loves his country... A true patriot will always demand the highest standards of his country and accept nothing but the best for and from his people. He will be outspoken in condemnation of their shortcomings without giving way to superiority, despair or cynicism."

In this enormous task before you, learned gentlemen of the Catholic faith, you have the social teachings of the Catholic Church to guide and direct you. The fundamental principles for the struggle towards the building of a just, democratic and peaceful modern society where individual human beings are respected, and utmost attention is given to the common good, are to be found in this body of teaching. Please familiarize yourselves with the social teachings of the church and get working. May God bless you.

CHAPTER THIRTY- SEVEN

Building Peace through Justice, Love and Forgiveness
(Written on November 2, 2002)

Widespread Violence and Heightened Tension in Nigeria

After years of military dictatorship, the worst form of which was manifested in the Abacha dispensation, Nigerians had hoped for a period of peaceful transition to a just, equitable, democratic and prosperous society. We had hoped for a new Nigerian society where we can once again have the opportunity to channel our enormous natural endowments to positive use for the advancement of our teeming population. We had hoped for a new Nigerian society where we can celebrate the richness of our diverse languages, cultures and religions. We had hoped for a new Nigerian society where we can take our rightful place in the comity of nations and compete in the advancement of science and technology.

Three and a half years have gone by now but rather than make progress towards the realisation of our dreams, the Nigerian nation appears to be more fragmented than ever before. Three and a half years into our new democratic experiment, Nigerians as a people seem to be more divided than they ever were since independence. This tense and gloomy political scenario is further compounded by the violent crimes of armed robbery and hired assassinations that have become very rampant.

The divisions and the resultant tensions are played out every day in violent conflicts on the streets, in marketplaces and in neighbourhoods, as Nigerians hound their fellow citizens to death and set their properties on fire at the slightest provocation. They are often reflected on the floor of the state and national assemblies, where the honourable men and women sometimes need the anti-riot police to keep the peace. They are implied in the frosty relationship between the executive and the legislature, that has reached its climax in the ongoing impeachment saga, making the Nigerian brand of democracy look like an exercise in mutual acrimony, rather than the "government of the people by the people for the people."

The many conflicts that have plagued post-military Nigeria, sufficiently demonstrate that we have been sitting on a pile of explosives that are now exploding in every direction, and sadly, there is no end to these crises. It has been an orgy of violence: From the onslaughts of the angry Egbesu youths of the Niger Delta, to the atrocities of aggrieved OPC youths of the Southwest, and from the senseless killings among the Ife/Modakeke, Aguleri/Umuleri, Tiv/Jukun and Egbura/Bassa, to the crazy Sharia campaign in many parts of the North that has shaken the very foundation of the nation, it has been a season of blood and tears. Precious human lives have been destroyed in their thousands, and property worth hundreds of millions of Naira have been set ablaze. We have witnessed thousands of internally displaced persons or refugees squatting in police and army barracks all over the place.

As a result of these sad developments, the Nigerian economy remains comatose. Investors have been scared away, in spite of President Obasanjo's numerous overseas travels. With the circumstance of widespread violence and great insecurity in the land, potential investors seem to have decided to watch and see. Unemployment remains high and the mass of the people are plagued by acrimonious poverty, with the lot of many worsening by the day. Thus, three and a half years after we said goodbye to military dictatorship, we are witnessing what appears sadly as another round of aborted dreams, broken promises and dashed hopes. Once again, our leaders have failed to deliver, and we are once again being challenged to go to the drawing board.

The unfortunate turn of events in the last three and a half years surely brings to the fore the imperative of forgiveness as part of the dynamics of conflict resolution towards national reconciliation and peaceful co-existence. Perhaps the people of Nigeria along with their leaders had underestimated the extent of the problems that had built up in the land over the years of debauchery, when social injustice, economic isolation and political banditry reigned, breeding widespread anger and resentment that were kept in check all the while only by military might. With the violent conflicts that have erupted in the North and South, and in the East and West, over unresolved ethnic, religious, political and economic differences, and over boundaries and the ownership of land and other resources, Nigerians must now realise that there are a lot of structural defects in the Nigerian society that are a potential source of conflict. This is a challenge we must take up and address courageously.

Many in the Igbo nation remain resentful of the rest of Nigeria for the injustices of the 1967 to 1970 civil war, the abandoned property imbroglio, and the alleged post-war marginalisation of Igbo people in some vital segments of the national economy. Many in the Yoruba nation are angry with the rest of Nigeria for the injustices associated with the

June 12 election annulment, and the alleged post-June 12 persecution and marginalisation of Yoruba people. The collocation of small ethnic nationalities which we call the Middle Belt are today vexed by the appendage status accorded them in the power structures of our nation. Many of them allege that they have suffered numerous injustices because of being falsely associated with the North all this time, while they gained nothing from the Northern hold on political power.

The citizens of the oil producing Niger Delta are poised for a showdown with the rest of Nigeria, and if recent clashes are anything to go by, their youths appear to be well equipped for war with the rest of Nigeria, because of the callous exploitation of their natural resources for decade, while they are abandoned in a state of destitution. Many among the Hausa and Fulani Muslims of the core North who desire to live under the supremacy of the Islamic Sharia are incensed that the rest of Nigeria wants to jettison what they see as their religious freedom. Within each group, there is often bitterness over past hurts and wounds which have never been seriously addressed.

Christ's Radical Message of Love

The passage of Luke 6: 27-38 forms the climax of Jesus' teaching on the new order, the order of mercy, compassion and sacrificial love, by which he seeks to replace the old order of hatred, vengeance, and violence among men and women. He says:

> Love your enemies, do good to those who hate you, bless those who curse you, pray for those who persecute you. To the man who slaps you on one cheek, present the other cheek too; to the man who takes your cloak from you, do not refuse your tunic. Give to everyone who asks you, and do not ask for your property back from the man who robs you. Treat others as you would like them to treat you... If you love those who love you, what thanks can you expect? Even sinners love those who love them... Instead, love your enemies and do good, and lend without any hope of return. You will have a great reward, and you will be sons of the Most High, for he himself is kind to the ungrateful and the wicked... Be compassionate as your Father is compassionate...for the measure you give out is the measure you will receive.

With these directives of Jesus, we see a complete reversal of the old-accepted order in human behaviour. What is characteristic about

Christian ethics is not mere love, for all religions seem to preach love in one way or the other. What is unique about the Christian faith is that it calls its adherents to love the enemy! My enemies include those who hate me, those who speak evil of me; those who accuse me falsely, those who persecute me; those who criticise me, those who irritate me; those who are aggressive towards me by their manner of thinking and acting; those who persecute me or my group; those towards whom I have an aversion. People generally love their friends and hate or at least resent their enemies, and no one sees anything wrong with that. The Israelites were expected to love and be kind towards their neighbours (that is fellow Israelites), but they did not see any reason why such gestures should be extended to non-Israelites or Gentiles who were often at war with them. These others belonged to pagan nations which had at one time or the other killed their people, enslaved them, exiled them, or pillaged their land. Even among the Israelites, enemies were meant to be tolerated, and not loved. Offenders or aggressors were supposed to be given the same kind of treatment as they have given their victims.

So, the prevailing law was that of *an eye for an eye, and a tooth for a tooth*. So, asking that such offenders, aggressors or enemies be loved and be prayed for was a totally revolutionary idea that hardly had any basis in their history, except isolated cases as the encounter between the young David and king Saul. Saul meant to kill an innocent man David and was out in the wilderness with troops in search of him. But as it turned out, David who was fleeing from the king, found him and his men in deep sleep. He had the opportunity to kill Saul and be free. His companion said to him: "Today, God has put your enemy in your power; so now let me pin him to the ground with his own spear." But David answered: "Do not kill him, for who can lift his hand against the Lord's anointed and be without guilt?"

Jesus not only taught his disciples to love their enemies and pray for those who treat them badly, he lived and died that way himself. In his life, Jesus had to put the ethic of loving generosity into action, and this was a painful and bloody affair. It cost him everything. He offered his love, even though he knew that the response of the people would be rejection. His love was not a matter of social contract. He never bargained love for love. He never loved so that he may get love in return. He loved because that is his nature, the nature of God. He often always overwhelmed, confused and disarmed his enemies by the outpouring of his immense love. St. Paul reflects on the life and death of Jesus and declared that what shows the depth of God's love for humanity is that while we were yet sinners, Christ died for us (Romans 5:8). The unusual kindness and generosity Jesus showed his enemies is demonstrated in the fact that he healed one of the soldiers who had come to arrest him, and whose ear was chopped off by Peter. And while reeling in pain on the cross of Calvary, he prayed for his executioners. He forgave Simon Peter who had denied him three times and made the same man the head of his Apostles.

The question is: Do we as Christians take our cue from the treatment we receive from others, or do we live in accordance with our nature and the nature of our merciful, compassionate and generous Father in heaven? When faced with hate, and when we are hurt by those who do not know any other way of living except by wickedness and violence, do we react with the logic of "an eye for an eye, and a tooth for a tooth," or do we react as Christians who appreciate the dynamics of sacrificial love? Jesus teaches his disciples with his own life example never to be provoked into taking retaliatory action for wrongs done against them. Their response should always flow from the nature of their discipleship, and not from the wrong they have suffered.

The love the Christian gives people is not related to the love they receive from others. The disciple loves because love is the fundamental character of Christian discipleship. The disciple loves because he or she is the son or daughter of the heavenly father who is so gracious that he does not withhold the sun and the rain from those who oppose him. What Jesus asks his disciples to do is simply to imitate God – God who is merciful, compassionate, loving and forgiving. The old law prescribed that the Jews must love their neighbours and hate their enemies. But in asking Christians to love their enemies, Jesus rejects the limitation of love to only those in our immediate environment. No one is excluded from Christian love, not even the persecutor of the Christian faithful.

Christian life is a continual attempt to transcend the values and conventions that are regarded as absolute in the human society. Like Jesus, the true Christian necessarily subverts the established order, when he put love, mercy and compassion over and above the demands of mere distributive justice. The true Christian who strives to live out the logic of Christ will often be regarded as a fool or an eccentric. The true Christian takes seriously Christ's admonition to be compassionate. He or she knows that those who hate are in need. They are often living with broken and divided hearts. Those who hate are often living with the misery and agony of fragmented and unfulfilled lives. Like everyone in need therefore, the Christian is called upon to show compassion to such people, never judging and never condemning them.

The action of Christians who attempt to live like Jesus with such a generous heart towards the enemy or aggressor often merits scorn. They often appear foolish in the eyes of the world and those who have reconciled themselves with the evil status quo. But that is the only way to break the endless cycle of violence which crushes the human society. By following Jesus' teaching, the Christian as it were, steps outside the spiral of violence to live in a different way. True, hatred can only be defeated by love, not by counter-hatred. Injury can only be healed by forgiveness, not by vengeance. Evil can only be controlled by goodness, not by more evil, for darkness cannot drive away darkness. This is Jesus' wisdom, the wisdom by which he saved the world.

Jesus expects his disciples to generously share the gifts they have received. The Christian therefore offers love, because he or she has been a beneficiary of God's tremendous love, and now he must share it with other, irrespective of their own disposition. The Christian offers love because there is someone somewhere who is harassed by hatred and who needs love, even when the person does not realise his or her need. The Christian offers mercy and compassion because someone somewhere is crushed by wrongdoing. Love, mercy and compassion are gifts of God which create worth in another person. They build temples in the wasteland of hatred, violence and death. Love, mercy and compassion are gifts which introduce people to the forgotten geography of paradise. And they stop the contagion of a meaningless existence. Love creates its own reality. It creates its own force for goodness.

True, love does not always transform the enemy into a friend. Love did not transform Jesus' enemies into friends. He loved graciously, but he got killed in the process. Yet Jesus stuck to his logic of love, because he is the Son of God. Love is his way of life, and he will live it, no matter what or who appears in front of him. He will love, even when confronted with the worst enemy. Does this logic of Jesus mean that God accepts evil? No! Never! God has nothing to do with evil. God condemns evil, but he loves everyone, even the person who practices evil. He hates evil but loves the evil doer. This is the mystery of God love, mercy and compassion.

The Christian Imperative to Forgive

The God of Abraham, Isaac and Jacob, the father of Jesus Christ, is known as the God of mercy and compassion (2 Chron.30:9; Psalm 100:5; Psalm 111:4). He is a God who is rich in mercy; whose anger is for a while, but whose mercy is everlasting. The God we serve is so merciful that he sent his only son to die in our stead, so that we may no longer have to bear the full consequence of our sins (John 3:16). The God we serve allowed his Son to be killed, as an act of mercy and forgiveness, so that his kingdom of love and compassion, his kingdom of forgiveness and reconciliation, his kingdom of peace and happiness, might be established.

Having sacrificed himself for us, the Son of God made love, forgiveness, mercy, and compassion towards those who offend us as the "conditio sine qua non" for our admission into his kingdom. He says in Matthew 5:7 "Blessed are the merciful for they shall obtain mercy. In Luke 6:36 he says: "Be compassionate just as your heavenly father is compassionate..." He adds that "the measure you give out is the measure you will receive." Jesus told those who challenged his dining with sinners: "Go and learn what this means, 'I desire mercy and not sacrifice.' For I came not to call the righteous, but sinners" (Mt. 9:13).

While explaining the Lord's Prayer to his disciples, he says (In Mt. 6:19), "if you do not forgive your neighbour who sins against you, your heavenly father will not forgive you your own sins also." And in the parable of the unforgiving debtor, whose debts were cancelled when he pleaded with the master, but who dealt ruthlessly with his fellow servant, Jesus said: "that is how the heavenly father will deal with you unless you each forgive from your heart" (Matthew 18:35). The author of Ecclesiasticus puts it powerfully thus: Resentment and anger, these are foul things too, and a sinner is a master at them both. Whoever exacts vengeance will experience the vengeance of the Lord, who keeps strict account of sin. Pardon your neighbour any wrongs done to you, and when you pray , your sins will be forgiven. If anyone nurses anger against another, can such a person then demand compassion from the Lord? Mere creature of flesh, yet cherishing resentment - who will forgive one for sinning? (Ecclesiasticus 27:30-28:5). Thus, nursing anger or cherishing resentment is dangerous for our health and salvation. It disables us and renders us defenceless when we seek the forgiveness of our own sins.

In what we know as the golden rule, Jesus told us to do unto others what we would like them to do unto us (Matthew 7:12). Christians believe that to show mercy is to live out the truth of our lives: we can and must be merciful because mercy has been shown us by a God who is love (I Jn 4:7-12). We cannot earn God's forgiveness. It is a gratuitous gift. It flows from God's mercy and compassion. But we can lose it when we jealously hoard the blessings that God gives to us. We can lose God's forgiveness when we refuse to share with others the quality of mercy, compassion and forgiveness we ourselves have received. Indeed the person who does not forgive is one who has never really experienced God's forgiveness. Those who truly belong to the household of God both experience and dispense the love of God through compassion and forgiveness on daily basis.

We owe a debt to God that is infinitely much more than the debt our neighbour (or even our enemy) could ever owe us. This is why in Jesus' parable on forgiveness we find such a big difference between the ten thousand talents owed the king by his servant and the one hundred denarii owed by the servant to a fellow servant. With sovereign majesty Jesus shatters all human calculations about the number of times an offence is committed, etc, and urges us to put no limitation at all to our forgiveness. The imperative to forgive always is not motivated with arguments from sociology or from any legal or ethical code of conduct. It is motivated instead by God's loving forgiveness of which we ourselves are beneficiaries. And regarding the measure of forgiveness, we are told that God is capable of forgiving absolutely everything. The sum of evil accumulated in the world is beyond reckoning. But God, moved with compassion, forgives the entire debt, and he challenges beneficiaries of this forgiveness to go and do the same.

Many Christians often think that the greatest miracles are those concerning the multiplication of loaves and the feeding of five thousand people, the healing of the blind, the lame and the lepers, the casting out of evil spirits, etc. Christians often think that the greatest gifts of God are those related to the wonders of Pentecost - the fire of the Spirit, the gift of tongues, etc. We often forget that the greatest demonstration of God's power and presence often come in calm and quiet. The greatest wonder of God, that is, the greatest miracle for us Christians is the miracle of God's love in Christ, Christ who died for us while we were yet sinners (Rom.5:8). The most graphic demonstration of this wonder of God's love, mercy and compassion, is shown on the cross of Calvary when Jesus Christ looked and his executioners and prayed: "Father forgive them for they do not know what they do." And the greatest gift which Jesus has poured forth upon the Church is the one related to the forgiveness of sins. He says in Jn.20:22-23 "Receive the Holy Spirit, for those whose sins you forgive, they are forgiven. For those whose sins you retain, they are retained."

John Paul II's Passionate Plea for the Practice of Mercy and Forgiveness

Pope John Paul II says that the practice of forgiveness is the only guarantee for lasting peace. In the Encyclical *Dives in Misericordia* which could rightly be described as a theological treatise on the mystery of God's mercy, the pope observes that the greatest weakness of the world today is its lack of mercy. He says there is a growing sense of justice in the world, and the Church shares the ardent desires of those who hunger for a more just society. Nevertheless, experience shows that negative forces, such as spite, hatred, and even cruelty, have gained the upper hand over justice. He says: "It happens that in the name of justice the neighbour is sometimes destroyed, killed, deprived of liberty or stripped of fundamental rights." He then declares that the experience of the past and of our own time demonstrates that strict (distributive) justice, by which we give to each his or her due, is not going to guarantee peace for the human society. It can lead instead to the negation and destruction of the right (social) order.

If the deeper power of love, is not allowed to shape human life in its various dimensions, the mere pursuit of justice will not bring peace. The Pope then challenges the men and women of the world to go beyond strict distributive justice, to embrace love, which includes mercy, forgiveness and compassion. The Church he says must introduce the mystery of love to the world. The Church must promote the civilisation of love which includes mercy and forgiveness, for a world without forgiveness will be a cold world of endless tension, violence and strife (See *Dives in Misericordia*, 12-15).

The Holy Father's Message for the World Day of Prayer for Peace (January 1, 2002) deals with the issue of forgiveness and justice. Coming shortly after the terrible events of September 11, 2001, the reprisal bombardment of Afghanistan and the overwhelming threat of terrorist violence in the world, the pope reflected on how to restore the moral and social order that is subjected to such horrific violence. He then declared that "the pillars of true peace are justice and that form of love which is forgiveness. He pleaded with Christians and to all men and women of goodwill to see that there is "no peace without justice" and "no justice without forgiveness."

He said there is no contradiction between justice and forgiveness. They are not irreconcilable. Forgiveness is not the opposite of justice, as if to forgive meant to overlook the need to right the wrong done.

Instead, forgiveness is the opposite of resentment and revenge, not justice. He noted that true peace is the fruit of justice, but because human justice is always fragile and imperfect, subject as it is to the limitations and egoism of individuals and groups, it must include, and as it were, be completed by the forgiveness which heals and rebuilds troubled human relations from their foundations. Thus, justice and forgiveness are both essential to true healing and wholesome restoration.

The Pope admitted that forgiveness is not a proposal that can be immediately understood or easily accepted. Instead, he said, it is a paradoxical message. He explained the paradox this way:

Forgiveness in fact always involves an apparent short-term loss, for a real long-term gain. Violence is the exact opposite; opting as it does, for a short-term gain, it involves a real and permanent loss. Forgiveness may seem like weakness, but it demands great spiritual strength and moral courage, both granting it and accepting it. It may seem in some way to diminish us, but in fact it leads us to a fuller and richer humanity, more radiant with the splendour of the Creator (See *L'OSSERVATORE ROMANO, 19/26 December 2001).*

During the Jubilee Year the Pope gave the world an example by asking for pardon for the past hurts and wounds caused by people who acted on behalf of the Church in its 2000-year history. He also on behalf of every Catholic offered forgiveness for all the injustices the Catholic Church and its functionaries have suffered from others over the ages.

True, if there is one gift of God the world so dearly needs in our day, plagued as it is by civil wars, religious and ethnic violence, social strife, violent crimes, and long-standing resentment, it is the gift of mercy, compassion and forgiveness. I agree with John Paul II that a world of revenge where each offender is punished according to his or her offence, will be a cold world of constant strife. Instead what we need is forgiveness. For it is only over the bridges of forgetful forgiveness that humankind will be brought together under the reign of the one merciful God. It is only through forgiveness that the perennial tension and sporadic violence between the Yoruba and the Hausa, the Igbo and the Yoruba, the Hausa and the Igbo, the Aguleri and the Umuleri, the Ijaw and the Itsekiri, the Modakeke and the Ife, the Tiv and the Jukun, etc, can be permanently overcome.

It is only through forgiveness that exploiters and the exploited, that plunderers and the plundered, and that oppressors and the oppressed in the world and in our land can be fully reconciled. It is only through forgiveness that warring brothers of Anambra and Taraba states, and the fighting sisters of Oyo and Osun states can be brought together as children of one household of God. It is only through forgiveness that warring husbands and wives and the fighting mothers-in-law and daughters-in-law can once again know peace. It is only through the generous exercise of mercy, compassion and forgiveness that our fragmented national polity and global society will be finally reconciled, and lasting peace, unity, security and prosperity restored. For if we continue with the jungle law of responding to evil with evil, when will the circle of violence in which we are now held hostage ever end? If we respond to evil with evil, where will evil ever stop?

No doubt mercy and forgiveness are among the most fundamental values of the civilisation of love launched by Jesus Christ. Those who wish to be identified as Christians must take time out to think about this and begin to practice forgiveness, otherwise, on the last day they may be told: "I do not know you, go away from me you wicked men."

Conclusion: The Challenge before Christian Leaders

The true Christian believes that evil does not have the last word in human history. The true Christian believes that God knows how to transform all things unto good, and how to touch even the most hardened of hearts and bring good fruits from what seems utterly barren soil. The true Christian believer has no doubt in his or her mind that mercy and forgiveness are among the most fundamental values of Christ's civilisation of love. The true Christian believer acknowledges that with the virtue of forgiveness, past hurts and wounds, and bitterness and resentment over such hurts and wounds, could be adequately healed, and wholesome human relationships can once again begin afresh.

However, the challenge of forgiveness is not only for Christians, but also for all peace-seeking men and women. It is a challenge that Nigerians must quickly summon the courage and take up, before the country collapses under the burden of long-standing mutual antipathy, divisions and violent conflicts. Individuals are in need of forgiveness. Families are in need of forgiveness. Ethnic groups are in need of forgiveness. Religious groups are in need of forgiveness. States too are also in need of forgiveness.

With so many un-addressed wounds and hurts over past injustices and inequities (as narrated above), our task of nation building must begin with an elaborate programme of, and an honest commitment to the building of a peaceful society through the preaching of justice and forgiveness. We must be resolutely committed to this task, or else our new preoccupation with democratic governance will lack the much-needed foundation, and end once again in disaster. The Christian Church in Nigeria must learn to feel the pulse of the nation, to hear the cry of the people, and to react with utmost sense of responsibility. We must be united in preaching the message of unity and peace that is based on mutual forgiveness for past hurts and wounds, and a mutual commitment to righting the wrongs of the past and building our society on justice and fairness.

In our kind of circumstances, the marriage of justice and mercy may not be an easy task. But Christian leaders are the ones to champion this noble cause. We must play the role of sentries, visionaries and dreamers even as the dominant culture pursues the culture of death and destruction. We must urge everyone to do an examination of conscience; to courageously address the hurts and wounds of the past; to offer forgiveness for these hurts and wounds; and to ask for forgiveness for those injustices which they have caused others. We must urge everyone to let justice and fairness, sustained by love and mutual respect, be the foundation of the peace we desire.

CHAPTER THIRTY-EIGHT

John Paul II: Hope in a Dying World
(Written on July 24, 2003)

IT was a major landmark in the history of ecumenism and inter-religious dialogue when on Sunday, May 6, 2001, His Holiness, Pope John Paul II took off his shoes and entered the Umayyad Mosque in Damascus, Syria, where he spent some time in silent prayer, thus becoming the first Pope to enter a Mosque in the 1400 years of the existence of Islam.

Addressing Islamic leaders, including the Grand Mufti of Syria, the Pope said that "we need to seek forgiveness from the Almighty and offer each other forgiveness, for all the times that Muslims and Christians have offended one another." He made a passionate appeal against religious fundamentalism from any side, insisting that "religious conviction was never a justification for violence." Violence, he said, destroys the image of the Creator and should never be considered as the fruit of religious conviction. Conflict in the name of religion is a terrible contradiction and a great offence against God. He said it is crucial for the young to be taught the way of respect and understanding, so they will not be led to misuse religion itself to promote or justify hatred and violence. He called on Christians, Muslims and Jews in the Middle East to take bold action to bring about peace in their region.

The Umayyad Mosque, one of the most precious historical monuments in Syria, which began as a pagan temple, was converted to a church in honour of St. John the Baptist in the 4th century when Christianity became the religion of the Roman Empire, and again became a Mosque when the Arabs conquered Damascus in AD 639. As the Pope took this unprecedented step, many Christians were shocked and perplexed. Some were scandalised or even repulsed. Others simply marvelled at such a great feat achieved by this enigmatic personality, who in the twenty-three years of his papacy has constantly plunged himself into deep dreaded waters, and scaled impossible heights, such that some observers say that John Paul II does not let history happen, he directs it!

Pope John Paul II, whose real name is Karol Wojtyla, was born of Polish parents and raised under Communist repressive rule, a man of unusual intelligence and charisma; he was professor of Social Ethics and Moral Theology at the University of Lublin and Archbishop of Krakow. Upon the death of Pope Paul VI, and shortly after, Pope John Paul I in 1978, Karol Wojtyla was elected Pope on October 16, 1978, assuming the name John Paul II. He became the first non-Italian Pope in 450 years and brought into the Catholic Church an impressive degree of dynamism.

Known widely as "the Pilgrim Pope," John Paul II visited and kissed the soil of more or less 130 countries, including some of the most troublesome spots in the world. In most of the countries visited, the Pope addressed not only Catholics but also non-Catholics and adherents of other world religions, including Islam, Buddhism and Hinduism. He took on the world and the issues of reconciliation and peace with a rare sense of mission and urgency. Some of the greatest records he set as Pope are indeed in the area of Ecumenism and Dialogue with non-Christian religions. In 1985 (as he entered the Synagogue of Rome), he became the first Pope ever to set his foot in a Jewish Synagogue. He has since then revolutionised ties with the Jews, with the Vatican restoring diplomatic relations with Israel in December 1993.

In 1986 John Paul II called a meeting of leaders of all the major religions in the world to pray for global peace. The event took place on October 27 1986, in Assisi, the birthplace of St. Francis, who distinguished himself as a universal peacemaker in the 12th/13th century when blood flowed freely in Europe at the hands of Christian crusaders and Islamic jihadists. World religious leaders responded to his invitation enthusiastically, and history was made, when under the leadership of the Pope, Roman Catholics and Orthodox Christians, Lutherans and Reformed Protestants, Jews and Muslims, Hindus and Buddhists, as well as leaders of other religions from across the globe, all interacted freely and begged God in their various ways, for the gift of peace in the world and among all people. No one could have imagined such a meeting taking place a few years before. It was one of the miracles performed at the hands of John Paul II.

As part of the fruits of the above kind of encounter, Venerable Master Hsing Yun, the leader of a global Buddhist organisation with headquarters in Taiwan, had the first-ever audience with the Pope in March 1997 to discuss Catholic-Buddhist ties. The main point of the meeting was to get Catholics and Buddhists to work together for world peace and to find the means to actualise this goal. Also, following the example of the Pope, the New York-based Council for Religion and

Peace acting under the auspices of the United Nations hosted (August 27 – September 5, 2000) a Conference on Religion and Peace to which major religious leaders from across the world were invited. The event was also a rousing success.

The Pope takes personal responsibility for uniting all people, not just Catholics or Christians. Responding to questions in his book, *Crossing the Threshold of Hope*, published in 1994, he says: "From the beginning, Christian revelation has viewed the spiritual history of man as including in some way all religions, thereby demonstrating the unity of humankind with regard to the eternal and ultimate destiny of man." He believes that "there is only one community, and it consists of all people."

In the Great Jubilee Year 2000, John Paul II went to the Holy Land on pilgrimage. On Sunday, March 26 of that year, the Pope was present as a symbol of unity in Jerusalem, a city torn by centuries of religious turmoil, a city that has played host to (Jewish) Zionists, (Islamic) Jihadists, and (Christian) Crusaders. His pilgrimage to the Holy Land was aimed at fostering a new relationship between people who have common religious roots. While there, he proclaimed his message of reconciliation and peace and gave powerful witness to unity by visiting in one single day the Wailing Wall, the Church of the Holy Sepulchre and the Al Aqsa Mosque. He joined Jewish pilgrims to pray at the Wailing Wall, and in a piece of paper he lodged at the Wall (as is the practice of Jewish pilgrims), the Pope wrote: "God of our fathers, you chose Abraham and his descendants to bring your name to the nations. We are deeply saddened by the behaviour of those who in the course of history have caused these children of yours to suffer, and asking your forgiveness, we wish to commit ourselves to genuine brotherhood with the people of the covenant."

He also visited the Yad Vashem, a memorial erected for the six million victims of the Jewish Holocaust. He said there were no words strong enough to deplore the event, which he blamed on a "Godless ideology." He then assured the Jewish people that "the Catholic Church is deeply saddened by the hatred, acts of persecution and display of anti-Semitism directed against the Jews by Christians at any time and in any place." Israeli Chief Rabbi said, as he came out to welcome the Pope: "We welcome one who saw it fit to express remorse in the name of the Catholic Church for the terrible deeds committed against the Jewish people during the course of the past 2000 years." And Ehud Barak, former Prime Minister of Israel, was so overwhelmed by the many conciliatory gestures of the Pope that he himself declared that John Paul

II had done more than anyone else to bring about historical changes in the attitude of the Church towards the Jewish people and to dress the gaping wounds that festered over many bitter centuries. True, the Pope did more than his predecessors to heal the rift between Jews and Christians after centuries of hostility.

With regard to those in the Christian fold, the Pope saw himself as the first servant of unity who must ensure the communion of all the Churches. He thus broke a number of historical taboos, such as the ones that nurtured and sustained the conflicts and tension that existed between Christian Churches of different denominations for hundreds of years. He stretched out a hand of fellowship to the Christian Churches and Ecclesial communities of Eastern and Western Europe who severed relationship with the Church of Rome at various points of history – the Church of Assyria in the 5th century AD, the Church of Constantinople in 11th century AD, and the Churches of the Reformation in the 16th century AD.

It should be noted that in the course of the Second Vatican Council, an event took place that is fundamental to the project and process of ecumenism. On December 7, 1965, the Church of Rome and the Ecumenical Patriarchate of Constantinople resolved to "condemn to oblivion" and to "remove from the heart of the Church" the memory of the mutual excommunication between Patriarch Cerularius of Constantinople (who represented the East) and Cardinal Humbert of Silva Candida (who represented the West) in the year 1054. This event marked the transition from the era of "excommunication" to the era of "fraternal dialogue," and this dialogue with the Orthodox Churches has grown ever more fruitful since then.

Long before the major schism of AD 1054, the Assyrian Church of the East had been separated from the rest of the Catholic Church over differences in the conception of the humanity and divinity of Christ. It occurred after the Council of Ephesus in AD 451, and the Assyrian Church had existed separately, having no relationship with the Catholic Church since then. But as a result of the powerful initiatives in the ecumenism of over thirty-five years, this early rift was mended to an appreciable extent. On November 11, 1994, Pope John Paul II and Patriarch Dinkha of the Assyrian Church of the East brought a formal end to the division (which existed between the Catholic Church and the Assyrian Church of the East for 1500 years) when they signed a common Christological Declaration, agreeing that "Our Lord Jesus Christ is true God and true man, perfect in his divinity and perfect in his humanity."

Two days before John Paul II's celebrated visit to the Mosque in Damascus, he was in Athens, Greece, where he met with Archbishop Christodoulos, Orthodox Patriarch of Athens and all Greece. This was the first visit by the head of the Roman Church since the Church of Constantinople severed its relationship with the Roman Church in AD 1054. On this occasion, the Pope emphasised the need for Christians of the East and West to be united. He prayed for God's forgiveness for the occasions, past and present when sons and daughters of the Catholic Church sinned by action or omission against their Orthodox brothers and sisters. While calling for the purification of memory, he noted that some memories are especially painful, and some events of the distant past have left deep wounds, an example of which is "the sacking of the imperial city of Constantinople."

The Great Jubilee Year 2000, whose celebration John Paul II proclaimed in November 1994, and which the Catholic Church worldwide took at least three years to make elaborate spiritual, pastoral and social preparations for, was to be among other features, a year of Repentance, Forgiveness, Healing, Reconciliation and Celebration. The Jubilee Year was to witness wide-ranging ecumenical initiatives. In the preparatory document for the celebration, *Tertio Millennio Adveniente* (As the Third Millennium Approaches), the Pope urged Catholics everywhere to take the challenge of Ecumenism seriously within the context of a new evangelisation, and work hard to see that the prayer of Jesus for his disciples in John 17:21 "that they may be one," will come to pass in the new millennium.

In 1995 John Paul II issued an encyclical letter dedicated entirely to the Church's commitment to ecumenism. With the title "Ut Unum Sint" (That They May Be One), the encyclical chronicles with a sense of gratitude to God the church's efforts at, and achievements in ecumenism and inter-religious dialogue since the Second Vatican Council, declaring that the Church is irreversibly committed to it. The Vatican Council indeed marks a watershed in the Church's commitment to ecumenism and inter-religious dialogue, with its landmark "Decree on Ecumenism" (*Unitatis Redintegratio*) and Declaration on Religious Freedom *(Dignitatis Humanae)* which provided the conceptual framework and set the impetus for the Catholic Church's relations with other Churches and other Religions. Since the Council, two major departments have emerged at the Vatican. They are the Pontifical Council for Promoting Christian Unity, then headed by Cardinal Cassidy, and the Secretariat for relations with

Non-Christian Religions, with Nigeria's Cardinal Arinze as head and Father (now Bishop) Matthew Kukah as one of its consultants.

Following the landmark achievements of the Second Vatican Council, the Catholic Church has also initiated a number of bilateral and multi-lateral dialogue commissions that are charged with the task of studying the theological differences that led to or have arisen since the separation of the Churches. Foremost among these dialogue commissions is the Anglican-Roman Catholic International Commission, which was established in 1970. The leadership of the Anglican Communion has shown the greatest cooperation in the project of ecumenism.

It will be recalled that on his way to the Holy Land in 1960, Archbishop Geoffrey Fisher of Canterbury stopped over in Rome to see Pope John XXIII. This encounter inspired the eventual establishment of the Council for Promoting Christian Unity. Relations between the Catholic Church and the Anglican Communion have steadily improved since then. A major achievement has been that in 1998 the Anglican-Roman Catholic International Commission approved a statement on how authority, including that of the Pope should be used in the Church. The title of the document is "The Gift of Authority."

Also, in November 1999, Lutherans and Catholics took a historic step in the process of ecumenism when they signed a Joint Declaration on the doctrine of justification at the Augsburg Cathedral. By the signing of this declaration, they removed their mutual condemnation over theological differences that date back to the reformation. Shortly after, and for the first time since the Reformation, theologians of the Catholic Church and those of the Lutheran and Reformed Protestant Churches debated the question of indulgence together. Indulgence is one of the issues that have divided the Church since Martin Luther's day. Theologians that took part in the study included representatives of the Pontifical Council for Promoting Christian Unity; the Lutheran World Federation, and the World Alliance of Reformed Churches. The study session was held in Rome at the invitation of the Vatican. When in March 2001, a group of Presbyterian Church leaders from the United States visited the Pope in Rome, he told them that their visit was "indeed a cause of great joy," because "it confirms our commitment to work for full Christian unity as we await His return in glory."

In "Ut Unum Sint" John Paul II insists that ecumenism is a priority project for the Church and "not just a sort of 'appendix.' He advanced three major reasons for the Church's commitment to ecumenism or the unity of Christ's faithful everywhere. First of all he said, "the Church must be obedient to Christ's prayer that his disciples may be one, living in communion." All Christians must be submissive to Christ's prayer for unity. To believe in Christ means to desire unity. Second, as a result of the Second Vatican Council's reading of the "signs of the times," an explicit mandate was given that the Catholic Church should follow the path of the ecumenical venture and pursue the project irrevocably. Third, division among Christian believers is a great scandal. It seriously damages the credibility of their testimony before the world.

Therefore, given the gravity of the Church's duty to foster Christian unity, John Paul II declared in the document that "the ecumenical task is one of the pastoral priorities of my Pontificate." He believed that "there are some things so urgent and so serious that they cannot be put off until tomorrow," The task of Christian unity is one of such things. He was convinced that the unity in the faith which he sought for the Christian Church is compatible with a diversity of expressions, in line with the example of the leaders of the early Church, who, acting under the influence of the Holy Spirit, resolved "not to impose any burden beyond that which is strictly necessary" (Acts 15:28-29).

On January 12, 2000, John Paul II opened the Jubilee Holy Door in the Basilica of St. Paul Outside the Walls, and solemnly walked through the door into the Basilica, accompanied by twenty-two leaders of different Christian Churches and Ecclesial Communities, including Archbishop George Carey of Canterbury, of the Anglican Communion, and Archbishop Athanasios of Heliopolis and Thera, who represented Archbishop Bartholomew I, Ecumenical Patriarch of Constantinople, and head of all Orthodox Churches. This event is unprecedented in the history of the Christian Church. In an address on this unique occasion, the Pope described the division among Christians as a grave scandal. He asked God to forgive all the sins committed by sons and daughters of the Church, which have compromised God's plan of unity for the Church.

On January 25, 2001, the Pope once again brought together representatives of all Christian Churches and Ecclesial Communities for an ecumenical celebration of the Word, at the close of the International Week of Prayer for Christian Unity. It was held once again at the Basilica of St. Paul Outside the Walls. As many as twenty-three different Christian bodies sent high ranking delegates to participate in the ecumenical celebration. Those represented include the Ecumenical Patriarchate of Constantinople, the Greek Orthodox Church, the Coptic Orthodox Patriarchate of Alexandria, the Orthodox Patriarchate of

Ethiopia, the Syrian Orthodox Patriarchate of Antioch, the Armenian Apostolic Church (of Armenia), the Assyrian Church of the East, the Anglican Communion, the Lutheran World Federation, the World Alliance of Reformed Churches, the World Methodist Council, the Baptist World Alliance, and the World Council of Churches.

On that occasion, the Pope noted that after centuries of separation, misunderstanding, indifference and conflict, there had been a rebirth among Christians in recent times of the realisation that faith in Christ unites them and that this faith is a force capable of overcoming all that separates them. He said that from being far apart and often adversaries, "we have grown closer and become friends. We have rediscovered Christian brotherhood. We know that our baptism incorporates us into the one Body of Christ, in communion that, while not yet full, is nonetheless real."

John Paul II observed that we were hostile and divided; we condemned and fought one another in the second millennium. He said now we must forget the shadow and the wounds of the past and strain forward towards the coming hour of God (Phil 3:13). Leaving behind distrust, the Pope said, "we must meet, know one another better, learn to love one another, and work together fraternally as much as possible." He said it is not up to us to create unity. Unity is the Lord's gift. And so, we must pray for unity. "Prayer for unity is the soul of the whole ecumenical movement. One of the fruits of the ecumenical movement, which the Pope noted with delight on this occasion, is the fact that in 2001, all Christians (from the East and West), were to celebrate Christ's resurrection (Easter) on the same day. This was never the practice since the separation of the Churches.

At a Mass in St. Peter's Basilica, during which rings were presented to 44 newly created Cardinals on February 22, 2001, John Paul II suggested that the role of the Papacy may need to be changed in the future in order to improve ties with other Christian Churches. He charged the new Cardinals to work and pray for the goal of reaching Christian unity in the new millennium that has just started. He said Christians had to return to the unity of the first millennium before Christianity was split by the East-West Schism of the 11th century and the Protestant Reformation of the 16th century. Then he said: "I would like today along with you, to pray to the Lord in a special way, so that the new millennium into which we have entered shall soon see the overcoming of this situation and the recovery of full communion."

The foregoing has been an overview of the initiatives of the leadership of the Catholic Church in Ecumenism and inter-religious dialogue on the international level for over thirty-five years and counting. It has been a chronicle of success, sustained in over twenty-two years by the Spirit of God and the rare courage, vision and charisma of John Paul II, who referred to himself as the first servant of unity. The Catholic Bishops' Conference of Nigeria, following these initiatives of the Pope with keen interest, called for the setting up of a dialogue commission on the national level that will work towards greater ties with the Anglican Church. An initial meeting took place, and modalities were worked out. A similar project with the Methodist Church of Nigeria was contemplated. Of course, in Nigeria, we already have the Christian Association of Nigeria, whose primary objective is to foster unity in the Christian Church. Over the years, Christian leaders of different denominations have acted together under the umbrella of CAN. Though there were initial hitches, some progress has now been made in the construction of the Ecumenical Centre in Abuja, a project jointly financed by the member Churches of CAN.

But on the whole, John Paul II was light years ahead in the project of ecumenism and inter-religious dialogue. For while the Pope was having sleepless nights agonising over the scandal of division in the Christian Church worldwide, and while he was breaking new grounds every day in the project of ecumenism which he viewed with a great sense of urgency and seriousness, Christian Churches in Nigeria are often tearing each other apart, and violating the principles that make for reconciliation and unity.

John Paul II is indeed very far ahead, for while he along with his Cardinals were offering apologies and doing penance for the sins of the sons and daughters of the Church, which are seen as partly responsible for the rift, the schism and the division experienced in the 5th, 11th and 16th century Christianity, we here in Nigeria, seem to be daily violating the integrity of Christ's Body, fragmenting and balkanising that One Body of Christ, with the registration of ever more new Christian Churches and denominations that are often professing disparate beliefs and conducting discordant liturgies.

We are truly lagging behind the Pope in these matters. For while the bilateral and multi-lateral dialogue commissions such as the Anglican-Roman Catholic International Commission, and the Lutheran-Roman Catholic International Commission are working hard towards a common understanding in matters of doctrine, morals and Church structures, in view of an eventual unity, Nigeria seems to be harbouring many new Church founders who appear totally oblivious of Christ's desperate prayer in John 17 "that they may be one."

It is most ironic that as we watched the Pope take up the challenge of being the servant of unity for the human race, gathering together all men and women who recognise God as Creator, forging the much-needed solidarity between Orthodox Christians and Catholics, Reformed Protestants and Lutherans, Jews and Muslims, Buddhists and Hindus, today in Nigeria many people are victims of religious oppression, as fundamentalists and extremists and power-seeking politicians continue to manipulate religious sentiments for selfish ends, causing violence and doing much harm to the psyche of young people.

As the *Sharia* zealots seem to be having a field day in Gusau, Kano, Katsina and Minna, denying Christians the right to build Churches and worship freely, condemning women involved in adultery to death by stoning, and violating the fundamental rights of non-Muslims in many other ways, Pope John Paul II presented himself as the greatest sign of contradiction for our times, the hope of a dying world.

CHAPTER THIRTY-NINE

Politics and the Manipulation of Religion in Nigeria
(Written on September 15, 2003)

Religion features at the very beginning of our nation's constitution. In the preamble to the 1999 Nigerian constitution, it is affirmed that we intend to live together as one united country under God. Indeed, the overwhelming majority of Nigerians are religious people. We believe in the supremacy of God. We believe that God is the very basis of our individual lives and our corporate existence. We believe in and relate with supernatural realities through prayers and supplications and through the offering of sacrifices. We find churches, mosques, shrines and sundry prayer houses everywhere in the land. We take part in crusades, worship sessions and vigils; we offer sacrifices and observe fasting days and religious holidays; and we go in large number on religious pilgrimages to Jerusalem and Mecca, taking pride in being called Jerusalem Pilgrim (JP) or Alhaji the rest of our lives.

While there is noticeable decline in religious fervour in many parts of the world, the religious enterprise appears to be thriving very much in Nigeria, as more and more company warehouses and private buildings are being converted to prayer houses, and our sports stadia all over the country are being used more for religious crusades than for sporting events. Streets within our towns and villages, as well as inter-state highways are often blocked these days by enthusiastic worshippers who flock to churches and camp meetings. In many of our urban areas, there are as many churches and mosques as there are streets! In an article that appeared last year in New York Times (March 13, 2002), the writer, one Norimitsu Onishi noted that "Christianity is growing faster in sub-Saharan Africa than in any other place on earth. Roman Catholicism and the major protestant denominations are gaining more followers every day, but new churches are leading the boom."

In the last few years, a new dimension has also been added to the thriving religious enterprise. It is the increased patronage of high-ranking public officials who not only openly call for and sponsor regular prayers sessions in different prayer houses but have themselves become born-again Christians and prayer merchants, often appearing at church crusades and prayer vigils with all the paraphernalia of public office, and sometimes grabbing the microphone to deliver sanctimonious homilies and earth-shaking prayers. At the end of last year, the Christmas carol service at the state house chapel in Abuja, which lasted several hours, was televised live on national television. And to usher in the New Year, Governor Ahmed Tinubu, himself a Muslim, had the Christian chapel he built in the Lagos state house dedicated with much religious fanfare. This gesture paid off for him, as many Christians contributed their votes to see that Tinubu retained the governorship at the April 19, 2003, elections.

President Obasanjo and a number of Christian governors have thriving chapels at the State House where prayer meetings, morning devotions, night vigils and praise worship sessions are regularly held to storm heaven and intercede for the nation and its leaders. There are palace prophets and priests who are engaged full time at the state house chapels to pray for the chief executive, drive demons away from him, to curse or call for fire and brimstone over the enemies of progress who may be making life difficult for the chief executive who God has anointed over his people. The palace prophets often lose sight of any prophetic dimension to their ministry, and become part and parcel of the regime, prodding the leader on, and assuring him that all shall be well, even when the rest of us can see that he is sitting on a pack of cards.

These days, prayer and preaching sessions are no longer limited to churches, mosques and homes. They are held at corporate boardrooms, in government offices, in commercial buses and in open markets. Nigerians going about their daily business can be seen brandishing the Bible or the Koran, the Rosary or Islamic prayer beads. The largest billboards in our towns and cities are those advertising upcoming religious crusades and faith healing carnivals. Religious exclamations such as "to God be the glory," "praise the Lord," and "Allahu Akbar," are often on the lips of Nigerians, at work or at play - from the exalted members of the National Executive Council or Council of State to the young ones who are about to sit Common Entrance examination. Thus, Nigerians are a chronically religious people. The whole environment is awash with religiosity. No wonder today's leaders have found it so easy to manipulate religion for political gains. While many critical Nigerians today see Obasanjo as a callous, vindictive and power-drunk dictator who was ready to compromise every principle in the book to stay put in power, he proclaims himself as a born-again Christian, and many Christian pastors have been dancing around him and proclaiming him as the messiah God has sent to save this country from disintegration.

While anti-corruption crusaders have accused many prominent politicians, including Senate President Pius Anyim of corrupt enrichment, these same politicians were always welcome at major Pentecostal Crusades where they often mounted the rostrum and took over the preaching from the pastor. Critical social commentators might have considered former Minister of Information, Professor Jerry Gana a shallow propagandist who was always available to do the dirty job for President Obasanjo, but he was a high-level minister in his church, and he justified everything he did with the fact that he was acting for God. And Governor Nnamani is alleged to be killing his people every day, but he appears on TV with the slogan "to God be the glory." The list of born-again Christians in government is endless. Yet Nigerian politics is dirty, and the environment stinks with corruption. Is what we have simply the manipulation of religion for political ends?

CHAPTER FORTY

Mother Teresa: A Challenge for Nigerians
(Written on Oct. 24, 2003)

ON Sunday, October 19, 2003, the whole world stood still in reverence of the diminutive Catholic nun, Mother Teresa of Calcutta, as she was beatified by Pope John Paul II before a capacity crowd of over 300,000 people from all parts of the world, which cut across religious and ethnic barriers. It was a similar situation when on September 13, 1997, this little nun of frail and fragile frame who served humanity in the simple life of charity, compassion, love and peace, was buried.

Coming just six years after her death, the beatification of Mother Teresa was one of the fastest in the history of the Catholic Church, which otherwise has a rigorous process in place for the cause of saints. However, to the outside world, the beatification ritual of the Catholic Church in respect of Mother Teresa was a mere formality. This small and fragile woman with a large heart who devoted the whole of her life to the service of humanity in the poor, the downtrodden, the sick and outcast and the unwanted child had attained sainthood even while alive. Hence, the beatification process as a prelude to her official recognition as a saint by the Catholic Church was considered an unnecessary ritual.

A remarkable dimension to Mother Teresa's beatification was the simultaneous celebration of the event by the people of Calcutta whose lives she most profoundly impacted upon while living. Thousands of Indians (including Christians, Muslims, Hindus, Buddhists, Sikhs, and those who do not profess any of the major faiths) came together to light candles in honour of the revered mother of the poorest of the poor who, before her beatification, they had already proclaimed as their saint.

Mother Teresa, whose real name is Sister Agnes Bojaxhiu, was born on August 26, 1910, in Skopje in Albania. The youngest of the six children of her parents, Nikola and Drane Bojaxhiu, her passion, desire and love for the underprivileged started blossoming at an early age. At 18, young Agnes joined the Institute of the Blessed Virgin Mary, also known as the Sisters of Loreto, in Ireland, where she received the name, Sister Teresa. She had her first profession of vows of poverty, chastity and obedience in 1931 and her final profession on May 24, 1937. She heard of the dehumanising poverty that is the plight of many in India and sought the permission of her superiors to move there and lend a helping hand.

By 1949 she had established a presence as a servant among the poorest of the poor and the lowest of the castes in India. On October 7, 1950, she founded the Missionaries of Charity (a congregation of young women willing to serve the poor) in Calcutta. This woman of great heroic virtues spent 49 of her 87 years on earth serving God in humanity by feeding the hungry, attending to the wounded, welcoming strangers, providing succour for the abandoned, comforting the dying and saving innocent babies. She saw the face of Christ in the wretched of the earth and ministered to these people as she would Christ. Information about Mother Teresa's compassionate work among the poor of India quickly spread throughout the world. The number of young women willing to follow her example also grew speedily, such that by the time of her death in 1997, the Missionaries of Charity had over 6,000 members working among the poor in 123 countries, including Nigeria.

By her life of simplicity in the service of humanity; through the common chores of daily life, Mother Teresa bequeathed a powerful legacy to the men and women of the world that are often so preoccupied with the struggle for power and prestige in the process of which many weak and lowly people are crushed. In recognition of her meritorious life, Mother Teresa got several awards from different organisations and countries all over the world, beginning with the Indian Padmashri Award in 1962 and culminating in the Nobel Peace Prize award in 1979. Her sobriquets include "Saint of the Gutters," "Friend of the Friendless" and "Angel of Mercy." Mother Teresa's passion for and close identification with the poor were played out for all to see by authorities in the Vatican when during her beatification ceremony last Sunday, the priority seats (of honour) at St. Peter's Square were given to lepers, the handicapped and other categories of poor people, instead of the dignitaries that flew in from various countries.

Congratulations to Pope John Paul II, the entire Catholic world and particularly her sisters, the Missionaries of Charity, for such a celebration of the successful life of one of their own, Mother Teresa of Calcutta. As the world honours this human symbol of altruism, her exemplary life provides wholesome food for thought for all Nigerians in our public and private lives. Today in our country, there exists many who are destitute on our roads and in our gutters; many sick people who are denied treatment; thousands of men, women and children groaning under the pangs of hunger and lack of shelter; scores of emaciated children roaming our streets begging or running dangerously after moving vehicles in an attempt to sell miserable wares; and several others deprived of justice, equity, peace and love. Many are dying daily not because of their own fault but as a result of a socio-political system bedevilled by corruption, injustice, manipulation, intrigue and hatred.

While the majority of Nigerians are suffering and in dire need of a Mother Teresa, there are those of the privileged class of leaders in politics or in business, living in affluence and conspicuous consumption, who feign helplessness amid the surrounding misery and destitution. To those in authority and indeed to all Nigerians, the life of Mother Teresa is an indictment as well as a challenge for us to be our brother's keeper through our service, love and care for the countless poor in our society.

We should therefore try to learn one or two lessons from the life of this Angel of Peace who stooped to conquer the world of power with nothing but her firm faith and her large heart. Mother Teresa emerged as the kind of leader that the world is longing for. Nigeria would be a much better place if we had a few men and women in positions of privilege who have sufficient interest in the plight of the multitude of poor people in our society. Nigeria would be a much better place if those whom we promote as leaders at all levels made the search for justice, equity and peace a matter of passionate commitment. Nigeria would be a much better place if those who seek to lead us saw every human life as inviolable and human dignity as non-negotiable.

The fact that the whole world literally stood still for Mother Teresa at her death in 1997 and at her beatification means that the men and women of today are able to recognise Godliness in a life of virtue and are prepared to identify with anyone of any faith whose life exemplifies and promotes the best qualities of humanity. This is very instructive for us in Nigeria who are often at each others' throats over the politics of religion and which group has conquered more political space than the other. What the universal acclaim of Mother Teresa teaches us is that the practice of humility, love and compassion, and the ardent commitment to peace and non-violence are more efficacious instruments of religious witnessing than the deafening noises of preachers that are the order of the day among competing religious groups in our country.

CHAPTER FORTY-ONE

Social Instability and the Quest for Peace in Nigeria
(Written on December 11, 2003)

Youth restiveness and social instability have become a major source of concern for many Nigerians, who, through the years of debauchery under the military, had hoped and prayed and looked forward to peace and security at the termination of the evil dispensation. But rather than experience peace and security, we are today confronted more than ever before with the tenuous nature of our national polity and the frightening dimensions youth restiveness and social instability have assumed in Nigeria.

From the sporadic exploits of the blood-thirsty sharia zealots of the North West and North Central Region, to the incessant display of violence by the angry mafia of the Niger Delta Region, and from the armed bandits that rule the highways of the North East, to the hired assassins that paint the political landscape in the South East with blood, and from the hot-headed ethnic militia known as the O.P.C in the South West and MASSOB in the South East, to the murderous secret cultists in nearly all our universities and polytechnics, it has been an orgy of violence and a season of blood and tears in which the very foundation of the nation is now threatened. Precious human lives have been destroyed in their thousands, and property worth hundreds of millions of Naira have been set ablaze in Odi, Warri, Lagos, Shagamu, Aguleri, Umuleri, Ife, Modakeke, ZakiBiam, Kaduna, Kano, Bauchi, Jos, and lately Abuja. We have witnessed thousands of internally displaced persons or refugees squatting in police and army barracks all over the place.

We have been through a season of madness here in Nigeria, and individuals and groups have often taken care of their own security by hiring police escorts, constituting vigilante groups or even forming private armies which operated largely outside the law. To combat the growing crime in our cities, some state governments constituted terrorist squads that were worse than the notorious "kill and go" arm of the police force. These killer squads often adopted such code names as "Operation Sweep," "Operation Crush," Operation Wedge," "Operation Flush" and Operation Fire for Fire." They were often mandated to shoot suspects at sight, and they often did their job with utmost recklessness. We would never know the number of innocent Nigerians who have been sent to their early graves as a result of the activities of these state-sponsored bandits. The young people of Nigeria have been growing up in this jungle and watching the Hobbesian existence that we call life – nasty, brutish and short. Our young people have been learning and playing out the jungle law of the survival of the fittest, and Nigeria is the worse for it.

Today the youths of the Niger Delta are at war with the Federal Government, with the Oil Companies and with one another, killing, abducting, maiming, raping and harassing innocent people. From Bori to Eleme and from Bomadi to Warri, the impression is that no one is in control. Instead what we are confronted with is total lawlessness or anarchy. In Lagos too the youth wing of the Oodua Peoples Congress has been credited with several killings at various locations in the city at various times. We are all familiar with the violent exploits of the "Area Boys" who command the streets of our major cities, harassing, extorting and terrorizing members of the public. Thus it appears that through all the years of debauchery, when the military held reign, an incalculable damage has been done to the psyche of the Nigerian youth. They no longer seem to be able to distinguish between good and bad, between virtue and vice, and between right and wrong. They seem to have lost faith in the adult society, in the leadership and even in their parents and teachers.

How indeed could the young people have learnt the lesson on the sanctity of life when daily they hear of adults and children being kidnapped, killed and dismembered for ritual purposes by members of the adult society? How could they have come to appreciate the truth of the inviolability of life when daily they are confronted with the reality of human corpses that are left to decompose and decapitate on our streets, while thousands of people pass by and only block their noses against the stench? How could our young people have accepted that violence is evil when everyday they watch the rich and powerful crush the poor and lowly with all the instruments of violence at their disposal, and when such criminals are treated as successful members of society? How could they have accepted the truth of human transcendence when they hear that government agents are sometimes involved in the sordid conspiracy that we call ritual murder?

How can you demonstrate to our young people that human life is not cheap, expendable, and disposable when (in the absence of a truly functional film censorship body) even the youngest and the most vulnerable among them are exposed to the most outrageous celebration of violence on TV by way of home videos? How can they accept the rule of law and respect the rights and freedoms of their neighbours, when everyday they watch innocent people humiliated, tortured and eliminated, while the culprits who are often well connected, go scot-free? How can our young people be made to value human life and respect the rights and dignity of persons when their leaders and elders have demonstrated to them that wealth and power are the ultimate values, when these leaders and elders would stop at nothing in the pursuit of these values, when they would blackmail, kidnap, torture or even eliminate anyone who may be on their way to the acquisition of maximum wealth and power. How can they accept that secret cults are bad when they observe that access to wealth and position is often guaranteed and safe passage through the corridors of power is often secured through one's enlistment in one of such adult cults as the Ogboni Confraternity or the Rosicrucian Order?

How can you make the young people in our schools and colleges sit down and concentrate on their studies when the leaders have messed up the educational set-up to such an extent that universities have been shut on many occasions for upward of six months, and there was no provision for any profitable engagement of their young minds during the period? Do we not say that the devil makes use of the idle mind? How can our students be eager to study, to pass their examinations and to graduate from the university, when there are no jobs awaiting them, when even for the mandatory Youth Service Scheme they sometimes have to bribe their way to be able to find placement, after having been deployed to such places as Lagos, Abuja, Port Harcourt and Warri? How can they value life amidst acrimonious poverty, when many young people are reduced to a state of destitution, when they are made to struggle with malnourishment, and when they have to study in an environment that is degenerate and decrepit, while they watch in amazement the conspicuous consumption of those who have stolen food off their hands?

True, we have not given our young people reason to live with dignity and responsibility. We have often been the cause of our young people's restiveness. It has been observed that "when life is worthless, fear is banished." Young people are highly impressionable. They are easily scandalised. They can easily be led astray. It is only by practical example from members of the adult society that they will learn that the fear of God is the beginning of wisdom; that human life is sacred, unique and inviolable; and that money, power and position are not the highest values for which other values may be so easily sacrificed.

Thus, after years of military dictatorship, the worst form of which was manifested in the Abacha dispensation, Nigerians had hoped for a period of peaceful transition to a just, equitable, democratic and peaceful society. We had hoped for a new Nigerian society where we can once again have the opportunity to channel our enormous natural endowments to positive use for the advancement of our teeming population. We had hoped for a new Nigerian society where we can celebrate the richness of our diverse languages, cultures and religions. We had hoped for a new Nigerian society where we can take our rightful place in the comity of nations and compete in the advancement of science and technology. But rather than make progress in these directions, multiple crises and conflicts have plagued post-military Nigeria.

As a result of these sad developments, the Nigerian economy remains comatose. Investors have been scared away, in spite of President Obasanjo's numerous overseas travels, and in spite of successfully hosting the 8th All Africa Games and the Commonwealth Heads of Government Meeting. With the circumstance of widespread violence and great insecurity in the land, potential investors seem to have decided to watch and see. Unemployment therefore remains high, and the majority of the people are plagued by acrimonious poverty, with the lot of the youth population worsening by the day. Thus, four and a half years after we said goodbye to military dictatorship, we are witnessing what appears sadly as another round of aborted dreams, broken promises and dashed hopes. Once again, our leaders have failed to deliver, and we are once again being challenged to go to the drawing board.

The unfortunate turn of events in the last four and a half years surely bring to the fore the reality of our tenuous existence, the restiveness of our youth in and out of school, and the imperative of social reconstruction towards national reconciliation and peaceful co-existence. This social reconstruction necessarily involves an ethical or moral revolution, the type that religious groups are best equipped to champion and promote. Perhaps the people of Nigeria along with their leaders had underestimated the extent of the problems that had built up in the land over the years of debauchery, when systemic corruption, social injustice, economic isolation and political banditry reigned, breeding widespread anger and resentment that were kept in check all the while only by military might. With the violent conflicts that have erupted in the North and South, and in the East and West, over unresolved ethnic, religious, political and economic differences, and over boundaries and the ownership of land and other resources, Nigerians must now realise that there are lots of structural defects in the Nigerian society that are potential sources of conflict. With our universities and colleges becoming breeding grounds for gangsters and murderers, perhaps the time has come for us to look critically at the very structure of our corporate existence, the management of our natural and human resources and what our developmental priorities are. This is a challenge we must take up and address courageously, perhaps as many have suggested, in a national conference.

The truth I have come to recognise is that many in the Igbo nation remain resentful of the rest of Nigeria for the injustices of the 1967 to 1970 civil war, the abandoned property imbroglio, and the alleged post-war marginalisation of Igbo people in some vital segments of the national economy. These are the sentiments behind the Movement for the Actualisation of the Sovereign State of Biafra (MASSOB). Many in the Yoruba nation remain angry with the rest of Nigeria for the injustices associated with the June 12 election annulment, and the alleged post-June 12 persecution and marginalisation of Yoruba people. These are the sentiments that sustain the activities of the Oodua Peoples Congress. The collocation of small ethnic nationalities which we call the Middle Belt are today vexed by the appendage status accorded them in the power structures of our nation. Many of them allege that they have suffered numerous injustices because of being falsely associated with the North all this time, while they gained nothing from the Northern hold on political power. These are the sentiments behind the activities of the Middle Belt Forum.

The citizens of the oil producing Niger Delta are poised for a show down with the rest of Nigeria, and if recent clashes are anything to go by, their youths appear to be well equipped for war with the rest of Nigeria, because of the callous exploitation of their natural resources for decades, while they are abandoned in a state of destitution. The Egbesu Youth best exemplify these sentiments. Many among the Hausa and Fulani Muslims of the core North who desire to live under the supremacy of the Islamic Sharia seem incensed that the rest of Nigeria want to jettison what they see as their religious freedom. These are the sentiments behind the 2000, 2001 and 2002 religious riots that rocked Kaduna, Kano and Jos. Within each group however, there is often bitterness over past hurts and wounds which have never been seriously addressed.

The orgy of violence all over the place and the restiveness of youth amidst our fledgling democracy may be an expression of the failure of state and the collapse of governance. There is nothing on the ground to demonstrate that ours is not a land run over by political bandits, ethnic warlords and religious fanatics. That is why the average citizen now seems to have lost confidence in the capacity of those in power to protect their lives and property. With a selfless, visionary and prudent leadership, the thousands of deaths we have recorded and the millions of Naira worth of property that have been destroyed in the last few years, could have been avoided. So we hold the current leadership of the Nigerian State responsible for the restiveness of the youth and the widespread violence and social instability that have resulted, because the leaders have remained indolent and insensitive in the face of very explosive situations.

With so many un-addressed wounds and hurts over past injustices and inequities, and with corruption having assumed epidemic dimension, our leaders have often carried on business as usual, dining and wining, taking chieftaincy titles and honorary degrees and conferring the highest national honours on themselves. But for serious-minded Nigerians, the task of nation building must begin with an elaborate programme of, and an honest commitment to social reconstruction and moral revolution as the first steps towards peaceful co-existence, or else our preoccupation with democratic governance will lack the much-needed foundation, and end once again in disaster. Instead of squandering our meagre resources on prestige projects and looking for every available opportunity to play the big brother to neighbouring countries and give lavish reception to international visitors, the leadership of Nigeria must learn to feel the pulse of the nation, to hear the cry of the people, and to react with utmost sense of responsibility to the desires and aspirations of the constituent units of the country for that kind of unity and peace that is based on mutual forgiveness for past hurts and wounds, and a mutual commitment to righting the wrongs of the past, and building our society on the principles of transparency, justice, fairness, and a passion among the leaders for the common good.

Before Nigeria collapses under the burden of monumental corruption, long-standing mutual antipathy, and violent conflicts, we hereby challenge peace-desiring Nigerians to champion the cause of national reconstruction through the promotion of the much needed moral and ethical revolution on the one hand, and a heavy investment in conflict resolution, the rehabilitation of our educational institutions and the provision of employment opportunities for the teeming population of our young people on the other.

We challenge the members of the Laity Council of Nigeria and indeed all Nigerian Christians to do an examination of conscience, and to take up the challenge of this moral revolution and national reconstruction. Members of the Laity Council must heed the wake-up call now, if there must begin a process of emancipation from a blighted future to which unborn generations seem to be condemned. We must develop a cohesive network for the incremental engagement of the nation's leadership on national issues, drawing on the sectoral specialisation of the members of the Laity Council across the country to educate and lead the masses.

The issue of impropriety in governance for example, whether in relation to electoral or constitutional manipulation, corrupt financial dealings in the Assemblies or such exploits as the celebrated Anambra state gubernatorial debacle, can be appropriately tackled by a group of Catholic Lawyers, acting as the arrowhead of civil society action, closely supported by an alert and committed independent press. And we cannot act alone. It is not possible to achieve the desired national transformation in isolation. We must seek out committed Nigerians and work assiduously to form and strengthen coalitions among such people across ethnic and even religious boundaries. As Church we must see ourselves as the light of the world. We must champion this noble cause of national transformation, for where there is no vision, the people perish.

CHAPTER FORTY-TWO

Death Penalty and the Imperatives of Change
(Written on February 16, 2004)

The question of capital punishment and the death penalty has in the last 50 years generated a lot of controversy in many parts of the world. Several humanitarian agencies have championed the cause of abrogating this form of punishment, which is seen as cruel, inhuman, and unworthy of civilised societies. A motion for its abrogation from our statute books has been tabled before the National Assembly. Also, a committee has been set up by the Attorney General of Nigeria to study the matter and make recommendations to government. I make this reflection on the death penalty question as a Christian who believes in the divine origin, the supernatural end, and the transcendence of the human person. I believe that every human person is created in the image of God, that is to say that each person has something divine or supernatural in him or her. Each person carries with him or her the seal of the Creator; and that includes villains, aggressors, and violent criminals. The life of each person remains sacred and inviolable, even when the individual chooses to be a deviant, a murderer, or an assassin.

With the death penalty in our statute books, hundreds of our brothers and sisters have been sacrificed to the "gods" of our land, their execution often carried out in a most callous and barbaric manner such as the public execution before a cheering crowd, of armed robbers, a gory site that presents us as modern-day gladiators. I have always considered that the summary termination of human lives (even the lives of hardened criminals), amidst a cheering crowd of spectators is a curious index of our social, moral, and spiritual degeneracy. Public execution, even of hardened criminals is an offence against human dignity, and an assault on human respectability. Every human person, precisely because he or she is a human person, deserves to die with some amount of dignity. For me it is symptomatic of a chronic pathology on the level of our communal psyche, that in this day and age when civilized people everywhere are pleading for the abrogation of the death penalty, thousands of our countrymen and women have often found pleasure in the tragic drama of public execution by firing squad.

Perhaps it is part of the psychology of an oppressed people that they often turn on themselves and unleash untold violence on one another. The more depressed they are, the more they enjoy such violent scenes as the torture and execution of a perceived social deviant or criminal. We all know that in Lagos today, one only needs to shout "ole" ("thief"), and the person concerned will be lynched within seconds by passers-by who have no idea at all what the person has stolen. Several innocent but poor citizens have died in this way at the hands of their fellow sufferers. This jungle justice, along with its officially sanctioned counterpart, the death penalty, is in my view nothing but a shameful descent to the lowest instincts in the human person.

There is a sacred dimension in every human being, including the sane and the insane, the hero and the villain, the innocent, and the criminal. I see capital punishment as a violation of this sacred dimension of the human personality. The widespread resort to capital punishment debases not only the victims but perhaps more seriously the perpetrators. It may be an easy way of dealing with violent crimes, but it carries with it unwholesome consequences for the society. Capital punishment harms the entire society in many ways because every form of violence, even the one carried out by the state, begets further violence. Human life is inviolable, and so every act of bloodshed, carries with it a curse of some sort. The government that authorises the killing of its own people is (perhaps unwittingly) sending waves of violence across the land.

It is becoming increasingly difficult to justify the death penalty in the modern society, except as a communal celebration of sadism, vengeance, and vendetta. We know that in our society as elsewhere, some of the most vocal proponents of the death penalty are often motivated by the desire for vengeance and vendetta. Yet vengeance and vendetta have no place in the life of a Christian who is called to champion the civilisation of love, to love until it hurts, to always forgive an offending neighbour. Desiring the death of an offending neighbour can hardly be justified in Christian morality.

Classical criminologists say that punishment is meant to achieve three main objectives for the human person and his or her society. The first is retribution. That is to say that the offender must pay for his or her offence. In the ancient Hebrew tradition, it was the "*lex talionis*" that reigned, that is the law of "an eye for an eye and a tooth for a tooth." This primitive practice did not help humanity in any way. It was and remains a serious obstacle along humanity's way towards a peaceful society. Those who relish in the logic of "an eye for an eye and a tooth for a tooth" are always caught up in the vicious circle of violence, as the build-up of resentment over unforgiven hurts provokes aggression and consequently further violence. It is this vicious circle of violence that Jesus Christ seeks to break with his prescription of love even towards those who are most undeserving, and that is to include enemies and criminals (See Matthew 5:38-48).

Perhaps the greatest weakness of the world and of our society today is its lack of mercy. Yes, as Pope John Paul II says, the pursuit of justice in the strict sense is not enough for a humane society. Our society must take a leap and go beyond strict distributive justice (that is giving each person his or her due), to embrace love which includes forgiveness, mercy, and compassion. A world without forgiveness will be a cold world of permanent tension, violence, and strife. A world without forgiveness has no hope of ever making any headway towards the civilization of love, the kind of civilization which Jesus Christ taught his followers in the Sermon on the Mount. Even in the case of hardened criminals which border on the demonic, the attitude of Jesus Christ implies that love is the most subtle form of exorcism. Jesus conquered Satan with an outpouring of immeasurable love. As Christians we should not imagine that we can conquer the demons of armed robbery, political banditry, hired assassinations and Advance Fee Fraud (419) with the same instruments of the devil. Christ came to offer something radically different from what the world is used to. Christians are the light of the world who must offer the world an alternative solution to the problem of violent crimes in society.

The second objective of punishment is said to be the reformation of the social deviant or criminal. It hardly needs to be stated here that capital punishment does not reform the criminal. The offender is killed. The punishment is extreme, ultimate and terminal. The offender is not given any chance for possible reformation and rehabilitation into the society. And in the case of a mistake in judgement as has often happened, the punishment is irreversible. There are many cases of wrongful execution that have been discovered in the U.S. DNA tests are beginning to help uncover many such cases of wrongful execution. In our own country, many legal experts would insist that the execution of Ken Saro-Wiwa and his companions on November 10, 1996, was a miscarriage of justice. Nasiru Bello is another Nigerian who was hurriedly executed while his appeal was pending before the Supreme Court. As Olisa Agbakoba said in the celebrated case of Onuoha Kalu versus the State, "capital punishment is incapable of correction in the event of an error."

The third objective of punishment is said to be deterrence. The killing of violent criminals, it is believed by some, will deter those who have similar tendencies. However, statistics the world over have taught many criminologists that the death penalty has not been an effective deterrent to violent crimes. Instead, those with criminal tendencies in society often become more vicious in their escapades when they know that if caught, they would pay with their lives. They often want to kill a few more before they are killed.

Many advocates of capital punishment talk of the protection of innocent citizens from the destructive tendencies of violent criminals as a reason to retain capital punishment for certain categories of crime. Yet considering the circumstances of today's society, including the reality of structural evil and long-standing injustices, and the various environmental, social, political and economic forces that marginalise a number of people and push some into crime, one wonders to what extent any individual in our society can claim to be truly "innocent." A lot of violent criminals today have ended up in the world of crime because of the neglect and abuse on the part of many of those who see themselves as "innocent citizens." These are part of the dynamics of crime and the responsible society.

The truth of human existence is that (in the words of Pope John Paul II) "we are each responsible for all." While growing up, a lot of our criminals lacked the conducive home they deserved, and the wider society showed no concern for their plight. Many of them grew up, lacking the basic necessities of life, including adequate food, shelter and clothing, parental love and care, and a minimum of social security. Many of them grew up without any positive role models in their lives. Some grew up without any moral training, so their consciences are ill-formed. The irony therefore is that our society breeds criminals, nurtures them to maturity and makes a public spectacle of the cruel termination of their lives.

The execution of armed robbers, drug pushers and any other categories of criminals, is in my view not a demonstration of strength on the part of the government and the rest of society. Rather for me it is an admission of defeat and a confession of weakness, helplessness and hopelessness. When the government goes ahead to terminate the life of one of its own citizens convicted of crime, what that government is really saying is that it has failed in its responsibility; that government is saying that it is incapable of protecting the innocent in the society from the violent criminal. Wherever capital punishment is practised, what the society is saying is that it has no means of controlling crime and reforming the criminal. Yet the truth is that we do not need to kill criminals in order to protect the rest of society, unless we are just looking for the easy way out. Capital punishment may indeed be an easy way out of the problem of violent crimes, but it carries with it unwholesome consequences for the entire society. While it terminates the life of the convicted persons, capital punishment harms the entire society in many ways, since violence begets violence.

In his 1995 social encyclical, *Evangelium Vitae*, Pope John Paul II observes that the modern society has devised different ways of protecting the innocent in society from the activities of those who tend to perpetrate violent crimes. He says that the primary purpose of punishment is to redress the disorder caused by the offender, to impose on the offender adequate suffering for his or her crime, while at the same time offering the offender an incentive and help to change his or her behaviour and be rehabilitated. "The nature and extent of punishment," he says, "must be carefully evaluated and decided upon, and should not get to the extreme of executing the offender..." The pope says that this is a view of penal justice that is "in line with the dignity of and inviolability of the human person. While admitting that in the extreme case of absolute necessity, when the State can otherwise not protect the rest of society from a vicious (murderous) criminal, the State could apply the death penalty, he quickly added that "as a result of steady improvement in the organisation of the penal system in the modern society, such cases are very rare, if not practically non-existent (See *Evangelium Vitae* no.56, and also *Catechism of the Catholic Church* no.2267).

Practically every society in the world at one time or the other applied capital punishment on some category of offenders. But in recent times the tide has changed. Up to 110 countries including Britain, Italy, Canada, Austria Australia and South Africa have either abolished capital punishment or at least declared a moratorium on the execution of persons. A number of agencies, both religious and secular, are today active all over the world in the campaign to abolish it. We salute the efforts of these agencies, and I pray that as we reflect on the imperatives of change in the application of the death penalty in our country today, in spite of the high rate of capital crimes in our society, Nigerians may soon be convinced that human sacrifice is not the best route to social security. May Christ who died for us while we were yet sinners (Romans 5:8), help us to get rid of this remnant of primitive barbarism from our statute books. In this matter of the death penalty as in the case of abortion or euthanasia, may Nigerian Christians be ready to stand up and be counted on the side of sacrificial love and life.

CHAPTER FORTY-THREE

Inter-Religious Dialogue in Nigeria: Present Challenges and Future Prospects
Report presented at the Conference organized by MISSIO in Germany, March 25, 2004.

Preamble

Nigeria is not an Islamic state. Christians and Muslims each claim 50% of the population. So this is one country with a sizeable Islamic population, but in which Christians do not accept a minority status. While population figures remain political and controversial in Nigeria, what is not in dispute is that the overwhelming majority of the population of the North is Muslim, while the overwhelming majority of the population of the South is Christian. It is also important at the outset to distinguish between the politics of religion and the actual practice of religion. Nigerians have hardly had to fight over the practice of religion. It is the politics of religion that has brought upon us so much trouble.

In Nigeria the politics of religion with its destructive consequences is epitomised in the fraudulent enlistment of Nigeria into the Organisation of Islamic Countries (O.I.C.) in the mid 1980s, and the unconstitutional declaration of the Shariah (with its criminal elements) as state law in 11 Northern States between the year 2000 and 2001. This latter development has done the greatest damage to the Nigerian polity since the (1967-1970) civil war against the secession bid of the Eastern Region. The fragile peace that existed between Muslims and Christians in Northern Nigeria from the time of independence in 1960, seems to have been destroyed by the Shariah phenomenon. What we now find in the area is tension, mutual suspicion, a feeling of insecurity, and occasional eruption of violence. Many non-Muslim and non-indigenes of the affected states in the North have had to relocate for fear that they might lose their lives during one of the now frequent conflicts, or have their hands cut off for the flimsiest excuse, or simply out of the realisation that their fundamental human rights are no longer guaranteed in these states.

Also, the people of the two religions existed peacefully together until the last 15 years. The ever-deteriorating socio-economic circumstances of poverty, distress and widespread frustration in the developing countries, including Nigeria are accountable in large measure for what is seen as religious tension in our country today. What some have identified as the "international imperialism of money" and the apparent ascendancy of a monolithic (western) world view is a major contributing factors to the rising religious tension in Nigeria and elsewhere.

Update on Inter-Religious Dialogue in Nigeria

1. Positive Developments

- ❖ The two women whose condemnation to death by stoning for adultery made headlines in the international media, Amina Lawal and Safiya, have been discharged on technical grounds. So far therefore, no one has been executed on the basis of the Shariah criminal law introduced in many states in the year 2000. A few people have had their limbs cut for petty offences, while others have been victims of corporal punishment and other acts that amount to violation of their rights according to the secular constitution of the Federal Republic of Nigeria.

- ❖ The Nigeria Inter-Religious Council (NIREC) comprising of 25 Christians and 25 Muslims, which was founded in the year 2000 and enthusiastically supported by the government continues to function, though the goals and strategies of the body are yet to be clearly defined, and though there is an apparent disconnect between this high profile body that brings together the national leaders of the two main religions, and the ordinary Muslims and Christians on the ground who, especially in the Northern part of the country have to live with perennial religious tension.

- ❖ The Catholic Church at various levels has organised a number of Workshops on issues of Inter-Religious Dialogue, bringing together not only Christians, but in many instances Christians and Muslims. One of such dialogue sessions which occurred in the year 2002 was organised in Abuja by the Catholic Secretariat of Nigeria in collaboration with Missio Aachen. Among the resolutions reached at that particular workshop are the following:

- Dialogue between Christians and Muslims is very important because it will help clear the cloud of misunderstanding and create a better atmosphere of mutual enrichment.
- Dialogue of action, communion and socio-political life should be promoted at all levels of society. These could include joint social projects, joint health projects, joint economic ventures, etc, that will promote community development and peaceful co-existence.
- Christian Women Organisations should reach out to counterpart Muslim Organisations and work out common grounds for dialogue.
- Christian and Muslim religious education should be tailored in such a way as to promote mutual respect and peaceful coexistence.

❖ The Catholic Bishops Conference of Nigeria invites the Secretary General of the Supreme Council of Islamic Affairs (SCIA) to the opening session of its annual meeting in March every year. At the opening session of its meeting this year, Dr. Lateef Adegbite was present, and he presented a very welcome Goodwill Message from the Islamic community. In the discussion that followed his presentation, the mutual desire for peaceful coexistence among Christians and Muslims was very evident.

❖ More Christian leaders, including a good number of Catholic priests are now studying Islam, with some doing specialized studies in Islamic Theology and Arabic. A few have gone to Egypt for that purpose. The Pontifical Council for Inter-Religious Dialogue in the Vatican has been in the forefront in promoting this study of Islam.

❖ The goodwill messages of the Holy Father, Pope John Paul II on the major Islamic feasts are now published in paid advertorials in Nigerian Newspapers every year by the Catholic Secretariat of Nigeria. In recent years, we have even published them in both English and Arabic.

❖ Above all, the dialogue of life continues, as the overwhelming majority of Nigerians of both faiths live together, work together, inter-marry and interact in an atmosphere of friendship and mutual respect. In many parts of the country, a number of community development projects are jointly embarked upon by Christians and Muslims.

2. Sources of Continued Religious Tension in Nigeria

Among the sources of continued tension after September 11, 2001 are:

- ❖ The bombing of Afghanistan in October 2001 - which was followed by a reprisal attack in the city of Kano, Nigeria, by extremist Muslim groups, who went on the rampage, burning Churches and destroying the property of some Christians.

- ❖ The war on and occupation of Iraq and the continued bombardment of Palestine by Israel. As long as these situations exist, Christians in the Muslim dominated parts of Nigeria can only sleep with one eye closed, as we perceive a strong bond of solidarity between Muslims of the Arab world and Muslims in the northern part of our country. And on the other hand, many Muslims believe that whatever the leaders of the West do, have the blessings of Christians everywhere, even though there is no rational basis for such an assumption in the contemporary society. It is nevertheless important for the leaders of the Western countries to know that their policies towards any Arab country can have far-reaching implications not only for the Middle East, but also for countries like Nigeria with a mixed population of Christians and Muslims.

- ❖ The worsening economic fortunes of the majority of people in Nigeria, following the Structural Adjustment Programme embarked upon by our leaders at the instance of the World Bank and IMF. With the increasing level of poverty and unemployment and decreasing access to the available resources, there is the tendency to resort to scapegoating - pointing accusing fingers to or holding the other group responsible for the economic and political woes of the land. This situation is often compounded with the problem of ignorance and illiteracy. Our circumstances in the last few years have demonstrated how easy it is to recruit poor and ignorant young people into the army of religious fundamentalists.

3. Obstacles on the Way of Wholesome Dialogue

- ❖ The absence of or the lack of commitment to, the Rule of Law.

- ❖ The apparent collapse of moral and family values in Western societies. What is perceived as moral decadence in Western countries is unfortunately often interpreted by some Muslims as the decadence of Christian civilization. And this is a fertile ground for the nurturing of fundamentalist or puritanical (extremist) orientations within Islam. The same tendency towards fundamentalism is noticeable today among fringe sects within Christianity.

- ❖ The "Globalisation of bad news," by which atrocities committed in any remote part of the world are beamed through satellite for everyone else to see, makes dialogue difficult today. Muslims in Nigeria can see all the violence in Iraq and in Palestine in a manner that would not have been possible before our technological age. There is need for international media corporations to know what to do with bad news. In my view there is too much bad news in the media today. A few good things do happen in many parts of the world, but it appears that good news is no longer newsworthy. This situation does not help our quest for global peace.

- ❖ The absence of a central (authoritative) interpretation of the Qur'an and Hadith, and the clear absence in Islam of any authority that can call aberrant or violent extremist groups to order. Thus, among the various groups of Muslims that exist in Nigeria and elsewhere, there is no common understanding of the Shariah legal system, the notion of a Secular (pluralistic or multi-religious) society, when capital punishment can be enforced, the status of non-Muslims in a majority Muslim society, the place and status of women, etc. We are beginning to have in Christianity also fringe (evangelical) groups which do not operate under any recognised authority or with any well-thought-out theology.

4. The Way Forward: Emphasis on the Rule of Law, Economic Growth, Justice and Fair-play and the Dialogue of Life

- ❖ Cooperation between Christians and Muslims in the task of building a just, peaceful and democratic Nigerian society. Working together in all the projects involved in our democratic transition, will enhance unity, mutual understanding and peaceful co-existence.

- ❖ Greater networking among civil society groups, including church NGOs and NGOs of Islamic origin in the promotion of human rights, and in the struggle for greater justice and genuine democracy in our country.

- ❖ We must encourage many more joint (Christian-Muslim) social welfare and community development programmes and projects.

- ❖ Common meditation and action to respond to the challenge of corruption, mismanagement of resources, bad governance, collapsed infrastructure, widespread disease, especially the epidemic of HIV/AIDS, the fallen standard of education, the collapse of moral and family values, and so on.

- ❖ Islamic fundamentalism has to be addressed internationally because the extremist groups are today strengthening their global networks, capitalizing on the poverty and ignorance of the third world countries.

- ❖ The international community must ensure that a uniform standard of human rights is applied everywhere. These human rights should emanate from some fundamental and universal human values that must be upheld by everyone who wishes to be part of the civilized human society.

- ❖ While recognising the right of individuals to practice their religion, religion as such must always be separated from state affairs in multi-religious or plural societies. When they are mixed together one religion will often be favoured against the others, and thus the seed of crisis will be sown.

❖ We must all come to recognise that even in the face of real or perceived injustice, violence does not solve any problem. It only begets further violence. Lasting peace can only come about through peaceful means. Thus, religious people everywhere, including Christians, Muslims, Hindus, Buddhists, and Jews must always condemn in the strongest terms the resort to violence by any groups whatsoever in the name of God.

Conclusion

Christians and Muslims in Nigeria lay claim to equal proportion in the nation's population of 120 million people. And so while Christians can continue to reject the imposition of the Sharia legal system in any part of the country, and while they insist on the secular character of the nation's constitution, they must nevertheless always leave the channels open for dialogue with the Muslim elite. The issue of the place of religion in the socio-political life of Nigeria can however not be adequately addressed if taken in isolation. The history of colonialism, the pitiable economic circumstances of many young, able-bodied people in the country and the real or perceived injustices in the political and economic structures of the country do have a direct bearing on the ethnic and religious tension in the country today.

The inability of certain segments of the population to access economic or political power is a dangerous thing that precipitates crisis. When people are poor and unemployed and have nowhere to look up to, their anger and frustration can often find expression through fundamentalist (extremist) religious activities. We must concede that the problem of poverty and infrastructural decay, brought about by the massive corruption of a succession of the ruling elite, as well as the "international imperialism of money" by which a large number of nations are unable to compete for global economic resources, have contributed a lot to the circumstances we find ourselves in today. In the face of these odds, while Christian leaders and moderate elements among the Islamic elite, as well as human rights and pro-democracy advocates continue the struggle, we shall require the assistance of the international community in many ways. Beyond the need for partner agencies to assist with funding such programmes and projects that will help reduce poverty and ignorance, and promote greater democratisation and conflict resolution towards peaceful co-existence, there is the major challenge for our friends in Europe and America to do some discernment on the root causes of these upheavals, to see how colonialism, neo-colonialism and the near exclusion of a number of poor countries from the global economic and technological progress of today have contributed to the social tension in those countries.

CHAPTER FORTY-FOUR

Religious Organisations and the Challenge
of Fighting Corruption
(A paper delivered at the National Seminar on Corruption Organised by the NASRUL-LAHI-IL-FATHI Society of Nigeria Lagos, August 5, 2004)

Introduction: The Place of Religion in the Modern Society

After our failed experiment in recent centuries with secularist fundamentalism expressed most graphically in the French Revolution which actually abolished religion for a while, and Atheistic Communism which effectively banished it from public life, the twenty first century society has come to recognize the resilience of religion as a factor in the private and public behaviour of citizens in many parts of the world. Along with the forces of culture and ethnicity, the importance of religion and the identity that derives from it have been very much highlighted in recent times. It has become clear to many leaders that the world cannot pursue truth, justice, transparency, accountability, peace, social integration and solidarity within and among nations while neglecting the place of religion in the life of people. Instead leaders are beginning to explore the immense potential for good to be found in all religions, and are asking how these can be exploited for the promotion of truth and justice and for the building of a more wholesome human society.

I understand that my task at this seminar is to highlight the role of religious organizations in the fight against corruption - corruption, that systemic evil which is responsible in large measure for the broken promises, the dashed hopes and the shallow dreams that have characterized the existence of the multitude of Nigerians for such a long while. I commend the NAFSAT, the organizers of this event for the laudable initiative, which I believe has come at a very auspicious time.

For indeed modern men and women in our country and everywhere today are becoming impatient with religious organizations and leaders. They seem to be challenging all religious groups to develop a critical social conscience or risk being dumped in the ashes of history as one of the past times of primitive humanity. Modern men and women are challenging religious organizations to demonstrate their usefulness to the 21st Century human society by uniting warring people, by giving hope and meaning to despairing people, by identifying with the poor and oppressed and doing something positive to improve their lot, and by promoting among their adherents such values and principles that will make for a wholesome humanity as truth, honesty, justice, accountability, respect for human rights and dignity, peace and non-violence, concern for the common good and care for the environment. In the Nigerian context, the ongoing seminar is one answer to this modern challenge.

Let me begin with the fundamental premise that all major religions in the modern world do have the potential and indeed the mission to promote truth and justice and to contribute immensely towards the emergence of a more wholesome, peaceful and prosperous humanity, since these religions often provide the spiritual force and the moral basis for the maintenance of social equilibrium, notwithstanding the many instances in the history of the world and of our own country when religious sentiments have been capitalized upon to cause havoc and unleash a regime of violence or social injustice.

Between the Politics and the Practice of Religion

In discussing the immense potential for the good ordering of society that religious organizations can make within the context of a society that has witnessed so much violence in recent times at the hands of religious fanatics and bigots, we must first make the distinction between the politics of religion and the practice of religion. In the course of history fanatics, extremists, fundamentalists, warmongers, conquerors, expansionists, crusaders, and jihadists (propelled by nothing but the primordial sentiments of greed and avarice and pride and arrogance and hatred and vengeance), have often jettisoned the best elements of religion and capitalized on the highly emotive nature of religion to kill and maim people and cause immense tension in the human society. But no matter how widespread this aberration may be and no matter how many highly placed people are involved, religious fanatics and extremists have never been acknowledged as the best examples of their faith.

Instead, their preoccupation with hatred and violence is a corruption of the very fundamental orientation of theistic religions, for as Pope John Paul II says, the God of peace is never glorified by human violence.

Thus, fanatics and extremists are not the best examples of their faith. They may make waves for a while, but in the end, they are often dumped in the ashes of history. Society never fails to take note of the other kind of religious power that shines through the humble disciple who draws people to his or her faith by the witness of a holy life, devoted to the pursuit of justice and peace, a life which constantly points the way to the rest of society. Think of the regard the world continues to give Mahatma Gandhi a devout Hindu. Think of the positive waves made by Mother Teresa of Calcutta, a devout Christian. Think of the respect we continue to have for the late Sir Ahmadu Bello, the Sardauna of Sokoto, a devout Muslim.

I am able to say without fear of contradiction that the genuine practice of Islam and Christianity for example will hurt no one in our land or in any land whatsoever. Instead, the faithful practice of Islam and Christianity, which include private and public prayer, fasting and acts of charity, the pursuit of truth and justice, generally avoiding evil and doing good, and living by the golden rule which admonishes that we do to no one what we would not like done to us, these tenets should normally hurt no one. Instead, the observance of these tenets of Christianity and Islam should ensure a just, accountable, corruption-free, non-violent, and peaceful polity. Yes, when devoid of hypocrisy and bigotry on the one hand, and the destructive politics that makes religion an instrument of violence, manipulation, and exploitation on the other, Christianity and Islam (and to a very reasonable extent the Traditional Religions of our people) should be a powerful instrument in the nurturing of a nation of integrity where corruption, fraud and social injustice have no place.

Religion in Nigeria: A booming enterprise

Very much unlike some other parts of the modern world, where the widespread practice of religious ritual is becoming an anachronism, our own is a country that is saturated with religiosity. Religion is not just thriving in Nigeria. Here in our country religion is a booming enterprise. Religion features at the very beginning of our nation's constitution. In the preamble to the 1999 Nigerian constitution, it is affirmed that we intend to live together as one united country under God. The overwhelming majority of Nigerians are religious people. We believe in the supremacy of God. We believe that God is the very basis of our individual lives and our corporate existence. We believe in and relate with supernatural realities through prayers and supplications and through the offering of sacrifices. We find churches, mosques, shrines and sundry prayer houses everywhere in the land.

Yes, while there is noticeable decline in religious fervour in many parts of the world, the religious enterprise appears to be thriving very much in Nigeria, as more and more company warehouses and private buildings are being converted to prayer houses, and our sports stadia all over the country are used more for religious crusades than for sporting events. We take part in crusades, worship sessions and vigils; we offer sacrifices and observe fasting days and religious holidays; and we go in large numbers on religious pilgrimages to Jerusalem and Mecca, taking pride in being called Jerusalem Pilgrim (JP) or Alhaji the rest of our lives. Within this religious firmament, bishops, pastors, evangelists, faith healers, prophets, and visionaries, as well as sheikhs, imams and gurus of all sorts are swelling in number and having a field day.

In the last few years, a new dimension has also been added to the thriving religious enterprise. It is the increased patronage of high-ranking public officials who openly call for and sponsor regular prayer sessions in different prayer houses, and the emergence of prayer merchants in and out of public service. These days, prayer and preaching sessions are no longer limited to churches, mosques and homes. They are held at corporate boardrooms, in government offices, in commercial buses and in open markets. Nigerians going about their daily business can be seen brandishing the Bible or the Koran, the Rosary or Islamic prayer beads. The largest billboards in our towns and cities are those advertising upcoming religious crusades and faith healing carnivals. Religious exclamations such as "to God be the glory," "praise the Lord," and "Allahu Akbar," are often on the lips of Nigerians, at work or at play - from the exalted members of the National Executive Council or the Council of State, to the young ones who are about to sit Common Entrance examination. Thus, from all outward indications, Nigerians are a chronically religious people. This must be why a recent survey came up with a declaration that Nigerians are the most religious people on earth.

The Embarrassing Contradiction in Nigeria

With all this show of religiosity or outward display of piety, one would have expected to see a very high degree of social morality in Nigeria, since all world religions generally promote truth, justice, honesty, and probity. But this is not to be the case with us. There is an embarrassing contradiction between the high ethical demands of the two religions which the majority of Nigerians profess, and the phenomenon of corruption, greed and graft that has earned our country the unenviable status of the "second most corrupt country in the world!" for the third year running in Transparency International's Annual Corruption Perception Index.

While the damning verdict of Transparency International may be contested on many grounds by patriotic Nigerians, we cannot run away from the embarrassing truth that corruption in Nigeria almost passes for state policy. Yes, some keen observers of the phenomenon actually say that corruption is so endemic in the Nigerian society that the socio-economic and political system can almost not function without it. Alongside religiosity, corruption in its many shapes and sizes is booming in Nigeria - from the petty bribery taken by the clerk in the office or the policeman at the checkpoint, to the grand corruption by which huge project contracts are hurriedly awarded, not for the sake of the common good, but because of the greed of the awarding official, who requires some money via contract "kick-backs."

Fraud, thievery and roguery are the order of the day, even as our environment is awash with prayers and ritual sacrifices to the God of truth, justice and holiness. It doesn't seem to be a matter of contradiction for many highly placed Nigerians that they embezzle or misappropriate stupendous amounts of public and company funds, while at the same time struggling to occupy the front seats in their churches and mosques. Examination malpractice is witnessed on a wide scale from the common entrance examination organised for the placement of 10-year-olds into colleges to the final qualifying examination at the Nigerian Law School. It is alleged that unscrupulous parents are not only accomplices, but sometimes initiators of these shameful practices.

Many Nigerians, including seemingly pious Christians and Muslims, who would go to war in defence of their religions, have no qualms of conscience when they pay to obtain yellow cards without the necessary inoculation for which the card is supposed to be evidence. Many of our countrymen and women who flock our churches on Sunday and fill the mosques on Friday are at one time or the other involved in such fraudulent activities as evading tax, issuing and obtaining of fake receipts, over-invoicing and under-invoicing, importation of fake drugs, petty and large-scale bribery, fake audit reports, "creative book-keeping," "round-tripping," advance fee fraud, etc. All these practices are so commonplace and so widespread that many young Nigerians are today unable to distinguish between good and evil or between right and wrong.

This evil of corruption in Nigeria has been described as systemic. And the unwholesome consequences are legion. Corruption has bred inefficiency and diminished productivity in both the public and private sectors of the economy. It has discouraged investment, fuelled capital flight, increased unemployment and inflation, created an acute degree of poverty, brought about a severe decline in the quality of life and life expectancy in Nigeria, and given Nigeria and Nigerians a terribly bad image in the eyes of the international community. Corruption is an affront on human dignity and an assault on the human conscience, apart from being a negation of the Muslim and Christian calling to promote holiness and righteousness in the world.

Religious Organisations and the War against Corruption

I have observed elsewhere that the struggle against corruption in our national landscape is one for the very survival of the nation itself. The choice before Nigerians is very clear: We either go to war against corruption in all its ramifications or we shall soon be consumed by this hydra-headed dragon. And in the fight against corruption, we religious leaders would first of all have to do a serious soul-searching. We would have to purge ourselves of our own acts of complicity in corruption, repent of the evils of the past and make an irrevocable commitment to a life of truth, probity, transparency and accountability in our individual and corporate lives and in our mosques, churches and institutions. Then we shall have the moral authority to teach our adherents the much-needed lessons in a life of integrity, for as the saying goes, *nemo dat quod non habet* (no one can give to others what he himself does not have). It is when as religious leaders we have purged ourselves of corrupt tendencies that we shall tell our followers who claim to be good Muslims and Christians, but who engage in sharp practices and dubious manoeuvres in the economy and in politics the truth that they need to know; namely, that the God of Abraham, Isaac and Jacob, is the God of holiness and righteousness, who in Leviticus 19:2 says "Be holy for I the Lord am holy!"

Yes, when we ourselves stand sufficiently secure on a moral high ground with regard to the many dimensions of corruption in Nigeria, we shall demonstrate to our followers that the God of Moses is the same one who on Mount Sinai presented the 10 commandments as the terms of his contract with his people, insisting that fidelity to this ethical code is what will distinguish his people from all others. Religious leaders can help fight corruption in Nigeria by constantly reminding the multitude of worshippers who flock to our prayer houses but who at the same time offer and take bribe, defraud, evade tax and circumvent just laws in numerous ways, that the God of Moses in Exodus 22:8 says, "You will accept no bribes, for a bribe blinds the clear-sighted and is the cause of the ruin of the upright." We can help fight corruption in Nigeria when we religious leaders constantly emphasise such passages in our Scriptures as Isaiah 33:15 where God says that the person who will be qualified to be in his presence is the one who "acts uprightly and speaks honestly, who scorns to get rich by extortion, who rejects bribes out of hand, who refuses to listen to plans involving bloodshed and who shuts his eyes rather than countenance crime..."

True, Nigerian worshippers who make a daily show of their religiosity should be constantly reminded of such passages as Micah 6:8 where we are told that what the Lord truly requires of those who know him is "to love tenderly, to do justice, and to walk humbly before your God." While preparing for the coming of Jesus, John the Baptist condemned the kind of religion that thrives side by side with corruption as empty ritualism. In Luke 3:13-14 he told those who had gathered to listen to him, among whom were soldiers and tax collectors: "Exact no more than the appointed rate...No intimidation! No extortion! Be content with your pay!"

Jesus Christ himself denounced the kind of religious practice that was not matched by high moral and ethical standards in private and social life. A comprehensive discussion of these standards can be found in the Sermon on the Mount (Matthew 5-7). They include a high level of truth and honesty in interpersonal and social relationships, a high sense of purity, modesty and humility, a profound sense of self sacrifice, a readiness to forgive as often as one is offended and a disposition towards peace and non-violence. He made his followers realise that not all who claim to be Christians (not all who say Lord, Lord) will enter the kingdom of heaven, but only those who do the will of the father in heaven. And the will of the Father in heaven is that they be perfect as the heavenly father himself is perfect (Matthew 5:48). Thus the Christian religion, like Judaism and Islam makes no room for crooks and fraudsters. It has no place for those who offer or receive bribe. It has no place for those who would lie and cheat. Authentic religion cannot accommodate the sum total of aberrations which is called "the Nigerian factor" today. It has no place for those who would use ill-gotten wealth to manipulate the political process. Instead, corruption is a negation of the fundamental orientation of all major religions of the world, which is to do good and avoid evil always.

Faced with the contradiction and the embarrassment of a booming religiosity in the midst of an environment that stinks with corruption and indiscipline therefore, religious leaders and organisations can contribute to the fight against corruption by demonstrating to their members that with the low level of social morality observed in our country, what camouflages as widespread religiosity may be little more than a mass movement with elements of religious ritualism, but one that is in large measure shallow, superficial, noisy and devoid of substance and depth. Religious leaders and organisations can contribute to the fight against corruption in Nigeria by attacking materialism and consumerism or the love of money which St. Paul says (in 1 Timothy 6:10) is the root of all evils. Authentic religion can help the generality of Nigerians find satisfaction for the profound hunger of the heart and recover a sense of ultimate meaning beyond material and physical gratification. For the loss of the sense of meaning and purpose is often linked to the preponderance of deviancy, delinquency and all forms of social pathology.

Religious leaders and organisations can help turn many Nigerians away from what appears to be an incredibly high sense of devotion to the cult of material prosperity and material success towards the spiritual values of truth, justice, holiness and purity. Christian leaders and groups can use the message of the cross to promote a modest and an austere lifestyle that will contradict the crass materialism and extreme economic liberalism of our age which is responsible for the worsening plight of the poor in our country and elsewhere. Muslims can do the same with the notion of sacrifice which is a key element of the three Abrahamic religions. Popular religion in contemporary Nigeria which lacks the essential components of sacrifice and a critical social conscience, has inadvertently supported the monumental pillars of corruption in the country. The challenge before us demands that we take a critical look at our penchant for scandalously expensive churches and mosques, harbouring stinking rich and nauseatingly flashy priests and pastors and imams, whose marks of success include palatial mansions, state of the art cars and fat bank accounts! No, Nigeria needs religious leaders and groups of austere disposition who would spearhead a moral revolution and an ethical re-orientation for a nation and its people that have been brought low in the course of a protracted midnight of debauchery.

Religious organisations in Nigeria can use their influence over people's consciences to bridge the gap between religious ritualism and social morality. To dislodge the evil dispensation by which Nigerians of all walks of life seem to have decided that the price to be paid for honesty, fidelity, truth, hard work and diligence are too high, and by which they have settled for the short cut and the quick fix, and by which they have resorted to mutual betrayal, calumniation, opportunism and manipulation in the bid to make it by any means foul or fair, religious organisations must take up the challenge of constantly highlighting to their members the deadly consequences for the body and the soul, of those seven social sins identified by Mahatma Gandhi, namely: "Politics without principle; pleasure without conscience; wealth without work; commerce without morality; education without character; science without humanity; and worship without sacrifice."

Conclusion

What we need in Nigeria is a reconstruction of our damaged corporate psyche. We need a fundamental re-envisioning, and that will involve a re-definition of our communal ethos, a re-appreciation of our social habits and a re-prioritization of our national values, and it is my contention that in today's Nigeria, there is no organ better placed than Religious organisations to champion this cause. Authentic religion teaches people that the meaning of human life is beyond humanity, and beyond this world, therefore the proper dissemination of the best principles of our two great religions, will help to checkmate the human instinct to grab and to accumulate for self, while neglecting the common good. I am convinced that the undiluted dissemination of the spiritual values in the two religions – not the message of convenience that we have become familiar with these days - is capable of purging Nigeria of the scourge of corruption, and salvaging our country from the gang of rogue nations in the world.

Yet, I must quickly add that religious bodies alone cannot do what every segment of the society must do to fight corruption in Nigeria. The generality of Nigerians must pay attention to the provisions of the Criminal Code against the various shades of corruption, especially involving public servants, and insist on the rigorous application of these provisions to all and sundry without fear or favour. To demonstrate its seriousness about prosecuting a war against corruption, the present administration must bring out the reports of the various probe panels that have been gathering dust in government archives, including the Oputa Panel Report about which so much fanfare was made and upon which so much premium was placed by Nigerians and the international community, but which appears to have been frozen by the very government that established the instrument. Concerted action must be taken on the most recent Auditor-General's Report and the one before it, which indicted practically all sectors of our public service including the Presidency, the

Legislature and the Judiciary. I am not aware that anyone has been sanctioned over those damning reports except the Acting Auditor General himself whose position was not confirmed after the release of the report. The perception created by this kind of disposition on the part of government does not help in the campaign against corruption.

The judicial system must be strengthened, and the law enforcement agencies must be thoroughly cleaned up, re-structured and re-oriented, so that they may become more efficient in detecting and fighting corruption. Religious organisations cannot do this for government. Employers of labour should strive to pay adequate salaries and wages to workers. And finally, the society in general should desist from conferring honours on people whose wealth is questionable. The conduct and processes of the National Merit Award scheme should be thoroughly reviewed to make it more meaningful and tailored towards acknowledging and rewarding true patriotism (not sycophancy), hard work, honesty and probity. All Nigerians must be at alert to ensure that their elected representatives operate with truth, honesty and accountability. Yes, even those who find their way to the presidency, the national assembly, the state houses, and the local government councils, by corrupt means, can be forced to become accountable by a nation that suddenly wakes up to the imperative of fighting corruption.

CHAPTER FORTY- FIVE

Nigeria and the Leadership Challenge
(Written on November 16, 2004)

It is widely acknowledged that a land devoid of visionary leaders and a nation without integrity can hardly experience stability and peace. That is the story of Nigeria in recent years. Leaders with vision inspire citizens and mobilize them for nation building. Leaders with crystal motives employ wisdom, foresight, sense of purpose and commitment, to galvanise a people towards self-actualisation and propel the national spirit in them. History throws up quite a few outstanding leaders, true heroes of their time, who set the moral and political tones for their societies. Such leaders as George Washington of America, Mahatma Gandhi of India, Winston Churchill of Britain, Charles De Gaulle of France, Julius Nyerere of Tanzania, Lee Kwan Yew of Singapore, and Nelson Mandela of South Africa, readily come to mind.

Where public figures exemplify the sterling qualities of leadership, they rub off on the society at large and invest citizens with the patriotic fervour. But whereas in this country, a society is plagued by rogue leadership, where it is dominated by treasury looting, election rigging, political brigandage and assassination - in such circumstances decent and public-spirited individuals are disparaged and discouraged from participating in the resultant dirty politics. Many with altruistic intentions who venture, end up being compromised and they join the bandwagon. And where a political system is dominated by greedy elements, such characters even if perceived to pursue politics with "blood-thirsty" devotion, cannot provide what it takes to lead a country to peace and prosperity.

Our lives in Nigeria have in recent times been dominated by a worsening security situation, manifested in sporadic violent skirmishes, armed robbery, arson, politically motivated assassinations, massive youth unemployment and acrimonious poverty. Ours remains a country where millions are under-nourished, where economic, education, health and social infrastructures are collapsed and tottering. In contradistinction to this national scenario is a political leadership class that wallows in financial and economic constipation and social self-adulation.

When we count our blessings in the year 2004, we note the unusual windfall from an unprecedented high crude oil price throughout the budgetary year, hitting up to $54 per barrel at some point, in contrast to the modest budgetary projection of only $27 dollars (that has turned out to be only 50% of what eventually got into our kitty). But how have Nigerians been better for it? How has the leadership been managing the difference in projected and actual income? How come we have experienced in this same year 2004 such increases in the price of petroleum products with the attendant inflation and the untold hardship on the masses of poor people and the labour unrest that followed? With a moribund economy under the tunnel vision of the type of leadership in place, what would happen if crude oil prices suddenly plunged?

No wonder then that in these convoluted times, many of our youths are taking to crime. No wonder our students are indulging more and more in cultism and perfecting the language of the underworld. No wonder our notoriety is growing with the most intuitive scammers in our climes, even as we are touted to be the happiest people on earth. Balanced against our endowment and potential, our circumstance in this country suggests that we have neither a listening or learning leadership in place. Despite all the tools and resources available to an otherwise committed leadership to refocus our society, the evidence abounds that what leadership we have in place at the critical national level and at other levels is often self-serving and opportunistic. In recent years so much resource has been wasted on grandiose projects and grandstanding endeavours, and no resource is spared in massaging the gargantuan egos and feathering the nests of the leadership class at the expense of the masses whose welfare they swore to labour for.

With the reality on the ground today where the masses are more and more depressed in all sectors, the gap is ever widening between them and a leadership feeding fat and getting richer by the day, a leadership enjoying self-awarded honours and perquisites, with their wards often comfortably ensconced in foreign lands. Only yesterday, many of these political parasites were out there, gaunt and hungry like the rest of us, bemoaning their lean fortunes. But today, they have metamorphosed into deities who are no longer sharing the pains in the land. The story of our kind of leadership is akin to the one told by Prophet Ezekiel in the book of Ezekiel Chapter 34, where the shepherds of Israel, rather than feed and tend the flock in their charge, chose instead to feed themselves on the sheep and the milk, to dress themselves in their wool, and abandon the sheep, putting them in harm's way. The Lord promises in that passage to rescue the flock from their vicissitudes and their abandonment in the wilderness and to disinherit the gluttonous and punitive shepherds and take over the task of shepherding the flock himself!

An overview of political and economic events in the year 2004 leaves little on our national horizon to cheer about, but merely reinforces the concern being expressed by serious minded citizens and cynics alike that Nigeria is in a state of anomie and perilously on a merry-go-round. Our national disaster has been in the making and has been nourished on virtually all segments by a pedestrian leadership long enough to demonstrate the manifest failure of the state. The spate of violence erupting now and again in different parts of the country, and especially the anarchy we witness in Anambra state, are a graphic statement on the security status of this country. True, the lawlessness displayed in high places and the brazen escapades of political kingpins now invade and intrude the political life of the entire citizenry, undermining national security and political discipline. The Police and other security agencies appear to have lost out entirely in the contest, yet they continue to talk tough while lives and properties are being destroyed.

Nigerians are hardly ever known to quit public positions on grounds of failure, incompetence, neglect, scandal or moral integrity. Even in the face of obvious neglect and mismanagement of public resource, it is not in our character to quit the stage, and when forced to do so following rotten scandals, our leaders are let off the hook to flaunt their ill-gotten gains and to worm their way back to political relevance at various levels, using the same ill-gotten wealth to buy up the people.

Many believe that a major factor in the Nigerian socio-political conundrum is the question of the moral credentials of those at the helm of our affairs. Evidence abounds that many just have bought their way into positions of leadership. Their true motive is not necessarily out of a passion to serve the people of this country but to take advantage of the prevailing political contradictions and economic distress for personal aggrandisement. Consequently, the average Nigerian political leader develops an imperial air of condescension and once in power treats people with utter disrespect, sometimes bordering on disdain.

It goes without saying that the government of the day is insensitive to the yearnings of the people and deaf to their cry of desperation. Those who are holding the reins of power believe too much in themselves, as if they know it all and they have everything in control. In their own eyes they are doing wonderfully well, but the signals everywhere are that this government has lost its bearing. And before such a deaf government, the people are praying as usual that the God of love will intervene. But if this country must make any headway, if the progressive decay in the polity must be halted, if an undemocratic monoculture in governance is to be avoided, and if the descent into anarchy in Nigeria must be averted, then change is inevitable, and so we shall need to pray harder, and get to work to bring the required change about.

Our situation is not irredeemable. Nigerians are not a different breed of human beings from citizens elsewhere such as in Singapore or Malaysia, South Africa or Ghana. Many of us do not believe that Nigeria is so difficult to organize and lead unto peaceful co-existence, political stability and economic prosperity. What we need is a paradigm shift from a reactive to a pro-active leadership and culture of governance. What we need is a different definition of perception of politics, where the paths to public service are not as smooth and attractive as they are now for rogues, thieves and brigands, and where the gains of office are not as rewarding as they are currently fashioned out to be. We need a shift in leadership focus sustained by transparency and accountability where civil society will engage the political leadership in balancing policy objectives against concrete acts of governance.

The generality of the Nigerian people who have had to put up with a succession of rogue leaders and whose sensibilities are today continually insulted by punitive overlords in the corridors of power, should wake up from their slumber and reaffirm their belief in the sovereign power of the people. Civil society must shake off its shackles and break out of the political inertia in which it presently finds itself and redefine the character of leadership for the Nigerian nation. The desired change will come about when civil society rejects the unfolding ignominious political system that is driven by a lack of moral credibility on the part of politicians who got into power with questionable electoral credentials.

The desired change will come about when civil society identifies and rejects the political parasites who are isolated and alienated from the social circumstance of the people, and who do not share in the economic austerity of the moment but whose interests lie in living on a different level thereby contributing to state failure. Current leaders and aspirants to leadership will do well to read the signs of the times and heed the admonition for change in leadership style and dream and actualise such positive dreams as will pull this country from the brink. Time is running out for our leaders, but if today they experience the much-needed conversion and toe the line of sanity, they may yet wean the people from the inevitable option of a popular revolt. Christians must intensify their prayer for the emergence of a God-fearing leadership in our land, and as individuals and groups, seek divine guidance on what we can and must do to see our country out of the present mess.

CHAPTER FORTY-SIX

Christmas and My Prophetic Imagination
(Written on December 28, 2004)

Christmas, the celebration of the birth of Jesus Christ the promised Messiah, is for me the triumph of prophetic imagination. Prophetic Imagination is a major plank of the Judeo-Christian religion. It is the power and the courage and also the inspiration to dream of, or envision a world that is totally different from the present one that is plagued by corruption, wickedness, social injustice, sickness and disease, violence and war. Prophetic imagination is the spiritual and mental attitude of defying the state of darkness and sin we find ourselves in today, and dreaming the promised future of bliss into the present. Prophets are the visionaries of their time. When all others are blind, prophets are the ones granted to see the light beyond the tunnel. Equipped as they are with superior knowledge and perception, prophets analyse the situation on the ground in the light of God's ultimate purpose and inscrutable design. Prophets refuse to be defiled by the corruption of the moment. They refuse to be engulfed by the darkness of the surrounding environment. Instead they possess the vision of life as it ought to be, and they hold on tenaciously to this vision, all appearances to the contrary notwithstanding.

Prophetic imagination is the spiritual defiance of what is, in the name of what God has promised. It visualises an alternative future to the one fated by the momentum of current contradictory forces. It breathes the air of a time yet to be into the suffocating atmosphere of present reality. Prophets who are totally committed to the new inevitability on which they have fixed their imaginations, can decisively affect the shape the future takes. Such prophets or dreamers are the shapers of the future. Prophetic imagination is the spiritual rejection of what the present reality is, in favour of what ought to be. It is the rejection of a world dominated by the powers of evil, in favour of the promised world of righteousness and peace which Jesus Christ calls the Kingdom of God.

In an environment of widespread debauchery and at a time of multiple tragedies, when the multitude of people will otherwise succumb to discouragement and to despair, prophetic imagination generates hope in the victims of injustice and in those who genuinely hunger for righteousness. Thus, prophets are harbingers of hope and heralds of freedom. Their prophetic imagination energises the poor victims of injustice and those who hunger and thirst for righteousness and peace with the powerful message that all is not lost – that soon, very soon, the Lord will intervene to turn things around for good. Thus, it was during the period of the Babylonian captivity, a time of great depression and distress in the history of Israel that such prophets as Isaiah and Zephaniah told their people to be strong, to fear not, for their God will come to save them. They encouraged their people with their powerful vision of the cosmic equilibrium that will occur when God visits his people. At that time, the wolf will live with the lamb, the panther will lie down with the kid, the lion will eat hay like the ox, the infant will play over the den of the adder; the baby will put his hand into the viper's lair, and there will be no hurt, there will be no harm, for the country will be full of knowledge of the Lord as the waters cover the sea.

At Christmas this year, therefore, I join the prophets of old in this dreaming exercise. Since the circumstances of our world and of my country are similar to those that inspired these prophets, and since I serve the same God of promise, I am daring to defy the present world with its multiple ills, and to imagine a different world and a different society that is possible by virtue of God's promise. So I dream of peace for our world and for Nigeria that has gone through a protracted nightmare by way of economic distress, political fragmentation and social decay. Though I have watched with sadness the negative trends in the economy and the sustained tension on the political front in Nigeria and elsewhere, I have not abandoned my dream of peace.

In spite of the mess of the moment, I have chosen to hold on to the dream of peace, security and prosperity for our confused world and for my country, the giant of Africa that today lies flat on its belly. I am not entirely distracted by the blood and tears I see. Nor am I overwhelmed by the selfishness, greed, hatred and violence all over the place that today render global and national peace impossible. I still dream of peace for the world and for Nigeria, for what will life be without a dream? How could I live without this prophetic imagination?

At Christmas 2004 I have decided to look at the world and my country with a great deal of optimism. That is why I dream of a new world order of peace and global solidarity, not one of First, Second, Third and Fourth Worlds. I dream of a strong, united, peaceful and prosperous Nigeria, one in which the teeming population of young people (who today lack pride in themselves and in their country), shall one day sing their national anthem and recite their national pledge with genuine pride. I dream of a transformed Nigerian, one in which everyone will have a place and have a say, one in which everyone will respect everyone else, Igbo or Hausa, Yoruba or Tiv, Itsekiri or Efik, Christian or Muslim, Catholic or Protestant, and affiliates of PDP, AD or ANPP. In spite of our chequered political history in Nigeria and the series of broken dreams and dashed hopes we have witnessed, I continue along the path of prophetic imagination. I continue to dream of freedom, justice, good governance, genuine democracy, the rule of law, mutual acceptance and peaceful co-existence, because I hold on to the promises of God.

Like the prophets of old I am able to imagine a time of peace for the world and for my society because I believe in the mystery of rejuvenation. I believe that out of the rubble of our shattered landscape, a rich, powerful, united people can emerge, if today we begin a serious reflection on the meaning and principle of corporate existence. I am going ahead with my fertile imagination of peace for our land, because I know that peace is possible if today we begin a revolution of hope that will include a genuine commitment to truth, justice and reconciliation. I shall hold on to the dream of peace because I am a believer who knows that with God all things are possible. Did he not create the world out of a formless void? Did he not bring water out of rock? Did he not put back flesh on dry bones? Did he not raise the dead back to life? Is faith in the resurrection not the cardinal point of Christianity?

As I imagine a time of peace and prosperity for the world and for my country at Christmas, I nevertheless acknowledge that peace is not without a cost. I know that peace will not come without some striving on the part of men and women. I know that the peace of my imagination is the fruit of justice; that the peace of my dream does not occur irrespective of the moral disposition of individual human beings that make up the human society. I know that the peace that is the fruit of my prophetic engagement is predicated on a prior commitment to truth, mutual tolerance, equity, and justice on the part of those who desire it. I know that a nation without integrity cannot have peace, and that where there is no vision, the people do perish.

Yet I continue dreaming of peace, notwithstanding the mitigating circumstances. And today I challenge all those who share this dream with me to dissociate themselves from the prevalent values, habits and orientations that make peace difficult to achieve. So let those who want the peace of my imagination to be realized for our country commit themselves to the task of demolishing those structures of sin all over the place that have made peace and prosperity such a tall dream. Let them join me in pulling down the mountains of corruption, selfishness, and social injustice, and in filling up the valleys of racial and ethnic prejudice, religious bigotry, and social discrimination. This is surely one way of defying the darkness of the moment and making our prophetic imagination become reality.

CHAPTER FORTY-SEVEN

The Good Shepherd and the Nigerian Situation
(Written on April 17, 2005)

The Fourth Sunday of Easter is traditionally observed by Catholics as the Good Shepherd Sunday. In the gospel reading of the day from John Chapter 10, Jesus Christ says that the sheep that belong to him will listen to his voice. He knows them, and they will follow him. He will give them eternal life, and they will never be lost. He says no one will ever steal them from him. Since he and the Father are one, and no one can steal from the Father, it means that the sheep that truly belong to him will never be lost.

This is very cheering news for us Nigerians at a time of widespread discouragement and disillusionment in our country at the hands of leaders that are not true shepherds but manipulators, exploiters and abusers of the people. In the desperate search for solution to the profound hunger of the individual heart and the hunger that plagues our entire country, we have indeed encountered many thieves, rogues and brigands who are only out to steal, to cheat and to destroy. Those who pretend to be shepherds in our land are often feeding themselves fat and abandoning the sheep to misery and destitution.

Jesus proclaims to a tired and famished people that he is the Good Shepherd who leads his flock to good pasture, and the sheep that belong to him listen to his voice. Those who do not belong to his sheepfold often hunger and thirst. They are also easy prey for wolves and other wild beasts. Besides him, other people who parade themselves as shepherds are not authentic. Like mercenaries or hirelings, they lack genuine interest for the flock. They are interested only in themselves and what they stand to gain. They will abandon the sheep as soon as they see the wolf approaching. He says such people are not shepherds but thieves, rogues and brigands. He says: "the thief has come to steal, to cheat, and to destroy, but I have come that they may have life and have it to the full" (John 10:10). Jesus Christ presents himself as the bread of life which offers the true satisfaction for the hunger of the heart (John 6:58), the true gate of the sheepfold through whom the hungry sheep can go in and out to find green pasture (John 10:9), the Way the Truth and the Life (John 14:6).

We remember that in Ezekiel 34 the Lord condemned the leaders of his people who failed to feed the flock, but instead cheated, sapped, looted, violated and manipulated those over whom they have been placed as shepherds. The Lord accused them of treating the sheep cruelly and harshly, of feeding themselves fat and clothing themselves with wool while letting the sheep go hungry and go astray. He subsequently threatened to take the flock out of their hands so that they may stop feeding themselves. He then promised to take care of the sheep himself as the true shepherd, feeding the hungry, bandaging the wounded, making the weak strong, looking for the lost one, and showing them where to rest. He promised to send a Messiah, an anointed one who will proclaim liberty to captives, bind up hearts that are broken, open the eyes of the blind, and set the downtrodden free. By his life and teaching, and by his passion and death, Jesus Christ presents himself as this anointed one of God, the Messiah, the Good Shepherd.

As I reflect on the Good Shepherd, I think of the hunger of our nation Nigeria. Our entire society is hungry. In the midst of our fledgling democracy that is threatened by all sorts of social and political crises, Nigerians are hungry for a stable polity that will make for peace and prosperity. Within the context of the clamour for resource control by states and ethnic nationalities that feel cheated in the present economic arrangement, Nigerians are hungry for equity in resource distribution. As various individuals and interest groups that believe they have been marginalised in the present constitutional arrangement call for a sovereign national conference, Nigerians are hungry for the justice that makes for peace. And as corruption becomes more and more entrenched at all levels of our country's political leadership, Nigerians are hungry for the integrity that makes for true prosperity. From Sokoto to Calabar, and from Maiduguri to Lagos, Nigerians are hungry and are yearning for true shepherds that will lead the country to the good pasture of truth, honesty, justice and accountability, where lasting peace and prosperity are to be found.

St. Augustine, at the height of inspiration had asserted that the Lord has created human beings for himself, and that their hearts will remain hungry and restless, until they rest in him. God is the God of Truth. Our peace and fulfilment as children of God will only come when we seek after, desire and embrace truth and justice at all times, in season and out of season. To the extent that we run away from the truth and justice and instead relish in falsehood, injustice and corruption, to that extent shall peace elude us. To the extent that we avoid the path of the truth that challenges and often embarrasses us, to that extent shall we remain a famished and restless people. Is it any wonder therefore that our economy doesn't seem to be improving and our democracy remains so fragile? If we reject truth, if we trample on justice, if we evade the Good Shepherd who alone is able to lead us to green pasture, are we not bound to starve, to wither and to eventually collapse?

Jesus invites all who hunger and thirst to come to him in order to find satisfaction, peace, consolation and salvation. In John 7:37 he says: "Let anyone who is thirsty come to me! Let anyone who believes in me come and drink." He promised that all who come to him will know the truth and that the truth shall set them free (John 8:32). He is the resting place for all who have laboured and are overburdened, for all who have borne the heavy yoke of poverty, sickness, oppression, discrimination, persecution, loneliness, rejection and abuse. He says in Matthew 11:28 "Come to me all you who labour and are overburdened, and I will give you rest. Shoulder my yoke and learn from me for I am meek and humble of heart, and you will find rest for your souls. For my yoke is easy, and my burden is light. It is in his name alone that even today wounded hearts can be healed, that broken families can be mended, that devastated countries like Nigeria can be redeemed, and that alienated humanity can be reconciled with God, with neighbour, and with the natural environment.

Jesus is the answer to the world's longing for light and truth. Amidst the darkness of sin and human depravity, expressed in idolatry and promiscuity, Jesus presents himself as the light and the truth. Within the midnight of hatred and wickedness, manifested in war, armed banditry, political manipulation, hired assassination, and jungle justice, Jesus presents himself as the Good Shepherd. In the dark tunnel of corruption, whose fruits are fraud, theft, bribery and the culture of settlement, Jesus says that the sheep that belong to him will listen to his voice that calls them to a life of truth and justice. In the midst of the jungle of Nigerian politics, where primitive greed and the manipulation of religion and ethnicity are often at the centre stage, and where justice, civility, and the rule of law are often discountenanced, Jesus says that the sheep that belong to him listen to his voice that calls them to a life of truth and justice. Even as discordant tunes are heard from North to South and from East to West, we hear Jesus say that the sheep that belong to him will listen to his voice of reason that calls them to a life of truth and justice. He promises that no one will steal his own sheep away from him, for no one can steal from the Father.

The feast of the Good Shepherd gives us the assurance that those who have always cast their votes for truth, justice and genuine reconciliation in our land need fear no harm, for while the visitation of the Shepherd spells doom for the agents of evil in our land, it also heralds the vindication and consolation of the faithful ones who have all the while persevered in a life of truth, justice and commitment to the common good. Soon the Good Shepherd shall be here. He shall dislodge the agents of darkness and corruption, and for once the children of light shall shine like the stars. Soon the Good Shepherd shall be here. He shall help the remnant faithful to rebuild the ruined landscape of our country, making it possible for those who were victims of the forces of darkness to sing the song of liberation. Soon the Good Shepherd shall be here. He shall establish the kingdom of justice and peace so that all who suffered harassment at the hands of thieves, rogues and brigands in our land, shall have the last laugh.

CHAPTER FORTY-EIGHT

Dress Codes and Social Dislocation in Nigeria
(A Paper Contribution to Education Today, A Quarterly Journal of the Federal Ministry of Education, June 2005)

Introduction

In recent times, indecent dressing among many young people in our society and the widespread advocacy for the application of dress codes especially in our institutions of higher learning have received a lot of media attention and generated quite an amount of debate amidst a cross-section of Nigerians. I have followed the debate closely and I have observed that the war on indecent dressing is being waged in many circles as if indecent dressing is the primary pathology that is plaguing the Nigerian socio-cultural and moral environment. Those who are spearheading this war, including University Administrators, Leaders of Religious Organisations and even Legislators, are responding to the very serious challenge of a major dislocation in our corporate existence with an inverted, passionate prescription of dressing.

Indecent dressing or immodesty in dressing, though a moral aberration is, in my view, among the least of the many social, cultural, and moral problems that are threatening to destroy this nation and its people. In fact, what we see today as widespread indecent dressing (as well as indiscipline) among the youths of our country is only indicative and symptomatic of the system collapse that is inevitable in a society run aground where, as it were, the fathers have eaten sour grapes and the children's teeth are on edge.

Quite apart from the overarching factors ruling the country's social pandemic, a good part of the debate on the subject of indecent dressing has often been devoted to treating the symptoms rather than the causes of the opprobrium that it has thrown up. To fully appreciate the contribution of dressing to today's social predicament and its implications for youth development, it is important not to concentrate on the linear and vertical considerations alone, but with a bit of lateral thinking to examine the wider socio-cultural dimensions of the problem.

Dress habits and their evolution in human societies

It is attested to by human experience all through the ages that dress is not just a symbiotic identification of a people with their environment but is also an evolutionary expression of their uniqueness. Before the boundaries of the world's communities became obfuscated with expedition, conquest and the overlap of cultures, dressing was closely linked to the habitat and reflected nature and the environment. Whereas the Eskimos fashioned their heavily laden dressing for maximum protection from the bitterly cold elements of their environment, the hot climatic conditions in our part of Africa under the tropical sun largely indicated a scanty dress code. The bare covering of the midsection would prove adequate for everyone including adults, and the sight of a young mother thus openly suckling her baby would hardly elicit any emotions of shame, arousal, or indignation. It was a normal, natural sight.

However, as new cultures and values found their way into our society with the advent of modern civilisation, dress seemed to have changed from being essentially a natural expression and identification with one's environment and became a symbol of acquired values, sometimes adorned for status or affectation and at other times for one to be seen to identify with the Joneses. Events have developed to a point in Nigeria where society has set formal and informal codes of dressing for virtually all occasions. Consequently, such professionals as lawyers and bankers are obliged to dress in suits sometimes under the most inappropriate weather conditions. For most social events, Nigerians are often heavily padded with layers of clothing even when the hot weather conditions and the incessant power failure clearly indicate light or scanty clothing. Anyone lightly (but otherwise appropriately) dressed in such situations could be greeted with condescending disapproval.

Every society is said to be self-regulatory - setting standards, providing basic social and economic infrastructures, rewarding exemplary demonstration of group values and imposing sanctions against deviants from societal expectations. In formative years in this country, uniform dressing in schools and colleges remains the code. Early in life this uniformity emphasizes discipline, orderliness, and identity. Later in life this dress regimen for minors is supposed to give way to maturity and freedom of choice and expression, the extent of which is now manifested in tertiary institutions where unbridled freedom is given flesh in unbridled dressing.

Nigerian Youth: Victims of a general systems collapse

Not much has been heard from the youth camp since the debate broke and so not all of the story can be told from the critical commentaries issuing from the older generation of Nigerians, some of who may be under the illusion that once our youth change their dress code our moral transformation is complete. The widespread disorientation, disillusionment and loss of the sense of values and meaning among the younger generation of this country must first be fully understood and appreciated in the context of the enveloping decadence in the nation. The social pressures at play in the national environment contribute in no small way to the behaviour of young people.

If all that is evident is the oppressive and limiting conditions of today, if all that is ringing out of today's leadership is the hollow message of perseverance without end, if all that our young people hear is the cacophony of misrule and discontent, if all that they feel are the pangs of hunger and the pains of poverty, if all they can hope for is a life of misery, of insecurity, of joblessness and frustration, and if all they can perceive is a nation wallowing in economic stagnation, in a jungle of political misdirection, corruption and immorality in high and low places, a nation more or less permanently in decline on many fronts, if that is all that is in store for them in a land of such promise and potential, what do they care what anybody thinks about the way they dress?

In Nigeria's convoluted social environment of today, dressing to please the crowd or to play to the gallery would come a poor second to other social imperatives in the minds of young people who form the vital majority in a country yet to find its bearing after decades of floundering. Whichever way we look at our nation, whether in its institutions, its organisation, its politics and economy, its religious structures, its cultural and ethnic interactions, in its social and administrative infrastructures and orientation, the question must be asked, in all sincerity and honesty, are we "properly dressed" as a people and as a nation? It just so happens that physical dressing is a tangible identity of human beings but beyond that there are these other 'dressings' that portray who and what we really are. So before we begin at all to enter the argument concerning our dress code, and before we reduce the debate on indecent dressing vis-à-vis the pandemic moral decadence to a chicken-and-egg situation, we must address this all-embracing global question.

True, our physical appearance is often perceived as the most visible evidence of our sense of modesty and decency. True, our young people, notably in tertiary institutions and especially many of the female members, are evidently often more guilty of running afoul of public morality in dressing. But out there in the wider society, there is another group whose legal status and social recognition are contentious and controversial but who nonetheless enjoy widespread patronage as they ply their trade in skimpy dresses. They are to be found in their thousands outside the best of hotels in cities across the nation, in sleazy joints in urban centres and smaller communities, and in the most unlikely holes in society. They are prostitutes who are given some respectability with the appellation of commercial sex workers. With HIV/AIDS ravaging many families and neighbourhoods, these people put their health and their society's health and well-being at risk in more deadly ways than their dressing alone could ever do. Society can certainly not deal with the menace of prostitution only by dressing prostitutes in flowing robes. But are we targeting them for any kind of social reform?

In a country where youth orientation and development get perfunctory attention of the nation's leadership across the board, we have bred a multitude of victims rather than a pack of rebels. In a situation of hopelessness and helplessness, young people are left to grow and mature in a state of abandonment. They are therefore easy recruits for pornography and prostitution, for drug abuse and violent cults, and for other social vices and negative tendencies. With no committed assistance and support, they seek understanding and acceptance from their peers rather than from parents, leaders or government. Trends in globalisation have deepened the distress for many and at the same time offered avenues to seek individual relevance in a socially dysfunctional environment. So for some, dressing becomes a means of attracting attention, of making a statement of rebellion and of provoking a dialogue with the adult society. And when confronted with a stare of righteous indignation, it is easy for them to retort in kind and with sublime abandon, "So what!"

On the domestic front, family values have become so degraded that our young people have lost touch with the traditional influence of parents and the immediate community. With little attention given by many parents who are preoccupied with the rat race of living and surviving in this country, what the child does with his or her time, and least of all, what they choose to wear no longer holds much concern for the parents. And of course morality is not an albatross on the conscience of young people alone. The adults are perhaps more deeply entrapped, which is why some have no qualms equipping the wardrobes of flimsy dresses that some young people have.

The moral bankruptcy by which some parents go to any length to aid and abet the corrupt and immoral passage of their wards through educational institutions is an example and an open licence for drifting into delinquency and portends difficult times for future leadership. Overwhelming social and economic decline has impacted heavily on many a family, practically consigning them to a lower status and standard of living. A consequence of this is the psychological stress that young people respond to by a reckless and lackadaisical approach to life - including the way they look, and from which promoters of crazy contemporary fashion trends gain a curious class of youth clientele.

Poor parenting may not be solely responsible for today's culture of loose dressing but is contributory to its taking root. Before society embarks on the wholesale condemnation of a vital segment of its population we must look closely at the genesis of our moral decline and how the pollution of our values crept on us. For indeed we could be confronted with the classic case of the children's teeth being on edge, the parents having eaten sour grapes. Today's manifestations of degenerate sub-cultures among the youth could be the partial outcome of yesterday's culture of indiscipline among the parents.

New cultural traits and how they impact on us

On the surface, what we see on our streets and on our campuses are indeed condemnable. The evidence of licentiousness and permissiveness is multi-dimensional in a society that has come under multiple attacks from prevailing global influences and foreign cultures. The clash of cultures that globalisation has brought about is partially evident in our changing dress habits. Elements of globalisation undermine cultural purity and freedom while promoting the integration and fusion of various cultural traits. With unrestrained access to television, the Internet, foreign magazines and other media, globalisation is homogenizing the avid interests of a large youth following, but often with invasive negative impact. Consequently, there are today those who would seek the right to being nudist or such other forms of sub-social behaviour. Young people are particularly vulnerable to a predilection for pornography and subliminal sexploitation. In Nigeria, marketing jobs in banks with subtle dress codes attached are a regular form of bait for female job seekers. Young people come under an assault of modern fashion represented by the catwalk displays of designers who sometimes use local fabrics for what some consider provocative dress designs.

We pride ourselves on being very religious people, the vast majority of us pitching our tents in the numerous religious camps in Nigeria. In our multi-religious national mosaic, we often witness the demonstration of extremism in the perceptions and practices of our beliefs - from the very traditional to the very liberal. And so even in the most intolerable weather condition we find advocates of a gender discriminatory dress code that seek to turn the human person into a near robotic masquerade. At the other extreme are those who are wont to give free reign to individual sartorial expression, pleading that the human spirit is a free spirit, that the human body is a gift of the Creator, and that freedom of expression extends to the way one chooses to dress.

But the traditional Christian position argues on the side of modesty in dressing and comportment (See Matt.5:27,28; Mark 9:42-50; Luke17:1-3; Rom.14,15; 1Cor.11:2-16; 1Tim.2:9-15). And that is why Christian religious leaders joined the fray in the virulent vituperations of critics against indecent dressing. Some of them have even gone further to prescribe punitive sanctions that strike at the very core of the offender's spirituality. We must however note that not all who dress poorly or scantily in our society necessarily dress to kill. Not all who affect today's fashion because of its currency necessary do so for immoral reasons. There are some, including students, for whom a clean T-shirt of any size, or a threadbare dress is the best available for Sunday worship! They include those whose social standing and economic well-being are low; those whose survival preoccupation is far removed from the aesthetic considerations of a dress code, but who nonetheless want to cling to a tenuous hope in a compassionate God and therefore would want to be welcome in Church.

These count among those who come seeking solace in the soothing words of the pastor. But what does the pastor do about the other very serious social vices of those who harbour in countless churches across the land, those whose 'peccadilloes' are not as evident as the sea of dresses in any church gathering? These would include 419ers, crooked contractors, dubious business tycoons, dealers in fake and substandard goods, corrupt officials, election riggers, and others. Would there be a motive to turn a deaf ear or a blind eye on these classes of worshippers? Or would the struggle not continue to win them over from their ungodly disposition to life? What would be the rationale for denying the believer succour in the sacraments and church processes when Christ himself would dine with sinners and tax collectors? (Matt.9:10-13; Luke 19:1-10). Pleading harassment of a kind in these circumstances, quite a number would opt to vacate their membership of one church, one parish or the other, in search of understanding, compassion and perhaps salvation elsewhere.

The legal dimension of the dress debate suggests that those who pontificate and moralize sanctimoniously on the question of an acceptable dress code may not have too firm a ground to stand on. It would appear that there is no law moderating dressing or setting for Nigerians any dress codes, but what are to be found are criminal provisions against illegal soliciting and prostitution. As it is, it would be difficult to defend successfully an action in court that challenges the enforcement of a dress code in the adult public domain. It would be seen as an encroachment and a constitutional infringement on the basic rights of a free citizen. It would rather be more productive to seek other means of appealing to the moral judgement of the individual.

There is a tendency for the self-righteous to categorise obscene dressing as the extraordinary mortal sin of society. Who indeed is the moralist rightly motivated and justified to set and enforce dress codes for society? Would the pastor abandon the primary duty of winning souls, including the souls of the offensively dressed? Or would it be parents whose failings have contributed to hatching the present generation of social deviants? Is it the institutional leadership which is saddled everywhere with a baggage of problems in campuses, problems of cultism, exams and admissions fraud, gang murder, vandalism, etc.? No study has located indecent dressing as the repository of these problems. Is it government which itself can hardly stand on any moral high ground? Society too is overwhelmed and overrun by prevalent decadence. For example, in the absence of viable public facilities and devoid of any coordinated control, the national environment is heavily polluted by a wayward garbage culture that includes the indiscriminate generation of human waste.

How does society prosecute a cleanup process and to what extent would that be impeded by a 'crisis' in today's dressing culture? It would seem then that making a scapegoat of dressing bases our social predicament on a faulty prioritization of our national engagements. The impression is not here being given that negative tendencies are to be condoned or glamorised, but we must situate the problem in context. The emphasis must be made here that the problem of dressing cannot be the causative factor to the ills of society. Our society is multi-cultural and pluralistic. Those who are in the business say that dressing is in a constant state of flux, but that our dressing responds to culture as well as fashion trends. Dress codes are dynamic, and like music, they are subject to constant change of variable duration. How long will male hairdo or earring last? How long will tattoos remain in vogue? The odd pieces of frilly female dresses may survive for only as long as they hold any attraction for those who use them. And perhaps for as long as there appear to be enough critics to accord them the attention they do not deserve.

The human person is created in God's image and endowed with high faculties. Part of God's gifts to the human person is a capacity to control emotions, and particularly with maturity, the adult human person learns to keep his or her instincts and passions in check. The sight of a stark naked mad person on the street often evokes quiet revulsion. The observer's perceptions are often tempered by the ability to suppress emotions of eroticism or arousal, often making the choice to look the other way. In the same way various levels of nudity may excite no more than controllable outrage in one who is imbued with enough maturity and self control.

As no empirical studies have proven otherwise, it is fallacious to claim that seductive dressing is the reason behind rape incidents. The perpetrator of rape would be more likely to need psychological or psychiatric evaluation and treatment, since most rape victims are not attacked on the basis of their dress. The randy university don or the sexual harasser is not enticed only by an inappropriately dressed female but is motivated by his sexual perversion. It is difficult for anyone to draw a neat line to determining the shapes and sizes of individual wardrobes. The moral strength of the human person as a superior species and one who has a working knowledge of the demands of the God of creation on the one hand, and sensitivity to the feelings of other members of the particular society on the other, can play down the tendency towards the idolatry of the human body. As we mature through life, we should normally become more appreciative of the beauty, innocence and purity of creation, and be less focused on the sensual, erotic dimensions. That way we would be better able to handle and control our sexual faculties.

Conclusion

A small segment of society cannot be an island unto itself, insulated from the environment. It would be an illusion to expect that our institutions can be oases of morality in a sea of moral degeneracy. Curbing the prevalent irresponsible dress habit should not be about prescribing solutions that would create fresh sociological problems. Society must aim at conscientizing its members using the social instruments and institutions available. Any attempt at enforcing dress codes as a means of compelling religious adherence or as an excuse for the restoration of values could be counterproductive. The challenge before society can be addressed on several fronts. At the family level parents need to pay closer attention to the values the children are imbibing. Friendly interactions with, and good examples shown to children by parents, would be far more beneficial than any orders handed down. The sentiments of love, mutual respect and responsibility can be effectively engaged. The home as the first school of life and parents as the first teachers, remain the primary source of moral development for children as they advance through life.

While religious organisations can be moral custodians and guardians for our youths, care must be taken to ensure that those who lead in the religious field do not wear the label of running a tyranny in religious habit. Religious leaders constructively engaging their youth organisations and blending the peer group activism in a positive way can turn the morality crusade into a vibrant youth initiative. A properly organised counselling network that places emphasis on persuasion rather than coercion would yield far more positive and durable results than enforcing ultimatums.

Government on its part must have a coherent development agenda for the nation, a segment of which will take in its stride the issue of moral and ethical behaviour of citizens, including the appreciation of an appropriate dress sense. This would mean taking into account the poverty dimension that demands adequate focus and vision. While they complement the role of the family in character moulding, government and leaders are key in the challenge of channelling a credible course for society.

The challenge that faces all manner of leaders at all levels in our country today is in my view one of pervasive social dislocation, where, due to years of abuse and neglect, many young people have lost all sense of values and meaning in life. Faced with such a crisis at the deeper and more profound level of life's meaning and values, an undue preoccupation with the dress habits of the youth population, or an obsession with dress codes, will amount to chasing rats when one's house in on fire. Let us not forget the truism that dress, like other ingredients of culture such as language, music and artefacts, reflect the generational transmission of values of identity in a society. Let us not forget too that inspired leadership can catalyse behaviour change in those being led. With all sectors of society playing their part in the project of moral regeneration, the proclamation of a dress code for any segment would be an idle exercise.

CHAPTER FORTY-NINE

Religion and National Integration: Past Experiences, Present Realities and Future Prospects
(Written on July 22, 2005)

The late Pope John Paul II made history in March 2001 by entering the Umayyad Mosque in Damascus, Syria. Out of deference for his Muslim brothers and sisters, he removed his shoes before entering the Mosque. When inside, he asked to be left alone for a while. He stood quietly and prayed! Addressing his audience on that occasion, the pope lamented over the numerous atrocities that have been committed in the history of humanity in the name of religion. He declared that religion can never be used as a justification for violence. He reminded Jews, Muslims, and Christians of their common patrimony in Abraham, and urged the warring parties in the Middle East to eschew hatred. This visit to the Mosque in Damascus was the first time in the history of Christianity that a pope would set his foot in a Mosque. The event threw up many lessons and challenges for those who are today concerned about the question of Religion and National Integration. That gesture of the pope is particularly challenging for those of us who live in Nigeria, where religion and ethnicity have often been manipulated or abused for political and economic ends, ends that are anything but religious.

Among the lessons we could learn from John Paul II's gesture, the first is that for all monotheistic religions, especially Judaism, Islam and Christianity, our mutual acknowledgement of the existence of one God who is Creator (and Father) of all, implies the concomitant acknowledgement and recognition of one another as creatures (and children) of the one God, who are endowed with equal dignity and sanctity. That is why Jews, Muslims and Christians, and to a very reasonable extent, adherents of African Traditional Religions, ascribe to the human person (all persons, including an unbelieving person), a divine origin, a supernatural end, and an existence that is imbued with transcendence. These are points of convergence for all monotheistic religions which modern pluralistic societies must capitalise upon in their search for peace and social integration, and in the task of nation building.

Furthermore, Jews, Muslims and Christians all have reference to Abraham as their father in faith. As we belong to one strand or the other in the Abrahamic progeny, we are therefore brothers and sisters who share a common ancestry that include such holy men and women as Abraham and Sarah, David and Elijah, and Jesus and Mary. It is right to say therefore that all who worship the God of Abraham, wherever they may be found in the world, and in whatever way they may express their faith in and worship of the one God, are one people – male and female, white and black, Jew and Arab, Hausa and Igbo.

Jews, Muslims and Christians share more than just a common ancestry. They share the fundamental elements in the ten Commandments of the Law as revealed to Moses. They mutually acknowledge the supremacy of charity and the "golden rule" as a workable moral principle for guiding human social relationships. They share a mutual aspiration for immortality, recognizing that human existence in this world is not all there is. They believe in an impending judgment after the human pilgrimage here on earth, and the existence of heaven – a place of reward for those who have lived good moral lives, and hell for those who have pursued evil ends. The three major monotheistic religions associate God closely with peace. That is why "shalom" is the standard greeting among the Jews. Islam itself is said to be a derivation of "salam" or "salem" which means peace. Christians on their own part call Jesus Christ "the Prince of Peace," whose kingdom shall be a kingdom of unending peace. It was Jesus Christ who taught: "Blessed are the peacemakers, for they shall be called children of God."

The foregoing is the truth of our common religious patrimony, which in the course of history has often been ignored or discountenanced by fanatics, extremists, fundamentalists, warmongers, conquerors, expansionists, crusaders and jihadists, who were often propelled, not by religious sentiments, but by the primordial sentiments of pride and arrogance, greed and avarice, and hatred and vengeance. Some of the most brutal wars in history were allegedly fought in the name of religion, and some of the worst atrocities and abuses against the human person have been committed allegedly in the name of religion.

Whole populations have been wiped out, cities have been sacked, groups and sects have been banished, and individuals have been tortured to death in the name of religion. Our own country has had its fair share of violence in the name of religion: From the *Maitatsine* crisis in Kano in the early 1980s to the Sharia riots in Kaduna and Jos in the year 2000 and 2001, we have sordid tales of brutal killings, torture and massive destruction of property, in the name of religion. And on the international scene, from the 9-11-2001 terror attacks on the Twin Towers in New York where some 3000 innocent people were killed, to the most recent incidents in central London (7-7-2005 and 21-7-2005), a number of suicide bombings have been carried out by alleged Islamic fanatics in different parts of the world, killing and maiming thousands of innocent citizens. Yet many of us recognize that those who in the course of history have killed, tortured and abused others in the name of religion were not true apologists of Judaism, Islam or Christianity. We know that those who have sacked, maimed and killed people in the name of religion only succeeded in giving religion a bad name, for as John Paul II once said, "the God of peace is never glorified by human violence."

In the last 200 years humanity has experienced enormous advancements in science and technology, but also in the knowledge of, and appreciation of human rights, dignity and freedom. With the age of Enlightenment, the Industrial Revolution, the French Revolution, and the two World Wars fought in the first half of the twentieth century, the very fabric of human society was shaken like never before, and subsequently, individual human beings and social groups have taken hold of their God-given freedom and they are not about to surrender it to any despot, even if such a despot is dressed in religious apparel. Strengthened by the United Nations Declarations on Human Rights, the African Charter on Human and Peoples' Rights, and similar charters and conventions, modern humanity is poised to resist any attempt at enslavement by primitive religious ideologies. They would rather throw religion overboard and order their affairs as purely secular societies than be bogged down or constantly distracted by the violent squabbles and skirmishes of the affiliates of competing religions.

Modern men and women guard very jealously their right to religious freedom, and they consider the choice of religion and the practice of such religion a private affair that should elicit neither special favours, nor discrimination from others. Instead, modern men and women seem to be challenging all religions to demonstrate their usefulness for the human society by uniting people, giving them a sense of meaning, and arming social groups with such values and principles as will make for reconciliation, integration, unity and peace.

To appreciate the infinite potential for good in all monotheistic religions, it appears that we must first make the distinction between the practice of religion and the politics of religion. I say without fear of contradiction that the genuine practice of Judaism, Islam and Christianity will hurt no one in our land or in any land whatsoever. Instead, the faithful practice of these three religions, which include private and public prayer, fasting, and acts of charity, and the dissemination of the fundamental teachings of the religions, will ensure a peaceful and united polity. Because of the transcendental values they share in common, and the elementary moral principles by which good is sought and evil is avoided, the faithful practice of Judaism, Islam and Christianity can only lead to a better human society, one that thrives on justice and peace.

On the other hand, it is often the politics of monotheistic religion that fuels the intolerance, discrimination, persecution, hatred, vengeance and violence that accompany religious expansionism. Fanatics and extremists have never been acknowledged as the best examples of their faith. They may make waves (often violent waves) for a little while, but in the end, they are often dumped in the ashes of history. Society never fails to take note of the other kind of power that shines through the humble disciple who draws people to his or her faith by the witness of a holy life, a life that constantly points the way to the rest of society. St. Francis of Assisi was a universal symbol of peace at the height of the crusades and jihads of the 12th century. He was acknowledged as a "man of God" by Muslims and Christians alike, because of his commitment to peace and universal brotherhood amid the deafening drums of war. Mother Teresa of Calcutta and John Paul II have been such symbols of peace in our own day. They, and not the fanatics are the best examples of religious witnessing. The way the world was united, speaking the same language and celebrating the same values around the death and burial of Pope John Paul II this year is a powerful testimony to how religion could unite humanity. His life as well as his death provided humanity with a moral leadership, such as the world has always craved for.

Religion indeed can be an instrument of reconciliation, integration, unity and peace. When devoid of destructive politics, religion at its best can constitute the underlying moral force behind society's just and peaceful ordering. When the political adventurists who camouflage as champions of religious causes are exposed for who they are and shown the way out, monotheistic religion (whether in the form of Judaism, Islam or Christianity), can become the soul of the modern society, even as it makes incredible advances in science and technology that are speedily transforming the face of the earth.

Religious people acknowledge that God has created us and sent us into the world for a purpose. Our destiny is in his hands. Our fulfilment in life is to be found in doing his will and accomplishing his holy design for us. To the extent that our individual and social lives are ordered in accordance with God's design, to that extent shall we have peace.

With its immense achievements in the last 100 years, modern humanity however stands the risk of missing its way and getting lost in the maze of goods and techniques it has acquired, if authentic religion does not help it to stay on course and keep its balance. Without authentic religion, modern humanity stands the risk of losing the sense of meaning altogether. We can already see signs of this malady in the more advanced segments of the world: Material well-being has reached an all-time high, but suicide rates are very high, divorce is rampant, abortion on demand and euthanasia are widespread, traditional institutions that are fundamental to the survival of society, such as the family, has become largely dysfunctional, gay unions are being recognized in the laws of many countries as of equal status with heterosexual unions, spiritual and moral values are being thrown away, and consequently, life is becoming meaningless.

Religion can protect humanity from the self-destruction that will arise, if men and women took their own destiny entirely in their hands. Religion will constantly teach the men and women of each generation that the meaning of human life lies beyond humanity, and that the most fundamental questions of the human heart cannot be answered by science and technology. Religion will enhance social integration when it gives men and women a sense of meaning and purpose. It will enhance wholesome existence for the individual and peace for the society when it teaches people that they are each other's keeper; when it teaches them to be charitable; and when it teaches them that they should do to no one what they do not want done to them.

And in a country like Nigeria, devastated by many years of dictatorship, with an economy that has been ruined by corruption, greed and graft, yes, a country that is today crying for moral rearmament or ethical revolution, authentic religion will play a pivotal role in the emergence of an accountable leadership and corruption-free nation, for our individual and social morality are often determined by our religious beliefs and practices, our attitudes and behaviours flow from our value orientations and spiritual dispositions, such as religion provides.

To dislodge the evil dispensation by which Nigerians of all walks of life seem to have decided that the price to be paid for honesty, fidelity, truth, hard work and diligence are too high, and by which they have settled for the short cut and the quick fix, and by which they have resorted to mutual betrayal, calumniation, opportunism and manipulation in the bid to make it by any means foul or fair, religious organisations can take up the challenge of constantly highlighting to their members the deadly consequences for the body and the soul, of those seven social sins identified by Mahatma Gandhi, namely: "Politics without principle; pleasure without conscience; wealth without work; commerce without morality; education without character; science without humanity; and worship without sacrifice."

Conclusion

What we need in Nigeria is a reconstruction of our damaged corporate psyche. We need a fundamental re-envisioning, and that will involve a re-definition of our communal ethos, a re-appreciation of our social habits and a re-prioritization of our national values, and it is my contention that in today's Nigeria, there is no organ better placed than religious organisations to champion this cause. Since authentic religion teaches people that the meaning of human life is beyond humanity, and beyond this world, the proper dissemination of the best principles of Islam, Christianity and African Traditional Religions, will help to checkmate the human instinct to grab and to accumulate for self, while neglecting the common good. I am convinced that the undiluted dissemination of the spiritual values in all our religions – not the message of convenience that we have become familiar with these days - is capable of purging Nigeria of the scourge of corruption and salvaging our country from the gang of rogue nations in the world.

CHAPTER FIFTY

Need to Re-invent the Nigerian Police
(Written on February 7, 2006)

The indictment and arraignment early last year of former Inspector General of Police, Mr. Tafa Balogun, the humiliating spectacle of Nigeria's former top cop in handcuffs over corruption and money laundering charges, and his eventual conviction and sentence to prison, must have sent elements of the police organisation into group psychological shock, for which the institution may need trauma healing. In the eyes of the public, the Police as an agency are besotted with corruption, manipulative intrigue, greed, impunity, and a palpable lack of moral discipline. A lot of issues around our jaundiced democracy remain unresolved because it is widely believed that the electoral process that produced the present crop of leaders who are bound in a permanent crisis of legitimacy was a sham and fraught with abuse, even though those who benefited by the crudity and deliberate manipulation of the elections claim otherwise. At every stage in our discredited electoral processes of the past, the police were implicated. They were alleged to have been passive onlookers, active collaborators and occasionally architects in the rape of democracy.

The abject performance and the lack of appropriate responsiveness in the primary duty of crime prevention and the provision of protection and security for the citizens and their property have scarcely ever endeared the police to the Nigerian public. The open extortion and transferred aggression of the police on the people of this country have further alienated Nigerians from their police and made the police the subject of ridicule and derision. The aggregate of these experiences has earned the police a bad reputation and thrown the institution into a quandary from which it requires structural rescue if it must remain relevant as a viable institution of state, as Nigeria progresses towards the democratic and electoral challenges of 2007 and beyond.

The Police no doubt are an important and necessary institution of state in a democratic society, as a watchdog of the rule of law. The Police are the frontline instrument of society that catalyses the provision of social justice and the institution that promotes the adherence to social order and democratic values. Democracy survives upon a single-minded devotion to such democratic principles as the supremacy of the rule of law, the separation of powers, the equality of persons, the sanctity of life and human dignity, and the recognition and respect for the institutions of state. Operating from the background, the courts as arbiters of justice have generally done well enough in our circumstance, though there are embarrassing incidents here and there, such as the dubious role of the acting Chief Justice of Oyo State in the recent impeachment drama in Oyo State. The Police however constitute perhaps the weakest link in the chain of justice and social order. The Police as a most crucial ingredient of democracy and as the most visible instrument for the maintenance of peace and good orderliness, must deeply understand the workings of the society and the law, if we must arrive at our desired destination.

Our historical antecedents portray a Nigeria Police that started as a colonial *force* not intended as a friend of the people but holding allegiance to the colonial masters to whip the erring natives into line. Forty-five years after the departure of the colonizers, our independence has bred generations of subtle promoters of home-grown neo-colonialism, and transferred police allegiance largely to the leaders that manipulate their way to power. Independence has thus not changed the mindset of the Police as instruments of manipulative coercion and enforcers of the will of the leadership. Their training has not transformed them into a friendly Civil Police but produced quasi-military operators with 'kill and go' anti-riot mentality. Nigerians have therefore not had the comfort of a police officer operating in peace time with a high sense of civil order.

A major factor in the deplorable state of our Police is that the majority lower cadre are poorly educated and poorly paid, are given archetypal rote training, and operate in the most austere and inhibiting living and working environments. The promoters and defenders of justice are themselves raised and bound in a most unjust and demeaning camp situation. The resulting low self-esteem is exhibited and poorly camouflaged with transferred aggression, intimidation, and extortion. Because their uniform as a symbol of oppression is a regular source of scorn, the police tote their gun as a source of recognition and now and again have used it irresponsibly to terminate the lives of innocent and unarmed civilians.

The leaders argue defensively against charges that the Police suffer deprivations bordering on criminal neglect of an institution that is so centrally important for the sustenance of the democratic tradition. At government level we hear of the financial starvation of the police where basic infrastructures are lacking or in a state of disrepair, where operational needs such as mobility, station materials, uniforms, arms and equipment are in short supply, and where personal emoluments are inadequate and often delayed. At the institutional level there are charges of target levies imposed on officers on point duty and other internal corrupt practices that in turn compel the police, gangster fashion, to fleece the hapless public.

The situation is not helped when the leadership of the country and the agency try to deny or rationalize the obvious. No one is deceived even when they sing the tired slogans of being among the world's best in providing effective crime and conflict prevention and control, combating corruption and indiscipline, enhancing police-public partnership, diligent investigation, contributing to the quality of justice delivery, enhancing the welfare of officers, and generally improving the operational standards, reliability, responsiveness, and image of the service. There is the moral question how we could ever achieve all of these goals, using a crop of personnel who are so materially and psychologically deprived and traumatized.

With this scenario and considering the state we are at in our democratic advancement towards realising good governance and a credible transition in 2007, the kind of police we have today can hardly take us home. Where the average police officer is so poorly informed that he or she has neither read the Nigerian constitution, the United Nations charter and other international conventions on human rights; where the defenders of the people and the law routinely entrap the innocent, humiliate suspects and mete out punishment outside the law; our police more often than not carry the image of the bully rather than the people's friend.

Whilst political parties, greedy politicians, corrupt office seekers, political king makers and gangsters, and other anti-social stakeholders are surreptitiously planning and scheming towards foisting their hidden agendas on Nigeria and Nigerians, if we must ensure better elections in 2007 and checkmate these negative forces, we must re-examine the basic ground rules and plug the exploitable loopholes. How can transparency be served and rigging neutralized in the process of credible voter registration, logistics, voting, counting, collating and announcement of election results? We must look at the courts to offer safe haven for the outmanoeuvred and aggrieved contestant, but before then a responsible police will offer a credible overview of security and confidence in this process, as neutral, non-partisan and dispassionate arbiters.

The crucial role of the police means that a restructuring of the institution has become an important national endeavour. This does not mean a partial half-hearted tinkering with the status quo. First, the entry qualification needs to be raised and the commensurate pay structure enhanced - possibly to university graduate level. This would mean virtually lifting the institution from the depths of inferiority and incompetence, and this is possible, considering the rate at which potentially jobless graduates are being churned out of our universities. The re-orientation of the police from the military mindset must be undertaken. Batch training and retraining of all personnel at all levels down the line must be factored into a time-structured programme to incorporate local and overseas elements involving modern tools.

A unified police has its merits. But while it may not be necessary to build a multi-structured police all over the country, it has been suggested that the community or neighbourhood police comprising of officers operating in their own immediate environment where there is mutual knowledge, familiarity and respect, would greatly impact on law and order and reduce crime. A re-orientated police should be helped to appreciate the cause and effect relationship between the acts of corruption in the system and the societal rot pervading the Nigerian environment. The many officers now in the system who cannot be re-trained should be re-channelled into other resettlement endeavours.

Nigerians, notably in the leadership, were up in arms over a recent American intelligence report that predicts a doomsday scenario of the disintegration of Nigeria within fifteen years. Alarming as the report might be it is clear to observers of this country that the dangers to nation building and democracy must first be recognised and confronted. It is also clear to observers in this country that once recognised, Nigerians possess the ingenuity and resilience to pull away from the precipice of destruction. The opportunity must therefore not be lost in recognising the place of a viable, patriotic and competent police in evolving a just, orderly, peaceful and democratic Nigerian society.

CHAPTER FIFTY-ONE

Lent: A Time for Repentance
(Written on February 18, 2006)

TODAY is Ash Wednesday, the day Nigerian Christians along with other Christians worldwide begin their 40-day season of Lent that is set aside to prepare for a worthy celebration of the central mystery of the Christian faith, the mystery of the suffering, death and resurrection of Jesus Christ. The Lenten season is characterised by prayer, fasting and abstinence, alms giving, and above all, repentance and conversion. For us in Nigeria, this year's Lent assumes a more poignant and urgent significance, due to our peculiar circumstances of crisis in various facets of our national life.

Lent 2006 is coming in the midst of multiple crises, with the worsening security situation in the Niger Delta, where the second set of foreign hostages are still being held by militants, the senseless killings and burning of houses of worship in Maiduguri and the reprisal killings elsewhere that have been the aftermath, the widespread political brigandage that has heated up the polity considerably, as well as the massive corruption that never seems to abate. Nigerians are familiar with the ominous signs of self-immolation hovering over a country given to dancing dangerously on the precipice.

Lent is a season of reflection, repentance, conversion and renewal. At a time of general anxiety and fear over the future of our nation state, Lent this year should provide an opportunity for individual and group soul-searching on the true quality of our religiosity. It is a time to take seriously and address the inherent contradictions in priding ourselves as religious people, and in our being brandished as the most religious nation on earth, while many in our rank exhibit some of the most irreligious, unholy and despicable behaviours, including the killing of one another in the name of religion, whereas we know that the God of peace can never be glorified by human violence. Lent is a time to address the anomaly of our ritual religiosity flourishing side by side with our widespread social immorality. Lent this year therefore is a good time to confront squarely the hypocrisy that has become a prominent feature of the Nigerian religious enterprise, and do something about it.

Piety is generally associated with the virtues of honesty, truth, selflessness, frugality, justice, non-violence, sacrificial love and concern for the common good. These among other qualities are the true marks of authentic religion, and truly religious people in the history of the world have tended to exhibit these virtues; but our practice of religion in this country does not seem to have yielded these dividends. This year's Lenten season therefore challenges the Nigerian elite (who are often seen taking front seats at churches and prayer grounds) to move away from a life of greed and politics of acrimony and brigandage which have held this country down this long. If we must lay claim to true religiosity, our leaders at all levels must imbibe the sterling qualities of leadership that inspire a people and edify a nation. As we travel the same route on the journey towards nationhood and democratic sustenance, all the citizens of this country should pause with Christians observing Lent, and together reflect upon and imbibe the lessons of the season.

The Lenten season this year challenges not only Christians, but all believers in God to recognise that the way to true greatness is the way of obedience, humility, generosity, kindness, poverty of spirit and self-sacrifice which Jesus' desert experience celebrated during the Lenten season, stands for. They should critically look upon the rat race for more and more power, wealth and fame, which often results in distress, conflict and violence. Indeed, Lent is the time to preach more passionately not only the need for prayer, fasting and abstinence, but also the message of repentance and conversion from hatred, greed, corruption and violence.

CHAPTER FIFTY-TWO

It's Another Good Friday
(Written on April 13, 2006)

TODAY, the Christian world celebrates Good Friday, one of the major events marking the climax of the prophetic essence of the life of Jesus Christ. Today, Christians worldwide are joined by millions in Nigeria to commemorate the death of Jesus, in hope of the ultimate promise of redemption and salvation. Good Friday is the day symbolizing the surrender of the human spirit by Christ in obedience to God's will and in fulfillment of the Father's promise to ransom the world with His only begotten Son. Christians believe that without the event of Good Friday happening, the Christian enterprise would lose its merit and its shine. In fact, it is said that Christianity subsists because among its many focal imperatives, Good Friday indeed came to be. Crucified on the cross of Calvary, Jesus had endured his ultimate humiliation in the hands of his traducers and torturers in what became a heart-rending enactment of the Passion that ended poignantly on Good Friday.

The events that led to Good Friday centred around the radical social paradigm that Jesus introduced and preached to the Jewish society, and subsequently to the world. The world of his time saw his style and message as an affront on their idolatrous and lascivious living. The new truths he revealed were too bitter for his accusers to swallow and so they unleashed the mob instinct to silence him. As he expired on the cross though, the power of his message was already legend.

Strands of the social teachings of Jesus remain evident across the world today, not least of all in Nigeria where the forces of greed and corruption continue to seek ascendancy in a national theatre of political intrigue, social distress and economic stagnation. In this season of the long knives along the dark alleys of political machinations, Nigeria is enduring in a sadly prevalent African leadership culture, by the sycophantic orchestration of tenure extension. Nigeria is living the lie of a convoluted democratic posture through the barefaced motive of the ambush of constitution mending - a rush to legitimize self-perpetuation. Nigeria endures in a season of the exercise of corruptible power at all levels of governance, growing brigades of decadent and illegitimate leaders, and an army of pretenders, aspirants, sycophants and acolytes.

The example that Jesus portrayed in his life and death on Good Friday has serious implications for us as a nation, and especially for our Christian leaders and their supporters. These are difficult times in our democratic odyssey as our politicians burn the midnight oil plotting how to get in on the governance act. Manoeuvrings are happening in the political arena that portend crises towards election year, 2007. The scandalous and contentious change of guard in state houses, the turmoil in the Niger Delta and other trouble spots, and the subtle infighting in the presidency all point to a troubled nation in crisis.

The Christian hope and confidence in the messianic gift of Good Friday remains a viable retreat as Nigerians grapple with the national crises of the day. The national environment calls for sober reflection on the moral imperatives of the political and economic choices before the nation. The values for which Christ died on Good Friday – love, truth, justice, humility, self-sacrifice..., remain relevant as Nigerians struggle for the soul of the nation.

CHAPTER FIFTY-THREE

The Challenge of Easter
(Written on April 14, 2006)

CHRISTIANS all over the world celebrate today the feast of the Resurrection of Jesus Christ. The innocent Son of God suffered a brutal crucifixion that was the climax of a short but remarkable life of commitment to love, truth, justice, humility, mercy, compassion, purity, peace and non-violence. In the course of passionately preaching and living out the truth as he knew it, condemning the injustices of the day and promoting a religion that emphasizes the spirit rather than the letter of the law, Jesus came in regular conflict with the status quo and those who benefited from it. He was betrayed by his own disciple, denied by his closest associate, handed over to the Roman authorities by the chief priests of his religion and condemned to death by Pilate. Death by crucifixion was the greatest symbol of the rejection of Jesus and everything he stood for by the religious and political authorities of the day. To highlight this point even more, the crucifixion took place outside the walls of the city of Jerusalem.

However, there was a dramatic turn to the story of Jesus. Three days after the gruesome event of Calvary, the disciples reported that he had risen from the dead as he said he would, and some witnesses confessed that they had indeed seen him alive. This unprecedented event and the devotion that followed it marked the beginning of Christianity as we know it. The resurrection of Jesus from the dead is for Christians of all generations the vindication of the innocent one who was taken for a criminal and treated like the worst of criminals.

Jesus died a vicarious death to take away the sins of humanity and open the way to eternal life for all who believe in him and in his message. His resurrection is, for believers, a powerful testimony to the ultimate victory of good over evil, the eventual triumph of light over darkness, and the much-hoped-for conquest of wickedness, aggression, violence and death by the forces of love, peace, non-violence and life. Thus Easter is for suffering Christians everywhere a time to rekindle hope in a God who would not allow evil to prevail but would now and again intervene to save his people.

In his Sermon on the Mount, Jesus had preached that it is the meek and gentle, not the arrogant and boastful who shall inherit the earth. His resurrection and the subsequent emergence and growth of Christianity prove him right. Indeed the life and teaching, and the death and resurrection of Jesus put together, are a lesson on the efficacy of humility, service, self-sacrifice and true love, by which one is prepared to die not only for one's friends but also for the higher values of truth and justice. Easter, therefore, teaches that there are values worth defending beyond physical human life. In fact, human life can be readily and voluntarily given away in the course of defending truth and justice.

Nigerians can learn a lot from the lifestyle and the supreme sacrifice of Jesus Christ. He taught a lot of lessons through his parables and miracles, but Jesus was more than a powerful teacher and a wonder-worker. The greatest lessons he taught are the practical lessons of his own life. For example, he taught his followers that there is no greater love than for a man to lay down his life for his friends, and that is exactly what he did. He taught his followers that those who seek to be first must make themselves last and servant of all, and that is what he did when he washed the feet of his disciples and accepted a humiliating death in order that they may live. Though as Son of God he was rich beyond measure, he made a preferential option for the poor, whose circumstances he graciously shared. His life was consistent with his message.

These are powerful lessons that the men and women of Nigeria, particularly those who desire leadership positions, need to imbibe. Our experience of leadership in this country has often been one characterized by primitive greed rather than service and self-sacrifice. Far from denying themselves that their people may live, our own leaders have often stolen food off the hands of their starving poor. Overwhelmed by the blind lust for power, and the desire to control and dominate others, our own leaders, have often manipulated, oppressed and abused their people. In the urge to grab political power and to sit tight even against the wishes of their people, we have recorded in our land many instances of political violence and high profile assassinations. Elections all over the nation witnessed an unprecedented level of rigging and political violence that remain a reproach for the Nigerian society and our experiment in democratic governance. The conduct of our political elite in and out of government is often a marked departure, indeed an affront on the model of leadership and service demonstrated by Jesus Christ.

Easter celebration, therefore, challenges incumbent and aspiring Nigerian leaders of all creeds to abandon the paths of selfishness and greed and the inordinate ambition for power at whatever cost, which have been the bane of our socio-political history. With Jesus' commitment to a life of love, humility, service and sacrifice eventually vindicated by the event of the Resurrection and celebrated annually at this time by believers through the course of history; Easter challenges Christians and non-Christians alike to embrace those higher values exemplified in Jesus that make for lasting peace and happiness.

As we celebrate Easter, we recall that an international agency some time ago released a report that identified Nigerians as the most religious people in the world. From the point of view of the outward manifestation of religiosity through massive public participation in the ritual activities of both Christianity and Islam, the assertion can be readily supported with facts and figures. However, the public morality of these otherwise spectacularly religious Nigerians is often at odds with the tenets of religion and constitutes a source of embarrassment to both Christianity and Islam. Is it not a matter of contradiction that the same Nigerians whose ritual preoccupations qualify our country to be recognized as the most religious in the world can conduct themselves in public life in such a way that the same country is identified (by Transparency International) as the second most corrupt nation in the world?

For Jesus Christ, whose resurrection Easter celebrates, the core of religion is not the outward display of empty ritualism where Nigerian worshippers seem to excel beyond all else. Thus, beyond the popular crusades, prayer vigils and miracle explosions, Jesus calls his disciples to the practice of authentic religion that is to be found in a passionate commitment to love, truth, justice, honesty, mercy, forgiveness and self-sacrifice. On this day, therefore, Nigerian Christians and other Nigerians are challenged to cultivate these elements of authentic religion for which Jesus died and rose from the dead. We wish all, particularly Christians who celebrate at this time, a very Happy Easter.

CHAPTER FIFTY-FOUR

The Mass Media and Social Responsibility: the Case of Religious and Cultural Symbols
(Presented at the "Times Media Conference," in Lagos, June 15, 2006)

Most people today recognise that information is power. To possess information is to possess power. To suppress information is to rob people of power. That is why the long-awaited signing into law of the Freedom of Information bill before the National Assembly shall constitute a major milestone in our democratic evolution as it is sure to give a measure of power to the people vis-à-vis their leaders. In the modern society those who possess the most information are the most powerful and sometimes the most wealthy people. The traditional agents of education - the home, the school, the Church, the Mosque and the peer group, have now been joined (if they are not being supplanted), by the mass media which are perhaps more powerful than all the other agents put together.

Advancements in Information and Communication Technology in our day have in certain respects conquered time and space, making it possible to reach people everywhere across the globe with information instantaneously. The modern mass media thus have an enormous potential for the service of the common good, to facilitate dialogue, collaboration and cooperation among peoples of diverse social, cultural and religious backgrounds, and to strengthen human solidarity. Ironically however, our experience so far demonstrates that immediacy of communication does not necessarily translate into greater understanding, collaboration and peaceful co-existence.

It is widely accepted today that as veritable instruments for the education, information, and entertainment of the people, the mass media exercise enormous powers towards shaping the societal values and influencing what perceptions or imaginations a group of people have about others who may be different from them. The mass orientation of the modern communication technology is such that there is the great tendency for media owners and controllers not only to use the media to acquire enormous wealth, but also to use the media as an instrument of social engineering. Media cartels on the global level are often tempted to manipulate news, information and advertisement in such a manner as to create a world of their own dreams, and disseminate their own values or counter-values. In plural societies, where religious and cultural differences and diversities are not widely understood as a source of strength, some practitioners of the media often play such differences against each other, profiting from the resulting sensationalism through widespread patronage, but in the process creating tension and setting the stage for conflicts.

Besides, there is a very strong tendency in the mass media industry of today (and within the context of an increasingly globalised society), to promote a global monoculture that is characterised by secularism, agnosticism, consumerism, crass individualism, moral relativism and economic liberalism, while ridiculing, maligning and caricaturing elements of society who think differently. It is my humble submission that this tendency towards imposing a global monoculture that has become very evident in the news, features, and documentary programmes, especially of the international media conglomerates of our day, dims creative genius, deflates the subtlety of complex thought, undervalues the specificity of cultural practices and violates the particularity of religious beliefs and symbols. What is more, this global monoculture that is gaining currency through the mass media is adopting an increasingly hostile and belligerent posture towards traditional religions and their symbols of identity and authority. Humanity as a whole will be the worse for it, when men and women everywhere think the same thoughts, eat the same food, dress the same way and speak with the same accent, and when their spiritual icons cannot be differentiated. But this anomaly will gain greater currency the more the media industry loses the sense of accountability to the common good, and becomes more and more self-serving, or the more it is propelled solely by the profit motive. Minority cultures and religions must be particularly sensitive to, and constantly protest against, this anomaly if they are not to be consigned to the margins of (so called) "progressive humanity."

The mass media indeed constitute an enormously powerful tool for the shaping of society. This enormous power however comes with an equally grave burden of responsibility for the practitioners: that of using the instruments at their disposal for the promotion of truth, justice, mutual respect, peace, non-violence and human solidarity. Practitioners and consumers alike must come to understand that though the instruments of modern communication, such as the press, the television, the radio, and the Internet, are in themselves wonderful human inventions, the news, information and entertainment we get through these media are not value-free. We need to understand that information dissemination and entertainment in the modern society is often ideologically conditioned, one way or the other in accordance with the orientation of the controllers of the various media. Indeed, there are ideological, cultural, political, and economic presuppositions underlying present-day information dissemination and entertainment.

Through the mass media we have, imposed on us, world views, ideas, opinions and situations that may well challenge not only our religion and culture, but our humanity as well. They can be either peace-building or war-inducing features, and either life-affirming values or life-denying counter-values. The media can present edifying models of human life, love and solidarity, but also images of human hatred and destructiveness that provoke vengeance, violence and war. The media can be used to inspire persons to take on heroic tasks and soar towards individual and group actualisation, but also they can be used to induce persons to lose completely their sense of humanity and plunge into the shameful abyss that human beings are always on the edge of falling. The audio-visual media particularly have a special power to stir up feelings of love, sympathy and compassion, but also feelings of anger, fear and insecurity, for it is widely acknowledged that images speak to our emotions much more than our reason.

The complex dynamic of the modern mass media as a double-edged sword outlined above, places an enormous burden of responsibility on practitioners as well as consumers. It is at this juncture that I wish to make a brief comment on the case of religious and cultural symbols and the need for these symbols to be respected by practitioners of the mass media, even when they are reporting factual events, if the mass media are to bring out the best, and not the worst in human interaction, and if they are to become veritable tools for the realisation of national, regional and global peace and human solidarity. The case of the Danish cartoon that was considered blasphemous against the person of the Prophet Mohammed and its publication in a number of Western media in September and December 2005, which many in the Western world thought was a good illustration of the freedom of expression and press freedom, turned out to be a very costly misadventure and a case of bad judgement on the part of the cartoonists and the Newspaper Editors, as protest marches and public demonstrations were staged against the alleged blasphemy by Muslims in different parts of the world. To this day we here in Nigeria are still counting our loses, as in February 2006 violent riots on account of the cartoon occurred in Maiduguri and spread to Bauchi and Katsina, in which hundreds of lives were lost and property worth hundreds of millions of Naira were destroyed, provoking reprisal killings and property destruction in Onitsha and elsewhere in the South.

A crazy artist in a post-Christian and largely neo-pagan Danish society could exercise what he/she considers his/her freedom of expression and made a caricature of the sacred symbols of Islam or any religion he/she wishes. If the outcome of this so called "freedom of expression" were confined to his or her studio in that environment where such artistic expression is not considered abhorrent, then perhaps the threat to peace from such a weird expression of freedom would have been minimal. But as soon as the blasphemous cartoon appeared in the mass media, which has turned the world to a global village, it generated widespread controversy, it offended the sensibilities of religious people everywhere and it provoked some militant Muslims to take to violence even in our own country, killing scores of innocent Christians in their midst, whom (by some skewed fundamentalist logic) they believe do have some affinity or share some common religious heritage with, and should therefore be punished for, the alleged crimes of the author of the cartoon in faraway Denmark. We could blame the tragic events of Maiduguri and elsewhere in our country on the irrationality of modern-day religious fundamentalism. But if wiser counsel had prevailed, the tragic events would never have occurred. If the Editor of the Danish Newspaper had sufficiently recognised the power of images in the mass media and exercised a greater sense of responsibility (through some form of self-censorship) over what is published in his or her Newspaper, the world and our country would have been saved one more major violent crisis.

In the last few years "The Da Vinci Code" book and lately the movie, have been making the rounds all over the world. The author, Dan Brown and the publishers of the book, as well as producers of the film have become instant celebrities, and are daily smiling to the Bank with millions of dollars they are making from their blasphemous account of the life of Jesus Christ, and especially his alleged amorous (or is it marital) relationship with Mary Magdalene that they claim produced children whose descendants can be traced to modern-day France. Though the publication of "The Da Vinci Code" book and the movie have generated controversy all over the world and a sense of outrage in many, devout Christians have however demonstrated utmost restraint in their reaction to the book. No violent demonstrations have been recorded anywhere. No bookstores stocking the books or cinema houses showing the movie have been razed down, and no individuals reading the book in public have been lynched, yet we must recognise that since religion is a highly emotive enterprise, this kind of (blasphemous) publications and their dissemination through the mass media could provoke explosive emotions of anger with a potential to degenerate into the kind of violence we witnessed in Maiduguri and elsewhere.

On the occasion of the widespread demonstrations over the Danish cartoon against the person of Prophet Mohammed, Pope Benedict XVI made a passionate plea to those who desire peace in the world, and especially the practitioners of the mass media, to be sensitive to, and to show respect for the religious symbols of adherents of the various religions in the world as a necessary pathway to peace. Peace does not just happen. Lasting peace is predicated on the practice of justice and respect for the rights of the neighbour, and this includes respect for the sanctity of the revered symbols and sacred personages of religious people even in a pluralist and secularist society. Otherwise there will be a build-up of anger, bitterness, resentment, and violence which, if care is not taken, may even degenerate to forms of terrorism, if the aggrieved parties consider that they have no other avenues of registering their discontent.

The globalisation of information in the modern society places an enormous burden of responsibility on media executives, producers and entertainers. If they are not to be agents of a mass culture that is antithetical to true human advancement, solidarity and peace, they must not allow themselves to be carried away by cheap sensationalism or blinded by the profit motive, and thus throw overboard the higher values upon which alone a wholesome humanity can thrive. If the media in our own society are not to become agents of a culture of death, then they must resist the temptation to surrender themselves to the destructive influences of an all too liberalistic, relativistic, and reductionist monoculture that is today being promoted from the West. Instead the practitioners of mass media are to see their involvement in information dissemination, education and entertainment as a providential opportunity to shape or midwife the emergence of a more wholesome world through an ardent commitment to all that makes for truth, justice and equity, wholesome dialogue, genuine freedom, non-violence, lasting peace, and human solidarity.

The globalisation of information also challenges media consumers on their part to take a measure of responsibility for what they and their children are exposed to through the mass media. The mass media are destined for the common good. They are the common patrimony of the people. Even if some particular entrepreneurs have invested heavily in them as business enterprises, they are nevertheless not the exclusive preserve of the rich investor, the executive directors, the producers, the editors and other practitioners. I therefore challenge media consumers to exercise the spirit of cooperation and co-responsibility and constantly demand utmost accountability from those who wield the enormous powers bestowed by the modern media. There is need for widespread media education at all levels. Media education is the art of provoking the right questions about the content and method of the communications and entertainment media, so as to establish and maintain a wholesome, meaningful and profitable relationship between the media and the consumers. If those of us who make up the elite in the modern society are uncritical about how the media work, we would miss the opportunity to respond to and to contribute towards the building of a new global culture. Media education equips individuals in the society to play their proper role in the shaping of their culture. It is in this way that both practitioners as well as consumers will contribute their quota towards the building of a society that is just, humane and peaceful.

We must become ever more enlightened and critical consumers, who are capable of discerning the values or counter-values promoted in the international and local media, discriminating between good and bad programmes, picking features that build up and edify, while rejecting those that appeal only to the base instincts of the human person. Consumers of media products could constitute themselves into pressure groups and advocacy cells that will regularly analyse the content of our mass media, make their opinions about the programme quality and content known to the producers and the supervising authorities, and in extreme cases where correction is not taken, court litigations may be required in order to protect society from the influences of a destructive media programme or an irresponsible media executive.

Finally, let me end this address by admonishing, encouraging and challenging media employers, producers, broadcasters, journalists, advertisers, film makers, corporate communicators and I.T. specialists, to recognise today that the enormous power of the media in our day is a responsibility. I challenge you media practitioners to use the instruments at your disposal to put us into human relationships in solidarity with each other. I challenge you to contribute to and nurture the unity in diversity between human beings that is meant to be a source of strength, not a liability. I challenge you to strive to observe high ethical standards and see that your entire industry and the tools of your trade are constantly enlightened and propelled, not by a narrow profit motive, but by the higher values of truth, justice, equity, non-violence, mutual understanding, and human cooperation, collaboration, solidarity and wholesome peace.

CHAPTER FIFTY-FIVE

The Nigerian Political Elite: A Plea for Compassion
(Written on July 27, 2006)

To a visitor with any time to spend there, Onitsha is today a sprawling slum city of chaos and disorder. A two-week retreat this month in the popular Eastern commercial capital presented a close-up of the urban degradation and collapse that has become a metaphor for a Nigerian nation grimly cast in a developmental free fall. Struggling vainly to cling on to its famous past, Onitsha wears the scars of the battles against slum dwelling, violence, joblessness, banditry and absolute infrastructural neglect. It has become a city carved up and 'governed' by groups holding dominion over segments of the social, economic and political life of the people.

Travelling up-country from Onitsha, en route the nation's capital Abuja, I began to reflect on what is becoming of this nation brimming with countless leaders at various levels who claim to be inspired and to be working 24 hours a day to "move the nation forward." At home in Okene, Kogi State, I saw again firsthand the level of unrelenting and unforgiving acrimonious poverty. Okene is a large, densely populated local government capital, the heartland of Ebira people and one of the central passageways to the federal capital from the south. The focal town of the iron ore belt spreading from Itape to Ajaokuta, Okene should exhibit the trappings of a booming economic activity of Nigeria's hinterland. Here again life for the people remains a grinding daily challenge for survival.

Degrading poverty is not just a common denominator but underscores the trauma afflicting families on a daily basis. I encountered cases of widows and widowers with scant resources to care for their children and their elderly; members of poor families dying because of the inability to afford the simplest of treatments for common ailments; school drop-outs whose education is truncated for lack of means to continue; and sundry cases dependent solely on begging for survival. This is a scenario replicated all over the country, the norm rather than the exceptions.

Do Nigerians truly deserve all this? Are they born and bound to a perpetual life of misery in a land of promise and opportunity? Have we truly been managing our affairs with the welfare of all in mind and with particular preferential option for the poor and needy in our midst? How many generations must be wasted before we can pull our people up from the pit of abject poverty and human degradation? Nigeria's privileged elite and leadership, those who enjoy the settled and the good life, do indeed have a lot to worry and answer for. The successive leaders of this nation as well as the current political and economic elite stand to be indicted for the deplorable plight of the neighbour who is at the mercy of a callously contrived national environment.

For indeed, the rich, the elite and the leadership at least have some of their relations in the poverty zone in this country. Yet the disposition of the privileged tends to accentuate the begging culture that has permeated the ranks of the poor. Among Nigeria's common folk of today there is the passionate aspiration to succeed and join the elite gang and once there to assume a newly acquired superior air of "I have arrived." In the comfort zone of sumptuous living, the sense of guilt and compassion for the poor are lost. It is thus a matter of course to send their children and wards to schools abroad, where they pay incredible amounts as fees. It is a matter of course for this class of elite to wine and dine regularly in first class restaurants and hotels, and for the young entrants to the club who have newly come into their own to have their babies in choice resorts overseas. Nigeria merely becomes the goose that lays the golden egg that keeps the poverty gap ever widening. And all of this in a country where families scrounge for a meal a day if at all; where the poor die by instalments with no social security and welfare of any kind; where high walls and electrified fences have created exclusion zones for the affluent and denied the poor of the 'Lazarus experience' for crumbs from the table of the rich, in a world where wealthy societies are setting up exclusive hotels for dogs!

In this unwholesome national environment, we are rapidly losing our traditional African sense of charity, compassion and mercy, and wearing the hitherto unfamiliar amour of dispassionate aloofness and cold economic statistics of hybrid alien cultures. It partly explains why many young Nigerians engage in sharp practices and put up with all sorts of indignities at foreign embassies in frenzied attempts to escape the hardship within. And it is partly encouraged by punitive and insensitive rulers of this country who have had neither the inclination nor the capacity for critical self evaluation.

In the face of these dispensations, I am inclined today to shift (even if momentarily) from harping on justice, transparency and accountability, to the desperate and critical plea for pity, compassion and mercy for the poor and suffering of this country. It is time to confront the truth of our failings and to ascribe the correct description of society's attitude to its disenfranchised and less privileged members. It is time to admit to the wickedness, callousness, meanness, and yes, sadism of many in our midst and to appeal for a change of heart, and for all to reach out to help the neighbour. It is time to call the insatiable greed and avarice of our political and economic elite by its real name, kleptocracy. The elite who have siphoned and stashed billions of naira away for themselves and their immediate families alone, and those who engage in conspicuous consumption, have killed millions of our people and left others stranded!

No one needs to be a millionaire to show compassion, to have fellow feeling for the plight of the neighbour. Jesus Christ and the apostles had no wealth to flaunt around. The account leading up to the first miracle of the loaves illustrates how Jesus abandoned and emptied himself totally for the multitude that hungered after him. He in fact came into the world out of pity for humankind and to teach the values of compassion and mercy. His sacrificial love for his flock is the model of good leadership for all times.

The human person is the dominant creature of the age, a higher order of creation endowed to reflect and act beyond mere impulse and instinct. Even lower animals feel and care for their own, how much more human beings. It has often been stated that the true measure of human civilization is not the number of expensive cars and palatial mansions the society can parade, but how the society takes care of the poor, the widow, the orphan and the handicapped in its midst.

A country with any pretensions to modernizing and democratizing must show greater concern for its people; the leaders must be true shepherds appointed for the people. Our leaders must recognise that they are part of a lopsided and unfair structure that perpetuates the yawning gap between the rich and the poor. And the generality of Nigerians must recognise the need for more kind-hearted people to come forward and touch the lives of the teeming poor. As a people, we need to rediscover the milk of human kindness. We need to nurture the virtue of compassion. We need to develop tender hearts that can easily collapse at the sight of the suffering of fellow human beings. We need sensitive consciences that will propel us to do something about the human degradation that is all around us. In this way countless Nigerians can be released from misery and empowered to live meaningful lives. I am pleading for compassion.

CHAPTER FIFTY-SIX

Towards the Globalisation of Human Solidarity: The Challenge of Social Responsibility
(Written on April 11, 2007)

Introduction: The Phenomenon of Globalisation

Globalisation could be described as the process of human interaction across borders and beyond frontiers which in our day has assumed unprecedented dimensions with the convergence of space and time, facilitated and accelerated by the dramatic advances made in recent decades in the Information and Communication Technology. Globalisation is the term generally used to describe the ever growing interdependence of people and countries or the worldwide integration of peoples, their economies, their politics and their cultures, a process that has witnessed among other benefits the collapse of the Berlin Wall, the end of the Cold War and the end to a world divided into ideological blocs.

Today people's lives across the globe are definitely linked more deeply, more intensely, and more immediately than ever before. Let me illustrate the phenomenon as follows:

> A woman could wake up in Germany this morning and drink coffee produced in Colombia, with sugar shipped in from Madagascar and milk from the diary farms of Australia, with a tea cup made in China. She could then jump into a car manufactured in South Korea and drive to the Frankfurt Airport to get into a Boeing 747 airplane produced in America and operated by Emirate Air for a flight to Dubai. She is welcomed to the flight by a Singaporean Captain and is served by a hostess of Indian origin. She gets into the shops of Dubai and comes back with clothing material from Hong Kong, jewellery from Israel, electronics from Japan, shoes from Italy, as well as choice wines from France. On her return to Germany the following day, the lady who works for a Multinational Business Consultancy Firm, moderates a video teleconference on Business Opportunities in the Republic of Uzbekistan. She sits at her desk in Bonn and connects a business associate in Ghana, another in Argentina, another in New Zealand, and yet another in Malaysia. This is globalization in action.

Though the process of interaction and integration between peoples and countries is not new to humanity, it has however witnessed in recent decades an intensification, and an acceleration that is unprecedented in human history, thanks to advances in science and technology and such inventions as the Telephone, the Television, the Internet and Satellite Communication that are poised to collapse distances between people and places and more or less "make geography history," and thanks to the discovery of the Microchip which has made it possible for us to store or carry around and share tones and tones of information in tiny little equipments. Perhaps one of the major catalysts for the contemporary process of globalisation was the epoch-making initiative of the leaders of the world to form in 1947 the United Nations Organisation and its various Agencies as well as the Universal Human Rights Charter which is premised on the belief that all human beings are created equal with a number of inalienable fundamental rights which must be protected at all times. A process that is increasingly breaking barriers between the peoples of the world, connecting them together more intensely and emphasizing their interdependence, is surely a blessing to humanity, and must be applauded and supported. But this is not the full story of globalization.

The Liberalisation of Trade and Investment

The process of globalisation has in recent time been characterized more by an ever greater liberalisation of trade and investment or the opening up of local markets to international goods and capital inflow, the weakening of local (governmental) controls over national economies, the gradual ceding of global and national economic governance to increasingly powerful Multinational Corporations and such International Financial Institutions as the World Bank, International Monetary Fund and the World Trade Organisation, excessive extraction/consumption of and depletion of non-renewable resources, the poisoning of the natural environment, as well as the centralization of global capital in the hands of a few super-wealthy and super-powerful individuals, corporations and countries, and ever worsening economic fortunes for a multitude of poor nations who are beginning to see themselves as victims rather than beneficiaries of the process of globalization. Furthermore, with the concentration of global economic power in the hands of a few International Corporations and Financial Institutions domiciled in the economically advanced countries, there is the growing fear of not only an emerging international imperialism of money, but also an attendant political and cultural domination of the poorer peoples of the world by the wealthy nations whose financial institutions and media conglomerates are presently the driving force behind globalization.

Globalisation and its Discontents

At the onset of the new wind of globalization in the 1980s and 1990s, the process which is decidedly driven by the doctrine of economic liberalism was celebrated with a great deal of euphoria and very high expectations in nearly every sector - political, economic, intellectual and cultural. At that time Martin Wolf, a Financial Columnist in America declared that "Globalization is the great economic event of our era... It is now bringing unprecedented opportunities to billions of people throughout the world" (Quoted in "Globalisation: The Hopes and the Fears" in AWAKE, May 22, 2002, page 3). At that time, developing countries that were caught in the web of poverty and weighed down heavily by a major debt burden came under immense pressure from the major controllers of international capital to get unto the train of globalization and adopt free market economy as the only way to prosperity. They were forced to adopt the Structural Adjustment Programme which as a package included the deregulation of local currencies, opening up of their local markets for competitive international trading, taking government's hands off business enterprises, reducing drastically government spending even on basic infrastructure and the wholesale privatization of public utilities.

Twenty-five years after the whirlwind of globalization gathered momentum, the economies of most of the rich industrialized nations have grown beyond their expectation. They have indeed produced many billionaires. And on account of the liberalization of trade and investment, which has opened up local markets of most countries, their big multinational corporations have made huge profits and in consequence have become major power brokers in the global community. A few developing countries, notably China and India have taken major strides along the path of economic prosperity and have therefore become major players in the global economy. But for the overwhelming majority of the poor developing countries, especially in sub-Saharan Africa, the story is totally different. After carrying out the prescriptions of the champions of globalization, their hopes have been dashed; their local industries have been crushed by a deluge of cheaper goods from abroad; their social infrastructures, such as schools and hospitals have largely collapsed, their citizens are experiencing widespread unemployment; there is a major brain drain as the worsening economic fortunes of these countries is forcing a good number of their qualified professionals and experts (trained with the scarce resources of the poor nations) to leave their homes in search of greener pastures in Europe and America.

Why for example would a qualified Nurse want to remain in Uganda and be paid the equivalent of 40 US Dollars a month, when her services are required in the United States where she could earn as much as 3000 US Dollars a month? Does this not explain why there are more Malawian Doctors practicing in and around Manchester, than all the Doctors in Malawi? Is that not why in the year 2000 alone, as many as 500 trained Ghanaian Nurses – 200% of the Nurses trained in Ghana that year, left the country for better placements in Europe and America? So it is part of the negative fallouts of globalization that many of the professionals and experts produced by the developing nations have often ironically ended up in the countries of Europe and America, taking care of the needs of the citizens and helping them to develop even further.

Along with their precarious economic circumstances, the poor developing nations are also undergoing a major social dislocation brought upon them by the incursion of foreign cultures, values and lifestyles that may soon result in a loss of identity. In many poor countries, American movies are more easily and cheaply available than locally produced films. Foreign fast food chains (like McDonalds, Kentucky Fried Chicken and Dominos Pizza) are now all over the place, offering cheaper (even if less healthy) food to consumers in the remotest parts of the world, and driving out of business the local food vendors that have provided these services for ages. Of course, with the opening up of the local markets, these fast-food chains find it easier and cheaper to import frozen chicken from Europe and America than to support the growth of local poultries.

The same story goes for clothing, music taste, house equipment, etc. On the whole traditional societies are very speedily losing their cultural identity, they are losing their peculiar values and ethos, they are losing their corporate integrity and communal cohesion to what could be called the globalization of materialism and consumerism, and the propagation of individualism and hedonism through the Television, the Internet and other mass media whose contents are often not sensitive to local values and ethos. Yet the new values and tastes are often unsustainable under the economic circumstances of the day. There is therefore heightened social instability, political turmoil and the quality of life has generally plummeted to a level much below where it was two decades before.

Thus, while globalization and the liberalization of trade and investment have brought prosperity for the industralised nation and provided employment for their citizens, they appear to have brought poverty, unemployment, the destruction of infrastructure and social dislocation to the poor developing nations. That is why today globalization is being discussed in many circles from the perspective of *beneficiaries and victims, winners and losers,* and some would add, "*conquerors and conquered people.*" Such a presentation of the stark reality of globalization may be controversial. Yet hardly anyone would deny that the world of 2007 is bifurcated between a part that is developing rapidly and successfully and a part that is stuck in a certain sense. This is where the countries of Sub-Saharan Africa find themselves, along with many in Latin America and in the Middle East. It is today estimated that the gap between the 20 most developed countries and the 20 most impoverished countries is something like 1-60! Even in the industralised nations, all does not appear to be going well, as globalization – driven largely by the profit motive, tends to concentrate the wealth of humanity in fewer and fewer hands, while an ever-increasing number of people are daily condemned to degrading poverty.

Furthermore, experts have demonstrated that the unrestrained consumption pattern of the beneficiaries of globalization especially in the area of energy, now constitute a major threat to the ecological system, as resources meant for countless generations of humanity are being recklessly squandered in one generation with the attendant emission of poisonous toxins, carbon and sundry non-biodegradable waste material. In consequence, the ozone layer that protects the earth from the excessive heat of the sun is being depleted at an alarming rate, and global warming is also taking place at an alarming rate. Ironically, the poor segments of the world are the ones who would bear the harsher consequences of an ecological system gone berserk, as they would be the least equipped to shield themselves against nature's vengeance.

All this and more account for the reason why the meetings of the major agencies and institutions whose liberal ideologies and policies are the driving force behind globalization are often a theatre for public protests by representatives of civil society that some now refer to as "globacritics" or "globaphobes." Recall the protests that stalled the Seattle World Trade Organisation meeting in 1999, and the protests that attend all subsequent meetings of not only this Organisation, but also the meetings of G8 and other institutions that are perceived to be fanatical apostles of economic globalization.

Social Responsibility: An Ethical Imperative

On the whole, the prevalent model or paradigm of global development that is promoted rather fanatically by the apostles of economic liberalisation is clearly dysfunctional and destructive, and must therefore be urgently re-visited, if the entire global mechanism (of politics, economy, culture, environment and civilisation) is not to undergo a systems-collapse with unimaginable consequences for everyone and everything. We must admit that ours is a world divided dangerously between the haves and the have-nots, between the powerful (super-developed) few who decide the fate of everyone else, and the multitude of powerless (underdeveloped) people who have been reduced to pawns in a global chessboard; a world of success in economics, science and technology, and a world of widespread discontent, disillusionment and despair, a world overwhelmed by the monologue of the terrorist and the monologue of the counter-terrorists, and a world of acute tension between a generation of unrestrained consumers of natural resources and a violated ecological system which, losing its equilibrium, is now poised to pay back through increased temperatures, cyclones, hurricanes and tsunamis. All perceptive stakeholders must do something to avert the impending disaster and doom.

The process of global integration is probably irreversible, for no one can afford to remain in primitive (sectarian, nationalist or cultural) isolation in a world continuously made smaller by knowledge and technology. Yet the process must be moderated or guided through some deliberate policy choices by all stakeholders and the introduction of certain fundamental ethical norms and values – of justice, of fair-play, of mutual respect, that would translate globalization into the true humanization of the world, recognizing that development is supposed to be (in the words of Pope Paul VI in Populorum Progressio) "the advancement of the person, the whole person and all the people."

1. We need a paradigm shift in our concept of growth, progress and development, from one of exclusivity, subjugation and conquest that has led to World Wars, Regional Wars, the Cold War, repression and
2. terrorism, to one of peace, security and the dialogue of civilizations. As stakeholders in the global project, there are certain policy orientations

in the old paradigm, such as those that place the pursuit of profit over the welfare of the poor, which we must now reject in favour of new policy orientations that are based not solely on the profit motive, but on the recognition of human dignity, justice, equity and fairness and the short and long-term greater good of all our fellow men and women and of all creation.

3. We need a global leadership structure that will take up the challenge of making the benefits of the modern world accessible to those who today only hear of the global village and the global market, but cannot participate in it because they have no access. We need a global leadership structure that can rise above the exigencies of politics and champion such policy choices as would make for a more inclusive, more just, more humanistic, and more peaceful and secure world. We need a global leadership structure that will put in place legal frameworks and formulate ethical standards to prevent an emerging multinational corporate hegemony from taking the world hostage and driving it into perdition. So far there is no alternative structure to the United Nations Organisation for such a global leadership, yet as presently constituted, the U.N. is highly handicapped because of its lack of true democracy. The fact that the General Assembly is not the most powerful body in the Organisation, and that any of the five members of the Security Council could veto a decision of the General Assembly does derogate very much from what would have been a very influential global governing body. However, since there is as yet no alternative to the U.N. and its Agencies for global governance, we must do all we can to strengthen and empower it to meet the challenge of global governance, and wrest the fortunes of humanity from the ravages of big capital.

4. Globalisation is too important a process to be left simply to "market forces." Market forces sometimes are often blind to ethical and moral considerations. We cannot leave the fate of humanity to such blind forces. The process of globalization must be democratized for the sake of the people who are now and again to be affected by the policy choices of the International Financial Institutions and the Multinational Corporations. Governments at all levels, Human Rights Advocacy Organisations, other N.G.Os, Churches, Workers Unions, Consumers' Unions, etc, must be involved in the process and help bring decision-making closer to the people who are to be affected by those decisions.

5. Individual countries need to work towards having strong, democratic, accountable governments that can protect the interest of the people before the homogenizing forces of globalization. Weak and especially undemocratic governments do make their countries very vulnerable before these forces.

6. The Media have a major role to play in the attempt to moderate and humanize the process of globalization. Media Executives must realize that no item featured in the Newspapers, on TV or on Internet is value-free. They should exercise a high sense of social responsibility on behalf of the masses of people that are the target of their enterprise. Therefore in an age of globalization, there is the need for some form of self-censorship in the conduct of the media, so that they do not easily become tools in the hands of big capital, so that at crisis times their publications do not aggravate tension, such as the Danish cartoon incident, or easily make themselves agents of societal decay, such as the promotion of pornography on TV and Video or racial hate websites on Internet. As they inform, educate and entertain, local Media must exercise utmost sense of responsibility and strive to preserve the people's cultural identities, positive values and ethos against agents of cultural imperialism that are working through the international media.

7. International Courts and Tribunals must be strengthened and enabled to adjudicate where there are cases of violation of international legal and ethical standards.

8. Since we cannot wish the process of globalization away, today's "Globophobes" and "Globacritics" must form a creative alliance of moderators of globalization, using generally accepted moral values and the highest principles of justice, equity, dialogue and cultural/religious diversity.

Conclusion

Let me conclude this reflection on globalization and the challenge of social responsibility with the exhortation of Pope John Paul II in his 2004 New Year Message: "The world needs a new international order to solve its conflicts and ensure peace. More than ever, we need a new international order which draws on the experience and results of the United Nations.... an order which is capable of finding adequate solutions to today's problems, based on the dignity of human beings, on integrating all society on solidarity, between rich and poor countries on the sharing of resources and the extraordinary results of scientific and technological progress."

CHAPTER FIFTY-SEVEN

Christian Development Professionals as Champions of 'Transcendent Humanism'

Keynote address at the 40th Anniversary Celebration of Paul VI's Populorum Progressio and the establishment of CIDSE, Soesterberg, the Netherlands, September 25, 2007

Introduction

I congratulate you all, participants at this Conference, the Board of the International Cooperation for Development and Solidarity (CIDSE) and its Secretariat team, functionaries of member organisations, as well as the partners represented here, on the occasion of this celebration of the 40th Anniversary of *Populorum Progressio* and the establishment of this very significant outfit that serves as a coordinating body for Catholic Development Agencies that have been established by the Bishops Conferences of various countries in Europe and North America to promote the Church's Ministry of Charity as enunciated and interpreted in the immutable but ever developing Catholic Social Teachings.

That prophetic document, which was clearly ahead of its time in the way it shed the light of the Gospel on contemporary issues of global justice and the courageous and far-reaching prescriptions it contained for a harmonious, integral development towards the achievement of a transcendent humanism characterised by justice, equity, peace and "solidarity," became the "Magna Carta" of CIDSE itself and the major reference point for the activities of its member organisations.

I congratulate the Board of Directors of CIDSE and the Secretariat team for putting together this major event to mark the 40th Anniversary of both CIDSE and *Populorum Progressio*. I commend the organizers particularly for giving the liturgy, gospel reflections and prayer such a pride of place in the entire programme. It is for me a refreshingly new and praiseworthy development amidst what appears to me as a dangerous trend towards the "dislocation" of the Catholic development enterprise from the mainstream of the Church's life and mission in recent times.

We have been brought together here to jointly celebrate the Stories of Change that are a chronicle of the success of the Church's Social Gospel so far, as witnessed to or lived with actual human beings in concrete situations across the world, such as emergency relief operations in Pakistan, the liberation of enslaved migrant workers in Lebanon, the empowerment of women domestic workers in India, mobilization of the poor for the reclamation of illegally acquired lands in Kenya, and courageous interventions on behalf of those suffering from or are intimately affected by the HIV/Aids pandemic in Uganda.

Even though the problems of injustice, poverty and underdevelopment in the world remain with us (and in some instances have become even more aggravated) forty years after *Populorum Progressio* and the establishment of CIDSE, we nevertheless have cause to celebrate in thanksgiving to God for the significant contributions that have been made to the integral development of peoples by the Catholic Church's organized ministry of charity, because the world would have been a much worse place without the timely interventions of Encyclicals like *Populorum Progressio,* and the gallant contributions of member organisations of CIDSE, some of which have entailed immense personal sacrifices on the part of Development Workers and Volunteers, apart from the enormous financial resources invested in various projects.

Many member organisations had been in existence before the establishment of such a coordinating body as CIDSE, yet with the emergence of CIDSE forty years ago, new vistas were opened for networking, cooperation, mutual support and mutual reflection, towards much stronger advocacy and lobby mechanisms by Catholic Development Agencies especially over issues of regional and international justice. The kind of solidarity that we have seen expressed among member organisations of CIDSE – even if imperfect - is what we would like to see operational in all spheres of the Church's life. By virtue of the Church's character and vocation as "sacrament" for the world, I pray that the CIDSE solidarity and our communion here today may be the much needed catalyst for the emergence of the (global) human solidarity that is the object of our collective development enterprise.

I have taken particular note of the fact that member organisations of CIDSE were founded by various National Bishops' Conferences who instituted annual Lenten Campaigns to raise funds for the support of development initiatives in Southern Countries. These Agencies were therefore meant to be the *Diakonia* or organized charity outfits of their founding Churches, equipped with the necessary expertise, funding and infrastructural logistics for carrying out the *"constitutive dimension of the Church's mission of Evangelization"* that we have come to know as Justice, Development and Peace work.

Thus, as we gather today to mark the anniversary of CIDSE and *Populorum Progressio*, amid the ever changing realities and configurations of life, not only in the secular society, but also within the Church, I wish to address myself in this presentation to the issue of our distinguished identity as *"agents of the Catholic Church's organized ministry of charity"* in a world of competing religions, conflicting ideologies, and contending development agencies, both governmental and non-governmental, secular as well as religious, and what challenges we are bound to confront in our self-perception and in our modus operandi, as we seek continued relevance in such a complex global society.

A critical reflection on our identity has become necessary, as a result of the emergence of new realities that have yielded new dividends and generated new opportunities for our development enterprise, but also have introduced new complications and are raising new questions; namely, the need to expand our operations to respond to ever more demanding issues of development, the quest for greater professionalism and technical expertise in our work, in line with the demands of the times, and the desire to access more and more public funding for our operations, as well as the necessity to collaborate and network with many other agencies and functionaries involved in development (who may not necessarily share our spiritual and moral vision and values). These new realities, compounded by the phenomenon of declining religiosity and the ever increasing wave of secularism in Western societies, are now posing serious challenges for Catholic Development Agencies and their staff – challenges on the level of not only our modus operandi, but also on the level of our self-perception, our individual and group identity, our fundamental orientation, our essential motivation, and what is supposed to be our spiritual inspiration.

I dare not speak of an identity crisis at this point, as the entire orientation of this Conference itself and a number of the "stories of change," do indicate that many functionaries in the Catholic Development Agencies are fully conscious of their vital link with the Gospel, and draw their inspiration from the Social Teachings of the Church. Yet, if there are instances where a crisis of identity is evident, it need not be taken as bad news. Crisis at this point in the evolution of Catholic Development Agencies may just be - as the famous Chinese translation of the English word "crisis" goes, *"a dangerous opportunity."*

Thus the many challenges that we are confronted with today in the conduct of this segment of the Church's mission of Evangelization, may well be a providential opportunity to sit back and take stock, and as individuals and groups, redefine the "fundamental inspiration," for our human development enterprise (See John Paul II, *Sollicitudo Rei Socialis*, no. 3).

Development: Part of the Church's Mission of Evangelization

The Lord Jesus Christ taught his disciples that the entire contents of the Law and the Prophets can be summarized into these two commandments: Love God with all your heart, with all your soul, with all your mind and with all your strength, and love your neighbour as yourself. He urged the disciples to let their light shine through the practice of love, through the pursuit of justice, and through being peacemakers, so that God may be glorified and men and women may come to believe in Him (Matthew 5:14-16; John 15:12). Motivated by the same love, Jesus showed His vocation and commitment to human liberation and integral human development when he said he came that men and women may have life and have it to the full; to proclaim liberty to captives and to preach the good news to the poor (John 10:10; Luke 4:18-19). With a number of parables, including the parable of the Good Samaritan, the parable of the Rich Man and Lazarus, and the parable of the Last Judgment, Jesus taught his followers that the love of God is inseparable from the love of neighbour. He then commissioned them to go out and teach the world all that he had commanded them (Luke 10:29-37; 16:19-31; Matthew 25:31-46; 28:19-20).

The early Christian community understood this fundamental Christian imperative and made spectacular efforts to live it out in their communities, to the admiration of all who knew them (See Acts 2:42-45; 4:32-37). As the Church grew however, it became clear that the informal, spontaneous ministry of charity exercised in the Christian community was no longer adequate. This gave rise to the establishment of the *"diaconia"* as one of the essential activities of the Church, along with the preaching of the Gospel (*kerygma-martyria*), and the celebrating of the sacraments – *leitourgia* (Acts 6:1-6). From the earliest times the Church has understood "charity" as a part of her very nature, *"an indispensable expression of her very being"* (Cf. *Deus Caritas Est*, no. 25). In the course of history, this organized charity of the Church or *"diaconia"* has come to include justice advocacy, conflict resolution and peace building.

Beginning from Leo XIII's 1891 Encyclical, *Rerum Novarum*, a new corpus of social teachings has emerged in the Church, setting the parameters for a new humanism that is based on the 2000-year-old Christian Civilization of Love, which can be summed up in the words of St. Irenaeus of Lyons, *"The glory of God is the human person fully alive!"*

The 1971 Post-Synodal document, *De Justitia in Mundo* (Justice in the World), makes the following declaration:

Action on behalf of justice and participation in the transformation of the world fully appears to us as a constitutive dimension of the preaching of the gospel, or ... the Church's mission for redemption (Justice in the World, no. 6).

This is one of the most unambiguous declarations by the leadership of the Catholic Church that it recognizes the pursuit of justice and development work as not an optional extra, but rather an integral part of its mission of evangelization, and thus the Catholic Agencies and individuals functioning in this area of the Church's ministry are part of its fundamental structure. They cannot be separated, isolated or dislocated from the other segments of the Church's mission of evangelization.

The implication of the foregoing is that the God of love, mercy and compassion revealed in the Incarnate Son, Jesus Christ, is our source of identity as workers in any Christian Development Agency, and that Jesus Christ the Redeemer is the reason for our *Being* and for our entire preoccupation. Our human development enterprise is *Opus Christi* – the work of Christ. It is His name that we carry around as we discharge our duties daily in the offices of our various organisations and as we relate with our development partners in the South and our collaborators and government authorities in the North. This is why John Paul II insists that the Social Teachings of the Church belong to the field, not of ideology, but of theology, and particularly of moral theology (*Sollicitudo Rei Socialis*, no. 41)

Development work in the Church is therefore to be understood as "pastoral work." It is not a 'secular' engagement. Far from it! Like the work of the Catechist who is engaged in the Church's *kerygma*, or the priest who is engaged in the Church's *leitourgia*, Christian development work is a vocation, a special calling, and it is Jesus Christ the Lord and Master of the vineyard who sends each one of us into the vineyard, and who in turn guarantees the success of our daily enterprise. He tells His disciples in John 15:5, "I am the vine, you are the branches. Whoever remains in me, with me in him, bears fruit in plenty; for cut off from me you can do nothing."

I say therefore that development workers in Church Agencies are *missionaries,* promoting the Church's mission of Evangelization in the social sphere, or shedding the light of Christ on contemporary social questions. Even though they are not directly engaged in proselytization - since Christ's followers are supposed to reach out in love to just any "neighbour" in need - their identity as believers in Christ the Redeemer and their distinctive character as agents of the Catholic Church's organized charity are neither to be compromised nor obscured in any way.

Among many of us Catholic partners from the South, there is a growing concern today that the social engagement of the Church, especially among the older Churches of the North, is gradually being dislocated from the mainstream of the Church's life and mission. It is as if in some cases the human development enterprise of the Church is taking a life of its own and (in competition with other development agencies in society), it is beginning to function almost independently of other organs engaged in the Church's mission of evangelization. But the troubling question however, is: "Can the Church's organized ministry of charity —the "diaconia" be separated or dislocated from the Church's "kerygma" and "leitourgia" and still retain its Christian identity?

We know that in the history of Christianity and in the social evolution of our Church, most of those whose radical commitment to integral human development, justice, peace and solidarity had yielded astonishing dividends in their lifetime and even in their death, were people of profound Christian faith, hope, love, and prayer life – some even belonging to the class of Christian mystics. Notable among these champions of Christian humanism are Francis of Assisi, Vincent de Paul, Peter Claver, Damian the Leper, Martin Luther King Jr., Oscar Romero, Dom Helder Camara, Mother Teresa, John Paul II, and (I would like to add to this list Jean Vanier, Canadian founder of the now well-known L'Arch Communities for the Disabled in many countries). These are people whose profound and intense interior life (in Christ) manifested so powerfully and so fruitfully outwardly in social activism.

Mother Teresa of Calcutta perhaps touched the hearts of more world leaders than any contemporary development worker, and in her death she has continued to be an inspiration to many. But this is the content of what she called her "Business Card:"

> The fruit of silence is prayer
> The fruit of prayer is faith
> The fruit of faith is love
> The fruit of love is service
> The fruit of service is peace.

It is my conviction that the deeply spiritual life of this "Saint of the Gutters" (which has been chronicled in a new book titled *"Mother Teresa: Come Be My Light*, Image, 2007), is the guarantee for the beneficial permanence of her life and work. A famous saying attributed to St. Vincent de Paul is: *"Give me persons of prayer and they will be capable of anything."*

Pope Paul VI challenges development workers to be the champions of a new Christian humanism that is rooted in the life of faith, prayer and contemplation. He notes:

If development work calls for an ever growing number of technical experts, even more necessary still is the deep thought and reflection of wise people in search of a new humanism, one which will enable our contemporaries to enjoy the higher values of love and friendship, of prayer and contemplation.... This is what will guarantee the human person's authentic development (*Populorum Progressio*, no. 20).

John Paul II says that human development work is essentially God's work, and it cannot be simply reduced to a "technical" problem. Thus he declares that the Church's development enterprise is aimed at supporting the efforts of all other agencies, (governmental and non-governmental), with her religious and human inspiration "in order to give them a 'soul' and an effective impulse" (*Sollicitudo Rei Socialis*, no.12 and 38).

Benedict XVI, on his part says:

> While professional competence is a primary, fundamental requirement, it is not of itself sufficient. We are dealing with human beings, and human beings always need something more than technically proper care ... they need to be led to that encounter with God in Christ which awakens their love and opens their spirits to others (*Deus Caritas Est*, no. 31).

From the foregoing therefore we can say that human development and justice advocacy work (done by anyone) is good work, and is in some way inspired by the God of love who is the fountain of all goodness. But without the spiritual, moral and ecclesial dimensions, without an organic relationship with Jesus Christ through an interior life of faith and prayer on the part of the worker, it is difficult to see how such work can be classified as part of the Church's mission of evangelization. If in the lives of the development practitioners the crucial element of transcendence is ignored or jettisoned it is difficult to see how such work can truly claim the Catholic Social Teaching as its inspiration.

This interpretation of the Church's human development enterprise as an organic, constitutive and inseparable dimension of her mission of evangelization raises a number of questions or poses multiple challenges for Catholic Development Agencies and their functionaries, especially in the contemporary Western society. Some of the more obvious questions are the following:

a. To what extent are development experts required to believe in Christ and his message of redemption in order to function properly in a Catholic Development Agency? Is it not enough that they show sufficient commitment to the promotion of those values (of human dignity, human rights, human solidarity and peace) which are commonly held by all contemporary humanists?

b. What place has Christian spirituality, prayer and community worship in the life of Catholic Development Agencies and their staff?

c. What are the fundamental principles and values to be upheld and guarded stringently by Catholic Development Agencies as they engage in the much needed networking and collaboration with secular agencies that are engaged in similar issues of human development?

d. As Church development agencies seek more and more public funding in the face of declining Church income, are there sometimes conditions that come with such funding that are capable of compromising their distinctive religious identity?

Perhaps with some of our agencies these issues have been discussed in the past and are more or less settled. But my observation is that since these issues border on our individual and group identity, they are bound to keep coming up and haunting us as it were. The nature of the questions are such that they cannot possibly be settled once and for all. Thus, as we celebrate the 40th anniversary of *Populorum Progressio* and of the founding of CIDSE with the sharing of these beautiful testimonies that we call "stories of change," I ask that you spare some moments to reflect on the vital link which the human development enterprise of the Church has with the Gospel of Christ, and to draw inspiration from the "cloud of witnesses" in the history of the Church, whose spectacular contribution to human development and social transformation was made possible by a profound interior life of faith, characterised by a passionate love for Jesus Christ that is often expressed in transparent piety.

Christian Development Workers as Champions of Transcendent (Christian) Humanism

In this third part of my presentation, I wish to outline briefly some of the challenges that Church Development Agencies in the Northern hemisphere, their functionaries and their Partners will have to grapple with urgently, if we are not to betray our calling as apostles of integral human development and champions of authentic human solidarity in our day.

i. Promoting integral human development

Paul VI defines development as the advancement of the person, the whole person and all the people (*Populorum Progressio*, no. 14). Thus at a time when humanity is confronted with the grave consequences of widespread dislocation and fragmentation on the personal and social level, and at a time when crass materialism and unbridled liberalism have blinded many against the true worth and meaning of human life, Christian development agents should see themselves as major apostles of integral development of the human person and of the human society. The mere accumulation of goods and techniques, the mere achievement of social freedoms and the mere attainment of democratic governance..., are not sufficient. Human development means much more than these, for as Jesus says in Matthew 4:1, "Man does not live on bread alone," and as he asks in Matthew 16:26: "What does is profit a man if he gains the whole world and loses his soul?"

Reflecting on this matter, Paul VI declares that the goal of the Christian development worker must be a full-bodied humanism, stressing that a narrow humanism closed in on itself and not open to the values of the spirit and to God who is their source, could achieve apparent success;

but "closed off from God," they will end up engendering new injustices, introducing new inequalities and bringing about new disorders (See *Populorum Progression*, no. 31, 39 & 42).

The challenge before us as Christian development practitioners is to be constantly working towards the harmonious integration of all development initiatives, economic, political, social, psychological, ecological, moral and spiritual. We must be constantly highlighting the divine origin, the supernatural end and the transcendence of the human personality. We must be constantly pointing the attention of men and women to the fact that the most profound longing of the human heart cannot be found within humanity. By the manner of our operation and the conduct of our own lives, we must be calling the attention of the men and women of our day to the fact that human beings are made for something higher, destined for greater perfection, even as we champion the struggle here below for the liberation of the oppressed, for greater equity, justice, peace and solidarity.

ii. From interdependence to solidarity: the ethical/moral factor

Thanks to the phenomenon of globalization, there is today an ever growing awareness of the reality of human interdependence, but this interdependence does not immediately translate into what we have come to identify as "human solidarity." Human interactions are still characterised by selfishness and greed, pride and arrogance, the all-consuming desire for profit and the insatiable lust for power on the one hand, and fratricidal wars, ethnic skirmishes, terrorist and counter-terrorist violence on the other, all constituting a major impediment on our way towards the desired solidarity or what Paul VI called "transcendent humanism."

The impediments are largely a fallout of human choices in the form of actions or omissions that are ethical and moral in nature. They are often a consequence of sin – individual and structural sin. Solutions to these problems therefore cannot simply be economic or political. They are also ethical and moral and unless these important dimensions are addressed in an integrated manner with the other technical factors, the human development enterprise may be all motion but no movement. Indeed, as John Paul II observes, when the growing human interdependence is separated from its ethical requirements, it has disastrous consequences on humanity (*Sollicitudo Rei Socialis*, no. 17). This is where we Christian development workers should make our most significant contribution to the global development enterprise: We must integrate the ethical and moral ingredients into the development enterprise, and in this way re-awaken in the contemporary society the spiritual energies and the moral forces necessary to translate today's growing interdependence to the higher level of human solidarity.

iii. The Interconnectedness of the Underdevelopment Question

It can hardly be contested that forty years after *Populorum Progressio*, and in spite of the praiseworthy efforts by Church Development Agencies, the various Organs of the U.N., International and Local NGOs and Government Organisations, and in spite of the high-level International Summits, Conventions and Protocols around the issues of poverty and underdevelopment, the conditions of the weakest and poorest segment of the human community have become notably worse. Humanity as a whole has witnessed unprecedented economic growth in the last forty years. Some of those that belonged to the class of "Developing countries" in the era of Paul VI, such as China, India, Malaysia and Brazil, are now gradually joining the club of the rich. Yet the scandal of today is that a significant proportion of the global community is actually undergoing regression. The poor of today are much worse off than the poor of forty years ago. On the whole, the gap between the richest countries of the world and the poorest countries has risen from a ratio of about 1-20 forty years ago, to a ratio of about 1-50 today! (See "Persistent Poverty" a 2007 study by The Tomorrow Project in the March 2007 edition of *Tomorrow Project Bulletin*. www.tomorrowproject. net).

Of course we must always acknowledge that there are a number of factors within many resource rich but poverty-stricken countries that impede their development, such as prolonged civil war in the Democratic Republic of Congo, Sudan, Angola, Sierra Leone and Liberia, or gross mismanagement and widespread corruption in Nigeria nad Cameroon, and callous dictatorship and repression in Zimbabwe. Yet there are many extraneous factors that have kept most of the poor countries in perpetual state of dependence, underdevelopment and social strife. Among such extraneous factors are the following:

a. Historical injustices. These include for example the monumental exploitation of sub-Sahara Africa in the form of slave trade and colonialism, with lasting negative consequences on economic growth, political stability, cultural development, and socio-psychological equilibrium in these territories that have not been sufficiently acknowledged, let alone addressed.

b. What Paul VI called the "international imperialism of money," a conspiracy as it were of the rich, by which certain mechanisms have been put in place to ensure the consistent economic growth of the already developed few at the expense of the multitude now condemned to degrading poverty, social insecurity, political instability and cultural decay.

c. The ascendancy of unbridled economic liberalism and the fallacy of limitless growth in an otherwise limited world, by which the rich in each nation and among nations are getting richer, while the poor are getting ever poorer, has in our day created a scandalous disparity between rich and poor that is unprecedented in human history. Even as the top-10 richest nations of the world are 1000 times richer than their poorest neighbours, economic relations between the rich countries and their poor neighbours are still dominated by the profit motive and the desire for even more growth among the rich. Experts say that today some Corporate Executives are earning an annual income that is 5000 times higher than the least earning worker in the same society, and sometimes in the same company! Excessive economic growth of rich countries is characterised by excessive consumption and depletion of limited and often non-renewable resources, as well as the poisoning of the natural environment. This will often imply more and more poverty and instability for the poor, not only of this generation, but also of future generations.

d. The arms trade from which the rich industrialized nations are making monumental profit, is killing and maiming millions of poor people and aggravating underdevelopment. A recent study by Oxfam reveals that between 1990 and 2005, as much as $300 Billion had been expended on the purchase of light weapons for sustaining civil wars and ethnic skirmishes in Africa. This amount, says the report, is equivalent to the total amount received as foreign aid by all African countries within the same period. It notes that 95% of the weapons were purchased from the industrialized nations (See *Los Angeles Times*, October 11, 2007, p.1.).

e. Excessive concern for (or paranoia over) security among the rich nations has upset global equilibrium and significantly retarded the progress of many nations. Vietnam, Cambodia, Afghanistan,

f. Argentina, Chile, Nicaragua, Honduras, Angola, and the Democratic Republic of Congo (formally Zaire), are among the many developing countries that were thoroughly destabilized as a result of the cold war and struggle for supremacy between the ideological blocs of the West and East in the period between 1945 and 1989. To this day, many poor nations are seen merely as "security outposts" for rich countries, while the internal peace and security of others are often discussed only from the point of view of whether or not they are "safe for investment." At a time when Information and Communication Technology has reduced the world to a tiny global village, at a time when International Financial Organisations and Multinational Corporations have become much more powerful than many sovereign states, poor countries have become more like parts of a machine or cogs in a gigantic wheel.

iv. Ongoing Critical Social Analysis

The realities outlined above call for an ever more critical social analysis (as an ongoing engagement) on the part of Christian development practitioners who are truly committed to authentic human solidarity. We need to develop even greater sensitivity to the cause and effect relationship between the damaging historical experiences of many poorer countries, that have carried the burden of slave trade and/or colonial exploitation as well as today's "international imperialism of money" and the widespread phenomenon of state fragility, social upheaval, civil wars, excessive migration, widespread poverty and disease in many of these countries.

The inability or failure to make these connections and advocate for fundamental structural changes that deal with the problems beyond the superficial level, may amount to treating the symptoms of the global injustice and underdevelopment dynamic, while leaving unchallenged the dysfunctional socio-economic and political framework or what may be called a superstructure of sin that pushes people into degrading poverty and renders equitable human development impossible. As Christian development workers however, we do have a prophetic role among all who are engaged in the development question.

We cannot afford to settle for only token, isolated, uncoordinated and un-integrated development interventions. Instead we must become more critical, perceptive, prophetic in our social analysis, and become even more creative in our global intervention strategies and mechanisms. Taking our inspiration from the forward looking Encyclical of Paul VI, we Christian development workers must be constantly giving a moral content to the emerging global interdependence, highlighting the unjust mechanisms and transforming those structures of sin that sustain the prevalent underdevelopment on both national and international levels.

iv. Seeking beauty, promoting goodness and sustaining hope

As champions of Christ's civilization of love, Christian Development Workers have the task of not only providing relief to the suffering and advocating for justice and peace, but also have the challenge of seeking beauty, promoting goodness and sustaining hope in the world. In an age of widespread discouragement in the face of monumental evil, we are challenged to open our eyes wide like treasure hunters, to discover what beauty that lies beneath the rubble of economic distress, social dislocation and even rampant criminality in a number of Southern countries. For in spite of everything – in spite of war, in spite of violence, in spite of poverty and in spite of dictatorship, there is still beauty in the world, there is still goodness in people, because they are created in the image of God.

Christian development workers must seek out this inherent beauty and goodness from the land and from among the people with whom they relate, and show the suffering people the dynamics of Christian hope, over and above their technical engagement. This intangible and unquantifiable contribution of the Christian worker in the process of integral human development, may to my mind, at the end of the day, be more valuable than his or her technical assistance and as Christ lives, this hope shall not disappoint. For all appearances to the contrary notwithstanding, light shall overcome darkness, truth shall dislodge falsehood, good shall triumph over evil, and love shall conquer hatred. Thus I join the Christian mystics in proclaiming my belief that: "It shall be well. It shall be well. All manner of things shall be well". Yes, with St. John of the Cross I declare my faith and hope in the fact that "Love shall be the last word of history."

CHAPTER FIFTY- EIGHT

Education for National Development: The Challenge before Christians & Christian Bodies
(Written on November 7, 2008)

Introduction

IN today's increasingly globalised world where life is mainly driven in the fast lane, thanks to the information and communication superhighway, quality education has more than ever before become a composite imperative for integral growth and development of the individual and the society. Even in the developing and under-developed countries and cultures which appear stuck on the fringes of this modern digital civilisation, it is increasingly dawning on visionary leaders that education is a critical prerequisite to fast-track human capital development for societal transformation.

But what quality of education are our leaders propagating in today's Nigerian social environment? What are the core values of our educational enterprise? What is the contribution of Christians and Christian Churches to the Nigerian educational enterprise? Education, in general, is the complex of processes of socialisation that would aid the human person in holistic development and wholesome existence from the cradle to the grave. Through these processes, the human person acquires specific value orientations, fundamental principles, life habits, qualities and necessary skills, not only to live successfully and make his or her contribution to the growth of human civilisation but also for us Christians, to advance the Kingdom of God inaugurated in the death and resurrection of Christ.

Home Education

The home is universally regarded as the domestic school where education and learning take root, where basic human behaviour, mores and values are observed, taught and imparted. The home is where parents and mentors teach practical lessons in discipline, self-control, etiquette, cooperation, love, tolerance, patience, compassion, selflessness, humility, respect and general good behaviour. The home thus plays a critical informal role in the character formation of members of the community.

The home is, therefore, where the essential rudiments of education are taught and learnt. Ultimately, the entry into traditional institutions of learning, from kindergarten to university, becomes an extension of home-grown education.

Education in missionary/colonial times

Modern western education in Nigeria was introduced by the Christian missionaries who came to the shores of our country about the same time as the advent of the British colonial administrators more than 140 years ago. Though the principal preoccupation of the missionaries was the spread of the Gospel of Christ, they nevertheless established schools, colleges and vocational centres that taught much more than religious knowledge. Thus, most of our earliest teachers, lawyers, and public servants were products of missionary schools. The colonial government made its contribution to education at various levels of administration, establishing government schools and colleges that trained those who were to staff various colonial establishments. Thus while colonial administration sought to provide secular education that would guarantee a workforce for the institutions of the state, the missionaries did something more: Their educational enterprise was imbued with Christian values. Yet, in less than 15 years after our national independence, many changes began to occur in the form, character, and conduct of education in Nigeria. The take-over or nationalisation of missionary schools started in the East Central State in 1973.

As a mark of the success of the late nineteenth century and early 20th-century missionary endeavour, one half of the Nigerian population is today, Christian. We rejoice at this fact. Credit must indeed be given to the missionaries and the pioneers of Western education in our country to whom we owe our early history of qualitative and functional education, as well as our introduction to the Christian faith. Our emergence as a nation state coincided with the landmark discoveries and advancements in science and technology, and our educational orientation should have taken full advantage of the global transformation. Yet, so far, much of our national potential seems to have gone largely unrealised.

Failed Leadership and Jaundiced Education in Nigeria

Today, there is a gradual degeneration in the value orientation of the adult class – a fact that now impacts very negatively on child development. So we may ask: To what extent has Nigeria's leadership succeeded over time in articulating coherent and sustainable education policies for national development? The answer to this question is located in many faltering attempts by previous national administrations to fashion out workable policies. The lengthy military interregnum throughout the last quarter-century before the new Millennium accentuated the misdirection and policy somersaults that characterised educational development. The scenario left little room for any assertive Christian dimension to a wholesome national educational development to take root and flourish after the pioneering influence of the missionaries.

Our institutions, too, are a reflection of the type and quality of education that we pursue. It cannot be overstated that over the years, our institutions have suffered widespread criminal neglect of infrastructure, content and administration. Once highly regarded and respected internationally, our institutions have plummeted in reputation and self-esteem. While some institutions whose leadership is sufficiently inspired have endeavoured to pull out of the morass and improve overall performance, others have drifted further into a comatose state. Everywhere one turns, the decay in structures and facilities and the fall in morale are palpable. Institutional corruption began to erode discipline badly in virtually all the processes of teaching and learning. Education in such climes became a reflection of the life of the nation where the leadership at all levels dumped much-needed development in preference for self-serving governance. Concerned observers recognised the need to arrest the decline and orchestrated the urgency for a paradigm shift in restructuring the nation's education framework.

Underlining the need for change is recognising an inherent weakness in our educational development on the individual level – a poor reading culture. This educational dysfunction has heightened our intellectual laziness, creating a gulf within the 'educated' and 'elite' classes. Often poorly informed because of a lack of reading habit, our students, and by extension, many of the leadership class, compensate for the resultant mediocrity by cutting corners and adopting unwholesome and unethical practices to cover up their inadequacies.

Our institutional and public libraries are generally antiquated, under-stocked and under-utilised. Without a good reading culture, there is no incentive to attract public support for improvements in our libraries. Likewise, very few writers turn out good books, and others who strive to be authors end up filling the void with substandard works.

Proverbs 29:18 says that "Where there is no vision, the people perish." The end product of our visionless educational misdirection is a legacy of poor planning, degraded institutions, fallen standards, examination malpractice, secret cultism, sexual harassment, administrative scandals, a high turnout of unemployed graduates, as well as a teeming population of unemployable products of tertiary institutions. The evidence of institutional failure shows clearly in a social environment inundated with a high incidence of armed robbery, political thuggery, drug addiction, and the 'area boy' syndrome.

"Knowledge without character," one of the "seven deadly sins" identified by Mahatma Gandhi, highlights the widespread tendency among Nigerians to place a greater premium on the material returns accruable from education over the higher value of character formation. In other words, rather than pursue education for wholesome personality development, we have often sought education merely for the purpose of wealth accumulation. In recent times, many parents have pushed their children into those courses of study that they believe will rake in more money, even when the children exhibit natural talent and flare for other disciplines.

Christians: Salt of the Earth and Light of the World

Faced with multiple crises of national development and corporate social morality, Nigerian Christians are today confronted with the challenge of sustaining and promoting the core Christian values of love, truth, justice and peace for wholesome national development. Jesus calls all His disciples, all those who profess to be Christians today, to be the salt of the earth and the light of the world (Matt. 5: 13, 14). We cannot fulfil this injunction if we fail or refuse to recognise those standards that make up the wholesome value-based education necessary to shine the light of exemplary character to dispel the darkness of the age. Whether as individuals or at the social or national levels of engagement, our pursuit of high moral standards can only succeed when we consciously and consistently work against the status quo.

What kind of education do we desire?

Good, wholesome education should ideally liberate one from the corrupting shackles of greed and graft, from the basal influences of primitive superstition, of ethnic and religious bigotry, and from the corrosive instincts of selfishness and parochialism. Good, wholesome education strives for excellence over mediocrity and promotes the patriotic spirit in place of blind sycophancy. Good, wholesome education should place a high premium on truth, justice, individual and social morality, as well as peace making. Good, wholesome education should be education in leadership, the kind that would throw up the leader as servant, mentor, inspirer and visionary. Good, wholesome education should emphasise civic and political awareness, training in human dignity and fundamental human rights and citizen responsibilities. Good, wholesome education should encompass training in the democratic culture and in popular participation in governance. Good, wholesome education today should include training in healthy living, ecological justice and environmental sustainability.

Christians and Christian bodies must begin to show the way in value-based education that is infused with the essential elements of human morality. We must now mobilise all our resources in the pursuit of excellence, diligence, discipline, hard work, selflessness and fairness and teach the men and women of our generation the value of "deferred gratification." As Christians, we must work against the ever-present tendencies among our people towards mediocrity, corruption, laziness, bigotry and pettiness. We must lead the campaign against such idle and retrogressive elements as "federal character", "state of origin", and the "indigene/settler" dichotomy.

The Role of Teachers

The pivotal role of teachers at all levels must be adequately recognised and appreciated. Much of the damage to our educational development is as a consequence of spawning poor-quality teachers while encouraging the flight abroad of well-trained and highly-skilled personnel – the so-called brain drain. Good education necessarily demands good teachers. Too often in this country, the place of teachers in educational planning suffers benign neglect from officials who are themselves beneficiaries of the work of teachers. In civilised societies, teachers are accorded appropriate status and recognition as implementers of a vital sector of national development policy. If we desire wholesome education for national development, we must place teachers where they truly belong in our national consciousness, and their welfare must have pride of place in our budgetary allocations.

Conclusion

In taking up Nigeria's serious development challenges in education, our leaders must first acknowledge the need to develop a coherent policy that will promote self-reliance. This visionary policy identifies and highlights core national values that become standard irreducible courses in our institutions. Our education must go beyond mere literacy to take up research and development challenges in the modern world. Our education planners must constantly advocate for adequate budgetary allocations for equipping our schools with teachers and material enough to meet UNESCO's minimum national budgetary level of 25% for education. Our planners must set up quality standards in academic and moral values in schools, colleges and vocational centres and hold the institutions' leadership to account. Likewise, rather than merely churning out half-baked graduates, our universities must be developed into centres of excellence. The controlling organ of government must establish collaboration with institutions whose courses and products must be tailored towards national development goals. Such development-based education policy formulation will de-emphasise the craving for paper qualification if it takes cognisance of the place of leadership formation and training in leadership skills and orientation. Such training will inculcate in our young people the moral discipline needed to live wholesome lives.

The Christian challenge lies in recognising the critical importance of education in national development and the need to articulate a new orientation towards a value-based national policy. It is a fact that there is so much religiosity in this country unmatched by a corresponding Christian commitment. The challenge is for Christian leaders to help raise the level of Christian commitment that would aid and sustain a new value-based national education enterprise. To be relevant in this national endeavour, Christian leaders must show the way. After the many years eaten by the locust, the task ahead is by no means an easy one, but we must take the bull by the horns, for where there is no vision, the people do perish!

CHAPTER FIFTY- NINE

The Challenge of Electoral Reform in Nigeria
(Written on May 13, 2009)

Introduction

Upon inauguration as President of the Federal Republic of Nigeria on May 29, 2007, after an outrageously flawed general elections in April of the same year, Umaru Musa Yar'Adua pledged to Nigerians that one of his priorities would be to reform the electoral process around which there has been so much controversy. This in the eyes of many Nigerians and outside observers was a tacit admission in the President's inaugural speech that the electoral system was flawed.

The confidence of Nigerians in the President's pledge to reform the electoral process was strengthened when on August 28, 2007, he inaugurated a 22-member Electoral Reform Committee with definite terms of reference that were agreeable to a cross-section of the people. The members of the Electoral Reform Committee are men and women of integrity who were seen to possess the capacity to rise above partisan politics, ethnic interests, and religious sentiments, and who could serve creditably on a national committee to lead Nigeria out of perennial electoral difficulties.

The need for the reform of the Electoral system in Nigeria arose out of the objective conviction that conducting credible elections that are deemed free and fair by both local and international observers is critical to political legitimacy and democratic stability in Nigeria. In effect, Nigerian electoral process has been lacking in credibility and elections in the country have generally fallen short of international standards and local expectations. The last general elections in April 2007 were so massively rigged that European Union observers, Commonwealth observers and local observers of various persuasions reported that they fell far below basic international standards and were not credible. The inability of Nigeria to conduct elections that are internationally accepted to be credible, free and fair has jeopardized and compromised the concept and ideals of democracy in the country.

While inaugurating the Electoral Reform Committee on August 28, 2007, President Umaru Musa Yar'Ádua said that the shortcomings in the electoral process, "have put a heavy burden upon us to evolve a means of endowing the electoral process with the highest internationally acceptable quality and standard." He then urged the committee to "evolve a practical roadmap to laying a solid foundation for the growth and consolidation of democracy" in the country.

The terms of reference of the Electoral Reform Committee consisted of six specific points:

- To review the whole electoral process and look at all the issues and laws that have bearing on the country's electoral process and make recommendations to government.
- To make general and specific recommendations (including but not limited to constitutional and legislative provisions and/or amendments) to ensure a truly Independent Electoral Commission imbued with administrative and financial autonomy.
- To look dispassionately at our peculiarities, specificities, historical experience, and those enduring dynamics which define us as a nation in arriving at decisions.
- To make general and specific recommendations necessary for evolving an electoral system on which we shall anchor our democratic culture firmly with everlasting peace, security and political stability.
- To call for, collate and make use of memoranda from individuals and groups.
- To make final recommendations to the government of the federation that will promote credible electoral system in Nigeria.

1. The Challenges of the Electoral System in Nigeria: There is no doubt that contemporary democratic practice must be anchored on an effective electoral process. This means that Nigeria can claim a genuine democracy, only and to the extent to which it is able to foster and sustain a democratic culture and the rule of law in holding democratic elections. This is because elections provide a peaceful democratic means for societies to channel competition for political power and make collective decisions. This means that elections are essential to democracy and to legitimate governments.

Genuine democracy involves the right and opportunity for citizens to choose a candidate as their representative in government, the freedom of assembly, the freedom of association and movement and freedom of speech for candidates, parties, voters, media, observers and others. In a genuine democracy, the political environment should be free of intimidation. This set of freedoms, in return, together constitutes the essential precondition for meaningful democratic election. Nigeria is today confronted with the crucial challenge of credible governments that will be solely concerned with the pursuit of social, economic and political development of the country.

The electoral system in Nigeria has indeed been haunted by several imperfections. These imperfections include: the lack of independence of the Electoral Commission from political and executive interference, the lack of administrative and financial autonomy of the Commission, the absence of an effective political party culture and the lack of internal democracy even within the parties, lack of popular participation and a highly flawed legal framework for the resolution of electoral disputes. After lengthy deliberations, these imperfections were in our opinion adequately addressed by the Electoral Reform Committee, as could be seen in their recommendations.

2. The Recommendations of the Electoral Reform Committee: The key recommendations of the Electoral Reform Committee involve the following crucial areas:

- Constitutional amendment to allow the involvement of independent candidates in elections;
- Disposal of electoral litigations before elected officials are sworn into power;
- Increased administrative and financial independence of the Electoral Commission (INEC);
- Removal of partisan considerations in INEC appointments by putting the power of appointment in the judiciary and legislature instead of in the executive arm of government;
- Punishment of electoral offenders by a special tribunal;
- Adoption of an "Open-Secret" Ballot System;
- Funding of INEC from the first-line charge on the consolidated Revenue Fund of the Federation
- Unbundling of INEC, and the creation of two more organs to handle some of the challenges regarding the conduct of elections, and
- Abolition of the State Independent Electoral Commission (SIEC)

The government of President Umaru Musa Yar'Adua rejected the most significant recommendations of the Electoral Reform Committee. The recommendation was to the effect that the appointment to the position of the Chairman of the Independent National Electoral Commission (INEC) should only be made after a recommendation by the National Judicial Council, and upon confirmation by the senior legislative house. This was rejected by the Federal Government. The other recommendation rejected by Government was that which sought to compel electoral tribunals to conclude election petitions within six months and prior to the inauguration of the elected officer.

3. A Failed Attempt at Electoral Reform: There is no doubt that the Electoral Reform Programme of President Yar'Adua has failed even before its take-off. Since the release of the Report and recommendations of the Electoral Reform Committee, there have been forces in the federal government contending the inauguration of a credible electoral process. Some of these forces derive the force of their arguments from the fact that most of the recommendations of the Electoral Reform Committee must be accompanied by a consequential amendment of the provisions of the Constitution in order to validate them; otherwise, they are rendered null and void.

However, the recommendations of the Committee anticipated the need for constitutional review in order to give effect to the Reform of the Electoral Process It is on this basis that the Electoral Reform Committee proposed changes and amendments to the 1999 Constitution so as to accommodate fundamental changes to the electoral process. The Committee considered some of those provisions and made recommendations on their amendment and or the insertion of new provisions into some existing sections and subsections of the Constitution.

4. A Challenge to the Nigerian People: The people of Nigeria must assume responsibility for their destiny by promoting the inauguration of a credible electoral process. There is no doubt that the electoral system in Nigeria does not protect the right of the citizens to elect public leaders of their choice. It is in this regard that the Justice, Development and Peace/Caritas Commission Nigeria, in February 2009 issued a statement calling on the Federal Government of Nigeria to implement the recommendations of the Justice Uwais Electoral reform Committee in its totality. Several other civil society groups have made similar calls. Nigerians must realize that it is their obligations to hold the President accountable for implementing the recommendations of such a

Committee whose recommendations on the desired Electoral Reform has been applauded by many citizens.

The various stakeholders within the Nigerian society, and friends of Nigeria in the international community must come to the aid of democratic forces within Nigeria to ensure the fundamental political rights of Nigerians are protected by law. We must all work hard to redeem public institutions in Nigeria from the stranglehold of primitive feudalists and a corrupt cabal who are resisting the emergence of a level playing field for all sectors of society to contribute meaningfully to the development of the country.

Every Nigerian must however assume responsibility for the reform of the Electoral process in the country. The electoral reform process should be viewed as an opportunity for the Nigerian people to contribute to the building and maintenance of an enviable democratic culture in the country. The present hypocrisy of government must be abandoned in favour of, and leaders must show true commitment to, the emergence of a truly just, democratic and peaceful society where all can participate in governance and contribute their quota to the development of the country.

CHAPTER SIXTY

LET THE SEED GROW: The Challenge of Mentoring the Future Generation in Purposeful Existence
(A speech delivered as Guest Speaker at the 14th Annual Prize-giving and Farewell Day of Regina Pacis College, Abuja, July 14, 2010)

A major paradox of human life is that we are constantly looking for the easy way out, even when we know that nothing good comes easy. We are constantly drawn to the glamorous path even when we recognise that not all that glitters is gold. We are continually looking for more and more comfort; for more and more pleasure, for more and more wealth, and of course, for more and more power, prestige and popularity, even when we know that they don't necessarily bring contentment and fulfilment. We put all our attention and all our energy into pursuing wealth, pleasure and power, seeking to find happiness thereby. Yet, we know that these things do not in themselves bring ultimate happiness. This is precisely what St. Augustine meant when he noted that men and women pursue happiness even when they live in such a way as to make happiness impossible.

With all the distractions of our age, many people find it very difficult to reflect on the fundamental question of life's ultimate purpose. We prefer to just live through each day, struggling for space, competing for power, and grabbing as many toys as we could lay our hands on along the way, rather than engage in the more philosophical question of the essence of our existence. We often get so engrossed in the rat race to succeed in business, to get to the top in politics, and to become social celebrities that we miss out on what truly matters in life and what really gives meaning to life. Indeed, today, we are all under such intense pressure to live on the fast lane, to be like the Joneses, to consume more and more goods, to indulge in more and more pleasures, and to acquire more and more personal freedom, that we have little time left to ask ourselves what meaning there is in all our earthly preoccupations. The Greek Philosopher Socrates observes that a life that is not reflected upon is hardly worth living.

As human beings, we are created for a purpose. Our ultimate fulfilment and happiness lie in the realisation of that purpose. We are designed in such a way that we can neither find happiness nor attain fulfilment within ourselves - no matter how much we try. We are wired in such a way that ultimate happiness and fulfilment for each one of us lie beyond us. No amount of material pleasure, no amount of wealth and no amount of power and security can provide for us the joy, the peace, the authentic happiness which is only available in God our Creator. Indeed, the human heart hungers and thirsts after something beyond all that is available to acquire in the material world. The author of Ecclesiastes came to this realisation when he wrote the classic poem titled "Vanity of Vanities, all is Vanity." He says in Ecclesiastes 1;1-15:

Vanity of vanities, the Preacher says, all is vanity. What profit can we show for all our toil, toiling under the sun? A generation goes, a generation comes, yet the earth stands firm for ever... What was, will be again, what has been done, will be done again, and there is nothing new under the sun... I Qoheleth, have reigned over Israel in Jerusalem. Wisely I have applied myself to investigation and exploration of everything that happens under heaven. What a wearisome task God has given humanity to keep us busy. I have seen everything that is done under the sun: it is all vanity, mere chasing after the wind.

Sadly, only a few get to discover this fact in their journey through life. So they spend a whole lifetime living destructive lives, and may also miss out on eternal salvation. St. Augustine discovered this truth in the middle of his life, and he exclaimed: "Lord, you have created us for yourself, and our hearts are restless until they rest in you." Indeed, St. Augustine, who had a spectacular Christian conversion experience in his early thirties, thereafter wrote a powerful poem, lamenting the years he had wasted, pursuing a life of vanity, lusting after the tiny little beauties along his way, while ignoring the Great Beauty and Creator of all beautiful things, who constantly beckoned on him: He said:

> Late have I loved you
> O Beauty ever ancient, ever new
> Late have I loved you
> You were within me
> But I was outside
> And it was there
> That I searched for you
> In my un-loveliness
> I plunged into the lovely things

> Which you created
> You were with me
> But I was not with you
> Created things kept me from you
> Yet if they had not been in you
> They would not have been at all
> You called, you shouted,
> And you broke through my deafness
> You flashed, you shone,
> And you dispelled my blindness
> You breathed your fragrance on me
> I drew in breath
> And now I pant for you
> I have tasted you
> Now I hunger and thirst for more.
> You touched me
> And I burned for your peace. *(From* The Confessions of St. Augustine*).*

Today, however, there appears to be an epidemic of widespread thoughtlessness or lack of vision, as a result of which many people are living very destructive and meaningless lives. That the Nigerian society is itself in such a mess today is largely a consequence of the successive generations of thoughtless, senseless, visionless, inept and corrupt leaders that we have been plagued with. Though there are a few positive examples here and there, the conduct of the younger generation does not particularly inspire hope in the immediate future.

The perpetuation of the culture of greed and graft and lack of ethics among many young up-coming Nigerian professionals, the continuation of the "money" politics among many young Nigerian politicians, and the heightened indiscipline and crass materialism among the generality of those we call leaders of tomorrow – these are not good indications of any major transformation to be expected in our society in the next few years. Ours is a society that is indeed plagued by what the Indian Sage Mahatma Gandhi identifies as the "Seven Deadly Social Sins," namely: Politics without principle; Wealth without work; Commerce without morality; Pleasure without conscience; Education without character; Science without humanity; and Worship without sacrifice. No society in which these sins thrive can expect a wholesome future, and individuals who operate along these destructive lines cannot possibly find lasting happiness, peace and ultimate fulfilment.

In Matthew 7:13-14, Jesus says: "Enter by the narrow gate, since the road that leads to destruction is wide and spacious, and many take it; but it is the narrow gate, a hard road that leads to life, and only a few find it." In an age of superhighways and digital broadways, of Cruise Ships and Jumbo Jetliners, daily transporting millions of people with ease across the globe, Jesus challenges us to be among the few who resolve to take the narrow and hard road that leads to life, for he says the road that leads to death and destruction is wide and spacious, and many take it. Yes, in an age and in an environment of crass materialism, when many are prepared to violate all the principles in the book in order to achieve maximum wealth and popularity; when many will do anything (including killing people) in order to get into high political office; Jesus presents himself to us as the Way, the Truth and the Life. He is the Way to a full, purposeful, abundant, meaningful and fulfilling life. He is the Way to the Heavenly Homeland, which our hearts truly desire. He is the Light of the world. Those who do not follow him do grope in darkness. He is the Bread of Life, the Only One that satisfies the deepest and most profound hunger of the human heart (John 10:10; John 14:6; John 8:12; John 6:51-58).

Martin Seligman, a Professor of Positive Psychology at the University of Pennsylvania, recently concluded an elaborate study wherein he demonstrated that in a world of acute competition for wealth, power and popularity, and in a world where human beings have more freedom, more choices, and more possibilities for pleasure than ever before, true, genuine, lasting happiness has not been enhanced in the life of many. He discovered that none of the indices of success celebrated in today's popular culture and mass media contributes in any significant way to genuine lasting happiness. He distinguishes between the Good Life, the Joyous Life, and the Life of Authentic and Lasting Happiness. The Good Life is symbolised by wealthy and well-placed people who can afford the good things of life, live in the best houses, spend time in the most exotic holiday resorts, and so on. The Joyful life is symbolised by sports, music and Hollywood celebrities as well as beauty queens who live lives of popularity and glamour.

The research found out, however, that the good life and the joyful or glamorous life does not necessarily lead to lasting happiness and fulfilment, as indeed there are many successful businessmen and women, and many celebrities who live the miserable and distressful life of depression and some end up in alcoholism, drug addiction or even suicide. The Professor observes, for example, that Britain, one of the most developed countries, with very good social, economic and political indices, has an epidemic of depression, anxiety and conduct disorder among its youth population. He says that Britain shares these attributes with many other developed nations. Thus, he concludes that there is no linear relationship between money or material success and overall human well-being. What we have instead is what he calls a "curvilinear relationship."

It simply means that true, authentic, lasting happiness can only be found at the higher level of meaning and purpose and not on the mundane level of material wealth, creature comfort, political power and popularity. That is to say, human beings do not achieve authentic, lasting happiness and fulfilment simply by acquiring wealth, power, high social status or popularity. Those who go to various extents in desperate pursuit of happiness do not often find it. Instead, the research shows that authentic happiness comes through a lifestyle of service and commitment towards the happiness of others. We achieve authentic, lasting happiness and fulfilment only in proportion to our commitment to enhancing the quality of life of others - especially the poor, the needy, the widow, the handicapped, the orphan, the victims of injustice, the less privileged. We achieve lasting happiness and fulfilment only in proportion to our commitment to family life, in proportion to our commitment to a religious community, and in proportion to our commitment to wholesome friendships.

I find Professor Seligman's study particularly interesting as it goes to confirm (from a purely sociological and psychological point of view) the central paradox of Christian faith, which even many who would like to be called devout Christians have constantly failed to realise. This is the paradox: "Anyone who loves his life will lose it, but anyone who loses his life for my sake (and for the sake of the Kingdom) will find it; and that: "Whoever wants to be great among you, must make himself last and servant of all." I find this work a very useful illustration of the teaching of Jesus Christ in the Sermon on the Mount, that the poor and those who serve them are blessed, that it is the narrow gate which leads to life, not the wide and spacious road, that small is beautiful, and that the first shall be last, and the last first. I consider these findings useful especially in an age and in an environment where material power and status are pursued with religious passion, and where wealth is made into an idol; an age and environment where many are plagued by a social pathology that has come to be known today as "acute celebrity syndrome," by which the cover-page girl, the beauty queen, the talk-show host, the movie star, the sports and music legend are elevated, adored and worshipped like deities.

St. Francis of Assisi understood the central paradox of our Christian faith very well and gave loud witness to the truth that "it is in giving that we receive, it is in pardoning that we are pardoned, and it is in dying that we are born to eternal life." That is why he prayed:

> Lord make me a channel of your peace; where there is hatred, let me sow your love; where there is injury, your pardon Lord; and where there is doubt, true faith in you. Oh Master grant that I may never seek so much to be consoled as to console; to be understood as to understand; to be loved as to love with all my soul. Make me an instrument of your peace; where there is despair, let me give your hope; where there is darkness, only light, and where there is sadness, ever joy. For it is in giving that we receive. It is in pardoning that we are pardoned. It is in dying (to self) that we are born to eternal life.

So how do we make this seed to germinate, grow to maturity and bear fruits for the upcoming generation? How do we disseminate this profound truth which as usual with the most fundamental truths of human existence, is buried in paradoxes? How do we convince the men and women of our age who have been socialised into believing that the big buck and fast lane are what make life worth the while, that it is not exactly so? How do we convince the growing child that it is the meek and humble who shall inherit the earth in a callous world of the survival of the fittest, where the siren blarer takes over the highway and the poor little ones scamper to safety? How do we popularise the wisdom of Qoheleth, the truth of Jesus Christ, the logic of St. Augustine, and the pathway to peace of St. Francis of Assisi in a society where Might is Right, and only the rich and famous get a hearing?

I am here to say to you today that the challenge of re-engineering society and effecting a paradigm shift in our social orientation and value prioritisation lies squarely on all of us who are sufficiently dissatisfied with the quality of existence of the majority of people in our society today. Those of us who accept the call to take responsibility for the future must now step forward and take the lead. Christians have been constituted into the Light of the world and the Salt of the earth. We are the ones to show the way to a world groping in darkness and to humanity that appears to have lost its sense of purpose and direction amidst a world of selfishness and greed, materialism and secularism.

Among Christians, the place of women is very critical. This I believe, is part of the rationale for the setting up of a school of this nature. My dear young women in the graduating class: In the course of the last six years, the Principal and teachers of this school would have done their best to inculcate in you some of the best humanistic and Christian values for your wholesome existence and for the transformation of our dysfunctional society. As you leave today, the challenge is for you to let the seed sown in you these past six years grow to maturity and to bear fruits for yourselves, for your families, for your country, for humanity and to the glory of God. With the quality of education you have received here, a number of you will surely get into positions of power and influence in the global society that is increasingly becoming gender-sensitive, and where women are beginning to take their rightful place in professions, in business and in politics.

But even if only a small percentage of you eventually rise to positions of power and influence in society, you all must nevertheless champion the cause of promoting purposeful existence as young women who eventually become mothers in the society. It is a truism that women – the so-called weaker sex - have more of what it takes to influence the future direction of society than the most powerful and influential of men. From the very cradle of life, the woman has not only the responsibility but also the opportunity to mould the helpless little creature in her womb or on her lap, and direct him or her to become the man or woman she wants him or her to become. Much of what we are is what our mothers made us to be. If Christian women who are committed to the dissemination of true Christian values become more conscious of their privileged influence over the growing child and (with the grace of God) use their feminine genius and maternal powers more pro-actively, and more creatively, we would soon witness positive changes in the configuration of society. This is not the time to feign helplessness or fall back immediately on the failed paradigm of power and domination long associated with the male species, which has fuelled the culture of greed and led to aggressive competition, violence and war. I challenge you all, and particularly our graduating students, to begin today to reflect upon and discuss seriously creative new intervention strategies towards changing the face of our society and our world to the glory of God.

CHAPTER SIXTY-ONE

Citizenship Rights and the Imperative of Constitutional Reform
(Delivered at the St. Thomas Moore Forum, Abuja, on July 28, 2010)

1. Introduction

Our country is a case study in political incongruity and social ambiguity. It is a land richly endowed by the Creator with oil and gas wells and countless other minerals, yet the mass of the people live in degrading poverty. It is a land awash with unusual display of religiosity, yet it is numbered among the most corrupt in the world. Ours is a land full of promise for greatness, peace and prosperity, yet today we feature at the lowest rungs of the United Nations' development index. However as a believing people, we cannot give in to despair. We must continue not only to hope for better days, but to take the necessary steps and to work assiduously towards the destination of our dream. That is why today I would like us to discuss the question of citizenship rights and national integration in the context of our ongoing constitutional reform process.

2. Ethnic/Religious Conflicts in Nigeria

Violent conflicts resulting in massive loss of lives and property are sadly a regular feature of Nigerian life. After the unfortunate civil war of 1967 to 1970, which is the outcome of structural defects and real or perceived injustices in the political arrangements of the First Republic, we have missed countless opportunities to achieve true national reconciliation and genuine integration. Among other epochs, we missed these opportunities at the end of the civil war in 1970, in the Constitutional Conference that gave birth to the 1979 Constitution, as well as the arrangements that produced the 1999 Constitution.

We have had many avoidable internal conflicts: from the mid-1980s when the Maitatsine riots first broke out in Kano, to the Sharia riots of recent years which have shaken the nation to its very foundation and highlighted the fragility of our nationhood, and from the intermittent inter-ethnic conflicts between the Tiv and the Jukun, the Ife and the Modakeke, the Itsekiri and the Urhobo, the Umuleri and the Aguleri, the Egbura and the Bassa, to the sporadic violence at the hands of ethnic nationalists such as the O.P.C. among the Yoruba and the Bakassi Boys and the MASSOB Fighters among the Igbo. In recent years we have had the Movement for the Emancipation of the Niger Delta Volunteer Force, armed with sophisticated weapons, and able to exchange fire for fire with the Nigerian Army, daily taking hostages, blowing up oil wells and shutting down flow stations, all in an attempt to seek justice and fair play in the management and disbursement of the oil resources that accrue from their area.

It is my belief that most of the conflicts that appeared to have pitched the North against the South, Christians against Muslims, and so-called Indigenes against so-called Settlers, are not inevitable. The differences between the diverse groups that make up Nigeria are not irreconcilable. Each one of the violent eruptions we have experienced in Nigeria could have been prevented. In my opinion the numerous conflicts we have had that camouflage as ethnic or religious crises are only a symptom of the failure of leadership and governance. They are a consequence of the failure of the leadership to harmonise and manage properly by constitutional arrangements and legal instruments, the discordant notes that emerged after the colonial amalgamation of the peoples of Northern and Southern Protectorates and following the (not altogether voluntary) unification of the over 250 ethnic distinct nationalities that make up the present day Nigeria.

The making of a nation does not end with the declaration of independence, just as democracy is not synonymous with the hosting of elections. It is this failure that ignited the series of crises which culminated in the bitter experience of the civil war. The failure of leadership and governance in this country shows itself perhaps most unfortunately in the critical questions of citizenship and national integration, land distribution and resource allocation, federalism, local governance and self-determination, religious freedom, the role of the state in a multi-religious nation, etc. The ambiguities in these areas, coupled with the absence of the rule of law and massive corruption on the one hand, and the habitual manipulation of not only the state machinery, but also religion and ethnicity for selfish gain on the other, are responsible in large measure for the multiple crises that have plagued our nation.

The leadership has often failed to put the structures in place to protect the innocent and law-abiding citizens from the nefarious activities of drunken ethnic nationalists, misguided religious fanatics, and the gang of
hooligans and bandits that a large number of our able-bodied but unemployed youths are now unfortunately turning themselves into. I am convinced that with a selfless, visionary and prudent leadership, the thousands of deaths we have recorded, and the millions of Naira worth of property that have been destroyed in the last few decades, could have been saved, and Nigeria would have taken its proper place in the comity of nations, instead of being something of a byword among the peoples of the 21st Century.

3. The Citizenship Question

The unresolved citizenship question for me holds the key to our national problematic: We refer to the lingering contradiction in Nigeria whereby there are "indigenes" and "non-indigenes" or "natives" and "settlers" among the people who lay equal claim to Nigerian citizenship, who have been engaged in cultural, religious, economic and political exchanges for over 100 years. Whereas the so-called settlers or non-indigenes are part of the society in every respect, worshipping with, socializing with, trading with, paying taxes with, and marrying the so-called indigenes, when it comes to sharing of resources, including ownership of land, scholarships, placement of children in colleges and universities, employment in the civil service, political appointments, and even appointments into the headship of academic institutions (which are supposed to be purely on merit), the indigene/settler syndrome is thrown up and the so-called settler often suffers the grave injustice of discrimination and persecution.

There is the ridiculous practice of requesting for what is called "citizenship certificate" from the local government Chairman of one's ancestral village to determine which part of Nigeria one belongs to, even if one's grand-father were born in the place of one's abode and the family had lived there all along! By this unjust and retroactive practice, the Nigerian who technically can migrate to the United States or to Canada and become a full citizen after 10 years or so, with all the rights, obligations and privileges of every other citizen of that country, the same Nigerian can live for a hundred years in a part of his country, do business there, pay taxes there, build houses and marry a wife or husband from there, and yet even his or her grandchildren will still not be recognized as citizens of that part of the country.

We recall the pains and dislocations that attended the creation of states and local government areas in this country, where many people have had to move, not because they wanted to, but because they were told they had no place in the newly created states, since they now had their own. The most ruthless examples of social dislocation as a result of state creation include the Anambra-Enugu saga after the creation of Enugu State, the Enugu-Ebonyi saga after the creation of Ebonyi state, the Oyo-Osun saga after the creation of Osun State and the Ondo-Ekiti saga after the creation of Ekiti state. On these occasions, so-called non-indigenes were treated so shabbily that you would think they were illegal aliens! The indigene/settler syndrome was again forcefully brought to national focus after the violent riots that occurred in Plateau and Kano States in the year 2005, and repeatedly in Plateau State in recent times where thousands of people have lost their lives. In both States, so-called non-indigenes suffered heavy casualties and lost billions of naira worth of property at the hands of their neighbours who considered themselves indigenes.

The questions that should arise in the minds of thoughtful Nigerians, and which a progressive leadership must provide answers for are the following: What does it mean to be a Nigerian citizen? Can one be a citizen of Nigeria and not be a citizen of his or her place of domicile? What rights and privileges (and of course duties and obligations) does a long-time resident of a state or local government have? What obligations does the so-called settler owe the so-called indigenes of a place before he or she is fully assimilated? How can this issue be resolved constitutionally and permanently? What legal instruments must we put in place to ensure that Nigerians who are resident in any part of the country are treated equally?

4. Towards a resolution of the Citizenship Question

A major contribution I wish to make to the topic of this conference is to highlight the need to resolve the crisis of citizenship, because for me it holds the key to the problem of our political instability and therefore our economic underdevelopment. Unless Nigerians perceive themselves as equal citizens who share common faith and destiny, they will never be able to show the kind of patriotism required to lift Nigeria from its sorry pass. Nigerians are either citizens in every part of Nigeria or they are not citizens at all. They cannot be citizens just of their own ethnic group or state in Nigeria, or put another way, they cannot be citizens of Nigeria and not be citizens of the state where they are domiciled.

We therefore recommend the following:

(a). That every Nigerian should hold a single citizenship with the right to reside in any part he or she desires and once resident, to enjoy the benefits of citizenship, while fulfilling the same obligations as the other citizens there.

(b). That residence should be the basis for enjoying the right of citizenship. The constitution should therefore provide a guarantee of citizenship in clear terms, such as determining how many years a person must reside in a state before he or she enjoys all the rights of a citizen.

(c) That a person who leaves a state and now resides on a permanent or long-term basis in another state should lose legal citizenship of that state, even though he or she can still maintain a cultural affinity with the state where he or she no longer resides.

(d). That a powerful constitutional declaration be made regarding citizenship rights, coupled with a legal regime of non-discrimination as a way towards genuine integration and national unity. To make this work, an agency should be established and empowered to investigate every allegation of denial of citizenship rights by any person, body or the State.

(e). That legal instruments be put in place to guarantee the property rights of every citizen in such a way that the government would be under obligation to pay adequate compensation to any innocent citizen whose property is destroyed during any crisis, since it is the primary duty of government to safeguard lives and property. In the same vein laws prescribing adequate sanctions on unjust aggressors and agents of violence should be in place in order to serve as a deterrent or make such dangerous ventures unprofitable.

(f). That a future constitution for the Federal Republic of Nigeria be very explicit on the place of Religion in our national life. To avoid the ambiguities and contradictions of the present constitution, the future constitution should stipulate a total disengagement of the State from religious affairs and all religious practices should be viewed as private obligation. Connected to the status of religion is the question of the *Sharia*.

There would hardly be any lasting peace in Nigeria until a new constitution emerges that proclaims in clear terms that no part of Nigeria should establish a state religion, or use the resources of the state to bestow privilege to any religious tradition. Also, as our recent experience has shown, the existence of dual or multiple legal systems in the country is a recipe for chaos. We recommend that the penal code should be harmonized with the criminal code, so that there will be only one unified legal system, even if the laws are derived from multiple sources, viz: natural law, Islamic law, African traditional morality, Christian ethics, etc.

CHAPTER SIXTY-TWO

Sacrificing for Others: Way to Lasting Happiness
(Delivered to the Knights of St. Mulumba, in Abuja, November 20, 2010)

A major paradox of human life is that we are constantly looking for the easy way out, even when we know that nothing good comes easy. We are constantly drawn to the glamorous path even when we recognize that not all that glitters is gold. We are constantly looking for more and more comfort; for more and more pleasure, for more and more wealth, and of course for more and more power, prestige, and popularity, even when we know that they don't necessarily bring contentment and fulfilment. We put all our attention and all our energy into pursing wealth, pleasure, and power, seeking to find happiness thereby, yet we know that these things do not in themselves bring ultimate happiness. This is precisely what St. Augustine meant when he noted that men and women pursue happiness even when they live in such a way as to make happiness impossible.

With all the distractions of our age, many people find it so difficult to reflect on the fundamental question of life's ultimate purpose. We prefer to just live through each day, struggling for space, competing for power, and grabbing as many toys as we could lay our hands on along the way, rather than engage in the more philosophical question of the essence of our existence. We often get so engrossed in the rat race to succeed in business, to get to the top in politics, and to become social celebrities that we miss out on what truly matters in life and what really gives meaning to life. Indeed, today, we are all under such intense pressure to live on the fast lane, to be like the Joneses, to consume more and more goods, to indulge in more and more pleasures, and to acquire more and more personal freedom, that we have little time left to ask ourselves what meaning there is in all our earthly preoccupations. The Greek Philosopher Socrates observes that a life that is not reflected upon is hardly worth living.

As human beings we are created for a purpose. Our ultimate fulfilment and happiness lie in the realization of that purpose. We are designed in such a way that we can neither find happiness, nor attain fulfilment within ourselves - no matter how much we try. We are wired in such a way that ultimate happiness and fulfilment for each one of us lie beyond us. No amount of material pleasure, no amount of wealth and no amount of power and security can provide for us the joy, the peace, the authentic happiness which is only available in God our Creator. Indeed, the human heart hungers and thirsts after something beyond all that is available to acquire in the material world. The author of Ecclesiastes came to this realization when he wrote the classic poem titled "Vanity of Vanities, all is Vanity." He says in Ecclesiastes 1;1-15:

Vanity of vanity, the Preacher says, all is vanity. What profit can we show for all our toil, toiling under the sun? A generation goes, a generation comes, yet the earth stands firm for ever... What was, will be again, what has been done, will be done again, and there is nothing new under the sun... I Qoheleth, have reigned over Israel in Jerusalem. Wisely I have applied myself to investigation and exploration of everything that happens under heaven. What a wearisome task God has given humanity to keep us busy. I have seen everything that is done under the sun: it is all vanity, mere chasing after the wind.

Sadly, only a few get to discover this fact in their journey through life. And so they spend a whole lifetime living destructive lives, and may also miss out on eternal salvation. St. Augustine discovered this truth in the middle of his life and he exclaimed: "Lord you have created us for yourself, and our hearts are restless until they rest in you." In fact St. Augustine, who had a spectacular Christian conversion experience in his early thirties, thereafter wrote a powerful poem, lamenting the years he had wasted, pursuing a life of vanity, lusting after the tiny little beauties along his way, while ignoring the Great Beauty and Creator of all beautiful things, who constantly beckoned on him (Augustine's Confessions Book 10, chapter 27)

Today however there appears to be an epidemic of widespread thoughtlessness or lack of vision, because of which many people are living very destructive and meaningless lives. That the Nigerian society is itself in such a mess today is largely a consequence of the successive generations of thoughtless, senseless, visionless, inept and corrupt leaders that we have been plagued with in this part of the world. And though there are a few positive examples here and there, the conduct of the younger generation does not particularly inspire hope in the immediate future.

The perpetuation of the culture of greed and graft and lack of ethics among many young up-coming Nigerian professionals, the continuation of the "Ghana Must Go" politics among many young Nigerian politicians, and the heightened indiscipline and crass materialism among the generality of those we call leaders of tomorrow – these are not good indications of any major transformation to be expected in our society in the next few years. Ours is a society that is indeed plagued by what the Indian Sage Mahatma Gandhi identifies as the "Seven Deadly Social Sins," namely: Politics without principle; Wealth without work; Commerce without morality; Pleasure without conscience; Education without character; Science without humanity; and Worship without sacrifice. No society in which these sins thrive on a large scale can expect a wholesome future. And individuals who operate along these destructive lines cannot possibly find lasting happiness, peace and ultimate fulfilment.

In Matthew 7:13-14 Jesus says: "Enter by the narrow gate, since the road that leads to destruction is wide and spacious, and many take it; but it is the narrow gate, a hard road that leads to life, and only a few find it." In an age of superhighways and digital highways, of Cruise Ships and Jumbo Jetliners, daily transporting millions of people with ease across the globe, Jesus challenges us to be among the few who resolve to take the narrow and hard road that leads to life, for he says the road that leads to death and destruction is wide and spacious, and many take it. Yes, in an age and in an environment of crass materialism, when many are prepared to violate all the principles in the book in order to achieve maximum wealth and popularity; when many will do anything (including killing people) in order to get into high political office; Jesus presents himself to us as the Way, the Truth and the Life. He is the Way to full, purposeful, abundant, meaningful and fulfilling life. He is the Way to the Heavenly Homeland which our hearts truly desire. He is the Light of the world. Those who do not follow him do grope in darkness. He is the Bread of Life, the Only One that satisfies the deepest and most profound hunger of the human heart (John 10:10; John 14:6; John 8:12; John 6:51-58).

Martin Seligman a Professor of Positive Psychology at the University of Pennsylvania recently concluded an elaborate study wherein he demonstrated that in a world of acute competition for wealth, power and popularity, and in a world where human beings have more freedom, more choices, and more possibilities for pleasure than ever before, true, genuine, lasting happiness has not been enhanced in the life of many. He discovered that none of the indices of success celebrated in today's popular culture and mass media contributes in any significant way to genuine lasting happiness. He distinguishes between the Good Life, the Joyous Life, and the Life of Authentic and Lasting Happiness. The Good

Life is symbolized by very rich and well-placed people who can afford the good things of life, live in the best houses, spend time in the most exotic holiday resorts, and so on. The Joyful life is symbolized by sports, music, and Hollywood celebrities as well as beauty queens who live lives of popularity and glamour.

The research found out however that the good life and the joyful or glamorous life do not necessarily lead to lasting happiness and fulfilment, as indeed there are many successful businessmen and women, and many celebrities who live the miserable and distressful life of depression, and some end up in alcoholism, drug addiction or even suicide. The Professor observes for example that Britain, one of the most developed countries, with very good social, economic, and political indices, has an epidemic of depression, anxiety and conduct disorder among its youth population. He says that Britain shares these attributes with many other developed nations. Thus, he concludes that between money or material success and overall human well-being, there is no linear relationship. What we have instead is what he calls a "curvilinear relationship."

It simply means that true, authentic, lasting happiness can only be found at the higher level of meaning and purpose, and not on the mundane level of material wealth, creature comfort, political power and popularity. That is to say, human beings do not achieve authentic, lasting happiness and fulfilment simply through the acquisition of wealth, power, high social status or popularity. Those who go to various extents in desperate pursuit of happiness do not often find it. Instead, the research shows that authentic happiness comes through a lifestyle of service and commitment towards the happiness of others. We achieve authentic, lasting happiness and fulfilment only in proportion to our commitment to enhancing the quality of life of others - especially the poor, the needy, the widow, the handicapped, the orphan, the victims of injustice, the less privileged. We achieve lasting happiness and fulfilment only in proportion to our commitment to family life, in proportion to our commitment to a religious community, and in proportion to our commitment to wholesome friendships.

I find Professor Seligman's study particularly interesting as it goes to confirm (from a purely sociological and psychological point of view) the central paradox of our Christian faith, which even many who would like to be called devout Christians have constantly failed to realize, namely, "Anyone who loves his life will lose it, but anyone who loses his life for my sake (and for the sake of the Kingdom) will find it;" and "Whoever wants to be great among you, must make himself last and servant of all."

I find this work a very useful illustration of the teaching of Jesus Christ in the Sermon of the Mount, that the poor and those who serve them are blessed, that it is the narrow gate which leads to life, not the wide and spacious road, that small is beautiful, and that the first shall be last, and the last first. I consider these findings useful especially in an age and in an environment where material power and status are pursued with religious passion, and where wealth is made into an idol; an age and an environment where many are plagued by a social pathology that has come to be known today as "acute celebrity syndrome," by which the cover-page girl, the beauty queen, the talk-show host, the movie star, the sports and music legend are elevated, adored and worshipped like deities. St. Francis of Assisi understood the central paradox of our Christian faith very well and gave loud witness to the truth that "it is in giving that we receive, it is in pardoning that we are pardoned, and it is in dying that we are born to eternal life." That is why he prayed:

> Lord make me a channel of your peace; where there is hatred, let me sow your love; where there is injury, your pardon Lord; and where there is doubt, true faith in you. Oh Master grant that I may never seek so much to be consoled as to console; to be understood as to understand; to be loved as to love with all my soul. Make me an instrument of your peace; where there is despair, let me give your hope; where there is darkness, only light, and where there is sadness, ever joy. For it is in giving that we receive. It is in pardoning that we are pardoned. It is in dying (to self) that we are born to eternal life.

So how do we disseminate this profound truth which as usual with the most fundamental truths of human existence, is buried in paradoxes? How do we convince the men and women of our age who have been socialized into believing that the big buck and the fast lane are what make life worth the while, that it is not exactly so? How do we convince the growing child that it is the meek and humble who shall inherit the earth in a callous world of the survival of the fittest, where the siren blarer takes over the Highway, and the poor little ones scamper to safety? How do we popularize the wisdom of Qoheleth, the truth of Jesus Christ, the logic of St. Augustine, and the pathway to peace of St. Francis of Assisi in a society where Might is Right, and only the rich and famous get a hearing?

The challenge of re-engineering society and effecting a paradigm shift in our social orientation and value prioritization lies squarely on all of us who are sufficiently dissatisfied with the quality of existence of the majority of people in our society today. Those who wish to take responsibility for the future, must now step forward and take the lead. Christians have been constituted into the Light of the world and the Salt of the earth. We are the ones to show the way to a world groping in darkness and to a humanity that appears to have lost its sense of purpose. We are not helpless. We must begin to reflect upon creatively new intervention strategies towards changing the face of our society and our world to the glory of God.

CHAPTER SIXTY-THREE

Meeting the Challenge of Environmental Justice
(Written on May 30, 2011)

Introduction: The Reality of Ecological Degradation

The times are frightening for our natural environment. There is an unprecedented climate change, global warming and ozone layer depletion, and this is happening at a very alarming rate. On account of the widespread abuse of the components of nature and the reckless destruction of plant and animal species that for millions of years ensured balance in the ecological make-up of the earth, we may be witnessing a radical mutation in individual species and in the constitution of the entire planetary system.

The human race, and along with us our animate and inanimate neighbours, are today face-to-face with a multiple ecological challenge: From the rapid deforestation and desert encroachment in the countries of the Sahel Region, to the seasonal floods, cyclones and tsunamis in the low-lying South East Asian countries; from the speedy disappearance of the tropical forests of Africa to the sudden recession of the rich Brazilian Amazon vegetation; and from the melting glaciers and ice surfaces of the Polar Regions to the rise in general sea levels across the globe, it is a gory tale of ecological degradation brought upon planet earth by human misadventure.

While the correct statistics may continue to be a subject of controversy among the experts, and while there may be divergent opinions on the ways out of the present predicament, the reality of an ongoing ecological disaster as such, has now been accepted as a matter of fact among the generality of people in the 21st Century. We do not need a microscope to verify the damage being done to the environment by the perennial gas flaring in the Niger Delta region of Nigeria. We do not need environmental experts to tell us of the devastating effects of the massive pollution (of carbon dioxide), oozing out of the over-crowded cities of our country. We do not have to be Bio-Chemists or Micro-Biologists to know something of the terrible harm being done to our water resources and delicate aquatic life by the frequent spillage of fossil fuels into rivers and ponds. And yes, we do not require the services of Geologists and Toxicologists before we know something of the impending danger in our reckless disposal of such non-biodegradable waste as tires and plastic bags upon land and water, and our practice of dumping such toxic wastes as used batteries, computer screens and air-conditioner or refrigerator compressors just anywhere and everywhere in our environment.

True, climate change, ecological degradation, and the depletion of non-renewable resources, which are already affecting the quality of life of the poor around the world, and may make life on our planet impossible for future generations of human beings, and species of plants and animals, have been caused by human activity, a result of the lifestyle choices of human beings. They are therefore to be recognised as a moral and an ethical challenge for humanity. For us Christians therefore, this matter falls squarely in the realm of social ethics. We must respond adequately to this great moral and ethical challenge of our time, beginning with a Christian understanding of the natural Environment as God's gracious endowment which we human beings are called upon to tend and nurture as responsible stewards.

Psalm 24 declares that the Lord's is the earth and the fullness thereof. The earth belongs to the Lord and the Lord alone. It does not belong to any other god, whether mythological or scientific, political or economic. It does not belong to any individual human beings, or even to the whole of the human race. The earth belongs to the Lord alone, the One "who founded it on the seas and established it over the waters." This brief statement of Psalm 24 stands on a rich and elaborate religious tradition that stretches from Genesis to Revelation, a tradition that has inspired many Christian saints, mystics, poets and scholars in the last two thousand years.

We human beings do not merely live within the natural environment as people live within a building. We are part of the building blocks that constitute the framework of creation. We are not disinterested observers of the web of nature. We are strands within this web. We are not bystanders that are able to watch as the mystery of natural life unfolds. We are participants in the wondrous workings of nature. We may be a unique dimension of the natural world, but we are not separate from it. We are part of nature, and nature is part of us. We may be able to discover the laws and the order of nature. But we are still subject to nature's inscrutable laws and mysterious order. As Dianne Bergant says,

We are truly children of the universe, made of the same stuff as are the mountains and the rain, the sand and the stars. We are governed by the laws of life and growth and death as are the birds and the fish and the grass of the field. We thrive in the warmth of and through the agency of the sun as does every other living thing. We come from the earth as from a mother, and we are nourished from this same source of life (Dianne Bergant, 1987, page 28).

The Bible is very clear on the point that the earth and all that fills it belongs to God and no one else. Human beings were created in the image and likeness of God and charged with certain royal responsibilities over creation. As representatives of God, caretakers, conservators, custodians, guardians, stewards and "advocates" for planet earth, they were to exercise some form of rule over creation. But in the discharge of these responsibilities, they were supposed to be fully accountable to God. They were certainly not meant to be autonomous in their governance or stewardship over a territory that belongs to God alone.

Human Greed and Acquisitiveness, Cause of Ecological Crisis

The roots of today's violent assault on the physical environment can be traced to human greed and acquisitiveness that is almost always accompanied by aggressive attacks and destructive manipulation. Pope John Paul II blames today's ecological crisis on what he calls "an anthropological error" that is unfortunately widespread in our day. He says, "in his desire to have and to enjoy rather than to be and to grow, man consumes the resources of the earth and his own life in an excessive and disordered way...thus provoking a rebellion on the part of nature, which is more tyrannized than governed by him" (John Paul II, 1991, #76).

Human greed and acquisitiveness are largely responsible for the reckless exploitation of the rich natural resources that the good Lord put at our disposal. The new civilisation has certainly made life easier for many. With the new civilisation, human life has been enriched and human dignity has been enhanced in many ways. But these have often been at a very high cost to both our human and non-human "neighbours" in the one planetary household: the poorer people of the world have been rendered helpless victims of the exploitative systems in place, while the natural environment has been so massively degraded that all present and future life species are now rendered perilous.

The new habits of consumption that accompanied the scientific revolution and technological growth, obtained as they are at the expense of the basic rights of the poor of today and future generations, and at the expense of a wholesome and integral ecological system, can in our day no longer be sustained for the ever-growing number of the human species. We now recognise that the natural environment may be able to endure a certain amount of imbalance, but that when its threshold of equilibrium is passed, it may no longer sustain human life or any kind of life for that matter (See Dianne Bergant, 1998, page 10).

Ecoharmony: A new way of looking at our relationship with the Environment

Ecoharmony raises the question of eco-justice. The challenge that faces us is no longer just a question of sustainability and human viability on planet earth, but that of justice to the rest of creation which are endowed with intrinsic value like ourselves. All creatures have value in and for themselves, for one another, and for God. They are interconnected in a diverse whole that itself has unique value for God. Benedict XVI observes that for true peace to reign on earth, humanity must be increasingly conscious of the links between natural ecology, or respect for nature, and human ecology. He declares that disregard for the environment always harms human coexistence and vice versa. Thus he says, "There is an inseparable link between peace with creation and peace among men. Both of these presuppose peace with God." Elsewhere the Pope speaks of the need to strengthen the covenant between human beings and the environment – a covenant which should mirror the creative love of God, from whom we come and towards whom we are journeying (See Benedict XVI, January 1, 2007, #8 and Benedict XVI, January 2008, #7. See also Charles Birch et al, Editors, *Liberating Life*, 1990, page 290).

Traditionally, the Africans understood that human beings are not the measure of all things; that the rest of creation are not there as objects simply meant to serve our needs. This is why they often had a more harmonious and less aggressive relationship with the rest of the created order. Over the years, we seem to have lost this traditional harmony. Perhaps the environmental challenges of today call for a review and an enrichment of some of the Christian prayers and songs we use in the Liturgy, so as to create greater awareness of, and deepen sensitivity to the splendour of the natural creation whose very existence and integrity reveals and glorifies the Creator. To enhance eco-sensitivity among Christians, perhaps we should begin to emphasise more seriously the sacramental role, but also the mystery and integrity of the natural elements we use in Christian prayers, sacraments and celebrations – water (which we use for baptism), bread and wine (which we use for the Eucharist), oil (which we use for anointing), fire and light (which we use to signify the light of Christ, colours (which we use to mark the seasons of the Church, the smell of incense and wax (which we use for prayers), as well as the dynamics of the liturgical cycles, including "hours," "days," and "seasons."

A New Dawn of Ecological Justice and Ecological Responsibility

Although the ecological scenario created by human neglect and abuse looks quite bleak, Christians by virtue of their faith in the resurrection, must continue to be harbingers of hope for the renewal of the whole of creation, which as St. Paul observes has been waiting with eagerness for the children of God to be revealed. He says, the entire creation has until now been groaning in endless travail, waiting for liberation from its slavery to decay (See Romans 8:19-23). Prophet Ezekiel had the vision of dry bones – a symbol of death and destruction. But with the breath of the Spirit of God, these dry bones came back to life and they became a powerful and an immense army (Ezekiel 37:1-10). Isaiah prophesied that the Spirit of God would "turn the wilderness into a fruitful field," that "the parched ground would be watered," and that a new paradise would be created, one that would encompass the entire world in peace. Isaiah's prophesy also includes the promise of "new heavens and a new earth" (See Isaiah 32:15; Isaiah 61:1-4; Isaiah 41:17-20; Isaiah 65:17-25 and Isaiah 66:22, and 2 Peter 3:13). In the book of Revelation, the Seer says,

> Then I saw a new heaven and a new earth; for the former heaven and the former earth had passed away, and the sea was no more... And the one who sat on the throne said, "Behold I make all things new" (Rev. 21:1,5).

It was science and technology that gave us the powers to do great damage to creation. Eventually, a new type of science and technology will enable us to repair the damage. There are rays of light on the horizon, raising hopes for a new day of ecological responsibility and ecological justice. The new day will call us to repentance and conversion for the sins we have committed against natural creation and lead us in a process of transformation of heart and mind which will involve the adjustment of some fundamental presuppositions we have had regarding ourselves and our environment. In this process:

1. We must recognise that the universe is a communion of subjects, with each one and the whole having intrinsic value, rather than a collection of objects which have only instrumental value.
2. We must recognise that the earth is a single reality that cannot function properly in fragments, but only in totality.
3. We must recognise the primary status of the earth. Human beings are derivative. We depend upon the earth for our existence. The earth does not depend upon us for its existence as such.
4. We must recognise that by virtue of the enormous intellectual gifts bestowed upon us as human beings, we are now involved in almost everything that happens to the natural creation. We must therefore exercise utmost responsibility and caution in the application of such intelligence in relation to the rest of the created order.
5. We must recognise that the core virtues that characterise authentic Christian life cannot be limited to the merely personal and social. They must now be extended to the ecological as well.
6. We must now develop a new set of ethical-moral principles as well as legal-political instruments that recognise the gravity of all acts of commission and omission that could be classified under "biocide" and "geocide," for if we continue to kill life forms, we will eventually kill the earth itself! (See Thomas Berry, 1991, pages 93-103).

To achieve a good measure of environmental justice and ecological harmony, the following virtues must also be cultivated by all who are committed to the survival of planet earth:

i. The virtue of sustainability. We must learn to live within the regenerative, absorptive and carrying capacities of the earth. This virtue in turn calls for adaptability and frugality. We must abandon the habit of excessive production and excessive consumerism, and learn to live simply, so that others may simply live. Others here include the poor of today and tomorrow, as well as the elements of creation whose existence and integrity are today threatened by our excessive consumption patterns.

ii The virtue of solidarity. We must live with an abiding consciousness that everything is connected to everything else, and they are mutually interdependent. Thus we must develop the virtue of solidarity with not only other people, but also other species and other elements of creation. This virtue will dispose us to respect biodiversity.

iii. The virtue of humility. We need the virtue of humility to recognise quickly enough the limitations of human knowledge, human technological
iv. ingenuity and human morality. This virtue will help tame our propensity to control and manipulate nature, to exaggerate our authority over other creatures, or to undervalue the rest of creation (See James Nash, 1991, page 66-67).

A challenge to the Nigerian Leadership

Our policy makers and legislators in this country must get serious and do more than pay lip-service to issues of the environment.

- Widespread air pollution from the dark fumes of old cars, motorcycles and generators are a common feature of our national life here in Nigeria.
- Mountains of refuse that contain not only human waste but also highly toxic and non-biodegradable materials dot our towns and villages unattended. Some of the toxic wastes end up in our rivers and ponds – poisoning what remains of aquatic life. Others are carelessly set on fire, thus adding to the air pollution from vehicles and generators already mentioned.
- Open sewages are also a common feature of not only our slums and ghettos, but even of places we would call middle-class settlements in Nigeria.
- Massive gas flaring remains a daily feature of our oil exploration and exploitation in Nigeria.
- In spite of the tremendous extent of recycling technology in the 21st Century global society, there is very little investment in recycling technology here in Nigeria, outside the crude and dehumanising engagement of the many young Nigerians who have become scavengers, rummaging through our stinking dustbins with their bare hands everyday. While the rest of the world is transforming organic waste to electric power, and effectively recycling glass bottles, papers, plastic containers and aluminium cans, here in Nigerians we simply pollute the environment with our used wares and buy new ones!
- We seem to have adjusted ourselves comfortably to a high level of noise pollution in Nigeria, with all the attendant health hazards. Senior public officers who drive around with deafening sirens are a major contributor to this noise pollution. They are not only destroying our ear drums and raising our blood pressures. They are also raising the level of resentment and aggression of the poor citizens against those who claim to be their leaders.

Effective policy and legal frameworks with accompanying sanctions need to be put in place to tackle these problems. The challenges may be enormous. But with adequate political will, they are not insurmountable. I hereby challenge all categories of leaders in both public and private sectors, to show good example and lead the way in the radical change of lifestyle that nurturing a sustainable environment would require of us all.

Conclusion

Christians have been commissioned by the Lord Jesus to be the "salt of the earth" and the "light of the world" (Matthew 5:13-14). We are to preserve the earth from decay by the message of truth and redemption which we possess. We are to shine out the Light of Easter before the men and women of our generation who would otherwise be groping in the darkness of violence and destruction. We have been sent out to teach the world about the beauty and integrity of each and every creature of God, and the dignity and sanctity of the whole of creation. We have been empowered to overcome evil in the world by the force of good, and to replace death with life.

As Christians we are constantly challenged by the Gospel to cooperate with the Spirit of God who makes all things new, in order to remedy the disorder within our own personal lives, to rectify the injustice within the human society, and to reverse the ecological devastation of our world. As true stewards of God's household, we must take responsibility for what happens to present and future generations of human beings and to the entire creation by advocating for a new environmental ethics and a new environmental politics in our country Nigeria, and across the world.

May the Good Lord send forth his Spirit and renew the face of the earth. Amen.

CHAPTER SIXTY-FOUR

The Christian Elite and the Challenge of Saving Nigeria
(Written on June 21, 2012)

KARL Maier, a renowned journalist, published a book on Nigeria in the year 2000 in which he critically reviewed the many failures and contradictions that make peace and prosperity a tall dream for our country. He gave the book the curious title: *This House Has Fallen* (Penguin Books, 2000). I read through the book with a sense of shame and embarrassment, for in the event of this house really falling apart, I do not carry another country's passport. I have no other place to call home. Yet I cannot fail to agree with the author, that as presently configured and with the inept, profligate and kleptomaniacal conduct of those who run our affairs at various levels – in and out of power - this political entity is only a pack of cards that may soon come crashing down, as events of the very recent past across cities in Northern Nigeria will illustrate.

It was Charles de Gaulle who said that politics is too serious a business to be left for politicians alone. The project of just structuring of society, equitable distribution of resources, maintenance of law and order, protection of lives and property, provision of social, economic, agricultural, industrial and health infrastructures, and protection of citizens of a country from external attack, which make up what we call governance, cannot, and must not, be left entirely in the hands of those who are popularly elected into power, those who steal their way, those who rig their way or shoot their way into power, as has often been the case for us in Nigeria.

Nigeria is a nation of multiple contradictions. It is a mosaic of religious affiliations, ethnic nationalities and language and cultural groups, knocked together by historical happenstance. Ours is a nation of vast human and resource potential, whose religious, ethnic, linguistic and cultural diversities, as well as an enormous population of talented people, could otherwise have made it truly the pride of Africa. But a conspiracy of punitive overlords has reduced the country morally and structurally to an open drain, stinking with the decaying blood of the innocent poor.

They have reduced it to a wasteland littered with the debris of dashed hopes, broken promises and squandered opportunities.

The Nigerian civil society, which includes religious groups, professional bodies, labour organisations, the press, students unions, civil rights and pro-democracy groups, market women organisations, road transport workers unions, okada riders unions, street traders associations, cannot afford to fold their hands, sit idly, or watch as it were helplessly, while criminal conspirators and terrorist gangs like the Boko Haram mortgage our collective bequest, destroy our common patrimony, and render desolate our national inheritance.

At a time like this, we cannot leave our fate and fortune in the hands of the office holders, whether of the executive or legislative arm, at the national or state level, since many of them have consistently demonstrated that they are not genuine democrats who have any real concern for the people. Many have shown that they are not honourable statesmen who are passionately committed to the progress of the society. Many have shown that they are not true patriots who would sacrifice some of their comforts and privileges for the sake of the people. Instead (as events of the very recent past show), many office-holders have consistently demonstrated that they are shameless remnants of primitive feudalism, greedy merchants of a thieving generation, and callous mercenaries in the corridors of power.

We are today as a people once again at the edge of the precipice, gazing peremptorily at the abyss of destruction. We can therefore not leave our fate and fortune in the hands of political prostitutes who have no idea of the dynamics of modern statecraft. We cannot entrust our fate and fortune to contract chasers who have no concept of just and equitable ordering of a modern society. We cannot afford to fold our arms and wait for a bunch of neurotics or a parade of blind kleptomaniacs who are incapable of figuring out the cause and effect relationship between mass destitution and violent eruptions in a society, or between successive generations of rogue leaders that we have been plagued with in this country and the heightened insecurity that we must contend with today, from Bonny to Damaturu, and from Yenagoa to Potiskum.

Indeed the exigencies of the times demand that all hands must be on deck and that all serious-minded groups and individuals of talent and vision must be passionately engaged in the project of national reconstruction, which in my view demands, first of all, an ethical revolution or moral regeneration, for indeed as we read in the Book of

Proverbs, "where there is no vision, the people do perish," and "a nation devoid of integrity cannot know peace."

Indeed Nigeria perishes for lack of knowledge. As a people, we are today groaning under the weight of our collective myopia. There is an acute shortage of vision, intellectual rigour, critical thinking, and discerning conscience even amongst the most learned and exposed Nigerians. What appears to be in place is the cult of mediocrity, whereby professors of political science for whom democracy is supposed to be an article of faith, legal luminaries who hold the title of "Senior Advocate of Nigeria," and who have sworn to defend the rule of law, and highly respected religious prelates, who are expected to hold truth as sacred, often violate their calling and now and again bow before corrupt rulers, canonise treasury looters and publicly anoint election riggers. Many of those whom Nigerians look up to for a sense of direction have today become shameless sycophants, despicable praise singers and contemptible propagandists for the violators of the Nigerian people – all for filthy lucre!

In the face of this bleak national scenario, Nigerians have obvious choices to make. Our dire state of affairs has not only been sustained by greedy lawyers, corrupt judges, rogue pastors, fraudulent priests, and cash-and-carry journalists but also by the widespread cynicism, apathy and despondency of the generality of Nigerians who simply "siddon look," as it were in utter helplessness, while the nation gallops along on reverse gear. Today, we can resolve to re-possess our land from the band of renegades having pretensions to leadership at various levels. This, of course, will be a daunting task because no conqueror, foreign or home-grown, ever gives up the hold on power voluntarily or without a fight. The Christian elite, and especially Christian professional groups like the Catholic Lawyers Association, must heed the wake-up call now if there must begin a process of emancipation from a blighted future to which unborn generations seem to be condemned.

Christians have been constituted as the salt of the earth and the light of the world. Jesus Christ came into the world so that human beings may have life and have it to the full (Matthew 10:10). He was anointed to proclaim release to captives, recovery of sight to the blind, and to set at liberty those who are oppressed (Luke 4:18). Jesus is the light of the world, and no one who follows him should ever walk in darkness (John 8:12). He is the Way, the Truth and the Life, and no one comes to the Father except through him (John 14:6). He calls all those who labour and are overburdened, to come to him and find their rest (Matthew 11:28).

Jesus assures his followers that if the Son sets you free, you shall be free indeed (John 8:36). He teaches the way of the Kingdom, and the civilisation of love. He cures the sick, he opens the eyes of the blind, he gives freedom to captives, he liberates the demonised, he feeds the hungry, he forgives sinners, he teaches the ignorant, he challenges the sinful structures in society that push people into sub-human existence, and he promises eternal life to those who follow him faithfully. In this way, Jesus' salvation is all-embracing. His liberation is integral and all-encompassing.

Christians, followers of Jesus the Light of the world and the liberator of humanity, are, by their very calling, supposed to be agents of social transformation and wholesome civilisation. Christians are called upon to regularly intercede for their societies, for they stand in the gap between God and their fellow men and women. That is why we are daily saying the Prayer for Nigeria in Distress, the Prayer Against Bribery and Corruption in Nigeria, and other private and public acts of intercession. Not long ago, the Catholic Bishops' Conference organised a very successful national prayer vigil in Abuja to ask for an end to the spate of violence in the land. Many individual Christians and groups are regularly offering masses, fasting and doing novenas for a change in our circumstances.

Yet, we Christians must do much more than simply pray. Our prayer must be supported by concrete acts of Christian witnessing. We must each make a commitment to the things that make for peace and be actively engaged in teaching Jesus' way of peace. Jesus commissions Christians to go teach all nations all he has taught us (Matthew 28:19-20). So we are the ones who must teach the world and our countrymen and women the fact that peace does not just happen, that peace is the outcome of a sustained life of truth, justice, and human solidarity. We are the ones who must help our countrymen and women come to understand that it is no use preaching peace unless we also do the things that make for peace. We are called upon to show the men and women of our society how to cultivate and promote love, compassion and forgiveness, which alone can bring peace and prosperity. We must teach Jesus' lesson to our generation that respect for human dignity and human rights, is the secret of peace and that the peace of all only comes from the justice of each. We must show our countrymen and women that if today we begin to cultivate these virtues, then we would be laying the foundation for a more wholesome future.

We Christians and Christian groups are called upon to free our people from the endless cycle of violence in which our society is presently trapped. We must teach them that darkness cannot drive out darkness, just as hate cannot drive out hate, and that returning violence for violence only multiplies violence, adding deeper darkness to a night already devoid of stars. We must help the men and women of our country come to recognise that the God of peace is never glorified by human violence; instead, as St. Iraeneus says, "The glory of God is the human person fully alive." We must keep proclaiming the truth, therefore, that those who use religious justification to slaughter their neighbours – whether they are Christians or Muslims, are blaspheming.

Possessing Jesus' gospel of life, Christians must constantly work against various manifestations of the culture of death in our society. We must work against the incessant terrorist bombing of Churches and other establishments that destroys innocent lives recklessly. We must work against so-called reprisal killings by which an entire society or a segment of it celebrates vengeance. We must work against the summary execution of mere suspects by angry mobs that is prevalent in our society. We must work against jungle justice and extra-judicial killings at the hands of security agents. We must work against hired assassinations by which perceived enemies are callously eliminated. Christians must never be tired of repeating to the men and women of our generation and of our country the age-old commandment of God, "Thou shall not kill."

The generality of Christians and, in a very special way Catholic Lawyers, must be quickly educated in the fundamental planks of the Catholic Social Teachings, which include:

1. The Principle of Human Dignity
2. The sanctity of all human life – from cradle to grave
3. The Equality of all persons
4. Option for the poor
5. The Principle of Human Solidarity
6. The Principle of Subsidiarity
7. The Priority of the Common Good over individual good
8. The right to participation in the ordering of society
9. The freedom of association
10. Stewardship over natural creation

Catholic lawyers and others that belong to the Christian elite must commit themselves to studying, living out and disseminating these well-thought-out principles of Christian social engagement for the desired transformation of our sick society. Furthermore, in an age of crass materialism and blind hedonism, when the overwhelming majority of people are guilty of the seven deadly social sins identified by Mahatma Gandhi as, "politics without principles, wealth without work, commerce without morality, pleasure without conscience, education without character, science without humanity, and worship without sacrifice," Christian elite must be in the forefront of promoting in our generation, a keen awareness of what Blessed John Paul II called in his first encyclical letter, "the priority of ethics over technology, the primacy of persons over things, and the superiority of spirit over matter."

Much is expected from those to whom much has been given. So in an environment of widespread profligacy of the leadership class and heightened insecurity, the Christian elite, and especially Catholic Lawyers and other Christian professionals, must constantly resist the triumph of mediocrity in our land and challenge the celebration of insanity in our society. The saner segment of Nigerian polity must not be caught in a conspiracy of silence while a hundred thousand lives are lost, and a hundred million dreams are damned in a conflagration that is contrived by the insatiable greed and lust for power of a few remnants of primitive feudalism.

All Nigerians who recognise the cause-and-effect relationship between the economic profligacy and political brinkmanship of a few prostitutes of power and the increasing destitution of the masses of the people must not look on passively while these pallbearers of a lost generation domesticate our commonweal and turn our land to ruins. We must all realise that it is only by promoting good governance through the just ordering of society that we can reduce the tension in the land and eventually bring an end to the senseless destruction of lives and property that today characterise our national existence. Good governance is the irreducible precondition for peaceful co-existence, national stability and prosperity.

CHAPTER SIXTY-FIVE

Moral and Ethical Formation of Christians in Nigeria
(Written on June 6, 2013)

The Moral Vacuum

ON account of the much talked about failure of leadership and the general systems breakdown in our society these last few decades, the moral fabric in Nigeria has suffered a fatal assault. Today's generation of Nigerians appears largely to have lost the sense of right and wrong, of values and vices, of what is desirable and what is condemnable, of what is good and what is bad. As a corporate entity, we seem to have lost quite a dose of our sense of shame and outrage at the preponderance of corruption and violence. Though we are acclaimed to be a very religious nation, many of us, Christians and Muslims, have lost the sense of sin and iniquity and the fear of hell and damnation. We, therefore, carry on our criminal exploitation of a dysfunctional and disdainful social system as if indeed we dwell in a jungle where might is right and where the gangsters and the fraudsters are the heroes and heroines that are constantly being adulated and decorated.

Today's generation of Nigerians appears in large measure to have lost the sense of the dignity, the sanctity and the inviolability of human life. We have become a very violent people, and our national landscape is now painted red with blood. For the slightest provocation or the most ridiculous malfeasance, fellow countrymen and women are daily being shot, slaughtered, set alight, lynched, beaten to death, or "wasted" - to use the callous and sadistic code name of the Nigeria Police for the extra-judicial killing of mere suspects in their charge! We fight and kill over elections. We fight and kill over religious differences. We fight and kill on account of boundary disputes. We fight and kill over chieftaincy titles. We fight and kill over minor disputes between cattle herders and local farmers, and of course, we fight and kill over the sharing of oil loot. The students of our universities and colleges have in recent decades set up violent cults that are now and again devouring the lives of young people in their prime, in what was meant to be citadels of learning and oases of sanity. We never seem to run short of excuses to fight and kill our kith and kin.

Corruption on its part is a pandemic social pathology. It is systemic. It thrives in its various dimensions and manifestations, and in practically all the sectors and departments of our national existence, including the political, the corporate and painfully also the religious. We witness what is generally referred to as Petty Corruption. It now appears to be the normal way Nigerians run their lives and do their businesses – cheating at exams, falsifying documents, pilfering public property, giving and taking bribes for pushing files, jumping queues, asking for sexual gratification in exchange for marks at university and college examinations or for bank deposits. Petty corruption is a key element of what many shamelessly refer to as "the Nigerian factor."

We have the Grand Corruption. It is that monstrous variant of corruption whereby for example, huge contracts are awarded by government departments, not for the good of the stated beneficiaries, but primarily to raise sufficient funds from the public treasury to out-rig the opponent in an upcoming election. Grand corruption is also manifested in cases where huge contracts are awarded, paid for, and certified executed, but the projects exist only on paper! We can almost say that today, corruption defines the character of the Nigerian statecraft, notwithstanding the checks and balances in our statute books and structural framework, and the existence of multiple anti-corruption agencies, including the Independent Corrupt Practices Commission (ICPC), the Economic and Financial Crimes Commission (EFCC), and the Code of Conduct Bureau.

There is indeed today what may be described as an ethical vacuum in Nigerian society. Our public square appears to have been stripped naked, and there appears to be no more taboos in these climes. Just anything goes, as moral leaders, men and women of thought, champions of the public good, torch-bearers, mentors and inspirers, have been driven underground. Now rogues and scoundrels, thugs and bandits, mediocre functionaries and charlatans, sycophants and greedy merchants of power are hanging around the corridors of power, destroying everything of value, championing the cause of national degeneration and setting the stage for an eventual collapse of our socio-economic and political system. The shoddy, knee-jerk response of our public institutions and security agencies to the ongoing menace of terrorist insurgency in parts of our country is evidence of the extent of rot in the land.

What then must we do?

No nation can survive for long as one corporate entity, let alone make progress and achieve any measure of peace and stability when it is plagued by such multiple self-inflicted ills as ethnic bigotry, rampant indiscipline, gross mis-governance, monumental corruption, political banditry, religious intolerance and widespread social discord. We must acknowledge, however, that not everyone in the Nigerian society is insane. Not everyone in Nigeria celebrates the triumph of mediocrity. There are little oases of sanity here and there whose small voices are often drowned by the cacophony of greed and avarice, political manipulation and the exploitation of religion for selfish gain, and who daily suffer the agony of isolation and alienation. So what must we do to resuscitate the dying giant? What must we do to salvage the collapsing superstructure? How are we going to be saved as a people from our collective death wish?

Nothing short of a true ethical revolution will save our sick nation from the destruction that accompanies a prolonged moral decadence in the polity. What we require is a radical turnaround, a national conversion experience as it were, if this superstructure is to be salvaged. Religious bodies are ordinarily the best placed and the most equipped to champion such an ethical revolution. In a country like Nigeria, where the overwhelming majority of people claim to be religious, Churches and Mosques, Religious Institutions, Pastors, Imams, by their very calling, must play a critical role in the project of national moral and ethical re-awakening.

Though Churches and Mosques have not been spared the devastating effects of the culture of violence and the moral decay in the land; though many Pastors and Imams have often not risen above the murky waters of violence and corruption in the land; and though many highly placed religious leaders have betrayed in the conduct of their own lives such elements of our national malady as ethnic and religious bigotry, indiscipline, greed and avarice, the society will nevertheless continue to look up to religious institutions and clerics to play critical leadership roles in the enormous task of moral regeneration.

Nigerians make a lot of noise in the name of religion. Still, their lives often betray a near-total lack of the sense of the fear of God, the sense of right and wrong, the strong desire for and commitment to the virtuous life and hatred for sin, commitment to the common good, care and concern for the poor, discipline or self-control, self-sacrifice, chastity, modesty, frugality and the aversion for violence that are traditionally associated with truly religious people. It does not matter whether it is Christianity or Islam, Buddhism or Hinduism; religiosity used to be closely associated with the practice of virtue and the cultivation and promotion of a life of discipline, frugality and self-abnegation. It is incredible how, now, we have found a way of practising and promoting a kind of pop religion devoid of the above critical elements of true religiosity. No wonder the widespread rot in the land.

The ethical and moral teachings of our various religions, however, remain intact and could be found in the Hebrew and Christian Bible, the Muslim Qur'an and Hadith, and the Hindu Gita. It is not difficult to see that the practical lives of many so-called religious people in this society run contrary to the best teachings of their professed religions. No one doubts, for example, that the high ethical standards and strict moral teachings of Jesus Christ and his early disciples as contained in the books of the New Testament will bring about a just and peaceful society if we could only imbibe and live by them. To what extent, however, are these high ethical standards and strict moral teachings being adequately taught to adherents today? Perhaps part of the challenge before us is how to rid our society of mediocrity and charlatans who parade themselves as religious leaders and teachers, proliferating superstition, promoting corruption and propagating violence, rather than teaching their adherents the core values of the religion they profess.

Structures for Ethical and Moral Formation in the Church

The Catholic Church, with the benefit of its 2000-year history, has very well-structured training programmes with adequate instructional materials for the moral and ethical formation of its members. The high ethical standards and strict moral injunctions of Jesus Christ and his early disciples constitute a significant part of the texts that are supposed to be used for teaching at the weekly and daily Masses, at Catechism classes for adults and children, in the formation of youths, and in the training of candidates for ordination into the priesthood and other ministries in the Church. Our entire religious pre-occupation is divided into three parts, namely: Doctrine, Morals and Worship. We believe, for example, that our God is love – that he is abundant in love, mercy and compassion, to the extent that he sent his only Son to die on the Cross in order that we may not perish on account of our sins.

Worshippers are admonished to honour the God of love by living a life of love. We believe that our God is a God of truth and justice. Worshippers are admonished to shun corruption and oppression and live a life of truth and justice, such as will honour the God of truth and justice. We believe that all men and women are created in the image of God, and that they are dear to the heart of God. Worshippers are admonished to respect the sanctity and inviolability of life from conception to natural death, and to shun violence as a way of honouring the God in whose image each person has been created.

Furthermore, worshippers are admonished to show concern and come to the aid of the poor and the weak, the widow and the orphan, the handicapped and the downtrodden, as a way of honouring the God who is described by the prophets as the Father of Orphans, Defender of the Widow and Friend of the Poor. The Catholic Church recognises and professes what is known as Jesus' preferential option for the poor. That is why it should always be a matter of embarrassment for Christians and especially Christian leaders to live in obscene affluence in an environment of widespread poverty. Therefore, the prosperity gospel that is today preached and propagated by many Christian leaders in an environment of massive impoverishment on account of corruption has no basis whatsoever in Catholic moral and ethical teachings.

The Social Teachings of the Church

There is a whole body of teachings - what we call the Social Teachings of the Church, addressed not only to Catholics and other Christians but to all men and women of goodwill, aimed at forming people in those values and virtues that can make for a wholesome, just, peaceful and harmonious society. The Social Teachings cover a whole range of issues of social concern, including:

i. The sanctity and Inviolability of the human person from conception to natural death
ii. The Equal Dignity of all persons
iii. The Universal destination of the goods of the earth
iv. The priority of the Common Good over individual and group goods
v. The Justice that makes for Peace
vi. The Universality and Inviolability of Truth

vii. Environmental Justice and the Stewardship of the human person over natural creation
viii. The Dignity of Labour and the Right of Workers to fair working conditions and a just wages.

Part of the Social Teachings of the Church today is the acknowledgement of the right to freedom of conscience. It is dealt with in great detail in the document of the Second Vatican Council known as *Dignitate Humanae,* and in order to promote mutual understanding and peaceful co-existence among people of different religious persuasions, there are Departments of Inter-Religious Dialogue all through the structures of the Catholic Church, from the Vatican, through the Bishops' Conferences, to the Provinces and Dioceses. Other religions are also studied in Catholic Universities and Colleges, such that today we not only have Catholic priests who are professors of Protestant Theology, but also priests who are professors of Islam, African Traditional Religions, Buddhism and Hinduism.

The social teachings are fundamental to Christian Social Ethics and Christian morality in general. They are meant to be a major part of the formation of the Clergy and Laity of our Church. They are expounded in Papal Encyclicals, the Pastoral Letters and Communiques of Bishops' Conferences and individual Bishops, and in the regular writings and teaching programmes of many Church ministers.

Conclusion

With the ethical and moral contents of our religion stated above, and the structures of formation just highlighted, if Nigerian Catholics and other Christians are not living by the above moral and ethical standards founded on the life and teaching of Jesus Christ and his disciples, then something is seriously wrong. If there exists such a great gulf between the ethical standards of the religion we profess and propagate and the practical lives of our people, then we religious leaders need to look inwards. It is either that as a people, we are all unteachable, deaf and dumb, or that we religious leaders and adherents must critically review our method of formation in Christian ethics and social morality, such that the gospel we profess will have its full transformative impact in the Nigerian society.

CHAPTER SIXTY-SIX

Easter and the Challenge of National Security
(Written on April 18, 2014)

It started in 2009 when the Boko Haram phenomenon stole into the consciousness of Nigerians with deadly effect. Nearly five years later, precisely seven days to Easter, the latest trademark bombing in Nyanya on the outskirts of Abuja capital city claimed hundreds of wounded and scores of the dead and counting. It was to be followed within hours by the news out of Chibok, a community in Borno State, of the forcible abduction of 100 female students. As if we need reminding, one of the critical objectives of the Boko Haram sect is the abandonment of western education, and particularly of girls.

In the intervening years and spanning these events, Nigerians have endured an unbroken chain of countless episodes of gruesome violence visited on the country. Abuja and the environs alone have witnessed the high profile bombings at the city centre, at the army barracks, the police Force headquarters, the UN building, St. Theresa's Catholic Church in Madalla and the offices of *Thisday* Newspapers. These occurrences have so far defied the containment efforts of the security agencies. What is frightening and alarming is the runaway rapidity with which this country is being bound hand and foot by the experiences of unchecked terror attacks, rampant kidnaps, wildfire communal clashes and intractable social violence of different hues.

Nigerians are thus living under a culture of death, with the regular gory pictures of decapitation and gruesome images of violence. In a country that is not at conventional war, how come we are living with the steady loss of so many lives? The traumatic effects on survivors are themselves a huge national challenge, with little or nothing by way of post-trauma psychological healing or economic compensation. The repeated message of the leaders that "We will get over this" does not soothe the pain the country is going through because the average Nigerian knows too well that it is a hollow message, the flip side of which is to tell Nigerians that they are on their own.

Whilst our leaders are preoccupied with consolidating and capturing political territory, and while they fiddle in government with all manner of administrative posturing, fresh targets may be under the radar of the terrorist groups. While they take steps to secure their own safety and that of a select few of the privileged, our hospitals and health facilities overflow with the maimed and the dead whose hopes, ambitions and aspirations are brutally terminated in mid-life.

We have a national talking shop currently set up amid the ongoing national crises, which to all intents and purposes is seen in many quarters as a diversionary ploy to take the heat off the back of government. The question is asked, to what extent does it add value to the quality of leadership that has charge of the affairs of this country? Here in this country, governance is all about political junketing and comradeship, which is why our national affairs cascade from one unresolved scandal to another. Our leaders are overwhelmed with the culture of instant gratification, unwilling to sow the seeds of deferred gratification that mark out leaders that truly serve their people.

As we succumb to mixed feelings of consternation, angst and frustration welling from what amounts to the betrayal of the leadership, Nigerians confront the rhetorical question: Where do we go from here? Are our leaders faced with the inappropriate engagement of the antagonism that is spawned by Boko Haram and their fellow-travellers? Are they so bereft of ideas? Are there no clues to unravel the psychology of the opposition? Are our leaders so ensconced in their comfort zones that they cannot read the script of our tormentors – which is to inflict maximum damage on human targets and deliver extensive collateral damage in razed homes and property? Are their attacks systematically tailored to avenge their losses? What the Nyanya bomb blast seems to have done is to further expose the soft underbelly of our security superstructure and to demonstrate our ineptitude. Each occurrence invariably erodes what is left of the confidence of our leaders who are fixated on simply carrying on ruling at whatever cost.

Faced with the intractable situation at the core of our national security at the moment, a saviour and redeemer is what Nigeria needs. Our experiences and lamentations of today are a cry for deliverance, a cry for divine intervention, a cry for protection and a cry for healing. A major prerogative of government is to protect citizens, but where we are left naked, betrayed and abandoned, we can take recourse in a superior saviour. Our brand of politics and governance is anchored on falsehood, pecuniary benefits, self-service, corruption and even banditry. The world has never been in need of a saviour and redeemer than as in these climes when we are living under the reign of darkness and evil with no one to turn to for direction. What we have as leadership in this country in many respects is brigandage by another name.

We need a deliverer like Jesus Christ who lived and preached love, peace, compassion, justice, truth, humility and non-violence. For those who believe in the ascendancy of truth over falsehood, in the supremacy of good over evil, and in the ultimate triumph of light over darkness, the example of Jesus now being celebrated at Easter suffices to offer the much needed hope for a distressed and traumatized people. In our current circumstance we need leaders after the fashion of Jesus of Nazareth, who lived out such universal virtues and eternal truths that our society urgently needs, namely, love, compassion, service, self-denial and commitment to the common good.

Part of the message of Easter is hope. No matter how dismal our circumstances may be, Easter challenges us to hold on to hope. The lessons of history assure us that many societies once plagued by violence and other destructive forces, have now and again experienced transformation and turned tranquil and peaceful. Modern-day Malta is a good example of such transformation. Malta and the neighbouring Island of Gozo have had a most chequered political history. For nearly two thousand years, inhabitants of these Islands were victims of foreign occupation, military conquests, mass deportation, colonial rule, and finally, reckless bombardment during the Second World War. Located in the middle of the Mediterranean Sea, the Islands of Malta and Gozo were repeatedly coveted, conquered, occupied and exploited by one Empire after another, beginning with the incursion of the Phoenicians in 800 BC and followed in quick succession by the Romans, the Normans, the Ottoman Empire, the Empire of Sicily, the Knights of Malta, then the French, and finally the British.

The transition from one imperial control to the other was often marked by brutal wars that ravaged and impoverished the local inhabitants. In the year 1551 for example, nearly all the people of Gozo (put at about 5000) were said to have been captured and transported by the agents of the Ottoman Empire to Libya for slave labour. Under Napoleon Bonaparte, the French were said to have engaged in such reckless looting of the ancient treasures of the land, that the poor peasants of Malta rose up in revolt against the occupation force. Malta became independent of colonial rule only in September 1964 and assumed the status of a Republic ten years later. It joined the European

Union in 2004. Malta is today a very peaceful society with a fast-growing economy and one of the lowest crime rates in the world. The people are generally simple, warm, welcoming and friendly. They exhibit a high degree of resilience - determined to build a new peaceful and prosperous country upon the ruins, the rubbles and the ashes of an inglorious past.

Malta's political history rekindles my hope that as God lives, Nigeria shall one day rise from the ruins and rubbles of the devastation to which the land is today subjected by local conquerors and their foreign collaborators. Yes, I believe that as in the case of Malta, the era of terrorist insurgency, of widespread kidnapping, of callous rape and reckless pillage by mercenaries that camouflage as leaders, shall pass away, and Nigeria shall rise again to become a land of peace, stability and prosperity. And this is the logic of the resurrection: that the Calvary humiliation being replicated in Nigeria today is not the end of our individual and collective story. With faith we can already see the light at the end of the tunnel.

Easter celebration challenges well-meaning Nigerians to start working for a new land of equity, peace, truth, solidarity and justice. We must commit ourselves individually and collectively to these values so that a new nation can rise and shine out of the rubble under which this country has been buried for so long. Giving active witness to these values is the most efficacious way of celebrating the glorious resurrection of Jesus Christ and keeping ourselves on the right side of history.

CHAPTER SIXTY-SEVEN

Ethical and Moral Imperative of Credible Elections
(Written on September 25, 2014)

I congratulate the Konrad Adenauer Foundation for hosting this Roundtable specifically designed for Religious leaders to discuss the roles we must play if the next rounds of elections are going to be free, fair and credible, and especially free of violence and thank the organisers for asking me to make this brief presentation. I commend KAF for this initiative and pray that our discussions here today may indeed contribute towards the credible, free and fair elections that we desire.

I consider the Ethical and Moral Imperatives of Credible Elections a very critical topic to address today, as many engaged in contemporary Nigerian politics do not seem to realize that there are ethical and moral dimensions to political conduct. Many do not seem to realize that almost all political, economic and legal issues that we are confronted with in our society today are also moral and ethical issues that should engage the human conscience. Concerning the conduct of elections in our society, for example, many Nigerians who camouflage as religious people do not seem to realize that the looting of national, state or local government treasury for the purpose of buying over political party chiefs and the electorate; the intimidation, killing and maiming of opponents and the destruction of their property; multiple registration and multiple voting; substitution of candidates names, diversion of electoral materials, selling of voters cards, stashing of and stealing of ballot boxes, falsification of figures; declaration of false results; receiving of bribes and the favouring of one candidate against another by agents of the law, corrupt deals and judicial malpractices at the election tribunals, are not simply electoral offences or an assault on universally accepted democratic principles. They are criminal offences and, over and above all, a violation of the elementary ethical and moral principles of Truth and Justice, Equity and Fairness, Honesty and Integrity that all religions profess.

Such violation of moral and ethical principles is known by Christians as SIN and ACTS OF INIQUITY. No one who engages in any of the above electoral offences can lay claim to any measure of moral probity. Such unscrupulous persons, who have no qualms of conscience, are not religious people. They constitute an evil force in the society that must be exposed and appropriately sanctioned if we are ever to make progress as a people or find peace, security and stability as a nation.

From June 15 to 17, 2007, the Protestant Academy in Loccum, Germany, had cause to host a workshop that brought together stakeholders from Nigeria and Germany to brainstorm on the Nigerian problem. Under the rather curious theme, "Nigeria: Too Rich for Dignity and the Law?" and coming shortly after the flawed 2007 general elections in Nigeria, the Workshop was an occasion to focus attention on the contradictions of the Nigerian State and attempt to draw up recommendations on the way forward.

At this Conference held in Loccum, one Heinrich Bergstresser, a German participant who has spent many years researching on Nigeria, observed that Nigerians are an extraordinarily creative and constructive people, but that there is in the country what he called "*a destructive undercurrent*" that accounts for the *fragile balance* which has been the fate of the country since its Independence from the British. According to this speaker, what is missing is "some *initial spark* that would turn the fragile balance closer towards the first stage of nation building." Unfortunately, whatever this "initial spark," it has remained elusive, and in my opinion the widespread acrimony that often attend our national elections does tend to render the "fragile balance" of our country even more precariously fragile with each succeeding election.

Many of our countrymen and women continue to approach politics with the killer touch. Party primaries at State and Federal levels have often been an exercise in high-level brigandage in which the infrastructures of state are used to intimidate the opposition, and looted resources of state, distributed openly to buy the allegiance of congress delegates, and as could be expected, the results have often gone in favour of the highest bidder. There is widespread lack of truth and justice and a prevailing culture of fraud in the political mechanisms and processes nearly across the board. The cumulative result is an unprecedented number of litigations in our courts, arising principally from party primaries, and a preponderance of anger and frustration among aspirants to political office. Political parties are dangerously split into warring factions, poisoning the polity and heightening the tension in the land. As election approaches, violence looms over the horizon, with threats of bomb blasts, direct assassinations, arson and sundry attacks. Some Nigerians prepare for the elections as if for war. As part of their preparation for elections, they import shiploads of arms and ammunition large enough to prosecute a civil war to the consternation of the generality of our people. What are the moral and ethical implications of all this for people who take pride in calling themselves religious people?

It is instructive that one of those present with me in Germany in the year 2007, at the Workshop referred to above, was Professor Attahiru Jega, now INEC Chairman. In his paper presentation, he described the succession of Nigerian leaders in the following words:

> With very few exceptions, our crop of so-called leaders have essentially been self-serving rulers, some even despots... They lack vision, focus, selflessness and even enlightened self-interest. Most of our so-called leaders are unimaginably corrupt; they are greedy, they are vindictive, they are callous and in many fundamental respects, senseless and even reckless... There is perhaps no other country in the world where power corrupts and absolute power corrupts as absolutely as in Nigeria.

Seven years after such a damning moral judgment on the Nigerian political elite, the situation is not much different. It is perhaps even worse. True, Nigerians of integrity and credibility have little chance in contemporary Nigerian politics, as greedy merchants, power mongers, common criminals, mediocre functionaries, and charlatans have often taken control of the political machinery, forcing men and women of reason and conscience to disengage. Many knowledgeable and principled Nigerians – who in saner climes should assume the responsibility of leadership - can often not make sense out of the elite madness and corporate death wish that we witness today, and so they have become cynical, apathetic, despondent and resentful.

The Nigerian situation is, however, not irredeemable. We read in 2 Chronicles 7:14, "If the people who are called by my name, humble themselves, and pray and seek my presence and turn from their wicked ways, I myself will hear from heaven and forgive their sins and restore their land." Nigerians are not a different breed of human beings from citizens elsewhere, such as in Singapore or Malaysia, South Africa or Ghana. Many of us do not believe that Nigeria is so difficult to organize and lead unto peaceful co-existence, political stability and economic prosperity. Yet, if this country of over 160 Million people must make any headway, if the progressive decay in the polity must be halted, if the descent into anarchy in Nigeria must be averted, if in the words of Heinrich Bergstresser, the fragile balance must be tilted towards the first stage of nation building, then it cannot be business as usual. There must be a paradigm shift. This paradigm shift must begin from the character and conduct of elections, as no illegitimate government can champion the moral and ethical revolution that Nigeria today desperately needs.

In the first Encyclical of Pope Benedict XVI, released in December 2005, the Pope observed that the just ordering of society and the State is a central responsibility of politics. Highlighting the words of St. Augustine, the Pope says that *a State or a government that does not function according to the rules of justice would be nothing but a bunch of thieves or a gang of robbers!* In our day, the Americans identify such governments as "rogue regimes." A rogue government, an illegitimate government, or a government with a stolen mandate can only hasten, rather than reverse our descent into anarchy, for as Proverbs 29:18 puts it, where there is no vision – where there is no integrity, the people perish. Violence-free and credible elections are indeed an element of social morality and an imperative to good governance, stability, peace and progress.

If the next round of elections turn out to be another exercise in elite brigandage, then as a people, we are doomed: In the best-case scenario, the level of anger in the land will increase; our courts and tribunals will be flooded with litigations that would render government practically dysfunctional; much more sophisticated weapons may find their way into the hands of thugs and criminally-minded people, and the plight of the generality of people will be worse than we have ever seen before. In the worst-case scenario, violence will erupt in many flashpoints across the country so as to render the country so ungovernable that the ongoing Boko Haram insurgency may be considered only a dress rehearsal. We can quickly shout "God forbid" at this point, but we acknowledge with the book of Proverbs that indeed, where there is no vision, the people do perish! We should remember that if we do not change our course, we will end up where we are headed.

We must all take responsibility for what becomes of our country, and each one of us must undergo a conversion experience and do what we must within our spheres of influence to change the people's perception of politics and governance and the processes and procedures for orderly change of government in the modern world. Nigerians need to learn a new leadership lesson as service to the people, not some kind of conquest. We need a fresh new perception of politics as the noble art of negotiating the stewardship of society along with the ethical and moral parameters of truth, justice, equality, transparency and accountability. Religious leaders have a major part to play in this much-needed reorientation of our people. Our Sacred Scriptures have all the ethical and moral codes needed to teach the required lessons and spearhead the desired change of orientation. But perhaps we must first rid our society of the burden of the con-men and women, rogue preachers and charlatans, madmen and murderous fanatics, as well as the elite prostitutes of power who parade themselves as religious leaders in this country.

Yes, as part of the desired ethical and moral revolution, we need to help our various institutions of state put in place new arrangements that would ensure that the paths to public service are not as smooth and attractive as they are now for rogues, thieves and brigands and that the gains of office are not as rewarding as they are today for men and women of easy virtue who have no business in leadership, but who are simply gunning for the keys of the national, state or local government treasuries. The desired change will come about only when the various stakeholders in the Nigerian society, including religious leaders, staunchly reject the ignominious status quo that throws up for leadership positions men and women of base character and dubious wealth.

Time is running out on Nigerian leaders and people. With the widespread disengagement, bitterness and resentment in the land, and with a violent culture already entrenching itself in several parts of the country, there are ominous signs on the horizon of an impending popular revolt, or what is called the revenge of the poor. For indeed, as presently constituted, the superstructure we have in place in Nigeria is only a pack of cards that will soon come crashing down. But if today the Nigerian people – including Christian and Muslim politicians experience the much-needed conversion and toe the line of sanity and integrity, we may yet pull back from the brink of disaster. There appears to me to be only one way out of the mess of the moment: the way of ethical and moral revolution, which naturally must be spearheaded by religious leaders, for it is better to light a candle than forever curse the darkness!

APPENDIX: Scripture Passages on Ethics in Politics

Exodus 18:21
Select capable men from all the people, men who fear God, trustworthy men who hate dishonest gain...

Exodus. 20:16 - You shall not give false testimony against your neighbour.

Exodus 23:1 - Do not spread false reports. Do not help a wicked man by being a malicious witness.

Exodus 23:7 - Have nothing to do with a false charge and do not put an innocent or honest person to death, for I will not acquit the guilty.

Deuteronomy 16:19-20
Do not pervert justice or show partiality. Do not accept a bribe, for a bribe blinds the eyes of the wise and twists the words of the righteous. Follow justice and justice alone, so that you may live and possess the land the LORD your God is giving you.

Deuteronomy 25:15-16
You must have accurate and honest weights and measures, so that you may live long in the land the LORD your God is giving you. For the LORD your God detests anyone who does these things, anyone who deals dishonestly.

Leviticus 19:11 - Do not steal. Do not lie. Do not deceive one another.

Proverbs 6:16-20
There are six things the LORD hates, seven that are detestable to him: haughty eyes, a lying tongue, hands that shed innocent blood, a heart that devises wicked schemes, feet that are quick to rush into evil, a false witness who pours out lies and a man who stirs up dissension among brothers.

Proverbs 10:9 - The man of integrity walks securely, but he who takes crooked paths will be found out.

Proverbs 11:1,3
The LORD abhors dishonest scales, but accurate weights are his delight. The integrity of the upright guides them, but the unfaithful are destroyed by their duplicity.

Proverbs 12:17 - A truthful witness gives honest testimony, but a false witness tells lies.

Proverbs 16:8 - **Better** a little with righteousness than much gain with injustice.
Proverbs 19:1 - Better a poor man whose walk is blameless than a fool whose lips are perverse.
Isaiah 33:15-16

He who walks righteously and speaks what is right, who rejects gain from extortion and keeps his hand from accepting bribes, who stops his ears against plots of murder and shuts his eyes against contemplating evil. This is the man who will dwell on the heights, whose refuge will be the mountain fortress. His bread will be supplied, and water will not fail him.

CHAPTER SIXTY-EIGHT

Nigeria at 54: Renewing Our Hopes
(Written on October 1, 2014)

THE need to fulfil our collective aspirations as a free people, led the founding fathers of our nation to struggle for self-determination from the British, which resulted in our independence in 1960. Fifty-four years on (2014), the dreams, hopes and aspirations of the founding fathers of our nation seem in the minds of many Nigerians to have been dashed, considering the poor economic fortunes of the generality of the people, in spite of God's generous endowments of intelligent people, rich and diverse natural resources, and good climate. Fifty-four years on, our democratic evolution has remained jaundiced by a combination of negative forces, including selfishness and greed, ethnic bigotry, and the politics of acrimony and brigandage among many of those who have found themselves in the corridors of power.

Fifty-four years on, our country Nigeria is held down by the evil of corruption in its many forms and shapes - from the petty bribery taken by the clerk in the office to the policeman at the checkpoint who extorts money from motorists; from the stockbroker who manipulates the market to the banker who defrauds shareholders and customers; from Judges who abuse judicial processes for monetary gain to politicians who rig elections. There is also the grand corruption by which huge project contracts are hurriedly awarded, not for the sake of the common good, but on account of the greed of the awarding official who uses the contract-award process to loot the national, state or local government treasury. Yes, corruption thrives in the Nigerian environment, and there is no sign of it abating, in spite of the existence of a number of anti-corruption agencies. The agencies have often failed to investigate diligently and prosecute successfully many corruption cases involving high profile and influential figures.

Fifty-four years on, we witness a precarious security situation across the country, now heightened and compounded by the Boko Haram insurgency. In the face of such tragic circumstances, many Nigerians are losing patience. Many, especially of the younger generation, are, in fact, losing hope. Yet, it is in circumstances like our own that the Christian faith must be put to work. Christians are harbingers of hope. We are a people whose faith is founded on, and sustained by the miracle of the resurrection. We are a people of hope, and our hope is not deceptive because we know that we serve a God of love who intervenes now and again in human affairs to save his suffering people. We believe that the God of Jesus Christ loves this country immensely, and so in spite of the machinations of the evil one and his human agents, we trust that our prayers for justice, unity, peace, and prosperity are even now being heard. So we believe that our land shall be restored, and our young people shall have a homeland to be proud of.

There is hope for Nigeria, in spite of the succession of failed political leadership, and our own individual and collective failings as a people. There is hope for Nigeria, in spite of our many socio-political and ethno-religious conflicts and in spite of other self-inflicted maladies. There is hope for Nigeria, in spite of the menace of mass murderers that camouflage as religious crusaders in our midst. There is hope for Nigeria in spite of the destructive activities of the many ethnic warlords and greedy merchants in our midst who are disguised as politicians. There is hope for Nigeria, because we are a believing people who cry to the Lord on a daily basis.

As we mark today the fifty-fourth anniversary of our independence as a nation, we must keep this hope alive. We must hold on firmly to the triumphant Christ in whom we have an assurance of the ultimate victory of good over evil, the eventual triumph of light over darkness, and the conquest of wickedness, aggression, violence and death by the forces of love, peace, nonviolence and life. Yes, as we struggle to bear faithful witness to Christ in our various spheres of influence even in an environment of widespread selfishness and greed, corruption and social decay, youth unemployment and restiveness, violence and criminality, let us continue to encourage one another in the Christian hope that all the social indices today notwithstanding, Nigeria will survive to the glory of God. Amen.

CHAPTER SIXTY-NINE

The Role Law in the Promotion of Justice and National Development
(Delivered at the National Conference of Nigerian Bar Association)
August 24, 2015

Introduction

I want to thank the Executive Arm of the Nigerian Bar Association, and especially the committee charged with organising this Annual Conference for asking me, a simple priest who has never attended even a "Law 101" class to address this distinguished body of Legal Luminaries, Senior Advocates of Nigeria, Revered Jurists, Teachers of Law, and other Learned Gentlemen and Ladies, on the Role of Law in National Development. On account of being perhaps the least qualified to pontificate on the topic of Law before such an intimidating audience of practitioners, I have decided not to approach the topic from the perspective of an academic. Instead, I will speak simply as a layman who has a passion for social justice, and one who over the years has been a critical observer of the practice of law, the conduct of lawyers and judges, as well as the administration of the various institutions, processes, and machineries that make up the Nigerian Legal System.

The Role of Law in the human society

Law, understood as the complex mechanism of rules, codes, pacts and conventions for governing human social interactions, is aimed preeminently at the attainment of justice – justice, that quality of social equilibrium that makes for peace, stability, and consequently, progress or development. Justice is expressed in rights and duties, and arranged in codes, pacts and laws that may not be infringed. They ensure the stability of society, as well as wholesome economic and cultural relations between peoples. Justice is the natural goal or objective of law. Thus, if law is what it ought to be, and if it is administered in the manner it ought to be administered, the resultant state of affairs is justice. This is why St. Thomas Aquinas says that "an unjust law is no law." From very ancient times, Western legal traditions recognise three broad domains of justice. They include:

(i). **Distributive justice**, which is concerned with how society will distribute finite goods, such as honour and property, or in modern societies, the right to vote, which ensures that "each should count for one and no one for more than one," or equitable taxation which ensures that the burdens of society are distributed in all fairness. Thus, distributive justice works to enforce fair division of social benefits and burdens among the members of a given community. This is perhaps the most fundamental domain of justice.

(ii). **Corrective justice**, which is concerned with how to correct the situation when one person hurts another, and the social balance or order is upset. When one member of the community hurts another, redress is sought for the victim. The redress is in the form of corrective measures that will help ensure that the right order is restored.

(iii). **Commutative justice**, which is concerned with ensuring equitable exchange of goods, and fulfilment of contractual obligations. When in modern societies we speak of Law, we refer to those rules and codes that are backed by the coercive power of the state, which we are bound to obey or face appropriate sanctions, such as fine or imprisonment for criminal offences, and damages or money compensation for civil offences. Law seeks to secure justice, to resolve social conflict, to protect interests, to moderate or control social relations, and to facilitate the means of social exchange. Law is supposed to serve the ends of justice and fair play at all times, if it is to be an effective tool for attaining a well-ordered society. Furthermore, law as a species of social engineering seeks to maximize the fulfilment of the interests of the community and its members and to promote the smooth running of the machinery of the society.

Laws like a living organism are a dynamic enterprise. Laws are constantly evolving to meet the demands of a growing sense or consciousness of justice and equity in the human community. In addition to giving flesh to such fundamental and inalienable rights as the right to life, modern laws embrace such political and civil rights as are aimed at curbing possible abuses in the execution of law enforcement by callous and overzealous agents of the state, as the guarantee against unreasonable searches and seizures, freedom of expression, the right to bail, the right to due process and equal protection, the right to speedy trial, and the right to be free from torture, or cruel, degrading and inhuman punishment among others. Violation of these rights is expected to result in government action, such as fine or imprisonment, when the injured party obtains legal judgement against the offender, even if such offender claims to be acting in the name of government. Laws serve to maintain the proper balance between the authority being wielded by the state on the one hand, and the constitutional rights to be enjoyed by its citizens on the other. Laws should therefore be a potent instrument of justice, especially when rights are exercised within the framework of legitimate laws, and conversely, when laws are enacted with due respect to human rights.

Though as we have stated above, the overriding purpose of drafting, codifying and administering law in the human society is generally understood to be the attainment of justice, history however shows that laws have not always been designed and managed in such a way as to promote greater justice. Laws have not always been designed and managed in such a way as to promote the priority of the common good over and above individual and group interests. Laws have not always protected the poor and the weak against the excesses of the rich and the powerful. Laws, rather than always promoting justice, have often helped to secure the dominant and privileged class with their undue advantage over the rest of society. Indeed experience has shown that laws and their administration can be a tool of oppression or an instrument of liberation, depending on who the practitioners are and what they make of them.

Yes, the whole mechanism of law making and administration can, and has often been manipulated by the dominant, powerful class in society to subvert justice and to subjugate, to impoverish, to marginalise, and to disenfranchise or further exclude the lowly poor. Examples include the 1890 "*Equal but separate*" law that instituted racial segregation in the United States of America; the 1911 Aborigines law of Australia that authorised the state to forcefully take away from their mothers any child suspected of being of mixed blood; the 1948 *Apartheid law* that accorded Black South Africans only second-class status in their own country; and the 1984 *Decree 4* of the military regime of our now democratic President which effectively removed the freedom of expression of Nigerians at the time. Thus, when written and administered by good leaders that are servants of the people, laws tend to promote justice, but when written by tyrants, laws are invariably unjust. We must add here that the legal practitioners who helped the dictatorial leaders in the course of history to draft such unjust laws, and the jurists whose unjust rulings upheld those oppressive regimes in power, often belonged to the dominant class themselves, and cannot escape condemnation for the evil cause to which they applied their privileged learning and expertise.

The Notion of Justice

The notion of justice derives from natural law and right reason. In the human consciousness, it belongs to ethics, to morality, and to good conscience. Justice derives from the recognition of the common humanity and therefore equal dignity, sanctity and inviolability of all human persons. Justice recognises that each human person has a worth or value that is not conferred on him or her by any state or institution, but that such worth or value is intrinsic or inherent. This is why we speak of fundamental human rights as inviolable. That is to say that they are neither conferred, nor can they be taken away by earthly authority. State laws do not confer, but only promote and protect the free exercise of these rights. Justice is rooted in the honest recognition and acceptance of this fundamental dignity and rights of each and every human person, as well as the concomitant commitment to render to everyone his or her due.

Our revered Jurist and former Justice of the Supreme Court, Chukwudifu Oputa of blessed memory, in a 1985 presentation titled, "Towards Justice with a human face," declared:

> Justice is the attitude of mind that accepts that others – all others – are subject of rights in their own rights; that one's own ego is not absolute; that one's interests are related to the interests of others; that my own rights stop where my neighbour's rights begin; that every man is free to do that which he wills, provided he infringes not the equal freedom of any other man. In this simple concession that each deserves his own *(scum cuique)*, the moral self comes to grips with the reality and value of other selves… We show what a person is worth by what we ultimately concede to him… if we deny persons justice, we have decided them worthless.

Just and Unjust Laws

This then introduces the concept of just versus unjust laws. Ancient Greek Philosopher Aristotle says that law is order, and good law is good order. Law and order indeed go together. They cannot be separated. This is why we regularly use the expression: "Law and order." An unjust legal system could uphold an order, even if momentarily. But such order is an unjust order. So, when oppressive, exploitative or dictatorial regimes speak of "social order" they mean no more than "organised disorder," or the dispensation of "stratified injustice." Yet even in societies that have a semblance of justice in their legal system, the law may be so skewed or badly administered that the resulting order becomes basically unjust. We recall St. Augustine's famous dictum, that "kingdoms devoid of justice are nothing but a bunch of bandits or a gang of robbers."

The role of lawyers

Lawyers have been described as ministers in the temple of justice. The legal profession is classically understood as a helping profession, not just one other means of livelihood, much less an instrument for wealth accumulation. The legal profession is in the western tradition perceived as a vocation, a divine calling, much like the medical profession or the priesthood. Whereas the contractor, the business tycoon or the entrepreneur sets out as his or her fundamental objective to amass wealth, and he or she measures his or her success in terms of the amount of wealth and property he or she is able to accumulate in the course of time, the lawyer on the other hand is expected to be motivated by an all-consuming passion for the common good, for the promotion of a just and equitable social order, and especially for the protection of the poor and the weak against the excesses of the rich and powerful in society. The lawyer is a custodian of civilisation. He or she is on a civilising mission in society. The lawyer is a freedom fighter after the fashion of Mahatma Gandhi, Nelson Mandela, our own Gani Fawehinmi and others.

In modern democracies, the lawyer is a leader in social change or social engineering, directing the course of social evolution towards greater justice for all, through regular engagement in law reform and social advocacy. In a country like Nigeria where repeated military interventions in our political history have had a major corrosive effect on our democratic culture, where we have been left with such terrible legacies of injustice as the widespread public display of executive lawlessness, torture, brutality and extra-judicial killings at the hands of the police and other functionaries of the state, reckless looting of public resources by those entrusted with the commonweal, arbitrary arrest and prolonged detention without trial of poor suspects, even for minor bailable infractions, and the general culture of impunity in the land, the work of the lawyer is clearly cut out for him or her.

In a country that has had more than its fair share of notoriously corrupt and abusive leaders, the lawyer cannot be inattentive or indifferent. Instead the lawyer must use his privileged learning and high standing in society as a minister in the temple of justice, to stand between the government and the citizens by resisting rights violations and abuses. In a country like ours where in spite of our enormous natural endowments, the poor and their children are largely denied opportunities for good nourishment, quality education, decent housing, decent but affordable public transportation, and adequate healthcare, the lawyer must be at the forefront of social engineering through creative social change advocacy mechanisms. Only bold affirmation of justice by lawyers on behalf of poor and helpless citizens can tear down the "organised disorder" that the political and economic elite have often erected around themselves in this country, and force them to submit to just, humane and democratic principles of governance.

The role of Courts and Judges

The courts in a democracy are supposed to ensure and maintain the rule of the law. The rule of law is today universally recognised to be reflected in, among other elements, the supremacy of the law, in the respect for fundamental human rights, in the equality of all persons before the law, in the observance of due process, and in the separation of powers and the checks and balances therein. Where they function optimally in administering the rule of law and dispensing justice promptly and impartially, courts are recognised as the bulwark of democracy and the last hope of the common man. The confidence the people repose in the judges is what constitutes the foundation of the court system. It is a tragic situation when judges are suspected of being corrupt or partial. The seed of social disorder is sown when judges yield moral authority to political influence, allowing themselves to be swayed from the path of truth and justice. Justice Oputa says in the same paper quoted above that "in the corridors of justice, there should be no sirens of wealth, power and influence, for the law is no respecter of persons, wealth, position or influence." Elsewhere, the revered Justice says:

Money, they say, is the root of all evil. The bench is definitely not the place to make money. A corrupt judge is, thus, great vermin, the greatest curse ever to afflict any nation. The passing away of a great advocate does not pose such public danger as the appearance of a corrupt and/or weak judge on the bench for, in the latter instance, the public interest is bound to suffer, and justice....... is thus depreciated and mocked and debased. It is far better to have an intellectually average, but honest judge, than a legal genius who is a rogue. Nothing is as hateful as venal justice, justice that is auctioned, justice that goes to the highest bidder(Justice Chukwudifu Oputa, Judicial Services Commission, Nigeria, 1985).

Conclusion

The legal profession has faced several challenges in these climes, navigating through the waters of colonial administration, then across the treacherous terrain of military dictatorship, and now over the bumpy alleys of an infantile democracy. We have a long way to go. Nigeria remains very far away from attaining the kind of justice that would facilitate any quality of national development. Much like what we witness in the fragile states of Zimbabwe, Somalia, South Sudan and Libya, life today in Nigeria is not very far away from the Hobbesian state of nature: nasty, brutish and short. The confidence of the Nigerian people in the legal system and judicial processes has continued to wane. No wonder they now and again resort to self-help, taking the law into their hands, by way of mob justice or extra-judicial executions. Lawyers and judges are perceived as belonging to the dominant class who do not care about the plight of the poor. This unfortunate impression must change as a matter of urgency.

Members of this exalted Body for whom the legal profession is not just another gateway to wealth and prestige, but who have a genuine commitment to the common good, have work to do. Members of the Nigerian Bar Association for whom the law profession is the expression of an all-consuming passion for the justice that makes for peace, must today take responsibility for the future of our country and stretch out hands of fellowship to network with other professionals in our society with whom they share a common belief in the cause-and-effect relationship between justice and wholesome development. Lawyers and Judges in our society can and must summon the political will to pursue with unrelenting tenacity and dogged determination the urgent task of consolidating the gains of our fragile democracy, through a series of legal advocacy mechanisms, as well as a deliberate regime of judicial activism.

CHAPTER SEVENTY

John the Baptist and Authentic Religion in Nigeria
(A paper presented to the Knights of St. John International and their friends on the Solemnity of the Birthday of John the Baptist, June 24, 2016, at Maitama, Abuja)

Nigeria: The Reality of an Ethical and Moral Vacuum

On account of the much talked-about failure of leadership and the general system breakdown in our society these last few decades, the moral fabric in Nigeria has suffered a fatal assault. Today's generation of Nigerians appear in large measure to have lost the notion of right and wrong, of values and vices, of what is desirable and what is condemnable, of what is good and what is bad. As a corporate entity, we seem to have lost quite a dose of our sense of shame and outrage at the preponderance of corruption and violence. Though we are acclaimed to be a very religious nation, many of us Christians and Muslims have lost the sense of sin and iniquity and the fear of hell and damnation. We therefore carry on our criminal exploitation of a dysfunctional and disdainful social system as if indeed we dwell in a jungle where might is right and where the gangsters and the fraudsters are the heroes and heroines that are constantly being adulated and decorated.

Today's generation of Nigerians appear in large measure to have lost the sense of the dignity, the sanctity and the inviolability of human life. We have become a very violent people, and our national landscape is now painted red with blood. For the slightest provocation or the most ridiculous malfeasance, fellow countrymen and women are daily being shot, slaughtered, set alight, lynched, beaten to death, or "wasted" - to use the callous and sadistic code name of the Nigeria Police for the extra-judicial killing of mere suspects in their charge! We fight and kill over elections. We fight and kill over religious differences. We fight and kill on account of boundary disputes. We fight and kill over chieftaincy titles. We fight and kill over minor disputes between herdsmen and local farmers. Of course, we fight and kill over the sharing of the oil loot. Students of our universities and colleges have set up violent cults that are now and again raping, maiming and devouring the lives of young people in their prime, in what was meant to be citadels of learning and oases of sanity. We never seem to run short of excuses to fight and kill our kith and kin. The social media is awash with gory images of these jungle-like killings.

Corruption on its part is a pandemic social pathology. It is systemic. It thrives in its various dimensions and manifestations, and in practically all the sectors and departments of our national existence, including the political, the corporate, and painfully also, the religious. We witness what is generally referred to as *Petty Corruption*. It now appears to be the normal way Nigerians run their lives and do their businesses – cheating at exams, falsifying documents, pilfering public property, giving and taking bribes for *pushing files*, jumping queues, asking for sexual gratification in exchange for marks at university, and college examinations or for bank deposits. Petty corruption is a key element of what many shamelessly refer to as "the Nigerian factor."

We have the *Grand Corruption*. It is that monstrous variant of corruption whereby, for example, huge contracts are awarded by government departments, not for the good of the stated beneficiaries, but primarily to raise sufficient funds from the public treasury to out-rig the opponent in an upcoming election.

There is indeed today what may be described as an ethical vacuum in the Nigerian society. How sad that recently the British Prime Minister declared that Nigeria and Afghanistan are fantastically corrupt countries. Many have argued that Britain is also corrupt. But that is not the point. The truth is that the Nigerian public square appears to have been stripped naked, and there does not seem to be any more taboos in these climes. Just anything goes, as moral leaders, men and women of thought, champions of the public good, torch-bearers, mentors, and inspirers, have been driven underground. Now rogues and scoundrels, thugs and bandits, mediocre functionaries and charlatans, sycophants and greedy merchants of power are often the ones hanging around the corridors of power, destroying everything of value, championing the cause of national degeneration and setting the stage for an eventual collapse of our socio-economic and political system.

The Imperative of Ethical and Moral Revolution

As he heralded the coming of Jesus with his civilisation of love, John the Baptist gave his hearers a moral prescription for the kind of change that

many Nigerians have desired, but towards which we have done very little over the years. When he (John the Baptist) saw many Pharisees and Sadducees coming for baptism, he said to them,
"You brood of vipers! Who warned you to flee from the wrath to come? Bear fruit worthy of your repentance. Do not presume to say to yourselves, 'We have Abraham as our ancestor,' for I tell you, God is able from these stones to raise up children to Abraham. Even now the axe is lying at the root of the trees; every tree therefore that does not bear good fruit is cut down and thrown into the fire... And the crowds asked him, 'What then should we do?' In reply he said to them, 'Whoever has two coats must share with anyone who has none; and whoever has food must do likewise.' Even tax collectors came to be baptised, and they asked him, 'Teacher, what should we do?' He said to them, 'Collect no more than the amount prescribed for you.' Soldiers also asked him, 'And we, what should we do?' He said to them, 'Do not extort money from anyone by threats or false accusation and be satisfied with your wages' (Matthew 3:7-9; and Luke 3:10-14).

No nation can survive for long as one corporate entity, let alone make progress and achieve any measure of peace and stability when it is plagued by such multiple self-inflicted ills as ethnic bigotry, rampant indiscipline, gross mis-governance, monumental corruption, political banditry, religious intolerance and widespread social discord.

We must acknowledge, however, that not everyone in the Nigerian society is insane. Not everyone in Nigeria celebrates the triumph of mediocrity. There are little oases of sanity here and there whose small voices are often drowned by the cacophony of greed and avarice, political manipulation and the exploitation of religion for selfish gain, and who daily suffer the agony of isolation and alienation. So, what must we do to resuscitate the dying giant? What must we do to salvage the collapsing superstructure? How are we going to be saved as a people from our collective death wish?

My dear friends, nothing short of a true ethical revolution such as championed by John the Baptist, will save our sick nation from the destruction that accompanies a prolonged moral decadence in the polity. What we require is a radical turnaround, a corporate repentance, a national conversion experience as it were, if this superstructure is to be salvaged. Religious bodies are ordinarily the best placed and the most equipped to champion such an ethical revolution. In a country like Nigeria where the overwhelming majority of people claim to be religious, and Christians claim at least 50% of the population, Christian individuals and groups, such as the Knights of St. John, by their very calling, must play a critical role in the project of national moral and ethical re-awakening.

Though Christian individuals and Churches have not been spared of the devastating effects of the culture of violence and the moral decay in the land; though many Priests and Pastors have often not risen above the murky waters of violence and corruption in the land; and though many highly placed Christians in business, politics and the professions, have betrayed in the conduct of their own lives such elements of our national malady as ethnic and religious bigotry, indiscipline, greed and avarice, the society will nevertheless continue to look up to religious institutions and organizations, and groups like the Knights of St. John, to play critical leadership roles in the enormous task of national moral regeneration.

Troubling Development in Contemporary Nigerian Religiosity

John the Baptist lived and died in the promotion and defence of an authentic religious practice, in place of the widespread hypocrisy and infidelity at the time. Today Nigerians make a lot of noise in the name of religion, but their lives often betray a near-total lack of the sense of the fear of God, the sense of right and wrong, the strong desire for and commitment to the virtuous life, and hatred for sin, commitment to the common good, care and concern for the poor, discipline or self-control, self-sacrifice, chastity, modesty, frugality and the aversion for violence that are traditionally associated with genuinely religious people. It does not matter whether it is Christianity or Islam, Buddhism or Hinduism; religiosity is closely related to the practice of virtue and the cultivation and promotion of a life of discipline, frugality, and self-abnegation. It is incredible how, in this country, we have found a way of practising and promoting a kind of pop religion that is devoid of the above critical elements of genuine, authentic religiosity. No wonder the widespread rot in the land.

The ethical and moral teachings of our various religions, however, remain intact and could be found in the Hebrew and Christian Bible and the Muslim Qur'an and *Hadith*. It is not difficult to see that the practical lives of many so-called religious people in this society run contrary to the best teachings of their professed religions. No one doubts, for example, that the high ethical standards and strict moral teachings of Jesus Christ and his early disciples as contained in the books of the New Testament will bring about a just and peaceful society if we could only imbibe and live by them. However, to what extent are these high ethical standards and strict moral teachings being adequately taught and accepted by Nigerians who claim to be religious today?

A major part of the challenge before us is how to rid our society of charlatans and con artists who parade themselves as religious leaders and preachers. These people are propagating primitive superstition rather than liberating the people from the shadows of a by-gone pre-scientific era of witches and wizards and evil spirits and demons. They are promoting corruption in the land instead of teaching the people the way of discipline, honesty, truth, and justice by denying, for example, the cause-and-effect relationship in the order of nature between hard work and prosperity. They are encouraging malice and vengeance rather than preaching the sacrificial love and forgiveness that make for peace and social harmony.

Indeed, the Christian Church has not been spared of the triumph of mediocrity that has plagued practically every sphere of the Nigerian society. Today our national landscape has been overrun by noisy prayer warriors, dubious contractors of healing and deliverance, and fraudulent prophets of prosperity and abundance. Yes, religion is the fastest growing business in contemporary Nigeria, and it is an all-comers affair. Just anyone can open a church and find followers from our ever-gullible population – from con men to cult men, from fraudsters to pop stars, and from comedians to magicians – they are all opening churches, cashing in on the gullibility of the generality of Nigerians, exploiting the ignorant poor of the land, and smiling daily to the bank.

A most embarrassing dimension of this ugly development in our country is the gradual incursion into the Catholic Church of the contemporary Nigerian pop Christianity - a noisy, shallow, hollow, and opaque enterprise characterized by an all-pervading fear of demons and evil spirits on the one hand, and on the other hand by a multiplicity of preaching crusades, prayer vigils, and healing and deliverance services, whereby government offices, corporate boardrooms, and motor parks, as well as long-distance passenger buses, have been turned into places of worship. Such multiplication of prayers and rituals, however, have no bearing with, nor impact on, the ethical and moral conduct of the worshippers, as everyone can witness with the growing level of corruption and violence, even amidst this upsurge in the outward display of religiosity.

My dear friends, we are witnessing in our country today what we may call a gradual ***de-spiritualisation*** as well as ***fetishisation*** of Christianity.

The religion that appears dominant in the consciousness of the generality of Nigerians today is what they seem to have received from the numerous half-baked preachers and cash-and-carry evangelists whose messages dominate our airwaves and websites, and billboards and signposts, and not the authentic religion of Christ preached by St. Peter and St. Paul, not the one propagated by St. Augustine of Hippo and St. Thomas Aquinas, not the one witnessed to by St. Francis of Assisi and St. Ignatius of Loyola, and certainly not the same religion professed by Blessed Mother Teresa of Calcutta, Blessed John Paul II or our own Blessed Cyprian Iwene Tansi.

There is no doubt in my mind and in the minds of many enlightened Catholics about the true identity of the Christian faith proclaimed by the Apostles, nurtured by courageous martyrs, kept aflame by austere monks, and witnessed to by self-sacrificing believers through the course of the last two thousand years – a religion characterised by purity of heart, mellowness of spirit, and calmness of soul; one whose fruits include frugality of life, sacrificial love, forgiveness, compassion, peacefulness, and self-control. Instead, what is spreading like wildfire in our country today is, in my critical assessment actually a new religion that is only marginal in resemblance to the Christianity handed over to us by the Apostles.

To illustrate this point: what is the relationship between the faith handed over to us by the Apostles and the celebration of vengeance and vindictiveness which we find among Nigerian Christians today, especially as championed by the Mountain of Fire and Miracle Ministries? What is the relationship between the faith witnessed to by St. Francis of Assisi with a life of poverty and frugality, and the prosperity gospel and such flamboyant display of vanity and vainglory as we find among Pentecostal pastors and preachers in our day? What is the relationship between the exorcism carried out by Christ and traditional Catholic exorcists on the one hand, and the widespread manipulation and abuse that go on today in the name of deliverance from demonic forces, whether real or imagined?

Yet, these days, many Catholic Priests, Religious and Lay faithful have fallen for these heretical and unorthodox beliefs and practices. Many agents of the Catholic Church have today resorted to the cheap gimmicks and unorthodox rituals invented by the untutored Pentecostal prophets and pastors as they have been discovered to be very attractive and appealing to our poorly educated Catholics. I will say that this unwholesome development in our Church is fast gaining momentum, first on account of critical failures and gaps in content and methodology in the formation of our Catholics right from childhood in families and in our Churches, and second, on account of what appears to be a close affinity between traditional African superstitious beliefs and practices and many elements of the new pop religion.

But the pop Christianity which majority of Nigerian Churchgoers seem to have embraced today, is a religion without sacrifice, a religion that has no place for the cross – which is otherwise the central doctrine of the Christian faith, a religion of instant gratification, a religion that elevates carnal desires and glorifies vanity and vainglory. The pop Christianity we refer to is a religion in which priests and pastors, prophets, and evangelists shamelessly display wealth and ostentation as evidence of their closeness to the God of abundance, even as we live in a country where the overwhelming majority of people are stuck in degrading and dehumanizing poverty.

Somebody has tried to identify or define the fundamental theological error behind this new religion that is sweeping through our gullible population. John Piper says it is an over-realized and an all-too materialistic eschatology, whereby no distinction is made between the already and the not-yet in the salvation wrought by Christ. For the prosperity Gospel and all who subscribe to it, Jesus has already won salvation and abundant life for us, and those of us who belong to God have a right to all the pleasures and riches of life here and now! The poor are poor because they are cursed or robbed of their riches by all kinds of demons, they have brought upon themselves or inherited from their parents! How could this theological error have spread so quickly and so massively across the land and even into our own Churches, such that many of those who celebrate the Eucharist with us on Sunday live the rest of their week with a religious orientation that is clearly at variance with, if not in contradiction to the theology and spirituality of the Catholic Church?

Perhaps we are witnessing today within the Christian fold something equivalent to the problem that has afflicted dominant groups in Islam for many centuries. The problem with Islam, as identified by Pope Benedict XVI in that controversial Regensburg address of 2006, is what he called the *de-hellenisation of Islam* – a situation whereby the religion at a time in its evolution abandoned intellectualism or any recourse to rational or philosophical inquiry. Perhaps what we are witnessing in what I call Nigerian pop Christianity of today is a combination of afflictions, namely: the de-*hellenisation of Christianity*, the *de-spiritualisation of the Christian Gospel*, and of course, the *fetishisation of Christian worship*.

Unfortunately, due to poor teaching of the faith or catechesis, our people have not been sufficiently vaccinated against deadly afflictions that have come upon our Churches. That is why many come for the Eucharist on Sunday, but the conduct of the rest of their week is largely inspired by the teachings and practices of Pastor T. B. Joshua of the Synagogue of All Nations, Pastor Chris Oyakhilome of Christ Embassy, or Pastor Daniel Olukoya of the Mountain of Fire and Miracle Ministries. Many healer priests and merchants of deliverance within the Catholic Church in Nigeria have fashioned their ministries along the theological parameters set by these pastors rather than the long-standing teachings and ritual practices of the Catholic Church.

A Re-Vitalised Catholic Evangelisation and Education to the Rescue

Christians are called to be the light of the world. We are to shine the light of Christ the Redeemer into an environment that is otherwise plagued by the darkness of greed and selfishness, ethnic bigotry and political banditry, violence, and crime. In an environment of widespread ignorance and poverty, we are called to be agents of individual enlightenment and social transformation. But how can we play this role effectively for our society when we are not firmly established on the same theological foundations? How can we truly be the salt of the earth for our generation when we have no unity of purpose and no common concept of what gives life meaning, or what the central focus of Jesus' salvific mission is all about?

The challenges that face our country and our Church today call for massive investment of men and materials in the project of religious and moral education at all levels, from Nursery School to University, and from Catechism and Sunday school classes to Seminary formation and the ongoing formation of Priests, Religious and the Lay Faithful. We must take responsibility for the future of our country and for the integrity of our faith by investing heavily in the intellectual, doctrinal, and moral formation of our children. We must accord children and youth formation programmes first priority in the Church, such that they attract even more funding than the building of Cathedrals, Parish Halls and Mission houses.

At all levels, Catholic formation programmes must be experienced as a transformative experience. The Gospel of Christ is the most potent agent of transformation. It is capable of and has indeed transformed individuals and whole societies in the past. Such transformation must be brought to bear on those who attend our Churches as well as those who pass through our schools, colleges, and universities.

We need to re-conceive our entire educational enterprise as a nation. We need education for character formation and for the realisation of meaning and purpose, rather than simply education for wealth accumulation. We need value-based education, an education that liberates from the shackles of corruption, from primitive superstition, from ethnic and religious bigotry, from selfishness and parochialism, from mediocrity and sycophancy, and from greed and avarice. Yes, we need a transformative education, an education that liberates the masses from an exploitative and abusive leadership, as well as from an apathetic and despondent citizenry. We need an education that inspires excellence, true patriotism, high-level individual and social morality, good, accountable servant leadership, respect for human rights and dignity, and respect for women and children's rights. We need an education that promotes the democratic culture and popular participation in governance. We need an education that promotes critical thinking, hard work, entrepreneurship, the spirit of creativity, and initiative. We need an education that promotes selfless service, the common good imperative, the principle of deferred gratification, high-level individual and social discipline, social harmony, national unity, peace, and non-violence.

Conclusion

With the ethical and moral contents of our Catholic faith, and the structures of formation that we have, if Nigerian Catholics and other Christians are not living by the moral and ethical standards founded on the life and teaching of Jesus Christ and His disciples, then something is seriously wrong. If there exists such a great gulf between the ethical standards of the religion we profess and propagate and the practical lives of our people, then religious groups need to look inwards. It is either that as a people we all are un-teachable, deaf and dumb, or that we lay and clerical leaders of religious groups and societies, including Bishops, priests and Catechists, Knights of the Church, CMO and CWO Chieftains, Church Council Members, Coordinators of the Catholic Charismatic Renewal, Legion of Mary, St. Anthony, St. Jude and other societies in our Church - must critically review methods of formation in

Christian ethics and social morality, and the quality of our own Christian discipleship as well as the manner of our witnessing. We must critically review the kind of Christian life we live and how we pass it on to our children, if the gospel we profess is to have its full transformative impact in the conduct of our individual and corporate affairs in the Nigerian society.

We must as a people each take an interest in leadership and in the quality of persons that assume public office. We must take responsibility for the future and do all we can to stop the thugs and the rogues, the charlatans and mediocre performers that often populate the corridors of power, but who have no sense of nation building, no sense of the common good, and no sense of sacrifice. Until now, it has been garbage in, garbage out, but the ugly trend can and must be reversed. So let those among us who have any serious commitment to the survival of our corporate entity invest some time and resources in cultivating leadership values and value-based leadership beginning from the conduct of husbands and wives in the family setting, through the practice of leadership in primary and secondary school prefects, to the level of parish priests and Church society Chairpersons, up to the level of local government chairmen, State Governors and the Presidency of our country.

We must all work towards helping our countrymen and women understand that in a nation desiring lasting peace and progress, rogues and brigands, murderers and assassins, and sycophants and charlatans have no place in the public square. We must all work towards demonstrating in various ways to our countrymen and women that true leadership is characterised by a compelling vision, an all-consuming sense of mission, an acute sense of sacrifice, rare courage, passion for the poor and the weak and commitment to the common good.

We must impress it upon our children and young people in families, in Churches, in schools, and in social groups the fact that "to live a good life is to impact positively on the lives of other people," and that true, genuine and lasting happiness is to be found in a life of service and sacrifice, not in primitive accumulation and personal aggrandisement. We must use the structures of all our religious and cultural groups, societies, and institutions to help those desiring leadership positions in our society to realise that political leadership is about passion for the common good, not an exercise in treasury looting and corrupt enrichment. Politicians and public office holders must be helped to recognise that governments exist to ensure the safety of the lives and property of the people they govern as well as provide the greatest good for the greatest number of the people, and not to secure the functionaries and provide for them at the expense of the generality of the people whom they claim to govern.

CHAPTER SEVENTY-ONE

The Common Good and Leadership Formation in Africa
(Paper delivered at the Continental Workshop on the Catholic Social Teachings, Nairobi, Kenya, February 23, 2017).

Introduction: The Critical Place of Leaders in Society

It is said, and it is indeed true that people are often able to be carried to as far a height as there are leaders who are willing and courageous enough to carry them. In a society or organisation, the combination of people, ideas, resources and time makes up only a basket of the potential force available to be mobilised. All these factors, important as they are, can achieve little without leadership. Leaders are the critical spark or the catalytic agents that make things happen. They are the defining factor in the pace and the direction an entire group moves, and thus they play a decisive role in determining the fortunes of the group for good or for ill.

Proverbs 29:18 says: "Where there is no vision, the people do perish!" Proverbs 29:2 says: "When the righteous are in authority, the people rejoice: but when the wicked rule, the people mourn." And following the recent inauguration of President Donald Trump, and his first set of rather disturbing executive orders, the social media was awash with the famous quotation attributed to John Calvin, which says that "when God wants to judge a nation, he gives them wicked rulers." This is how critical the subject of leadership is in the affairs of men and women, in the determination of the fortunes of a people, and towards the promotion of the common good. Yet, in spite of all our rhetoric, still very little attention is being paid to initial and ongoing leadership formation in the structures of our Church.

An Ignominious Legacy of Authority and Power

The historical misfortunes of the African continent and its people, including the infamous slave trade that lasted over 400 years, and the exploitative colonial administrations that held sway for another 100 years, can be blamed to a reasonable extent for the absence of good, visionary, purpose-driven, self-sacrificing leadership. We had thoughtless rulers, who, like the proverbial wolves in sheep's clothing, made profit selling their kith and kin to wicked slave dealers. We had senseless rulers who conspired to mortgage the future of generations yet unborn with callous colonisers.

More recently, we have had notorious despots and brutal dictators like Idi Amin Dada of Uganda, Kamuzu Banda of Malawi, Jean Bokassa of Central African Republic, Mobutu Sese Seko of Zaire, Gnassingbe Eyadema of Togo, Sani Abacha of Nigeria and Charles Taylor of Liberia, who with brute force ascended the sacred precincts of power in their countries, banished all civility and then proceeded to loot the country's resources, and suppress, subjugate and massacre their people. Today, military regimes are no longer fashionable. Most African countries claim to be running some form of democracy. But what manner of democracy are we having in Zimbabwe, in Angola, in Cameroon, in Uganda, in Equatorial Guinea, and in the recent drama of Yahya Jammeh's Gambia?

These callous rulers that presided over the affairs of African countries at various times constitute something of a curse on a land that is otherwise endowed by the Creator with talented human beings, a rich patrimony of human cultures, and abundant natural resources. On account of their misadventure in the corridors of power, African countries and peoples became a metaphor for poverty and destitution, youth unemployment and youth restiveness, fratricidal wars, ethnic skirmishes, religious conflicts, diseases and epidemics, corruption and human rights abuse, as well as the scandalous phenomenon of having floating islands of affluence amidst a sea of dehumanising poverty. Yes, Africa has produced many *kleptomaniacal* despots who callously plunder the resources of their homelands and store them away in the already overflowing vaults of Switzerland, the United Kingdom, the United States, and now Dubai. Indeed, as the Bible says, "when the wicked rule, the people mourn! This ugly scenario is playing out in nearly all of sub-Saharan Africa, where for over a hundred years now Christianity has taken root, and Catholic Churches, Catholic Schools and Universities, Catholic Seminaries and Convents, etc. are flourishing, and now and again we even speak of vocation boom and overcrowded seminaries in some of our countries.

Impact of the Gospel of Christ and the Catholic Social Teachings

Jesus says by their fruits, you shall know them. So, the questions must arise: What is the impact of Christian evangelisation and catechesis in the many African countries where Christians are in the majority, or where at least they form a significant proportion of the political and economic elite? What impact has the Catholic Social Teachings made on Catholic politicians, Catholic entrepreneurs, Catholic intellectuals, and Catholic Media practitioners, etc., in African countries, as they shape the fortunes of their societies or as they influence the formulation of policies and legislations in their countries? To what extent has the common good imperative, so prominent in Judeo-Christian social morality and in the Catholic Social Doctrine, been embraced by Catholic politicians, intellectuals and entrepreneurs as the path to authentic human development and sustainable peace and stability in these countries?

A critical view or dispassionate assessment of our socio-economic and political circumstances today in African countries will show that a major gap does exist between the lofty ideals expounded in the social doctrine of the Church for the right ordering of society, and the reality of structural injustice, human rights abuse, monumental corruption, senseless exploitation of natural resources and abuse of the environment, etc. In the face of large-scale and widespread urbanisation and such negative effects as the degrading and dehumanising life for millions of people in sprawling slums and ghettoes around African cities, for instance, many of our pastoral agents have not been trained or equipped with the proper orientation and necessary skills to work with the flock of Christ in the slums. Yet, if no remedial action is taken by all stakeholders in society, the slums could easily become the incubators or training grounds of tomorrow's terrorist insurgents, warlords and purveyors of genocide.

Church leaders are rightly disturbed by the apparent discordance between flourishing Christianity on the one hand, and on the other, an abysmally low level of commitment on the part of many who occupy leadership positions in African countries to the common good imperative, to high level social morality and social justice, to leadership accountability, to the promotion of human rights and dignity, to brotherhood and solidarity among men and women of diverse cultural backgrounds and religious affiliations, to the protection of the rights of women, to the protection of the natural environment, and to peace and reconciliation in these countries.

Perhaps after centuries of exploitative governance by foreign powers and home-grown despots, sub-Saharan Africans appear to have lost the sense of leadership as service of the common good. Perhaps the present generation of Africans do not have many people to look up to for purposeful, visionary, self-sacrificing, servant leadership. They have few models to emulate in the high art of leadership as an exercise in mentoring. So, they compete for power largely for personal aggrandizement, they become ethnic warlords, or they see their ascendancy to high political office as state capture and territorial conquest. The crisis of leadership that emerged in most African countries within the first decade of political independence, which in many cases resulted in a succession of military coups and despotic regimes, each becoming worse than the regimes they overthrew, sufficiently demonstrates how ill-equipped these politicians and military rulers were politically, spiritually, emotionally and psychologically, to lead modern democratic societies, notwithstanding the fact that some of them were educated at some point in top-level Catholic institutions run by Jesuits, Dominicans, White Fathers, Salesians or members of the Society of African Missions (SMA). There is a moral and ethical vacuum in our society, which explains why agents of the civil society in many of our countries have often fought to bring down a particular dictatorship or set of corrupt leaders, only for them to be replaced by an equally bad set.

Echoes from the First and Second Synod of Bishops for Africa

The First Special Synod of Bishops for Africa which was held in 1994, and the Second one which was held in 2009, after reflecting at length on the dire circumstances of the African continent, recommended the widespread dissemination of the Social Teachings of the Church as a major pathway towards the emergence of a more just social order, and more wholesome and peaceful societies in the continent. The 2009 Synod was specifically devoted to the Christian vocation to be salt of the earth and light of the world: our vocation to be architects, builders and promoters of justice, peace and reconciliation, in our troubled countries. Among other recommendations in "Africae Munus," the Post-Synodal Apostolic Exhortation of Pope Benedict XVI, we have the following regarding the dissemination of the Social Teachings of the Church in paragraph 95 of the document:

...the Compendium of the Social Doctrine of the Church is a guide to the Church's mission as "Mother and Teacher" in the world and in the society, and is therefore a pastoral tool of the first rank. Christians who draw nourishment from the authentic source, Christ, are transformed by him into "the light of the world" (Matt 5:14), and they transmit the one who is himself "the light of the world" (John 8:12). Their knowledge must be shaped by charity. Knowledge, in fact, "if it aspires to be wisdom capable of directing man in the light of his first beginnings and his final ends... must be 'seasoned' with the 'salt' of charity.

In paragraph 137 of the document, the Pope recommends that "in order to make a solid and proper contribution to African society, it is indispensable that students (of Catholic Universities and Institutes) be taught the Church's social doctrine."

The Imperative of Leadership Formation

But it is my opinion that besides the need to disseminate the Catholic Social Teachings widely across all the segments of the Church and beyond, what is called for today is a massive investment of the structures and resources of the Church at all levels in leadership formation for social transformation. The two Synods emphasised the importance of forming the laity for leadership positions, and for socio-political engagement towards the transformation of their societies. Yet the modalities and specificities of this formation of the laity were to be worked out by the various local churches according to their peculiar circumstances. Now 23 years after the First Synod, and over 7 years after the second, only few and isolated programmatic steps have actually been taken in most of our local Churches towards achieving this all-important goal.

One of the visible steps that have been taken by the Justice and Peace Commission in some countries with support from some partner agencies, since the First African Synod of 1994 is the periodic monitoring of elections by agents of the Church. Yet the mere monitoring of elections and issuing of reports afterwards may not achieve the desired result, if those who emerge from ostensibly free and fair elections have no solid value base such as is contained in the Catholic Social Doctrine, have never known models of good leadership they could emulate, have never undergone any serious training in the dynamics of visionary and purposeful leadership, have a warped notion of political office, and have a poor sense of service.

We shall continue to be long in talk but short in action until leadership formation is given priority attention in the evangelisation, education and pastoral care mission of dioceses and congregations in Africa. Many observers within and outside the Church today recognise that the mere issuing of powerful exhortations, communiqués and pastoral statements against social injustices and their perpetrators, has proven to be thoroughly inadequate. It often amounts to sitting on the sidelines and watching things happen, and then making value judgement of the events after the fact. Should the leadership of the Church in many countries continue to function like a weeping child in the face of widespread social injustice, gross human rights abuse, monumental corruption, poverty and disease, and violence and war? No. For it is better to light a candle than to curse the darkness.

Concrete Recommendations

The crisis of leadership in Africa challenges Church leaders to invest a reasonable proportion of the Church's material and human resources into training and nurturing purposeful, visionary and committed servant leaders that will transform our societies with the values and ethos of the Kingdom of justice and peace as enunciated in the Catholic Social Teachings. If we are to take our vocation seriously as salt of the earth and light of the world, the Church's ongoing intervention in leadership formation must be properly structured and mobilised with adequate funding and the required expertise, as follows:

1. Establishment of CST Inspired Leadership Training Institutes

Regional and National Bishops Conferences, Dioceses, Religious Congregations, as well as individual Catholics who have the required means should think of establishing Leadership and Management Training Institutes - inspired by the fundamental values of the Catholic Social Teaching, which not only teach leadership and management courses, but also project and showcase good practices and exemplary models in good leadership and the service of the common good. It can also be part of the mandate of such Institutes to engage in research and documentation on issues of leadership, management and governance in the particular country and in the world, and network with like-minded organisations in policy and legislative advocacy, such that they gradually come to be recognised as centres of excellence in leadership formation. Such Institutes, even though unapologetically inspired by CST, should be open enough to accommodate the involvement and participation of non-Catholics and even non-Christians who share the social values of the Church. This is the direction towards which the Lux Terra Leadership Foundation where I have been engaged in the last nine years, has been moving, and the modest results we are seeing here and there show that it is a viable path to take.

2. *Turning All Our Catholic Education Programmes into Instruments of Leadership Formation*

It is not enough to have the Social Teachings of the Church as a course in the Social Science Faculty of our Catholic Universities, or simply a unit in a Moral Theology or Social Ethics course. We must move beyond this basic level. The challenges of the times in our continent demand that the fundamental values contained in the Social Teachings, such as the common good imperative, leadership accountability, the fatherhood of God, the brotherhood of all mankind and human solidarity, the equal dignity of all men and women, the sanctity and inviolability of all human life from conception to natural death, and our stewardship relationship towards natural creation, , etc., must be reflected in the content and presentation of all the courses offered in our Universities, Institutes, Schools and Colleges, down to the level of the Kindergarten! Our Christian initiation programmes for young people and adults alike, should contain core elements of the Catholic Social Teachings. Yes at all levels, Catholic education must be felt as a transformative experience. Africans must be made to recognise that the Gospel of Christ is the most potent force for personal and social transformation. Such transformation must be brought to bear on those who attend our Churches as well as those who pass through our schools and colleges.

3. *We need a New Pedagogy of Social Transformation*

It is time to re-conceive our entire homiletic, catechetical and educational enterprise, and repackage their content and methodology in line with the spirit of the new evangelisation and the exigencies of the times. We need a new kind of pedagogy for character formation and for the realisation of meaning and purpose, rather than simply for the acquisition of some body of knowledge. We need a paradigm shift from a pedagogy focused on knowledge acquisition, to one focused on (personal and technical) competency building. We need value-based pedagogy, a pedagogy that is firmly anchored on the rich patrimony of the Catholic Social Doctrine. We need a pedagogy that liberates men and women from the shackles of corruption, from primitive superstition, from ethnic and religious bigotry, from selfishness and parochialism, from mediocrity and indolence, and from greed and avarice.

Yes, we need a transformative pedagogy, a pedagogy that liberates the masses from an exploitative and abusive leadership, as well as from citizen apathy and despondency. We need a pedagogy that inspires excellence and heroism, high-level individual and social morality, the principle of deferred gratification, volunteerism, selfless service and the common good imperative. We need a pedagogy that promotes the democratic culture and popular participation in governance, as well as good, accountable, courageous and visionary leadership. We need a pedagogy that promotes critical thinking, hard work, entrepreneurship, the spirit of creativity and initiative. We need a pedagogy that promotes high-level individual and social discipline, social harmony, national unity, peace and non-violence.

Modern researchers from across a multiplicity of disciplines are discovering that the generality of people often do not act on what they know or what they think. Too many highly knowledgeable people make the wrong choices in life, and as a result they ruin their lives and the lives of others. Human beings are more what they love than what they think. To be human is to be animated, oriented and motivated by some picture of the good life. Human beings generally gravitate towards that picture of the good life, which attracts them, or which captures their imagination. Yes, human beings put their energies into pursuing that goal, that vision of "flourishing" - where happiness is to be found. The critical questions we must now ask are: What vision of the good life have we succeeded in transmitting to the members of our Churches, and others who have passed through our educational institutions? In what direction have we fired the imagination of those whom we have trained in our various institutions? Towards which ultimate goals have we inspired, animated, motivated and mentored our people to direct their energies? It is not enough that we educate the mind. More important is what we educate the mind with, what the content of our education is, and towards which goal we are shaping the mind.

We need a pedagogy whose principal objective is to re-calibrate the people's ultimate quest, their most profound desire, their deep-seated longing. Yes, we need a new pedagogy that will seek to influence the people's fundamental orientation in life towards the logic of the Beatitudes:

- making sense of deferred gratification
- taking pleasure in serving the common good
- defending the lowly poor, the oppressed and the marginalised
- finding joy in pursing justice, reconciliation and peace
- leaving a lasting legacy of love and compassion

By championing such a pedagogy, the Church in Africa will be laying a solid foundation for more just, peaceful and wholesome societies that are superintended by visionary, purposeful, accountable, and self-sacrificing leaders.

4. *Evangelising Agents of the Mass Media*

The challenge of evangelising the Mass Media must now assume a particular urgency, as the Radio, the Television and the Billboards, along with the Internet and social media, are in our day proving to be stronger and more formidable agents of socialisation than all the traditional agents of socialisation combined, viz: the family, the Church, the School and Peer Groups. We must set up institutions not only to train experts that will project the programmes and values of the Church to the public, and make optimum use of the old and new media in our programmes of evangelisation and pastoral care, but also more critically, we must develop the mechanisms for the much required evangelisation of the secular media itself, whose programme content is today often driven by the profit motive or market forces, appealing more to the base instincts of our young people than to their higher aspirations which require the cultivation of such habits as discipline, sacrificial love, and deferred gratification.

The new independent media on their part are often avenues for endless entertainment and sometimes sadistic entertainment, senseless consumerism and hollow populism. We cannot make much progress in our desire to transform society with Gospel values, if we are not able to evolve creative ways of reaching out to and engaging the powerful agents of the international and local media, as well as the celebrity bloggers and entertainers - who today often command more following and may be winning more hearts with whatever beliefs and ideologies they hold, than many political leaders and perhaps many Bishops and Religious Superiors.

Conclusion

We have tried to demonstrate in the foregoing presentation that the widespread lack of appreciation of the common good imperative in most African societies, is largely a consequence of the centuries' long ignominious legacy of slave trade, colonialism and military dictatorship which combined to present a portrait of leadership that is synonymous to enslavement, conquest, domination and exploitation. Many African societies have no experience, and no example of the leader as mentor, inspirer or servant of the common good, to look up to. So our emerging leaders have often been fumbling along with the fortunes of their people, abusing and violating, rather than promoting the common good. The Church however under these circumstances does possess the Compendium of the Catholic Social Teachings, which contains *the Principles for Guidance, the Criteria for Judgement, and the Directives for Action* that could be used to form a new generation of Africans that will be committed to building a new culture of good, visionary, purposeful, democratic, accountable and self-sacrificing leadership, as well as a mass of enlightened, active, solidary citizens, who will constantly set high standards of leadership conduct for those who volunteer to serve them.

Since we have to contend with a long entrenched negative culture of political power and authority, the Church's leadership formation for the promotion of the common good will entail a well-structured programme designed to transform the men and women in our environment and re-calibrate their hearts to begin to desire service of the common good as a veritable means to human fulfilment. The strategies outlined above for such leadership formation towards the eventual transformation of the African socio-political landscape, will demand some major adjustments in the content and methodology of our education and formation programmes from Kindergarten to University, and from the level of Children in Catechism class to the level of graduate students of Theological Institutes. It will also call for a re-prioritization in the management and allocation of the Church's personnel and financial resources. Some of our best human resources may henceforth need to be directed towards formation for leadership and the media apostolate. The comprehensive and multi-sector leadership formation we are advocating for here will also call for the commitment of a sizeable percentage of the Church's financial resources to the project. In this way our Church will position itself as salt of the earth and light of the world, nourishing and shaping her members with the Word and Sacraments, and then equipping and sending them out to promote the common good, to practice good governance, to pursue justice, and to be agents of peace and reconciliation in the world.

CHAPTER SEVENTY-TWO

The National Question and Nigeria's Stability
(Presented at a Workshop organised by the Department of State Services, in Abuja, August 2, 2017).

Introduction

I congratulate the Department of State Services for hosting this Seminar on Security and National Development and thank them for inviting me to contribute to the debate on the National Question at this critical time when the call for restructuring of our nation has become ever more strident and perhaps never before since the end of the civil war has the call for restructuring of the Nigerian state been ever more persuasive.

This seminar, like others happening around the country, is timely and necessary, because we are living through a season of rampant violence and intermittent strife. We are living through precarious times, as we watch our motherland being devoured by murderous insurgents from the North, perverted by drunken militants from the South, ravaged by rancorous bigots from both the East and the West, shattered by hostile herdsmen and vengeful farmers in the Middle Belt, wrecked, corroded and rendered desolate by a succession of degenerate rulers that have camouflaged as leaders at all levels and in nearly all sectors.

Violent conflicts resulting in massive loss of lives and property are sadly a regular feature of Nigerian life, which the Buhari regime of the last two years has unfortunately failed to quell. On account of the bitter economic recession that accompanied the emergence of the present regime, and the dashed hopes and broken dreams of many who looked forward to real change in 2015, some even think that the policies and political posture of the new regime have aggravated rather than mitigate the political tension and security challenges that we have always lived with. Thus, security agencies are today perpetually on red alert in an environment of widespread anger and bitterness, and hatred and resentment, on account of age-old ethnic antipathies, historical injustices, and real or perceived religious persecution, political isolation, ethnic marginalisation and economic exploitation and disempowerment - none of which has been seriously addressed in our structural arrangements, notwithstanding the many national conferences and commissions of enquiry that have been hosted or set up by successive governments and to which huge resources have been committed over the years.

Yes, we live in a land, and our security agencies carry out their business in a land where the political, economic and religious elite have become thoroughly blinded by the lust for power and greed for money; where the middle class has become criminally maladjusted; and where the poor masses have become so thoroughly malleable and gullible that otherwise dangerous religious and ethnic sentiments are now regularly mobilised in individual struggles for economic opportunities, for high-level public office, for private sector positions and for social status enhancement. Nigeria is once again teetering on the edge of the precipice, as it struggles to contend simultaneously with terrorist insurgents in the north, secessionist forces in the South, and the vanguards of restructuring in between the north and the south.

A Brief Survey of Violent Conflicts in Nigeria

Violent conflicts resulting in massive loss of lives and property are sadly a regular feature of Nigerian life. From the operation *wetie* that rocked Western Nigeria in 1964, through the unfortunate civil war of 1967 to 1970, to the Niger Delta militant uprising of recent years; and from the Sharia riots of year 2000 and 2001, through the sporadic carnage in Jos and its environs that has not abated since the year 2004, to the yet ongoing *Boko Haram* terrorist bombing campaigns, it has been a litany of violent conflicts that have tended to pitch the North against the South, Christians against Muslims, and the so-called Indigenes against the so-called Non-Indigenes, highlighting very graphically the failure of the critical institutions of state and the fragile and tenuous nature of our corporate existence as a nation.

If we identify the above incidents as high intensity internal conflicts, then there are others that will fall into the class of low intensity conflicts, even if equally devastating of our national landscape. We have witnessed intermittent inter-ethnic and inter-clannish conflicts all over the country, such as between the Tiv and the Jukun of Benue and Taraba States, the Ife and the Modakeke of Osun State, the Ijaw and the Urhobo of Delta State, the Umuleri and the Aguleri of Anambra State, the Egbura and Bassa of Nasarawa State, and that between Fulani herdsmen and local farmers across the entire stretch of the Middle Belt. We have seen sporadic violence at the hands of ethnic nationalists, such as the O.P.C. among the Yoruba and the Bakassi Boys and MASSOB Fighters among the Igbo. Local Government, State and Federal elections have often seemed to some like a war to be prosecuted with machetes, machine guns, hand grenades and even home-made bombs, resulting in a flood of blood and tears. In a number of locations across the country, election days often feature soldiers in military fatigue, armoured personnel carriers and tanks and bomb detection and disposal squads on peacekeeping operations. This workshop is holding on the threshold of the 2015 general elections, and what we have today are clear indications of desperation, as many contenders to political office are once again approaching politics with a killer touch, and demonstrating that they would rather burn down the country than lose the election.

The High Cost of Conflict in Nigeria

On the whole, even though we are not prosecuting a war against another country, and though there are no natural disasters, hundreds of thousands of Nigerians have died, hundreds of our children have been abducted and enslaved, while many others have suffered various degrees of physical injury, and property worth hundreds of billions of Naira have been destroyed. We have witnessed hundreds of thousands of internally displaced persons (or refugees), moving from North to South or squatting for prolonged periods in police and army barracks all over the place. Cameroon, Chad and Niger now play host to hundreds of thousands of refugees who have fled from their now inhospitable homeland. Indeed, many Nigerians have suffered emotional, psychological, economic and social trauma and dislocation on account of these crises, with little compensation from the authorities. The unfortunate impression has been left in the minds of many Nigerians that human life here is cheap, very cheap, and easily expendable. With the repeated failure of institutions of state to come to their aid when face-to-face with a violent aggressor, Nigerians have often resorted to jungle-style self-help, acquiring deadly weapons for self-defence and taking on revenge for losses suffered, and thereby aggravating the tension that already exists.

I am not aware of anyone or any group that has embarked on a comprehensive analysis of the cost of the numerous conflicts we have witnessed in our society since independence in 1960. We are not likely to ever be able to calculate in any detailed manner the cost of the many conflicts we have witnessed: from wasted lives to wasted property that could be reckoned in trillions of naira; the opportunity cost of school closures that keep the lives of young intelligent people on hold; the incessant dislocation in family life, the destruction of social infrastructure; the loss of investment opportunities on account of widespread insecurity; the environmental degradation and the destruction of the social and moral fabric of the nation; the effect of all this on our international image, etc.

The Prevailing Angst in the Land

My dear friends, as we speak here today, there is anger and resentment all over this country, for real and perceived injustices that are yet to be addressed sufficiently in the structural configurations of our country. You only need to glance through the Newspapers or the Social Media these days to come to the recognition that – besides the latest Nnamdi Kanu-led Biafra secessionist campaign - many in the Igbo nation have remained resentful of the rest of Nigeria for the injustices of the 1967 to 1970 civil war, the abandoned property imbroglio, and the alleged post-war marginalisation of Igbo people in some vital segments of the national economy and politics; many in the Yoruba nation are angry with the rest of Nigeria for the injustices associated with the June 12 election annulment, and the alleged post-June 12 persecution and marginalisation of Yoruba people, and they have never ceased to call for restructuring; and many from the collocation of small ethnic nationalities which we call the Middle Belt, are vexed by the appendage status accorded them in the power structures of our nation. They too have been calling for restructuring. And in spite of the Amnesty Programme implemented during the Yar'adua and Jonathan regimes, many aggrieved people of the Niger Delta Region remain poised for a showdown with the rest of Nigeria, because of the exploitation of their natural resources and the senseless devastation of their ecological environment for decades, while they were abandoned in a state of near destitution. There are many among the Hausa and Fulani Muslims of the core North who reject the ideology of the Boko Haram insurgents, but who nevertheless desire to live under the supremacy of the Islamic Sharia and are often incensed that the rest of Nigeria wants to jettison what they see as their religious freedom.

Ah yes, with practically every group in Nigeria, there is often bitterness and resentment over past hurts and wounds and structural injustices which have never been seriously addressed. The 2014 Justice Kutigi-led Conference discussed some of these grievances, but like the Oputa Panel of the year 2001 and 2002, and other conferences before it, the Kutigi Conference has ended up as just one other exercise in futility. Today across the country, there is intense anger, bitterness and resentment among the unemployed and impoverished youth population who have seen their dreams and aspirations for a meaningful life truncated and frustrated by a callous and profligate adult society. Some of them are now taking to crime – resorting to armed robbery, kidnapping high profile personalities for a ransom, engaging in internet fraud, emigrating by any means or at any cost overseas. Some of them are drowning daily in the Mediterranean sea, while a number of others who arrive in Europe, sell themselves off into the shameful trade of prostitution.

There is therefore more than enough work for all the overt and covert security agencies in the country. There is no dull moment for us in these climes, because the harvest of violent conflicts is indeed plentiful and the labourers are few. The indications are that we shall be requiring many more security officers to prevent crime and conflict as well as apprehend criminals and agents of violent conflict. True, there are no indications as yet that we are about to see any reduction in either crimes or flashpoints of violent conflict across the country.

Between Peace Building and Nation Building

Ladies and Gentlemen, let me highlight at this point what in my view are the dynamics of nation building, what constitutes the substructure or foundation of a nation, what the fundamental ingredients of nation building are, who and who constitute the real architects and engineers of the project of nation building, and what will make for peace, security, stability and prosperity in our dear country. I am convinced beyond reasonable doubt that there are fundamental ingredients for nation building that must be present in the right proportion in order for a stable, peaceful, harmonious and secure nation to emerge or evolve from a collection of disparate ethnic groups, with distinct historical experiences, different cultural orientations, diverse political interests and multiple religious affiliations. The tragedy of Nigeria has been the preponderance of missing ingredients in the project of nation building and democratic consolidation. This reality throws wide open the floodgate of violent conflicts that appeared yesterday under the camouflage of religious bigotry and terrorist insurgency and today under the guise of secessionist agitation and ethnic hatred. If this fundamental ailment is not addressed, it may yet take another form tomorrow, such as the popular rebellion of the destitute poor across the country against their rich oppressor. And it may happen so quickly and so massively that our entire security infrastructure may be too overwhelmed to be able to put the situation under check or protect the privileged rich against the angry poor who have resolved that they have had enough and that they have nothing to lose.

Ladies and Gentlemen, nation building refers to the internal, organic (and of course dynamic) process by which a society identifies, discusses, contests, considers, and reaches consensus (or agreement) on shared values, principles and norms, galvanises a sense of national cohesion, consolidates a national identity, and forges a sense of common purpose and a set of common goals to which the society is oriented. It is the process of moulding diverse groups into a unified, cohesive, harmonious and stable national entity with a shared vision and a collective mission. Nation building and democratic consolidation, if they are to be successful, necessarily involve the active participation of all segments in the society, and the creative engagement of all citizens in the constituting processes of the emergent nation. Essential to the project of nation building and democratic consolidation is a purposeful, visionary, courageous, self-sacrificing and therefore legitimate leadership. Such leadership assumes the role of the Architects, Engineers and Project Managers of the emergent nation.

With the above ingredients in place, anchored as it were by purposeful leadership, nation building, and democratic consolidation will become the solid foundation for lasting peace, security, stability, prosperity and harmonious co-existence. But when many of the above ingredients that are fundamental to nation building are missing, as appears to be our predicament in Nigeria, what we have is a free-for-all: intermittent conflicts, sporadic skirmishes, incessant strife, secessionist attempts, perennial social discord, political banditry, rancorous electioneering campaigns, the kidnap-and-settle syndrome, general lawlessness, and jungle-like anarchy etc. I must emphasise here that strong, stable, unified nations are built fundamentally on values, and experience has shown that such values must proceed from leadership, if they are to take root in society.

Yet, what quality of values for nation building can we expect to emerge from the succession of rogue leaders, treasury looters, coup plotters, election riggers and punitive overloads that this land has endured (with only few exceptions) since independence? What quality of values for nation building can we get from the prebendal, self-serving, cash-and-carry politics that have held sway in these climes since independence and have constantly propped up a gang of self-perpetuating conquerors who have had absolutely no clue about what it takes to build a viable nation, let alone lay the foundation for a peaceful, stable, secure and harmonious society? What quality of values for nation building can proceed from the rent seekers, contract chasers, and elite prostitutes of power who rely on corrupt godfathers, unlettered witchdoctors and village thugs to clinch power, and who change political affiliation each time they lose an election?

Nation Building Values also make for Democratic Consolidation, Security and Peaceful Co-existence

Modern nations are built on certain shared values, norms and interests, which come to be known simply as core national values. They include patriotism (or the love of one's country to such an extent that one is ready to sacrifice one's life for it), an unwavering commitment to justice, discipline, the rule of law, the equality of all persons under the law, the equal opportunity for all segments in the federation, mutual respect for cultural and religious diversities among all constituting units and members, the priority of the common good over individual and group interests, the protection of the weak against the possible excesses of the rich and powerful in society, and the assurance of security of all persons who live and carry out legitimate trade anywhere and everywhere in the society, as well as leadership accountability. These are among the ingredients that make for true nation building, and they are consistent with the ingredients that make for peace and security.

We can hardly make progress towards resolving our multiple political crises and consolidating our democracy, or securing our country, until we address very critically and in an honest and dispassionate manner the leadership deficit that has continued to plague our nation, and put in place appropriate structures and institutions for the formation of a sufficiently large pool of potential leaders, as well as programmatically nurture the disciplines and habits of life that will bequeath the country with truly enlightened, patriotic, selfless and development-focused leaders in the near future.

There are examples through the course of history, of leaders whose very lives symbolised and encapsulated the core national values upon which their nations were built and which to this day have continued to hold such nations together. They include George Washington (1732 – 1799), hero of the American Revolutionary war, first President of the United States of America, and champion of the most comprehensive democratic principles ever before applied in national governance. Washington is known by Americans as the "first in war, first in peace, and first in the hearts of his countrymen." We also have Giuseppe Garibaldi (1807 – 1882), hero, founder and unifier of modern Italy. There is Otto von Bismarck (1815 – 1898), hero and unifier of the German nation. There is Lee Kuan Yew (1923-), first Singaporean Prime Minister, who saw to the transformation of his country from a resource poor and terribly underdeveloped colonial outpost at independence in 1965 to a First World Asian Tiger by the time he left office in 1990.

Nearer home we have Julius Nyerere (1922 – 1999), perhaps the godliest African statesman to date, who united two separate countries - Tangayika and Zanzibar into what has come to be known as Tanzania, and kept the diverse people of his otherwise resource poor country in peace throughout his reign. He was fondly called *Mwalimu*, (or Teacher) and *Baba waTaifa*, (meaning Father of the Nation). His legacy of integrity has continued to sustain Tanzania in peaceful co-existence over twenty-five years after he left office, while many other African countries have gone up in flames soon after their founding fathers left office. Finally, we have Nelson Mandela (1918 - 2013) Nobel Peace Prize winner and first President of post-apartheid (democratic) modern South Africa. He was an anti-apartheid activist who spent twenty-seven long years in prison, and upon his release, led his devastated country through a process of reconciliation and the complex negotiations leading up to the country's new democratic constitution. He stepped down after just one term as President and remained until his death a foremost international statesman.

The Challenge before Security Agents and Conflict Management Experts

Now what is the role of security agents and conflict management experts in addressing the challenge of peace, security and the consolidation of democracy in our country? Our security agents surely have a lot to do in this volatile security environment. Over the years a lot of Nigerians engaged with the security enterprise have performed gallantly in their task of securing the nation and its people, and especially protecting the innocent citizen from the criminally minded. Yet our country remains precariously insecure, because among other reasons in a nation of widespread discontent such as we have, we cannot even be sure of the sense of patriotism and nationalism of those charged with the task of securing us. Many Nigerians have reasons to doubt that the average soldier, the average policeman, or the average agent of the secret service on the streets has any serious commitment to securing the life and property of the common man or woman. Instead many Nigerians believe that they are on their own when it comes to the security of their lives and property. That is why they so easily resort to self-help in the face of threat or provocation.

However, building peace and security in the nation involves much more than the multiplication of security agencies or equipping them with state-of-the-art equipment and sophisticated gadgets. The task of building peace and securing the nation includes among other elements addressing very seriously the historical injustices against individuals and groups, whether real or perceived, and the current inequalities and inequities in our socio-political and economic structures and arrangements, because lasting peace, security and the consolidation of democracy cannot be discussed, let alone achieved, in a vacuum. Sustainable peace and security in the polity, within which context democracy can be truly consolidated, cannot be achieved where a few smart alecks and their friends and family members now and again seize the key of the national treasury, capture the resources of the land, and live in criminal and provocative opulence, while the vast majority of the population subsist in dehumanising poverty.

It was St. Augustine who in the 5th Century A.D. made that famous declaration that *"A state where there is no justice is nothing but a gang of bandits or a bunch of robbers."* Thus the challenge is for us to adopt a more and more holistic and integrated approach to the keeping of security, the management of conflict and peace building. It is not enough for us to vote billions of naira in purchasing expensive hardware such as armoured tanks and surveillance helicopters. We must see it as part of the task of securing our nation and ensuring peace to invest time and resources in promoting good governance, justice and equality in all sectors and facets of our national life, otherwise we would be continually overwhelmed by crime and violence all over the place. This of course is a challenge for all peace lovers and indeed all patriotic citizens in general, as well as friends of Nigeria, and particularly the international development community.

Conclusion

I am convinced beyond reasonable doubt that Nigeria remains today in such crisis, and continues to be so prone to conflict and insecurity, largely on account of the fragility of our nation state, which has a direct link to the injustices and inequities in our structural arrangements or what some have referred to as fundamental flaws in the structural configuration of our country, and for which many are today calling for restructuring. In the foregoing presentation I have identified the problem as "missing ingredients in our nation building project." These missing ingredients are values, principles and norms that are critical to nation building. They include patriotism, commitment to justice, human dignity and equality, discipline, the rule of law, the common good imperative, mutual respect for cultural and religious diversities, equal opportunities and access to the resources of the land, etc. To anchor these values and entrench them in the very structures of the society, we require a crop of purposeful, visionary, self-sacrificing and accountable leaders, whose very lives are an embodiment of such core national values, and whose disciplined conduct in public and in private affairs, are an exercise in mentoring and an inspiration to future generations of their countrymen and women.

These value-based ingredients have unfortunately been in very short supply, if not entirely missing from our national landscape, and we as a people have continued to pay lip-service to the project of nation building. But there are no short cuts to nation building and the consolidation of democracy. Nigerians desirous of peace, security and stability in this polity must invest today in what has been established as the critical building blocks of a modern nation state, if we are ever going to have a viable nation with sustainable peace. We must invest heavily in leadership training and in the dissemination of the nation building values outlined above, for they also happen to be the values that make for peaceful co-existence. We must each take interest in politics, in the quality of political discourse, in the quality of electioneering campaigns, and in the quality of persons that assume public office. We must take responsibility for the future and do all we can to stop the thugs and the rogues, the charlatans and mediocre performers who now populate the corridors of power and who are bent on ruining this nation.

Until now it has been garbage in, garbage out. But the ugly trend can and must be reversed. So I urge those of you who are security agents to now and again look beyond the merely technocratic dimension of your work, which is very useful, but often does not strike at the root of the problem and does not guarantee lasting security peace in the nation. I challenge the leadership of our various security outfits to collaborate with other segments of society in investing some time and resources into the project of promoting what we have identified as the value-based ingredients of nation building and peace building, including a selfless and visionary leadership elite, towards the emergence of a viable nation of lasting security and peace, and vibrant democracy and economic prosperity.

CHAPTER SEVENTY-THREE

The Critical Role of Faith Communities in the Task of Building a Nation of Freedom, Security and Peace

(A presentation at a Roundtable on Freedom, Interfaith Relations and Civil Society in Nigeria; Abuja, March 15th to 16th, 2018)

Introduction

LET me begin by congratulating Prof. Lamin Sanneh and his Yale University collaborators for initiating the Freedom, Interfaith Relations, and Civil Society in Africa project, and for this very timely conversation in Abuja. Nigeria is at this point in time confronted with multiple political, economic and security challenges that many believe are largely on account of inherent contradictions in its structural configurations, on account of real or perceived historical injustices that have remained unresolved, on account of a succession of rogue leaders who were often incapable of helping Nigeria to realise its full potential, and finally on account of the many flashpoints of violence in recent times (often assuming religious and ethnic colourations), that now have heightened the political tension in the land, and rendered our unity ever more tenuous.

The Widespread Call for Restructuring

Besides the mega challenge of terrorist insurgency in the north, secessionist agitations in the east and the marauding Fulani Herdsmen's violence in the Middle Belt, there is today widespread discontent over the conduct of leadership and administration of the Nigerian commonwealth, and a strident call from practically every quarter for the restructuring of the Nigerian polity or even a renegotiation of the space we call Nigeria. Nigerians are today calling for a wholesale reconfiguration of our federal arrangement, a re-delineation of the sub-national entities that make up the federation, the re-definition of the fundamental elements of our socio-political and cultural connectivity, and the clarification of what citizenship in Nigeria entails, or which rights and freedoms are to be taken for granted by Nigerian citizens anywhere and everywhere in the land. Nigerians want to put an end to the contradiction whereby one can be said to be a citizen of Nigeria, and yet not be a citizen of their place of residence, even if the person was actually born there, and has paid taxes there all their life!!! This vexatious element of the restructuring debate – the citizenship versus indigeneity conundrum – has a bearing with elements of religious freedom, including the right to worship freely the God of one's choice, and obtain land to build houses of worship anywhere in the country.

The Ethical Vacuum in the Nigerian Public Space

Meanwhile, the Nigerian unique experience of colonial rule, and the multiple crises that have plagued our nation since its independence in 1960, appear to have taken their toll on the nation's moral fabric. For, though Nigeria is generally acclaimed to be a very religious nation, today's generation of Nigerians appear in large measure to have lost the sense of right and wrong, of values and vices, of what is desirable and what is condemnable, and of what is good and what is bad. As a corporate entity, we seem to have lost quite a dose of our sense of shame and outrage at the preponderance of violence and corruption. Yes, in spite of our loud and open display of religiosity, many Nigerian Christians and Muslims appear to have lost the sense of sin and iniquity, and therefore we carry on our criminal exploitation of a dysfunctional and disdainful socio-political system as if indeed we dwell in a jungle where might is right, and where the gangsters and the fraudsters are the heroes and heroines who are constantly being adulated and decorated.

There is indeed today what may be described as an ethical vacuum in the Nigerian society. Our public square appears to have been stripped naked, as there appears to be no more taboos. Just anything goes, as moral leaders, men and women of thought, champions of the public good, torchbearers, mentors and inspirers, appear to have been driven underground. Now rogues and scoundrels, thugs and bandits, charlatans and comedians, sycophants and greedy merchants of power are hanging around the corridors of power, destroying everything of value, championing the cause of national degeneration and setting the stage for an eventual collapse of our socio-economic and political system. The shoddy and insensate manner in which the Federal Government and the security agencies have been handling the ongoing menace of murderous herdsmen all over the Middle Belt and beyond, is evidence of the degree of leadership failure and the moral vacuum that have become our lot in this country.

No nation can survive for long as one corporate entity, let alone make progress and achieve any measure of peace and stability, when it is plagued by such multiple self-inflicted ills as the senseless exploitation and manipulation of ethnic and religious identities, gross mis-governance, executive lawlessness, monumental corruption, political banditry, legislative rascality, and widespread social discord. Yet, nothing short of a true ethical revolution will save our sick nation from the destruction that accompanies a prolonged moral decadence. What we require is a radical turnaround, a national conversion experience as it were, if this superstructure is to be salvaged.

Need for Ongoing Dialogue

The remnant few in Nigeria, who have refused to join the madding crowd in the dance of death, and all those who are poised to bequeath a better society to the upcoming generation, have a lot of work to do. We must seek out one another and join hands across the artificially constructed walls of religion, ethnicity and political affiliation. It will not do any good to continue to simply bemoan and lament our shameful and embarrassing circumstances. We must now engage in the critical task of nation building or national regeneration. For a nation of 180 million people of diverse ethnic and religious identities, we require much networking and collaboration with like-minded agents of civil society. This is where a robust and ongoing interfaith dialogue is not only necessary, but a matter of priority importance. The good news is that a significant number of the participants at this Roundtable are actively involved in one interfaith dialogue platform or the other. We must continue to intensify these efforts, in spite of our challenging circumstances.

I see our inability to achieve true freedom, security, peace and prosperity as a failure of fundamental nation-building values, rather than a consequence of religious and ethnic diversities or even the failure of techniques, strategies or expertise in political engineering, financial planning or security management. Corruption has thrived, insecurity is rampant, and terrorists, as well as marauding herdsmen, appear to have overwhelmed us, not so much because of conflicting identities, but because ours is a corporate entity that is not solidly founded on values - those critical building blocks upon which more successful modern nations stand. Yes, Nigeria is today embroiled in multiple crises, as a result of the fragility of its very foundations.

Very critical, in my opinion, is the absence of the essential ingredients that make for nation building or that are necessary for national regeneration. These vital but missing ingredients are fundamental values, principles and norms. They include patriotism, commitment to justice and fairness to all segments of the society, the rule of law, common good imperative, mutual respect for cultural and religious diversities, equal opportunities and access to the resources of the land. To anchor these values and entrench them in the very structures of the society, we require a crop of purposeful, visionary, self-sacrificing and accountable leaders, whose very lives are an embodiment of such core national values, and whose disciplined conduct in public and in private affairs, are an exercise in mentoring and an inspiration to future generations of their countrymen and women.

Role of Religious Bodies

Religious bodies are ordinarily the best placed and the most equipped to champion the ethical revolution and value re-orientation that we require urgently in our society. In a country like Nigeria where the overwhelming majority of people claim to be religious, Churches and Mosques, Religious Institutions, Pastors and Imams, by their very calling, must play a critical role in the project of national moral and ethical re-awakening or they will soon be considered irrelevant and anachronistic.

Though Churches and Mosques have not been spared the devastating effects of the culture of violence and moral decay in the land; though many Pastors and Imams have often not risen above the politicisation of religion and exploitation of ethnic identities for personal gain, and yes, though many highly placed Nigerian Christians and Muslims have often betrayed in the conduct of their own lives those sad elements of our national malady that have made our nation so fragile and its landscape so combustible, the society will nevertheless continue to look up to religious institutions and clerics to play critical leadership roles (along with other civil society agents), in the enormous task of national regeneration.

The Politics versus the Practice of Religion

As we discuss freedom, interfaith relations, security and peace in Nigeria, I would like us to distinguish clearly between the actual practice of religion, which does not hurt or threaten anyone, and the politics of religion, which is responsible for some of the worst atrocities in human history and is today constituting a major threat to the security and stability of the Nigerian state, along with the manipulation and abuse of ethnic identities. Difficult as the enterprise may be, especially for our Muslim brothers and sisters, it is imperative that we distinguish between the freedom to practice one's religion, and the insistence by some elements on having a Muslim society, run by Islamic law.

Those who would go to war over religious identities, fighting and killing their neighbours, or denying their neighbours what they are entitled to in justice, so as to facilitate the spread of their own faith or gain some political, economic or social advantage over others, are definitely not among the best examples of religious people. By the moral standards of Jesus Christ as enunciated in the Sermon on the Mount, and as demonstrated in the lives of many saints of our Church, such misguided zealots, such senseless fanatics, such religious politicians, whether they be found among Christians or Muslims, are doing a major disservice to the religious enterprise, and they should be helped to recognise that.

With regard to Nigeria, a starting point for interrogating the relationship between the politicisation of religion and national stability is understanding the nature of political relations in our country and the role of state power in what the American social scientist Harold Lasswell would call the art of "who gets what, when, and how."

In a fragile, highly polarized and low-trust society like ours, state power is often seen as the most critical instrument for material accumulation, for the dispensation of privileges, for redressing perceived historical injustices and for meting out punishments. In such a society, there is a pervasive fear that the group that wins state power could use it to unfairly corner privileges for its group and, in some cases, punish others. In such an environment, politics and the struggle for state power tend to be very anarchic and brutal, and every form of identity is mobilised and manipulated, including gender, ethnicity, religion and regionalism, to capture power.

Essentially because religion is such an emotive matter, it is especially easy to exploit and manipulate in a society where believers are largely poor, uneducated and desperately looking for someone to blame for all their woes. In such an environment, not many people are able to see that the politicization of religion is often merely a mask over intra-elite struggles for political power and lucre. Of course, the foot soldiers who lose their lives in the violent conflicts that often result, are never these politicians or their children, but ordinary Nigerians struggling to eke out a living and provide for their children.

Conclusion

Violent conflicts are not an inevitable consequence of diversities in religion, ethnicity and culture. Our security challenges and the fragility of our nation are not principally on account of our diverse ethnic and religious identities, but a direct consequence of failed leadership and the absence of what I have identified as core nation-building ingredients. The task before all religious communities and other civil society agencies that are committed to the security and stability of our nation, therefore, is the promotion of those values that make for nation building and a massive investment in the formation of the kind of leaders that will galvanise the disparate identities and harmonise the competing interests, towards the emergence of a stable, harmonious society.

Religious communities and other civil society agencies must each take an interest in leadership and in the quality of persons that assume public office. We must take responsibility for the future of our society, constantly interrogate the leadership selection processes, and do all we can to stop the thugs and the rogues, the charlatans and mediocre performers who now populate the corridors of power and who are often bent on ruining this nation. Until now, it has been garbage in, garbage out. But the ugly trend can and must be reversed. All of us who have any serious commitment to the survival of our corporate entity must invest some time and resources in cultivating leadership values and value-based leadership from the very cradle in the family up to the presidency.

We must all work towards helping our countrymen and women understand that in a nation desiring lasting peace and progress, rogues and brigands, murderers and assassins, sycophants and charlatans, have no place in the public square. We must all work towards demonstrating in various ways to our countrymen and women that true leadership is characterised by a compelling vision, an all-consuming sense of mission, a strong sense of justice, sacrifice, courage, passion for the poor and the weak, and commitment to the common good.

Those desiring leadership positions in our society must be made to realise that political leadership is about passion for the common good, not an exercise in treasury-looting and corrupt enrichment. Politicians and public office holders must be helped to recognise that governments exist to ensure the safety of the lives and property of the people they govern as well as provide the greatest good for the greatest number of the people, and not to secure the functionaries and provide for them at the expense of the generality of the people whom they claim to govern.

The ordinary members of our faith communities must be helped to recognise that they have a major stake in the governance of their society. They must learn to participate actively at every stage of the political process, defend the rule of law, work against impunity and protect the commonwealth against any attempt by a crop of rulers to domesticate or privatise their common patrimony. In a democratic society, the people must be vigilant, constantly dragging the feet of those occupying positions of power to the fire of democracy. These are among the ingredients that must be in place if we are ever to have a stable, harmonious, peaceful and prosperous nation. May this roundtable that we are having in collaboration with researchers from Yale University bear fruits towards the emergence of a more wholesome, peaceful and secure Nigerian society. Amen.

CHAPTER SEVENTY-FOUR

The Nigerian Christian and the Imperative of Judicial Activism for National Transformation
(Homily at the formal Opening of the 2018/2019 Legal Year for Judicial Officers of the Federal High Court of Justice, Abuja, September 17, 2018)

Sisters and brothers in Christ, it is an honour and a privilege, for me to be asked to preach the homily at this Eucharistic celebration that marks the opening of the Legal Year of the Federal High Court of Nigeria. I am glad to know that in spite of your high learning and experience in the dispensation of justice; in spite of the fact that we call you Honourable Justices and Your Lordships, you nevertheless recognise that you are mere mortals, and that as judges in the Court of justice, you act in the name of the Most High God who alone is the real Judge of his people. So, like King Solomon requested of God in 1 Kings 3:9, to begin a new legal season, we are here to join you in praying for *"a heart to discern good and evil,"* because your judgements will affect the lives of individuals and groups, and sometimes through legal precedents, your judgements will affect the future direction of our entire country.

This annual celebration of the opening of the legal year with religious service allows us as Church and as God's people to honour the sacred character of the law, and the vocation entrusted to you, its guardians. This is also a day for you hopefully to remember why you chose this profession in the first place, and to prayerfully reflect upon how you can become even more effective servants of truth, justice and the common good. You embrace quite a serious responsibility that causes people to hold you in high regard – calling you Esquire, Your Lordship, My Lord. People are generally awed by the responsibility you shoulder each day for all of us. It is indeed an awesome responsibility and an immense moral burden that is placed upon your shoulders, and for which you are bound to render an account before the Almighty God at the end of the day. You need the presence and grace of God in your lives. So, we pray today for you and for all members of the judiciary, that you may be given the gift of wisdom and discernment to enrich your knowledge and experience. May the Holy Spirit fill you with wisdom to know how to apply the laws of our land with both impartiality and mercy. May the good Lord protect you from bad decisions and wrong judgments. Amen.

God's word is filled with stories of judges and lawyers. Not all of them are flattering or praiseworthy. We have many stories about lawyers and judges in the Scriptures, because even the authors of the sacred texts recognise how important you all are to the well-being and stability of society from time immemorial. Scripture views the members of the judiciary often as the very substitute of God himself. You are therefore asked to tend to the issues of law as God would. We need you to be wise and fair, insightful and accommodating, prudent but not naïve, as you decide the many complex issues that come before you each day. Our courts and its officers are the bulwarks of the security and well-being of our nation itself. We look up to you for wise and balanced opinions that safeguard us all. Your service must be animated by passion and the energy of fire. May your service be praiseworthy and faithful to the laws of our country. May you be abundantly rewarded for being servants of justice and mercy in everything that you do during this new legal year. The law itself must be a bastion of security and harmony for all of us in the country. Judges and lawyers are our first line of defence against mob rule, elite criminality, executive lawlessness and the arrogance of power. Yours is a very noble and lofty vocation. And this nobility and sacred character of your profession is the reason why any unsavoury legal practice among your members so infuriates and scandalises people everywhere, in the same manner as the scandal of priests and pastors horrifies and outrages people everywhere. This annual prayer service guarantees our well-being as well as yours. This mass, and all the prayer services you hold each year, are a wise investment also for all of us who depend on your wisdom, your impartiality, your balanced perspectives and your commitment to the common good, to make this nation a more secure, stable and peaceful society.

The theme of my brief reflection with you this morning is "*LET YOUR LIGHT SHINE: The Nigerian Christian and the Imperative of Judicial Activism for National Transformation.*" Let me begin with the declaration of Prophet Isaiah while announcing the coming of the Messiah, in Isaiah 9:6. He says: "the people who walked in darkness have seen a great light; those that lived in a land of deep darkness – on them light has shone." And on coming into the world Jesus proclaims (in John 8:12) that "I am the Light of the world; no one who follows me will ever walk in darkness."

Christ is the light that breaks through the darkness of human misery. He is the persistent and defiant light that darkness cannot overpower as we read in John 1:5. St. Paul tells us in Roman 13:11-13 that with the coming of Christ, the night is over, and daylight is here. Yes, those who come to Christ in darkness go away bathed in light. What the Scriptures teach us is that on account of the coming of Christ, the people that walked in darkness have seen a great light. That is why Jesus tells his disciples and ourselves that: "You are the salt of the earth. But if salt loses its taste, what can make it salty again? It is good for nothing and can only be thrown out to be trampled under people's feet. You are the light of the world. A city built on a hill-top cannot be hidden. No one lights a lamp to put under a tub; they put it on the lamp stand where it shines for everyone in the house. In the same way your light must shine in people's sight, so that, seeing your good works, they may give the praise to your father in heaven" (Mt.5:13-16).

Christ has shared his light with us and now asks us to be what we are. He says: Be light to the world. Let your light dawn over the darkness of corruption, hatred, vengeance, violence and war. You are the light of the world. So let your light dawn over the darkness of ethnic bigotry, executive lawlessness and political banditry in your country. Be light, dispelling the darkness of greed and selfishness on the part of the privileged few in your society, which has driven the multitude into misery and destitution. He also says: You are the salt of the earth. Be salt to your country. Preserve your society from spoiling because of widespread injustice, deceit and manipulation. Preserve your country from decaying on account of rampant indiscipline and widespread impunity. Be salt to your country, transforming it through the values of truth and justice, love and compassion, hard work and sacrifice for the common good.

Therefore, confronted with elite debauchery and popular despondency, our light must shine through the passionate pursuit of human rights, the defence of human dignity and the promotion of freedom and abundant life for all in our society. The socio-political and economic circumstances of today's Nigeria truly challenge those of us who lay claim to Christianity to act as the conscience of the nation. We must assume our responsibility as salt of the earth and light of the world. Our faith must become a faith that does justice. We must be forthright and consistent in working against individual evil and evil structures in our society. As the multitude of Nigerians are plagued by poverty and all manner of human degradation, and as our worsening economic fortunes has pushed a lot of our kith and kin unto the slums, where they live subhuman lives, we cannot afford to look the other way. We enlightened Christians must stand alongside the oppressed, the impoverished, the marginalized, the sick, the handicapped, the prisoners, those denied their just rights and those discriminated against. We are called upon to defend the right of poor workers to just wages, to affordable housing, to descent transportation, to health insurance, and to adequate retirement benefits.

The Christian elite must at all times resist the temptation to apathy and despondency. We must be patriotic but fearless Christians who will demonstrate to the men and women of this land that a true patriot is one who cares deeply about the happiness and well-being of his country and all its people; not one who applauds or defends any government in power, or one who is simply concerned with climbing the ladder of professional or career success for personal aggrandisement. We must demonstrate love for our country by demanding the highest standards from our leaders and by accepting nothing but the best for and from our people. We must be ready to stand up and be counted on the side of truth, even as falsehood reigns in the land.

True, many who belong to the Nigerian Christian elite have paid only lip service to the social imperative of the Gospel of Jesus Christ. We have often lived like hypocrites, preferring to have our little pleasures and comforts, rather than rocking the boat and getting hurt. We have often avoided as much as possible any occasion of confrontation with the status quo of power and privilege for a tiny minority, while the overwhelming majority are denied a modicum of dignified existence. We have put up with unjust structures; we have accommodated ungodly dispensations; and now and again we have conspired with callous oppressors of God's children, only so that we may indulge in our miserable pleasures and be ensconced in our privileged positions. To that extent we have betrayed our Christian prophetic calling, and if we do not repent and change our course, we shall someday answer for it before the Most High. We need to put an end to this season of betrayal and abandon our erstwhile posture of hypocrisy and complacency. The embarrassing socio-political realities of our day are a constant reminder that if we do not stand up for something we will fall for anything.

My dear friends, whereas the foregoing has been directed at all Christians – all baptised persons, among baptised persons the critical role of Christian lawyers and jurists in the project of social transformation must be particularly emphasised. The legal profession is in the western tradition understood as a vocation, a divine calling, much like the medical profession or the priesthood. Whereas the contractor, the business tycoon or the entrepreneur sets out as his or her fundamental objective to amass wealth, and he or she measures his or her success in terms of the amount of wealth and property he or she is able to accumulate in the course of time, the lawyer or the jurist on the other hand is expected to be motivated by an all-consuming passion for the common good, for the promotion of a just and equitable social order, and especially for the protection of the poor and the weak against the excesses of the rich and powerful in society. Lawyers and Jurists are therefore prime custodians of human civilisation, which is why they are often referred to – even in secular terms - as the light of their society (Advocatorum quae societas luci suae).

In a country that has had more than its fair share of notoriously corrupt and abusive leaders, lawyers and jurists cannot be inattentive or indifferent, nor can they feign helplessness. Instead, lawyers and jurists must use their privileged learning, their constitutional prerogative and their high standing in society, to stand in the gap between the distressed people of Nigeria, and those who preside over their economic, political and social affairs – convicting corrupt officials, condemning acts of impunity and resisting rights violations and abuses. In a country like ours where in spite of our enormous natural endowments, the poor and their children are largely denied opportunities for good nourishment, quality education, decent housing, decent but affordable public transportation, and adequate healthcare, Christian lawyers and jurists must capitalise on their constitutional prerogative and social standing to achieve social transformation, through creative application of the law for social change, and through a number of legal advocacy mechanisms.

Justice is radically intolerant of injustice; justice seeks out injustice to destroy it. Justice knows neither father nor mother; justice looks to the truth alone. Judges must be in the front line in the defence of human rights, and in the project of giving every human being his or her due, simply because he or she is a person; simply because justice requires it. This is the honour of law and the honour of jurists. Only bold affirmation of justice by lawyers and jurists on behalf of poor and helpless citizens can tear down the "organised disorder" that the political and economic elite have often erected around themselves in this country. Yes, only bold affirmation of the rule of law can curb the arrogance of those who exercise power and force the agents of primitive feudalism in our day to submit to just, humane and democratic principles of governance. On the other hand, a judicial system (including the criminal justice regime), which betrays or undervalues the equality and the dignity of all persons, compromises its calling, and violates humanity as a whole.

We read in Psalmist 18 that *"the law of the Lord is perfect. It revives the soul."* The Lord requires that everyone be given fair judgment and treated with equal dignity, whether poor or rich (Lev 19:15). Injustice is an abomination to God (Deut 25:16) because God is righteous and there is no injustice in him (Deut 32:4). The prophets lashed out against unjust laws and judges (Is 10:1-2; Amos 5:7, 15). He who sows injustice will reap sorrow (Prov 22:8). It is by justice that a king gives stability to the land (Prov 29:4). Prophet Micah sums it up when he declared that what the Lord desires of us is "to do justice, to love kindness, and to walk humbly before our God."

Ancient Greek Philosopher Aristotle says that law is order, and good law is good order. We recall St. Augustine's famous dictum, that *"kingdoms devoid of justice are nothing but a bunch of bandits or a gang of robbers."* The challenge before your Lordships and our Christian lawyers today is how to put the law at the service of the common good, instead of allowing it to become a tool at the hands of the oppressors of God's children. Lawyers are ministers in the temple of justice, and by their training and practice, they cleverly harness, canvass and persuade the judges to sway the judgment in favour of their clients. But as the judiciary is the last hope of the common man, judges ought to constantly beware of the manipulation of the technicalities of the law in order to ensure the dispensation of substantial justice in our courts.

The confidence the people repose on judges is what constitutes the foundation of the court system. It will therefore be a tragic situation if some judges are suspected of yielding their moral authority to political influence. When there is the growing impression that smart lawyers are increasingly able to persuade jurists to exploit the technicalities of the law in order to exonerate corrupt rulers, rogue politicians and greedy business tycoons, then we will begin to set the stage and lay the foundation for the coming anarchy or the revenge of the poor. And it should be noted that such revenge of the poor will not spare lawyers and judges as well as bishops and priests, who in our society are seen to belong to the privileged elite class. The French revolution (of 1792 to 1802) should continue to be taken as a bloody reminder of what dire consequences all of us who belong to the elite class will face, if we do not change our course today, and show greater commitment to upholding and defending the fundamental and inalienable rights of every human being in our society. What is called for today therefore is a measure of judicial activism by which forthright lawyers and godly judges, moved with passion for the common good and inspired by their commitment to God, will courageously engage in the necessary project of social engineering, overcoming the shackles of the literary provisions in our statutes, in order to ensure substantial justice in all cases.

Let me conclude by recognising along with the Psalmist that unless the Lord builds the house, the labourers labour in vain, and unless the Lord watches over the city, the sentries keep watch in vain (Ps 127:1). And indeed, Jesus told his disciples in John 15:5 that "cut off from me you can do nothing." May the Lord grant you all lawyers and jurists the abiding presence and power of the Holy Spirit, so that you may live out your faith with truth and justice, and discharge your sacred duties with integrity and authenticity, even as you navigate your way through the valley of darkness that our society has become today. Amen.

CHAPTER SEVENTY-FIVE

Beyond Ballots and Numbers:
The Moral Imperative of Credible Elections

(Paper delivered at the Nigerian Bar Association Organised Voter Education Workshop, Lokoja, Kogi State, January 10, 2019)

I congratulate the Voter Education Committee of the Nigerian Bar Association, for organizing this one-day Workshop for all the stakeholders in the forthcoming gubernatorial elections of Kogi and Bayelsa states. Such an initiative of the Nigerian Bar Association is very laudable. I only wish a Symposium of this nature was held much earlier in the electioneering process, and not on the eve of the election proper. Recall that as a process the 2015 Elections started soon after the conduct of the 2011 National and State Elections, with the litigations and court rulings that resulted in the discordance we now have in the electoral calendar of several states, including Kogi and Bayelsa. The electioneering processes include the amendment of electoral law (whenever such is called for), the registration of political parties, the setting up of election timetable, the voter registration exercise, the conduct of party primaries and the emergence of candidates, and the campaigns leading up to the conduct of the elections on election day. Elections are won or lost on account of what happens throughout the entire process, and not just the singular event of election day; and elections would be judged credible or non-credible, free and fair or rigged on account of the integrity of the entire process, and not simply what happens on election day. Nevertheless, I commend the Nigerian Bar Association for this initiative, and I pray that even at this eleventh hour in the process of preparation for the elections, this Symposium would prove to be a very useful exercise for the active participants and for all stakeholders at large.

I have decided to reflect in this Keynote address on the Ethical and Moral Imperatives of Credible Elections, and hope that it can generate or stir up the kind of discussions envisioned by the learned organisers of the Symposium. My impression is that many of those engaged in contemporary Nigerian politics do not seem to realize that there are not only legal, but also ethical and moral dimensions to political conduct.

Many do not seem to realize that almost all political, economic, and legal issues that we are confronted with in our society are also moral and ethical issues that should engage the human conscience and consciousness. With regard to the conduct of elections in our society for example, looting of national, state or local government treasury for the purpose of buying party chiefs and the electorate; intimidation, killing and maiming of opponents and the destruction of their property; multiple registration and multiple voting; substitution of candidates' names, diversion of electoral materials, selling of voters cards, stashing of and stealing of ballot boxes, falsification of figures – if any of these crimes are still possible in the era of card readers; declaration of false results; receiving of bribes and the favouring of one candidate against another by agents of the law, corrupt deals and judicial malpractices at the election tribunals, etc, are not simply electoral offences or an assault on universally accepted democratic principles. They are criminal offences and over and above all a violation of the elementary ethical and moral principles of Truth and Justice, Equity and Fairness, Honesty, and Integrity.

Such violation of moral and ethical principles is known by Christians as SIN. No one who engages in any of the above electoral offences can lay claim to any measure of moral probity. Such unscrupulous persons – who have no qualms of conscience – constitute an evil force in the society which must be exposed and destroyed, if we are ever to make progress as a people or find peace, security and stability as a nation.

In the month of June 2007, a Conference was held in Loccum, Germany, to discuss the Nigerian political situation. It brought together stakeholders of diverse backgrounds from Nigeria and Germany to brainstorm on the Nigerian problematic. Under the rather curious theme, "Nigeria: Too Rich for Dignity and the Law?" and coming shortly after the 2007 general elections in Nigeria that generated a lot of controversy, the Workshop was an occasion to focus attention on the contradictions of Nigeria and attempt to draw up recommendations on the way forward.

At this latter Conference in 2007, one Heinrich Bergstresser, a German participant who has spent many years researching on Nigeria, observed that Nigerians are an extremely creative and constructive people, but that there is in the country what he called *"a destructive undercurrent"* that accounts for the *fragile balance* which has been the fate of the country since its Independence from the British. What according to this speaker is missing is "some *initial spark* that would turn the fragile balance closer towards the first stage of nation building." Unfortunately, whatever this "initial spark" is has remained elusive, and in my opinion the terribly heightened anxiety and palpable fear that characterize each electioneering period in this country, the widespread acrimony and cash-and-carry party primaries that precede most of our gubernatorial and national elections, seem to have rendered what Heinrich Bergstresser called the "fragile balance" of our country, even more precariously fragile.

Ladies and Gentlemen, let us face it: Many of our countrymen and women continue to approach politics with a killer's touch. Party primaries at State and Federal levels have often been an exercise in high-level brigandage, by which the infrastructures of state are used to intimidate the opposition, and looted resources of state are distributed openly to buy the allegiance of congress delegates, and as could be expected, the results often went in favour of the highest bidder. There is often widespread lack of truth and justice and a prevailing culture of fraud in the political mechanisms and processes nearly across the board. The cumulative result is the outrageous number of litigations in our courts, arising from party primaries and the elections proper, as well as a preponderance of anger and frustration among aspirants to political office. Political parties are often dangerously split into warring factions, poisoning the polity and heightening the tension in the land. This is why violence looms over the horizon, where it is not already being prosecuted through bomb blasts, direct assassinations, arson and sundry attacks as we have witnessed in several flashpoints in this country, including Kogi and Bayelsa States. Yes, today many Nigerians do prepare for the elections as if for war. For a cross section of politicians, it is a do-or-die affair. We have witnessed situations in the past where arms and ammunition large enough to prosecute a civil war, are being imported in the build-up to state and federal elections, to the consternation of the generality of our people. What are the moral and ethical implications of all this for a people who pride in calling themselves religious?

Professor Attahiru Jega, former INEC Chairman, was a participant at the 2007 Conference in Germany referred to above, and this is what he had to say about the succession of leaders in Nigeria:

With very few exceptions, our crop of so-called leaders have essentially been self-serving rulers, some even despots... They lack vision, focus, selflessness and even enlightened self-interest. Most of our so-called leaders are unimaginably corrupt; they are greedy, they are vindictive, they are callous and in many fundamental respects, senseless and even reckless... There is perhaps no other country in the world where power corrupts and absolute power corrupts as absolutely as in Nigeria.

It is now twelve years after such a damning moral judgment on the Nigerian political elite was made, yet the situation is not much different today. I just pray that it has not gotten worse. The truth is that Nigerians of integrity and credibility have little chance in contemporary Nigerian politics, as greedy merchants, power mongers, common criminals, charlatans, and mediocre functionaries, have often taken control of the political machinery, forcing the men and women of reason and conscience to disengage. Many knowledgeable and principled Nigerians – who in saner climes should assume the responsibility of leadership - can often not make sense out of the elite madness and corporate death wish that we witness in our political, and particularly electioneering engagements, and so they have become cynical, apathetic, despondent and resentful.

Many ordinary Nigerians have almost completely lost faith and trust in government and in the electioneering processes that they have over the years come to see as a monumental fraud. This is why in many areas of life they simply resort to self help. Yet these ordinary Nigerians are daily sinking further into dehumanizing poverty, while the insecurity of lives and property in our towns and villages and on the highways and alleys may soon degenerate into a state of anarchy.

The Nigerian situation is however not irredeemable. We read in 2 Chronicles 7:14 "If the people who are called by my name, humble themselves, and pray and seek my presence and turn from their wicked ways, I myself will hear from heaven and forgive their sins and restore their land."

Nigerians are not a different breed of human beings from citizens elsewhere such as in Singapore or Malaysia, South Africa, or Ghana. Many of us do not believe that Nigeria is so difficult to organize and lead unto peaceful co-existence, political stability and economic prosperity. Yet, if this country of 180 million people must make any headway, if the progressive decay in the polity must be halted, if the descent into anarchy in Nigeria must be averted, if in the words of Heinrich Bergstresser, the fragile political balance in Nigeria must be tilted towards the first stage of nation building, then it cannot be business as usual. There must be a paradigm shift. And this paradigm shift must begin from the character and conduct of elections, as no illegitimate government can champion the moral and ethical revolution that Nigeria today desperately needs. If the fragile political balance in Kogi and Bayelsa states is to be tilted to peaceful co-existence and wholesome development, then the processes leading to the emergence of new leaders at the executive and legislative arms must be sufficiently inoculated from the menace of corruption, acrimony, rancor and violence. The Rule of Law must be brought to bear on the entire electioneering mechanisms and processes. And law here must be aimed preeminently at attaining justice and equity, not one that is manipulated by smart jurists and attorneys to protect and defend the all-powerful villain against the innocent victim.

The central responsibility of politics and obligation of politicians is the just ordering of society. The task of ensuring justice and equity in the entire polity belongs to those who answer the call to public service. St. Augustine observes that *"a State or a government that does not function according to the rules of justice would be nothing but a bunch of thieves or a gang of robbers!* Americans identify such governments as "rogue regimes." A rogue government, an illegitimate government, or a government with a stolen mandate, cannot tilt today's delicate political balance towards a stable and progressive polity. Instead, a government with a stolen mandate can only hasten the society's descent into anarchy; for as Proverbs 29:18 puts it, where there is no vision (or where there is no integrity) the people perish.

Free, fair, and credible elections are an element of social morality, an ingredient of the rule of law and an imperative of good governance, stability, peace and progress. If therefore the forthcoming elections in Kogi and Bayelsa states turn out to be another exercise in elite brigandage, then the political elite in these states and the co-conspirators in INEC, the security agencies, the BAR and the BENCH, must be held responsible for the crime of under-developing the people of these states at this point in history. Failure to execute the remaining stages of our electioneering processes with all civility and justice, and with utmost commitment to peace and the security of lives and property in these states, will result in an increase in the level of anger in the land. If the elections are rigged by any means whatsoever, our courts and tribunals will be flooded with litigations that are capable of rendering government practically dysfunctional; many more private militias will emerge; much more sophisticated weapons will find their way into the hands of thugs and criminally minded people; and the plight of the generality of people will be worse than we have ever seen before. Indeed, where there is no vision, the people perish!

It is a truism that if we do not change our course, we would end up where we are headed. We must all take responsibility for what becomes of our country, and each one of us must undergo a conversion experience and do whatever we can to change the people's perception of politics, governance and the processes and procedures for orderly change of government in the modern world. As a people we need a new definition of leadership as service and a fresh perception of politics as the noble art of negotiating the stewardship of a society along the ethical and moral parameters of truth, justice, equality, transparency and accountability.

As part of the desired ethical and moral revolution, we need to put in place new arrangements that would ensure that the paths to public service are not as smooth and attractive as they are now for rogues, thieves and brigands, and that the gains of office are not as rewarding as they are today for men and women of easy virtue who have no business in leadership, but who are simply gunning for the keys of the national, state or local government treasury. The desired change will come about only when the various stakeholders in the Nigerian society staunchly reject the ignominious status quo that throws up for leadership positions men and women of base character and dubious wealth. The desired change will definitely not happen without the critical contribution of functionaries of INEC who are the umpires, the judges and lawyers who are ministers in the temple of justice, and the security and law enforcement agents, whose principal responsibility it is to ensure compliance with the rules of engagement. If these critical sectors do not undergo a major ethical and moral transformation in the discharge of their duties, then as a people we are doomed. If in the course of the forthcoming elections in Kogi and Bayelsa states and such future exercises, custodians and agents of the law could be bribed, bought over, rented or arm-twisted by unscrupulous and desperate politicians, to violate the integrity of the electoral process as easily as has been the case in the past, then there is little chances of a better Nigeria emerging soon.

We need a shift in leadership focus in a new culture of patriotism and responsibility in governance, sustained by transparency and accountability, where politicians, public office holders, civil servants, security agents, civil society groups and the members of the public will engage the political process with the highest ethical and moral standards and the most noble democratic principles. We need a major reform of the various security and law enforcement agencies and the retraining and reorientation of their officers and men, so that they may begin to be more accountable to the generality of the Nigerian people - in whom resides our national sovereignty – rather than continue to see themselves as only accountable to and protective of the interests of the ruling elite at any time.

Indeed, the generality of Nigerians have an enormous task ahead. Those of us who have had to put up with a succession of punitive overlords in the corridors of power will not arrive at the Promised Land without some effort on our part. We must wake up from our slumber and reaffirm our belief in the sovereign power of the people. The Nigerian citizenry must shake off its shackles, break out of its reactive disposition, become more proactive, engage the leadership more constructively, demand the highest standards of probity and accountability from public officers, and begin to mould a new culture and redefine a new character of governance for the Nigerian nation.

Our society is today plagued by pathological greed for money and mindless lust for power. Our national security is criminally undermined by high level corruption and crass indiscipline at all levels. If today the Nigerian people – including politicians, INEC officials, judges, lawyers, and law enforcement agents, experience the much-needed conversion and toe the line of sanity and integrity, we may yet pull back from the brink of the disaster that stares us in the face. There appears to me to be only one way out of the mess of the moment: the way of ethical and moral revolution that would involve all stakeholders, for indeed where there is no vision, the people do perish!

CHAPTER SEVENTY-SIX

Finding Happiness and Salvation Trough Work
(Written on February 24, 2020)

> "The toil of fools wears them out,
> for they do not even know the way to town"
> (Eccl. 10:15)

Work, a major part of human life and culture

The word work is on everyone's lips, almost everyday. We talk of going to work, coming from work, looking for work, having no work, etc. Work is for most people the ordinary means for the provision of their own sustenance and that of their families. Through work the human person comes to grips with nature, with his environment, with the neighbour – with all that surround him.

Work, a means of resolving problems

Through work, the human person resolves problems.
We humans are endowed with not only a body and two hands, but also with a mind and will. The primitive man invented the flint, the arrow, the bow, the wheel, the raft and the dagger, etc. to solve problems. Faced with critical problems of survival, the other animals either adjust to them or they succumb and become extinct. The human being on the other hand is able to think through and resolve many problems of survival and leisure through work. With the aid of science and technology the human person has solved many problems of shelter, transportation, communication, diseases and natural disasters.

The human person is able to create for himself a habitat, a dwelling, a village or a city, to satisfy his personal and social needs. Through work the human person receives recognition by his fellow men and women as having achieved or acquired this or that. Work therefore manifests not only what one has (externally), but also what one is (internally). It is through work that cultures and civilisations are built.

The human person however also initiates some problems through some form of work. Desertification, environmental pollution, ozone layer depletion, bomb explosions, nuclear plant disasters, land mines, lead poisoning, etc, are some of the problems we face today on account of human misadventure with science and technology.

Between Work and Toil

Work is often understood simply as a means to amass wealth and survive, with no other end beyond survival. But this is very unfortunate. Such is the enterprise of the fool described in Ecclesiastes 10:15. Work according to Chambers' dictionary is a physical or mental effort to make or do something. This is why we speak of a good work, or a work of art or "this is my work." Toil is described as exhausting labour or effort. It implies that the self-exertion of labour is accompanied by a certain suffering or pain. But work is not synonymous with toil. Whereas all human toil may be called work, not all work is toil.

Work is specifically a human activity, because it requires

- the human capacity for higher cognition,
- the human capacity for love and service,
- the human capacity for creativity,
- the human capacity for decision making, and
- the human capacity for problem solving.

Work is SERVICE

Through work the human agent serves his or her neighbours as he or she for example heals the sick, nurses the wounded and cares for the weak and the handicapped. This form of work is understood by many as among the most noble of human activity. The human being is engaged in wholesome service of society when he or she engages in wholesome politics and governance, securing life and property, maintaining law and order, administering justice, initiating and executing policies for the care of the environment, and promoting other common good causes.

Work Promotes Beauty and Advances Creation

Human beings promote beauty in the world and in creation through their work. Prominent among those whose work promote beauty are Musicians, Artists, Poets, Environmentalists, Beauticians, etc. Through work human beings build upon, develop, repair and maintain the physical and environmental structures needed for wholesome existence. Architects, Engineers, Surveyors, Town Planners, Estate Managers, Landscapers, Horticulturists, Florists and Environmentalists are among those who advance creation in this way.

Work enhances Human Self-Realisation

As human beings engage in the collaborative enterprise of co-creating, serving God and their neighbour as well as developing and maintaining the structures that make for wholesome existence, the products of their imagination, creativity and physical and mental exertion are a major source of human fulfilment. From this point of view, not to have work is a major tragedy... to be engaged in work which brings no fulfilment, or with which one is most unhappy, is suicidal... to be engaged in a particular work only because it puts food on the table is most undesirable.

Work reveals the inner quality of persons – "By their fruits you shall know them" (Matt 7:16).

There is a critical relationship between a person's character and integrity and his or her work. Just as the artist is known in his works, the teacher, the mason, the nurse, the banker, etc., reveals himself or herself largely through the work he or she does. A person of integrity, discipline, diligence, order, etc., is easily known through his works. On the other hand, an un-disciplined, disorganised, shabby personality is easily revealed in his or her works. A good man or woman does good work, and conversely a bad man or woman does bad work. So, we could deduce from watching someone consistently do bad work that he or she is a bad person.

Work as a Vocation – a way to temporal and eternal happiness

Many Christians see their work as a vocation – a calling, an avenue to daily answer God's call to love and care for the neighbour and to be stewards over creation. Doing our work daily with devotion and commitment, no matter how humble the work, and whatever challenges may be involved, is perfecting God's creation. There is a close link between our work and our overall happiness or fulfilment here on earth, and indeed our eternal happiness in heaven. Since we spend such a high percentage of our lifetime in work, our happiness depends to a reasonable degree on our attitude towards our work or what we think of the work we do. Thus, if our work has meaning, it becomes a blessing. But if it has no meaning or very little meaning, it becomes almost a curse. Perhaps the first major task a human being has to grapple with is the task of finding the work he or she is meant to do in the world. The renowned painter Vincent van Gogh spent many years trying to find out what he wanted to do with his life. He finally discovered that he was meant to be a painter. From that day on his life changed.

Those whose work is a vocation do the work because they consider that they are serving God, not just man; because they love to do the work, because their hearts are in the work. Those who find such a vocation have found a treasure of inestimable value. Such work may be difficult and unspectacular, the work nevertheless glows with a lot of meaning, because it is a labour of love. People can work long hours as long as they feel that their work is making a difference.

Those however who feel that their efforts are being wasted, that no matter how long and hard they work, it won't make a difference, will experience a feeling of weariness and exhaustion. What is important in the choice of work therefore is not whether the work is difficult or how much money it brings, but whether or not it has purpose. What really saps one's energy is giving oneself purposelessly. Purposeful giving does not sap one's energy so much. Work that absorbs one completely gives a person tremendous strength and energy.

When one does work that is a vocation, the work may contain many difficulties and hardships, but deep down one is contented, because a happy life is not the same as an easy life. In fact, the harder the task to which we give ourselves for love's sake, the more it will exalt us. Happy indeed are those who have found their work in life, no matter how humble that work may be. They are saved from half-heartedness, and from the tragedy of only half-living their lives. The work brings out the best in them. Their work is a service to others. Their work becomes a route to salvation.

Jesus' work was that of a Good Shepherd to the Father's flock. He knew his sheep. He cared for his sheep. He gave his life to save his sheep. (John 10:11-18). Jesus' work absorbed him completely. He did his work passionately. On one occasion he had no time to eat, and when his disciples expressed some worry, he told them, "I have a food of which you know nothing. My food is to do the will of the one who sent me, and to complete his work." (John 4:33-34).

CHAPTER SEVENTY-SEVEN

Information as Public Good and Press Freedom
(Lead Paper presented at the World Press Freedom Day Media Stakeholders' Roundtable, Abuja, May 5, 2021)

A: **Introduction**

1. The theme for the World Press Freedom Day, May 3, 2021, is "Information as a public good" per UNESCO, and the day was observed in Nigeria as elsewhere according to tradition. It is a day to Promote the Freedom of the Press, to Fight Against Oppressive or Tyrannical Governments that seek to curtail this fundamental right, and a day to honour our fallen heroes – innocent journalists like Dele Giwa, Bagauda Kaltho and Chinedu Offoaro who lost their lives at the hands of brutal dictators or "disappeared" on account of simply discharging their duties! We pay tribute to the likes of Tunde Thompson and others who spent years in jail, for simply doing their work as journalists during the dark days of military dictatorship in Nigeria. We pay tribute to functionaries of the Newswatch Magazine, Tell Magazine, the Guardian, Tribune, Punch, Champion, Vanguard, and Daily Trust Newspapers among other print media outfits that risked everything while providing space for champions and advocates of democracy and free speech, through those years often described as "years eaten by the locust."

Yes, I agree with Lanre Arogundade that *"there cannot be information for public good where journalists are in chains!"* Yes, there cannot be information for public good when governments or agencies of government routinely weaponize the law, to punish individuals and group that express dissenting views. We cannot have information for public good when journalists and media houses are targeted mainly for uncovering uncomfortable truths, reporting failures of government or exposing high-level corruption.

What is a public good? "Public Good," also known as *"the Common Good"* is one of the nine cardinal principles in the Catholic Social lexicon, along with: t*he principle of Human Dignity and Inviolability, Participation,*

Distributive Justice, Peace & Non-Violence, Subsidiarity, Preferential Option for the Poor and the Vulnerable, Solidarity, and Human Stewardship over Natural Creation. In this lexicon the common good is defined as *"the sum total of social conditions which allow people, either as individuals or as groups, to reach their fulfilment more fully and more easily."*

In ordinary political discourse Common or Public Good refers to those provisions and facilities – whether material, cultural or institutional – that a community provides to all members in order to fulfil a relational obligation. They all have to care for certain interests that they all have in common. Typical examples of the common good in a modern liberal democracy include: the road system; public parks; police protection and public safety; healthcare; courts and the judicial system; public schools; museums and cultural institutions; public transportation; civil liberties, such as the freedom of speech (which includes press freedom) and the freedom of association; the system of property; clean air and clean water; and national defense. The term itself may refer either to the interests that members have in common or to the facilities that serve common interests. For example, people may say, "the new public library will serve the common good" or "the public library is part of the common good". (See Waheed Hussain, "The Common Good," *Stanford Encyclopedia of Philosophy* https://plato.stanford.edu/entries/common-good/). Societies are organised, and governments exist, fundamentally to protect, to promote and to defend the public good. The whole raison d'etre of the modern state is the realisation of the common good of all.

And how is information a "common" or "public good?" In 1954, Paul Samuelson, then a young economist defined public goods as "…those which we all enjoy in common in the sense that each individual's consumption of such good leads to no subtractions from any other individual's consumption of that good." In other words, a public good is non-rivalrous in consumption – A's benefit of it, does not deny B access to it. A public good is also non-excludable in the long run in the sense that A's access to it does not pose a threat to B. When there is exclusivity of access, that is when one party can prevent the other from the use of a public good. This is potentially a situation that leads not to public good, but public bad or public evil. Exclusivity could be in the form of secrecy, insistence on property rights over the public good, or the use of power or advantages to shut others out, and deny them access, either by force or coercion.

2. Information a public good: UNICEF has chosen this as the theme for the World Press Freedom Day 2021. This is a follow-up to the key message for the 40th anniversary of UNESCO's International Programme for the Development of Communication on 24th November 2020. The theme is well-articulated by Joseph Stiglitz, American, and leading expert in the economics of information and globalization, who has argued that "information is a public good… and (as) a public good, it needs public support". We shall interrogate this a little further.

3. From the traditional communities when early man used his voice to communicate with others in his community, to the Guttenberg Revolution of the 16th century which produced the printing press, the emergence of the computer and latter-day cybernetic revolution, information has always been at the centre of culture, knowledge, and the advancement of humanity. Information is central to the knowledge ecosystem. It is a critical tool for human self-expression, human empowerment, and ultimately human actualisation. It has been established that access to information is a fundamental human right in global order.. This is an acknowledgment of individual's rights, and the importance of the media as a vehicle for promoting that right. Section 22 of the 1999 Constitution of Nigeria in defining the obligation of the mass media states: *"the press, radio, television and other agencies of mass media shall at all times be free to uphold the fundamental objectives contained in this Chapter and uphold the responsibility of the Government to the people"*. The Chapter of the 1999 Constitution under reference here is Chapter Two, titled "Fundamental Objectives and Directive Principles of State Policy". The main assignment of the media is *information dissemination, analysis, agenda-setting, knowledge diffusion, and entertainment.* Section 22 acknowledges the value of information in the governance and democratic process and as a key tool of development in all ramifications.

4. The right of an individual to be part of this process is later upheld in the same Constitution in Section 39 wherein it is stated that *"without prejudice to the generality of subsection (1) of this section, every person shall be entitled to own, establish and operate any medium for the dissemination of information, ideas and opinions"*. This idea of the media and free flow of information is on all fours with the American Constitution, the First Amendment thereof. But more importantly, Article 19 of the International Covenant on Civil and Political Rights (ICCPR) describes information as "the oxygen of democracy" and most essentially, a human right. Many other

international organizations including the African Union, the Council of Europe and the Organization of American States hold the same position that the right to freedom of information is sacred and inviolable. Internationally, the standards and the basic principles with regard to right of access to information include people's rights, obligation of the state to publish information, to be transparent and accountable, and to run an open government, to ensure good governance, to run a limited scope of exceptions where applicable, to provide mechanisms for facilitation of access, as well as adequate mechanisms for the protection for whistle-blowers.

5. The ideological acknowledgment of the value of information as vehicle for achieving these standards and principles has led to the emergence of a Freedom of Information regime within the international system. The *desideratum* is that the people have a RIGHT TO KNOW. If the people are informed, then they will be more knowledgeable about how their societies are governed; they will be able to ask questions, to demand information, and to use the media and other non-state instruments (to compel institutions of state) to enforce their rights under the Constitution.

B: Challenges

The biggest challenge to the people's right to know has been the refusal of authority systems at various levels of state to allow that part of the international covenant to flourish. The depth and scope of this has varied over the years among jurisdictions and media systems. Dictatorial governments, including some of those with pretentions to democracy have routinely adopted repressive measures, legislative processes, economic policies, and sheer use of force to debar or restrict the people's access to information. Whereas international covenants refer to "limited scope of exceptions," usually with regard to national security, privileged state information, or doctor-client confidentiality etc, many governments have opted for a regime of secrecy and repression. Nigeria provides a convincing illustration in this regard through the following, among other instances:

(i) The Official Secrets Act of 1962 (No.29 of 1962 Laws of the Federation) (see AG Federation vs. Dele and Concord Press). In 2011, Nigerian President Goodluck Jonathan passed into law a Freedom of Information legislation. This was hailed as a major breakthrough for the information regime in Nigeria, but the state has since then continued to act as if it is still under the old military regime, even if the FOI Act states clearly that it supersedes the 1962 Official Secrets Act.

(ii) Some of the repressive decrees imposed on Nigeria's information space include Newspapers (Prohibition of Circulation) decree no 17 of 1967,

(iii) Public Officers (Protection Against False Accusation) Decree No 11 of 1976, Newspaper (Prohibition of Circulation) (Validation) Decree No. 12 of 1978, and the infamous Decree No 4 of 1984.

(iv) Under the military in Nigeria, journalists were routinely harassed and abused, media houses were often shut down, and newspapers were seized and destroyed. Since the return to democratic rule in 1999, not much has changed. As recently as October 2020, during the #EndSARS protests in Nigeria, journalists ended up as victims. At least one media house in Lagos was set on fire. Journalists were detained for simply doing their work. To ensure that information serves its purpose as public good, those in the business of information dissemination must have the freedom to do their work.

(v) It is important to note that the conflict between the people's right to know as guaranteed by the Constitution, and promoted by the media, and the unholy determination and desperation by authority figures to annul or circumscribe the people's rights on the grounds that they do not have the need to know, has been responsible in large measure for our continued experience of mis-governance, authoritarianism, unrelenting corruption among public officers in Nigeria and such other countries where the right to freedom of information is not duly recognised and protected. The attempt to impose exclusivity rights over news by states and powerful institutions, amounts to using information for public evil rather than public good. Now, what should be done to turn information into the public good that it is meant to be?

C. Digital Disruption of Information Transmission: a Turning Point?

There have been major turning points in the global information ecosystem but perhaps the most impactful would seem to be the "technical *reproduceability* of the age" as defined by Walter Benjamin. The emergence of the cyberspace or cybersphere has changed the information space as we knew it. Technological innovations have now created new norms:

(a) An information age, which generates information at the speed of light. The speed is now so frenetic that it is difficult to keep up with it.

(b) Interactivity and networked technologies have produced a convergence system that threatens the print media. Are we on the verge of witnessing the "death of the print?" This is something that was unimaginable a century ago. But should we allow the newspaper to die? Shouldn't newspapers be reinvented in digital format in keeping with the spirit of the age?

(c) News was something we waited for, but not anymore. News now travels at the speed of light! A decade ago, we talked about the emergent 24-hours news cycle. That has now become obsolete. News now goes viral with the touch of the button, or a computer click.

(d) We are in the age of the citizen journalist, and the democratization or liberalisation of information, with its many implications that must be constantly interrogated by media practitioners and non-practitioners alike.

(e) This is a new age, the digital age, the age of the new media. Everything has changed: the way we conceive and manage the social contract, the way we participate in politics, the way we do business, the way we engage in teaching and learning; even media theory and the economics of information too. Everything is constantly changing.

Have we arrived at Nirvana (paradise)? Perhaps not. It will be wrong to assume so. The cybernetic revolution in information has brought its own challenges as well, and perhaps therein lies the biggest threat to the promotion of information as a public good. While the democratization of news, the elimination of exclusive rights to information, the empowerment of the citizen, a re-mapping of the global information order, are enticing fallouts of the new information trajectory, these are not without new challenges. We can reflect on a few:

(a) The rise and proliferation of FAKE NEWS, MISINFORMATION and DISINFORMATION. The golden rule in information processing and distribution has been *accuracy, truthfulness, objectivity* and *fairness*, but now that everyone is a journalist, and the ownership of a smart phone creates an unrestricted and undeterred access to a global information gateway via Facebook, Google, Instagram, Twitter, TikTok, Webo, etc, anyone at all, in any corner of the world can manufacture news, garnish or manipulate such news and then broadcast it. Not even major global institutions and systems are safe.

(b) The democratization of information has not necessarily reduced the resolve of authoritarian governments and state actors to limit access to information. Many countries have introduced social media monitoring applications, and others have introduced repressive legislations to curtail access. In Africa, Sudan, Zimbabwe, Chad, DRC, Ethiopia, and Cameroon have had to cut off internet services at one point or the other in the last three years. Nigerian legislators have attempted several times in the last few years, and despite widespread public rejection, they are yet to give up on the *"Social Media Bill,"* which was re-christened as the *"Protection from Internet Falsehoods and Manipulation Bill."* Indeed, many governments in Africa and elsewhere constantly seek to restrict access to the internet and ignore the value of media diversity and plurality.

D. Saving the Information Ecosystem: What to Do

Joseph Stiglitz, quoted above, says as a public good, information "needs public support". Yes, but how? A few suggestions:

(a) Multilateral organisations and sub-national actors must continually insist on the right to information as a universal human right as indicated, and agreed upon, in international covenants.

(b) National parliaments must exercise appropriate watchdog functions with regard to the right to information and good governance.

(c) Civil society organisations must develop the capacity to protect the civic space, and to defend and promote the citizens' right to know, by ensuring that constitutional and legal provisions regarding access to information are not mere window-dressing.

(d) Media institutions need to be rescued, salvaged or supported in the public interest. They deserve a special status as institutions that are not only providing a public good, but also protecting and promoting the other ingredients of the public good. This may imply that their operations should be subsidised in certain instances, even as they jealously guard their editorial independence. Such subsidy could come by way of tax exemptions such as exemption from corporate income tax or tax breaks as may be so determined.

(e) Media houses also must consider the following:

(i) There is the need to take a second look at the business model of media houses. Do the challenges of the times not call for more media outfits to go public? Notwithstanding the desirability of plurality and diversity, isn't it time to consider the possibility of mergers that allow for the pooling of resources?

(ii) Isn't it time for us to advocate that our government begins to impose taxes on international social media platforms that are now taking adverts away from Nigerian Print and broadcast media houses? I am thinking of the proceeds from such taxes being used to subsidise some of our traditional media operations here in Nigeria.

(iii) Has the time not come for an expansion of niche journalism instead of every newspaper doing what others do much better in the now crowded and competitive space?

(iv) Isn't it time for Media Proprietors and professional organisations like NUJ and IPC to pay serious attention to the welfare of journalists (including better remuneration and hazard insurance packages) as well as matters of ethics and professionalism?

(f) The social media remains a major area of concern. Yet, any form of government regulation in that direction in Nigeria is bound to be abused. Can we then reflect on other possibilities, such as putting pressure on owners and managers of social media platforms, to redefine and enforce their community guidelines more strictly?

Conclusion

The media is a cornerstone of a free society. The freedom to source information, to process such information, and to disseminate it, is critical for the nurturing and sustenance of a free, democratic, and prosperous society. Democracy is understood as self-government. It implies that the people as a whole shall govern themselves. Such self-government is not possible or is doomed to fail without an independent and free press. Governments must change their attitude towards media outfits and journalists that express views that are critical of government policies and programmes. When in a constitutional democracy agents and spokespersons of the president openly refer to critics as "enemies of the country," then we know that it is time to mobilise all the resources at our disposal to wrestle our freedom of speech out of the hands of tyrannical elements in the corridors of power who seek to return Nigeria to the dark ages of military dictatorship.

Freedom of any type is not cheap. It does not come on a platter of gold, as those who hold power often seek to intimidate, coerce into submission and silence dissenting voices in the society. Thus, press freedom, as indeed the freedom of expression from which it ensues, will hardly ever be simply given in our society or anywhere else. Such freedom must be wrestled and seized from the authorities, and thereafter guarded jealously. For as Roseanne Barr says, "nobody gives you power – you just take it." Therefore, while calling on conscientious Journalists and committed Media houses to remain courageous and be ready to take risks in sourcing for and disseminating information, I call on the generality of Nigerians to support journalists and media practitioners in advocating for wide-ranging reform of outdated laws in our statute books that curtail or undermine in any way the free exercise of the right to freedom of expression and press freedom. Broadcast media practitioners are these days constantly on edge, because of certain sections of the 1992 NBC Broadcast Code, which emerged during the military dictatorship of Ibrahim Babangida. It goes without saying that some sections of the said broadcast code may be at variance with democratic norms and standards regarding freedom of expression in general and press freedom in particular.

CHAPTER SEVENTY-EIGHT

Strategic Communication in Governance and Security:
The Role of Traditional and Religious Institutions
Presented at the Crisis Management Seminar
of the National Institute
for Security Studies, Abuja, October 18, 2021

Introduction: Dynamics of Effective Communication

Communication is defined as the mutual exchange of information and understanding between two or more parties by any means possible. Communication is also described as the mutual exchange of meaning, which is characterized by the dispositions of empathy and compassion, acceptance, and respect. Communication involves an ongoing process of 'coding' and 'decoding,' because if the recipient of communication cannot successfully decode the content, then no communication would take place. For Effective Communication to occur, **truth** and **trust** are indispensable among the required ingredients. In the first instance the content of the communication must be true, and it must be communicated truthfully. Secondly, the parties in the communication enterprise must have earned the trust of each other before any effective communication can take place. It was Abraham Lincoln who advised that, "If you would win a man to your cause, first convince him that you are his sincere friend, that you have his interest at heart, that you care..." Thus, effectiveness in communication often depends to a reasonable extent on the credibility of the communicator in the eyes of the other parties involved. The parties need to have wide areas of shared experiences and shared meaning, and the content of the communication must be credible, relevant, beneficial, tested and owned by all the parties involved, if communication between them is to be effective.

Trust is critical in the effectiveness of communication. But such trust cannot be earned through acts of coercion and intimidation. Acts of coercion and intimidation rather lead to further breakdown in communication. In the face of the breakdown of trust between the leaders and those they lead, no real progress can be made in the direction of effective communication for governance, security, and sustainable development, until a measure of trust is re-established. And how do the leaders facilitate the re-establishment of such trust? By disposing themselves to know and embrace the truth of their local or national circumstances, no matter how uncomfortable such truth might be; for as Jesus Christ says, "You shall know the truth, and the truth shall set you free." Yes, by demonstrating sincerity of heart and sincerity of purpose, and by being consistent on this path of sincerity, the people will eventually come to believe that the leaders truly care for them, and they will reciprocate with not only personal loyalty, but also some commitment to assisting their leaders in the task of strategic communication of policy frameworks and policy directions with the people.

Information dissemination and announcements are not the same as communication. A series of monologues do not qualify to be called communication. And attempts at the indoctrination of a population are antithetical to effective communication. What is more, the mismanagement of public relations by reactive rather than proactive messages from official channels of the government have in recent times often aggravated potentially volatile situations, rather than calm down such situations. Instead of strategic proactive communication, we have often been fed on a diet of strategic denials and distractions regarding facts, figures and realities that are in the public domain. We have also been treated with what has now become regular demonization of Nigerian stakeholders who happen to voice out their disagreement with certain policies of government or those who express their displeasure and frustration over the obvious failure of government to improve the economy, to reduce corruption or to effectively address the heightened insecurity in the land. Such crude attempts at communication or such public relations practice on the part of government officials can hardly elicit any measure of loyalty and patriotism in the citizens. The result has indeed been widespread resentment among a significant portion of the Nigerian polity, and a proliferation of groups that are now seeking self-determination. Sadly, there are elements in some of these groups who today have resorted to armed insurrection.

Agents of the government who react too quickly and often in the most impetuous manner to every critical comment regarding the failures and perceived injustices of the government should be told in very clear terms that they are often heating up the policy and rendering an already dangerous situation even more precarious. Senior officials of government, who react too quickly and often too impulsively to critics of the administration should be educated on the fact that democracy only thrives when there is a government in power, and there are opposition voices, whose duty it is to constantly drag the feet of those in power to the fire of good governance. In a democracy, critics of government policies and political actors should never be called enemies of the state. Yes, spokespersons of the administration who take on critics of the government often in the most uncivil manner, should be told that if all Nigerians become sycophants, minions, and praise singers of the captain of a sinking ship, then we are all doomed, when the inevitable occurs. Finally, in a volatile environment such as our own, all those who speak for government and their principals should be mandated to take a short course in the dynamics of nonviolent communication, which is now widely available, even online.

Critical Elements of Human Security

On the subject matter of security, I need to emphasise here that all of us stakeholders in this country, and especially functionaries of our security agencies, need to begin to understand national security beyond regime protection and the safety of the incumbent, to include or take into consideration all elements of the human security of Nigerians. We need to begin to understand the remote causes of insecurity, and appreciate that justice and equity, the availability of social infrastructure and a robust social welfare system, a generous provision for universal education and youth employment, as well as the amount of trust the leadership has succeeded in earning from the various segments of the diverse population, etc., are the most critical elements that make for security and peaceful co-existence in any society. The very serious trust deficit between the leadership and the people they lead today, the widespread perception of injustice and inequity in the distribution of opportunities and benefits as well as in the application of sanctions and penalties in the Nigerian polity – and especially the widespread perception of nepotism and sectional bias, to whatever extent it is true, or if such impressions are not satisfactorily addressed, the situation will often generate resentment, bitterness, and political tension, and this will ultimately culminate in the breakdown of law and order, which now and again require crisis management and the intervention of security agents towards restoring some measure of order.

The Place of Traditional and Religious Leaders

With regards to culture, my understanding is that what the framers of my part of today's topic mean is "the role of traditional institutions and religious bodies in addressing the challenge of strategic communication for governance, security, and sustainable development." Traditional and religious institutions are naturally supposed to be custodians and stabilizers of the fundamental values that nurture and sustain human societies. Traditional and religious institutions ordinarily hold the key to the realization of good conduct (among leaders and followers alike), and the promotion of social cohesion, harmonious interaction, peaceful co-existence, and wholesome development in the polity, as they help to formulate and disseminate such core values as truth and justice, equity and fairness, as well as the common good imperative in the society.

Since the onset of colonialism up to this day however, our traditional institutions have been progressively polluted and increasingly bastardized by successive governments, which unjustly appropriated to themselves the right to enthrone and dethrone traditional rulers at will, and the right to determine their salaries and allowances. Is it surprising therefore that the loyalty of many of these traditional rulers has often shifted from their people and what the legitimate demands of their people may be, to the will of the one who pays the piper? Is it surprising that ever since colonial days traditional rulers have often conspired with foreign and local conquerors to subjugate their own people? Is this not why many of these rulers have often lost the trust of their people, as they are now and again seen to be dancing to the tune of whoever is in power at any particular time? And to what extent can an institution that has been destroyed to such a level contribute meaningfully to promoting the higher values that make human societies thrive? To what extent can such a thoroughly bastardized institution play the role of custodians of truth and agents of social cohesion? And to what extent can such an institution (which itself is needing to be salvaged from the forces of degeneration), be engage in any reasonable measure of effective communication for security and sustainable development?

Religious organizations too and their leaders have not been spared this onslaught of decay and triumph of mediocrity in our society, as successive political actors have often sought to manipulate the religious sentiments of the people for their partisan designs. Some religious leaders have now and again been recruited by unscrupulous politicians to promote their nefarious agendas, sometimes even using the pulpit to disseminate sectional, partisan, parochial and divisive messages, and thereby heating up the polity, and worsening the already dangerous security situation. Instead of using their platforms for critical, constructive and objective analysis of societal issues and strategic communication engagement between the people and their leaders, a number of religious leaders have sometimes allowed their institutions to be reduced to platforms that simply project the positions of the government of the day – positions that have sometimes been found not to be on the side of the common good of the people. Rather than insist on our sacred mandate as custodians of lasting values and purveyors of truth, many of us religious leaders have often vacillated and equivocated, when now and again the hard, direct, uncomfortable truth needed to be told to power. True, when in the last few decades, traditional and religious leaders started to dance to the tune of whoever was in power at any particular time, Nigeria as a nation truly began to lose its soul.

Rising to the Challenge of Communication for Justice, Good Governance and Peace

Under our present circumstances, what can traditional institutions and religious organisations do to foster strategic communication in governance for security and sustainable development? The challenge is for those of us who are leaders in these institutions to get back to the drawing board and rediscover our identity and mission in society as custodians of lasting values (including governance values), purveyors of inviolable truth, defenders of the common good and promoters of justice and fairness. Religious leaders (in particular) have a transcendental reference point. This means that we have a divine mandate that should never be compromised or undermined if we are to be true to our calling. In a country like Nigeria that is today in dire need of moral leadership, we religious leaders must find our proper place as truth bearers, as prophets and as sentries, and work hard to earn credibility and trust in the eyes of the generality of the people.

We must constantly assert our independence and neutrality in partisan political matters and insist on our sacred mandate to defend the common good of all, to function as the voice of the voiceless, to speak truth to power, and to advocate for justice, equity and fairness, even when now and again such advocacy will rattle the people in power or make them uncomfortable. We religious leaders must see it as part of our duty to interrogate the persistence of feudalist orientations in our democratic governance. As teachers of good conduct and chastisers of those who oppress and exploit the people of God, we must be constantly addressing the staggering degree of corruption that thrives not only in the conduct of governance at all levels, but also in the leadership recruitment processes themselves. Yes, we religious leaders must clean up our acts, take our rightful place, and address courageously the crisis of legitimacy, the trust deficit and the widespread alienation and disengagement of the population that presently bedevil our political system.

Index

A

Abacha, Sani, 53, 54, 55, 58, 93, 109, 137, 139, 160, 167, 171, 189, 221, 416
Abdul Azeez Atta Memorial College, Okene, 49
Abrahamic religions, 248
Abuja, 160, 167, 209, 212, 219, 221, 234, 299, 341, 349, 355, 372, 381, 403, 427, 439, 447, 469, 493
Achebe, Chinua, 89, 188
Adegbite, Lateef, 235
Afghanistan, 197, 236, 324, 404
African Charter on Human and Peoples' Rights, 277
African Union, 472
Agbakoba, Olisa, 229
Aguleri/Umuleri clashes, 179
Ajaokuta, 96, 299
Ajegunle, 151, 158, 179
Al Aqsa Mosque, 203
Ali, Chris, 53, 125
Allahu Akbar, 212, 244
Amnesty Programme, 430
Anambra state, 225, 253, 179, 428
Anglican-Roman Catholic International Commission, 206, 209
Anti-Riot Police, 150
Anti-Semitism, 203
Anyaoku, Emeka, 41
Argentina, 103, 304, 325
Armah, Ayi Kwesi, 25
Arogundade, Lanre, 469
Aso Rock, 59
Assyrian Church of the East, 204, 208
Australia, 231, 303, 397
Austria, 231
Autochthonous, 31

B

Babangida, Ibrahim, 25, 37, 39, 40, 41, 54, 477
Bakassi Boys, 186, 350, 429
Balogun, Tafa, 281
Banda, Kamuzu, 139, 416
Baptist World Alliance, 208
Barak, Ehud, 203
Basilica, 175, 207, 208
Bello, Lateef, 243
Benue State, 47, 179, 428
Bergant, Dianne, 362, 363, 364
Bergstresser, Heinrich, 386, 388, 456, 458
Biko, Steve, 103
bin Laden, Osama, 180
Bishops' Conference of Nigeria, 38, 209
Blessed Virgin Mary, 215
Bomadi, 158, 220
Bonny, 370
Bori, 158, 220
Brazil, 323
Brown, Dan, 296
Buddhism, 202, 378, 380, 406
Buhari, Muhammed, 25, 427
Burundi, 110, 114

C

Calabar, 129, 262
Calcutta, 215, 216, 243, 278, 318, 408
Cameroon, 323, 416, 429, 475
Campaign for Democracy, 42
Cardinals, 208, 209
Castro, Fidel, 123
Catholic Bishops Conference of Nigeria, 78, 183, 235

Catholic Charismatic Renewal, 411
Catholic Church, xi, xii, xviii, 77, 123, 145, 173, 184, 188, 198, 202, 203, 204, 205, 206, 207, 209, 215, 231, 234, 314, 315, 317, 318, 378, 379, 380, 381, 407, 408, 409, 410
Catholic Development Agencies, 313, 314, 315, 320
Catholic Laity Council of Nigeria, 73
Catholic Men Organisation (CMO), 78
Catholic Secretariat of Nigeria, 234, 235
Catholic Theological Association, xii
Catholic Women Organisation (CWO), 78
Catholic Youth Organisation of Nigeria (CYON), 78
Champion, 469
Christ Embassy, 410
Christ the Redeemer, 317, 318, 410
Christian Association of Nigeria, 209
Christian prophetic calling, 18, 450
Chukwumerije, Uche, 41
Church of Rome, 204
Churchill, Winston, 251
Code of Conduct Bureau., 376
Cold War, 303, 308
Committee for the Defense of Human Rights, 42
Common Entrance examination, 212, 244
Commutative justice, 396
Conscientizing, 273
Council for Religion and Peace, 203
Council of Europe, 472
Cross of Calvary, 90, 91, 193, 196, 287
Cuba, 123
Cybersphere, 473

D

Daily Trust Newspapers, 469
Damascus, 201, 205, 275

Damaturu, 370
De Gaulle, Charles, 251
De-hellenisation of Islam, 409
Democratic Republic of Congo, 323, 325
Denmark, 296
Distributive justice, 396
Dominos Pizza, 306
Dress habits, 266
Dubai, 303, 416

E

Eastern Region, 233
Ebira Muslim Association of Nigeria, 95
Ebiraland, 95, 96, 97, 98, 99
Economic and Financial Crimes Commission, 376
Ecumenical Patriarchate of Constantinople, 204, 207
Ecumenism and Dialogue with non-Christian religions, 202
Egbesu youths, 168, 171, 190
Ehusani, George, xvii
Electoral Reform Committee, 335, 336, 337, 338
Eleme, 158, 220
Empire of Sicily, 383
Enugu, 129, 352
Equatorial Guinea, 416
Eskimos, 266
Ethical Revolution, 25
Ethiopia, 475
Evangelium Vitae, 184, 231
Eyadema, Gnassingbe, 416

F

Falana, Femi, 42
Fanatics, 278
Fawehinmi, Gani, 42
Feast of the Good Shepherd, 263
Fetishisation of Christian worship, 410

First Special Synod of Bishops for Africa, 418

G

Gana, Jerry, 213
Gandhi, Mahatma, 93, 103, 133, 142, 243, 249, 251, 280, 330, 343, 357, 374, 399
Gentiles, 192
Ghana, 25, 254, 304, 306, 357, 387, 458
Giwa, Dele, 469
Globacritics, 310
Globalisation, 237, 303, 305, 309
Globophobes, 310
God of Abraham, 143, 148, 195, 246, 276
Good Friday, 287, 288
Good Samaritan, 316
Gospel of Christ, xvii, 321, 328, 411, 417, 421
Grand Corruption, 376, 404
Grand Mufti of Syria, 201
Great Jubilee Year 2000, 203, 205
Guinness Book of Records, 63, 83

H

Hadith, 237, 378, 406
Hausa and Fulani, 21, 173, 191, 223, 430
Hinduism, 202, 378, 380, 406
Hitler, Adolf, 138, 139
HIV/AIDS, 238, 268
Hobbesian state, 157, 181, 401
Holy Father, 124, 197, 235
Holy Land, 203, 206
Holy Sepulchre, 203

I

Ibadan, 30
Idi-Araba, 186
Igbo people, 172, 190, 223, 430
Ijaw, 147, 158, 198, 428
Ikeja Cantonment, 186
Ilaje, 158
Independent Corrupt Practices Commission, 376
Information and Communication Technology, 293, 303, 325
Instagram, 474
Interim National Government, 42, 43, 44, 45, 54
International Covenant on Civil and Political Rights, 471
Itape, 96, 299
Itsekiri, 147, 198, 259, 350

J

Jammeh, Yahya, 416
Jega, Attahiru, 387, 457
Jerusalem Pilgrim, 211, 244
Jesus of Nazareth, 103, 383
Jews, 193, 201, 202, 203, 210, 239, 275, 276
John Paul II, 123, 125, 173, 174, 181, 184, 197, 198, 201, 202, 203, 204, 205, 206, 207, 208, 209, 210, 215, 216, 229, 230, 231, 235, 242, 275, 277, 278, 310, 316, 317, 318, 319, 322, 363, 374, 408
John the Baptist, xii, 88, 140, 144, 201, 247, 403, 404, 405, 406
Jonathan, Goodluck, 430, 472
Judicial Services Commission, 401
Jukun, 147, 190, 198, 350, 428
Justice Uwais Electoral Reform Committee, 338

K

Kabba Teachers' College, 49
Kaduna State, 21, 25
Kaltho, Bagauda, 469

Kano, 30, 179, 180, 210, 219, 223, 236, 276, 349, 352
Kentucky Fried Chicken, 306
King Jr., Martin Luther, 88, 318
Kingdom of God, 145, 175, 257, 327
Kleptocracy, 301
Konrad Adenauer Foundation, 385
Koran, 99, 212, 244
Kukah, Matthew Hassan, xii, xiii, 206
Kuti, Beko Ransome, 42
Kwara State, 47, 137

L

Lagos, 21, 110, 129, 151, 153, 157, 158, 160, 161, 179, 183, 186, 212, 219, 220, 221, 228, 241, 262, 293, 473
Lasswell, Harold, 443'
'Lazarus experience, 300
Legal Luminaries, 395
Legion of Mary, 411
Liberation Theology, 137
Lincoln, Abraham, 88, 493
Loccum, Germany, 386, 456
Lutherans, 202, 206, 210
Lux Terra Leadership Foundation, xx, 421

M

Machiavellian junta, 37
Madagascar, 303
Maier, KARL, 369
Malaysia, 254, 304, 323, 387, 458
Malta, 383, 384
MAMSER, 25
Mandela, Nelson, 251, 399, 434
Marcos, Ferdinand, 139
MASSOB, 219, 223, 350, 429
Methodist Church of Nigeria, 209
Middle Belt agenda, 169
Middle East, 201, 236, 275, 307
Modakeke, 147, 168, 172, 179, 190, 198, 219, 350, 428

Mother Teresa, 215, 216, 217, 243, 278, 318, 319, 408
Mountain of Fire and Miracle Ministries, 408, 410
Mugabe, Robert, 142

N

NAFSAT, 241
Nasarawa State, 179, 428
National Assembly, 227, 293
National Association of Catholic Lawyers, 183, 185
National Merit Award, 250
Newswatch Magazine, 469
Niger Delta region, 161, 179, 361
Nigeria Inter-Religious Council, 234
Nigerian Bar Association, 395, 401, 455
Nigerian Clergy Association, 78
Nigerian Federation of Catholic Students, 78
Nobel Peace Prize, 216, 434
Nyanya bomb blast, 382
Nyerere, Julius, 251, 434

O

Obafemi Awolowo University, 157
Obasanjo, Olusegun, 149, 180, 190, 212, 213, 222
Obiora, Francis Ike, xxi
Oduduwa, 169
of Chibok, 381
Offoaro, Chinedu, 469
Ogar, Peter, 137
Ogboni Confraternity, 159, 221
Ogunde, Hubert, 63, 83
Okene, Kogi State, 299
Olagboye, Amos, 47, 51
Olukoya, Daniel, 410
One Body of Christ, 209
Onitsha, 295, 299

Oodua Peoples Congress, 158, 161, 220, 223
Operation Crush, 149, 158, 219
Operation Fire for Fire, 219
Operation Flush, 149, 158, 219
Operation Sweep, 149, 158, 219
Operation Wedge, 149, 158, 219
Oputa Panel, 249, 431
Organisation of Islamic Countries, 233
Organization of American States, 472
Orthodox Christians, 202, 210
Orthodox Patriarchate of Ethiopia, 208
Oshogbo, 109
Ottoman Empire, 383
Oxfam, 324
Oyakhilome, Chris, 410
Oyo State, 199, 282, 352

P

Pontifical Council for Inter-Religious Dialogue, 235
Pope Benedict XVI, 297, 388, 409, 418
Pope John XXIII, xix, 206
Populorum Progressio, 308, 313, 314, 315, 319, 320, 321, 323
Port Harcourt, 160, 221
Potiskum, 370
Prayer Against Bribery and Corruption in Nigeria, 372
Prayer for Nigeria in Distress, 372
Prophet Ezekiel, 252, 365
Prophet Mohammed, 295, 297

Q

Quran, 30

R

Rapid Response Squad, 151
Reformed Protestants, 202, 210

Resurrection, 289, 291
Romero, Oscar, 103, 318
Rosary, 212, 244
Rosicrucian Order, 221

S

Saint of the Gutters, 216, 319
Sanneh, Lamin, 439
Sardauna of Sokoto, 243
Saro-Wiwa, Ken, 229
Second World War, 383
Senior Advocate of Nigeria, 88, 188, 371
Seven Deadly Social Sins, 343, 357
Shagari, Shehu, 25
Sharia, 168, 169, 172, 173, 179, 180, 181, 185, 190, 191, 210, 223, 239, 277, 349, 354, 428, 430
Sharia campaign, 168, 172, 180, 190
Shonekan, Ernest, 41
Siddon look, 371
Sikhs, 215
Singapore, 251, 254, 387, 458
Skopje, Albania, 215
South Africa, 103, 139, 231, 251, 254, 387, 434, 458
Southern Protectorates, 350
Sovereign National Conference, 55
St. Francis of Assisi, 278, 346, 359, 408
State Independent Electoral Commission, 337
Stiglitz, Joseph, 471, 475
Structural Adjustment Programme, 50, 236, 305
Synagogue of Rome, 202
Syrian Orthodox Patriarchate of Antioch, 208

T

Taiwan, 202

Tangayika, 434
Tansi, Father Cyprian Michael Iwene, 123, 126, 408
Tanzania, 251, 434
Taraba State, 179, 198, 428
Taylor, Charles, 416
Tell Magazine, 469
Thisday Newspapers, 381
TikTok, 474
Tinubu, Ahmed, 212
Tiv, 147, 190, 198, 259, 350, 428
Tower of Babel, 44, 74
Traditional Religions, 243, 275, 280, 380
Transparency International, 178, 245, 291
Traore, Karim, ii
Tribune, 469
Trump, Donald, 415
Twin Towers in New York, 277

U

Umayyad Mosque, 201, 275
United Nations Declarations on Human Rights, 277
United States, xii, xx, 123, 132, 181, 206, 306, 351, 397, 416, 434
Universal Human Rights Charter, 304

V

Vatican, 32, 184, 187, 202, 204, 205, 206, 207, 216, 235, 380
Vatican Council, 32, 184, 187, 204, 205, 206, 207, 380

Von Bismarck, Otto, 434

W

Wailing Wall, 203
Wallace, Mike, 29
War Against Indiscipline, 25
Warri, 158, 160, 219, 220, 221
Wojtyla, Karol, 201
Wolf, Martin, 305
World Alliance of Reformed Churches, 206, 208
World Bank, 236, 304
World Council of Churches, 208
World Day of Prayer for Peace, 197
World Methodist Council, 208
World Press Freedom Day, 469, 471
World Trade Centre, 181

Y

Yad Vashem, 203
Yar'Adua, Umaru Musa, 335, 337, 338
Yenagoa, 370
Yew, Lee Kwan, 251, 434
Yoruba people, 172, 191, 223, 430
Yun, Hsing, 202

Z

Zaire, 139, 325, 416
Zamfara State, 180
Zangon-Kataf, 21, 25
Zanzibar, 434
Zeraphtah, 144
Zimbabwe, 323, 401, 416, 475
Zionists, 203